WHAT DARWIN BEGAN

Modern Darwinian and Non-Darwinian Perspectives on Evolution

EDITED BY

LAURIE ROHDE GODFREY

University of Massachusetts

Allyn and Bacon, Inc.

Boston   London   Sydney   Toronto

To my husband,
Paul Joseph Godfrey

Library of Congress Cataloging in Publication Data
Main entry under title:

What Darwin began.

Includes bibliographies and index.
1. Evolution.   2. Darwin, Charles, 1809–1882.
I. Godfrey, Laurie R.
QH366.2.W52   1985   575.01   84-20375
ISBN 0-205-08379-X

Production Coordinator: Helyn Pultz
Production Services: TKM Productions
Cover Coordinator: Christy Rosso

Printed in the United States of America

10 9 8 7 6 5 4 3 2 1   89 88 87 86 85

Contents

Preface

When Loren Eiseley wrote *Darwin's Century* in 1958, organized anti-evolutionism was at an ebb in the United States and the primacy of natural selection was unquestioned by virtually the whole community of evolutionary scientists. There was a remarkable consensus in biology. The modern synthesis was firmly entrenched in the evolutionary literature. It was more narrowly Darwinian than Darwin's Darwinism; it had completely rejected Lamarckian use inheritance and had raised Darwin's natural selection to a primacy that would have surprised even Darwin himself. Evolution was expressed in mathematical models documenting changes in gene frequency. Mendelian population genetics gave natural selection a new mathematical legitimacy, and natural selection had become the sole agent of directional change in gene frequency. Charles Darwin, author of a theory of descent with modification by natural selection, was universally acclaimed as author of *the* theory of evolution. The mood has changed a little in today's academic world. There is more polarization today than there was in the late 1950s, and the primacy of natural selection as *the* mechanism of evolutionary change is under renewed scrutiny.

Some of the basic premises of the current evolutionary orthodoxy, neo-Darwinism, have been challenged by several leading evolutionary biologists. Meanwhile, evolution is being attacked, defended, revised, and reviled in the popular press and the pulpits. For a subject so widely discussed by the media, most people little understand the current issues and debates in scientific journals, and the quality of the popular debate reflects this problem. Evolution, a fundamental concept in Western culture, has itself evolved since its formal nineteenth century origins, and it continues to change, although some public discussion still centers on century-old arguments.

There are three basic kinds of criticisms of evolutionary theory. (1) Within the life sciences, specialists debate issues and revise, refine, and challenge basic ideas, with the goal of building a better evolutionary theory (the neutralist/selectionist debate; the cladist/evolutionary taxonomist debate; the punctuationalist/gradualist debate; the debate over neo-Lamarckism, and so on). (2) On logical rather than substantive or empirical grounds, some philosophers and writers, such as Arthur Koestler and Norman Macbeth, have argued that "natural selection is dead," even though they still agree a yet-to-be-explained evolution does take place. (3) Finally, people who are openly hostile to evolution as well as to natural selection argue from a directly opposite ideology—most commonly religious fundamentalism and creationism. These three kinds of critics communicate to the broader public in varying degrees, and anti-evolutionist polemicists seize on all kinds of critiques in an effort to portray evolution as a crumbling citadel defended by a powerful but wrong-minded Establishment. A muddled public perception of evolution frequently results.

But evolution is not a crumbling citadel. Neither, for that matter, is Darwinism—the real target of Arthur Koestler's graphic metaphor. Evolutionary biology is actually in a period of rapid and healthy growth. That growth centers in part around controversies. Not all of these controversies are about Darwinism per se, but it is certainly in the past decade or so a host of alternatives to strict Darwinian explanation have been proposed. For the first time since the modern synthesis, or synthetic theory of evolution, emerged between 1930 and 1950, some of the basic premises of Darwinism are under serious attack from within evolutionary biology. The alternatives to Darwinism enjoy varying degrees of popularity within the profession as a whole: some are decidedly peripheral to the mainstream of evolutionary thought, while others have gained broad acceptance. But whatever the strength of their constituencies, the very existence of plausible and actively debated alternatives signals not the death of Darwinism but the life and vitality of modern evolutionary theory.

Perhaps the most controversial arguments in any discipline prove in the long run to be neither the most interesting nor the most important. Yet they are the issues that generally capture media attention, and they are the most likely to be distorted or misused by people who, for one reason or another, want to destroy the credibility of that discipline. To hold the arguments of non-Darwinian evolutionary scientists in disdain merely because they have attracted the attention of the popular press, or because some of them have been misused by anti-evolutionists, would be a bad mistake. What is needed is a better understanding of what those arguments *are*. This book is intended to accomplish precisely that. Its goal is to help students understand the bases of current professional disagreements without getting lost in the hoopla of media debate.

My own belief is that some elements of Darwinism will indeed be replaced eventually by non-Darwinian evolutionary theory. This has not really happened yet, a century and a quarter after the publication of Darwin's quintessential book. But the most radical essays in *What Darwin Began* were not selected because their authors had convinced the majority of practicing evolutionary biologists of the strength of their positions; rather they were selected because they represent sober challenges to some aspects of the current orthodoxy. It is my hope that these essays will clarify current issues for students and lay readers who have had some exposure to Darwinian theory and who may be confused or tantalized by some of the more flamboyant announcements of its burial.

What Darwin Began is divided into four sections. The first section, "Historical and Philosophical Perspectives on Darwinian Explanation," reviews Darwin's contribution to evolutionary theory, and asks just what Darwinism attempts to explain. The second section, "Modern Challenges to Neo-Darwinism," focuses on current critiques of natural selection and Darwinian evolution—the debates between *neo*-Darwinian and *non*-Darwinian evolutionists. The third section, "Evolution and the Public," focuses on two ongoing and lively media debates—the first over creationist objections to the teaching of evolution in public schools, and the second over just how natural history museums should present evolution to the public. This latter debate is actually far more complex than it might initially seem. Taxonomists at the British Museum (Natural History) in London and at the American Museum of Natural History in New York are embroiled in a debate over the best methods of classifying organisms and of studying evolutionary processes. But it is the claim some cladistic taxonomists have made—that evolution is irrelevant to the proper classification of organisms—that has piqued the curiosity of the press and the public. The last section of the book, "The Edge of Discovery," focuses on debates on the origins of the cosmos, the earth, life on earth, complex organisms, and (why not admit our vanity?) our own genus, *Homo*.

It is difficult to give a book such as this a sense of cohesion. The arguments of different authors are, in fact, quite distinct, and the lack of cohesion necessarily derives from the nature of the current debates. A book that tries to present the best of the challenges to the current orthodoxy can also be criticized for being unfair to that orthodoxy, which is not allowed to properly respond. This is a valid criticism; this book reviews Darwinism only briefly. The reader unfamiliar with neo-Darwinism can only be urged to attain greater familiarity elsewhere.

No attempt is made to present groundless arguments as valid challenges to the current orthodoxy. Thus the arguments of the so-called scientific creationists are not treated here; the interested reader is referred to the spate of books now available that not only present those arguments but refute them quite successfully. The essay on the creationist movement included in this book deals more with the nature of this anti-evolutionist movement than with the details of its arguments. In my view, this is the most interesting aspect of religious anti-evolutionism today.

Criticism, controversy, and confusion notwithstanding, Darwin's genius is acclaimed just as vigorously today as it was when Loren Eiseley commemorated the *Origin's* centennial. Eiseley's poetic conclusion of *Darwin's Century* rings just as true today as it did when it was first written:

> *As a young man . . . Charles Darwin saw a vision. It was one of the most tremendous insights a living being ever had. . . . None of his forerunners has left us such a message; none saw, in a similar manner, the whole vista of life with quite such sweeping vision. None, it may be added, spoke with the pity which infuses these lines:* 'If we choose to let conjecture run wild, then animals, our fellow brethren in pain, disease, suffering and famine—our slaves in the most laborious works, our companions in our amusements—they may partake of our origin in one common ancestor— we may be all melted together.'
>
> *Darwin was twenty-eight when he jotted down this paragraph in his notebook. If he had never conceived of natural selection, if he had never written the* Origin, *it would still stand as a statement of almost clairvoyant perception. There are very few youths today who will pause, coming from a biology class, to finger a yellow flower or poke in friendly fashion at a sunning turtle on the edge of the campus pond, and who are capable of saying to themselves, "We are all one—all melted together." It is for this as much as for the difficult, concise reasoning of the* Origin *that Darwin's shadow will run a long way forward into the future.* ∗

"*We are all one—all melted together.*" This seems so naively obvious to us today that we tend to forget how counterintuitive it was in Darwin's day. We tend to forget the ridicule heaped on the very idea of biological evolution prior to Darwin's century. Evolution is basic to all of modern science. What seems radical and exciting about evolution in the twentieth century is not its mere existence, which we take for granted, but the nitty-gritty details of its operation. Out of the twentieth century have grown new startling visions, including the notion that the existence and evolution of life on earth are tied to the evolution of the cosmos—that "we are all stardust." Inanimate and inanimate objects on earth today are elements born many billions of years ago in the stars. We are living in an exciting period of growth in evolutionary science—of building upon what Darwin began. *What Darwin Began* reflects that growth—and its growing pains.

L.R.G.

∗ Loren Eiseley, *Darwin's Century* 1958 (Garden City, N.Y.: Anchor Books, Doubleday, 1961), pp. 351-352.

SECTION ONE

Historical and Philosophical Perspectives on Darwinian Explanation

The Dawn of Evolutionary Theory

KENNETH A. R. KENNEDY
Division of Biological Sciences
Cornell University

Introduction

The idea of human fossils is very recent in Western thought. That particular mineralized bones discovered in caves and river gravels might be vestiges of mankind who lived thousands or millions of years ago is a speculation that did not trouble the best minds of Hellenic and Roman antiquity or of the European Middle Ages. When a few daring writers of the eighteenth century first proposed the notion of fossil man, the moral majority scornfully dismissed the idea as ridiculous and irreverent. Indeed, it seems remarkable that the idea of human fossils was conceived at all, so humiliating to the ego is its implication of human affinities with anthropoid apes, monkeys, and even "lower" forms of life. To this day, denials of claims that humans descend from beasts are delivered with disgust and apprehension. Even those people who would approve of scientific methods of research may hold strong biases on this issue. Everyone knows educated people who are prepared to accept the fossil evidence for the evolution of nonhuman organisms but reject the applicability of paleontological data to theories concerned with human biological origins and histories. How, then, did a theory of organic evolution that encompasses mankind ever achieve the essentially universal acceptance it enjoys today among scientists and other educated people?

The modern theory of organic evolution maintains that processes operating in nature bring about the origin of new species by descent from earlier species that have undergone adaptive modifications over time. This view of the succession of living things is not the child of any *single* academic discipline or philosophical-theological school. To understand human evolutionary history is to understand the

Theodore D. McCown, Kenneth A. R. Kennedy, *Climbing Man's Family Tree: A Collection of Major Writings on Human Phylogeny, 1699–1971,* © 1972, pp. 1–14. Adapted by permission of Prentice-Hall, Inc., Englewood Cliffs, N.J. The author thanks Dr. Laurie Godfrey for her generous and welcome comments during the preparation of this reading.

history of the *idea* of evolution as this concept emerged from the cultural configuration known as Western civilization. The theme of this reading is that these beginnings are to be found within the very heart of theological and philosophical doctrines of the Judeo-Christian tradition and earlier classical sources.

But while evolutionary theory finds its roots deeply implanted in many aspects of Western orthodox thinking within the Western religions, the same may not be said for the idea of human fossils, nor for the use of the human paleontological record as evidence that humans evolved and are evolving. Indeed, the possibility of human evolution has been admitted by scientists for only the past 125 years. Today, when paleontologists, anthropologists, and other biological scientists debate the issues of human evolution and the evolution of other organisms, their concern is not with establishing evolutionary proofs. That battle was waged and won by evolutionists of the last century. Rather, they are concerned with the patterns of evolutionary development over time; the degrees of affinities among organisms; and the determination of specific evolutionary mechanisms operating in the past and present that may explain taxonomic diversity and the adaptability of organisms to different and changing ecological settings.

The Shape of Time

Christian and Judaic cosmology favors a single-world view. There was one Creation, and from this unique event emerged a basically static world. Explanations of the universe were to be found in Scripture, particularly in the episodes described in the first eleven chapters of Genesis. Scholars of these texts assumed the kinds of plants and animals observed in the world today are lineal descendants of the prototypic creatures appearing for the first time in the cosmic week of Creation. Not only had the biotic kinds, or species, remained identical, but it seemed improbable that any of these ancestral forms had ever become extinct in this static universe.

Christian theology laid the groundwork for evolutionary ideas in the fifth and thirteenth century writings of the great scholars Saint Augustine and Saint Thomas Aquinas. Augustine interpreted the creation story of the Bible to mean that, at the time the plants and animals were created, God infused into the earth the necessary energy or potency so that it could thereafter produce living things by a natural process—the unfolding of his plan. The earth was the giver of life, because God had given it the power to generate a natural evolution of forms. However, these writings did not receive much attention in the nineteenth century when organic evolution became an issue. Before the dawn of the eighteenth century, the question of organic evolution was hardly an issue at all.

Most thinkers of the Greco-Roman cultural tradition held a multiworld view conditioned by the precept that time was cyclical and that nature was an entity analogous in its behavior to the life cycle of the human body. Such a temporal concept satisfied the canon of classical aesthetics that only an orderly and finite universe could be virtuous and real. Cycles were the dynamics of perpetual and beneficent change that reflected the nature of a cosmic intelligence. Humans were, of course, part of this system, for as the seeds of decay were intrinsic in each new world, so humans themselves gradually became corrupted as the cycle in which they lived progressed. As each cycle neared its end, and as humans descended to the nadir of their destruction, the earth and all its living things were doomed to destruction in a vast cataclysm of fire and flood, until saved at the critical moment by the intervention of the Deity. This event was followed by another cycle. The duration of a completed cycle ranged from Plato's estimate of 72,000 years to Cassander's 360,000; but Pythagoras lamented that no one might know the number of the cycle in which he or she lived. The doctrine of the Five Ages of human history was synchronized with these concepts of cycle, degeneration, catastrophism, and divine intervention, the earliest and most felicitous period being the Golden Age at the commencement of each cycle. Aristotle's assertion that there was only one world, rather than many, received little popular favor.

The church fathers of the first centuries A.D. were faced with the problem of synthesizing the prestigious pagan literature with the scriptures of Christian tradition. While many of the pagan concepts did survive in the single-world view of Christianity, the notion of cycle was a threat to belief in the one Creation, the single Atonement through Christ, and the final Day of Judgment. Augustine declared that the cyclic concept was incompatible with orthodoxy, in reaction to some of his theological predecessors who had favored the incorporation of the idea into Christian doctrine. The world view of Christianity was that of a universe created by God in the manner described in Genesis. The world was subject to constant divine intervention, as witnessed by the occurrence of natural catastrophes and miracles—the manifestations of divine wrath and approbation. The earth, whose existence extended back in time but a few millennia, was destined for imminent dissolution. Whereas the thinkers of the ancient world saw an orderliness and an intelligence inherent in the cycles of nature itself, the Christian philosophers considered these qualities imposed on the world by a supernatural cause beyond the physical limits of nature. In the Ptolemaic universe, humans were set to the task of working out salvation—if, by the grace of God, they

were to escape the everlasting damnation incurred through the in-
discretion of the very first member of the species. Thus while degra-
dation and divine intervention were pagan concepts congenial to
Christian philosophy, cyclic time was inadmissable and catastrophes
were limited to the biblical Deluge and Day of Judgment.

In the sixteenth century the circumscribed universe of the
Middle Ages was replaced by the wider world view of late Renaissance
scholars—a world with expanded celestial and geographical horizons.
The Copernican system revealed that the earth was a decentralized
planet adrift in a limitless sea of astral bodies. "Natural philosophers"
saw in astronomy, physics, and mathematics the possibility of discovering natural laws created and maintained by the Creator. While
final causes might forever remain unknown, such natural laws were
within the power of the human mind to understand; thus it fell to
scholars to decipher the plan of Creation. To study nature was to
become familiar with divine effort. Thus, during the sixteenth and
much of the seventeenth centuries there was little conflict between
science and religion *per se*. Atheism was ascribed to individuals'
moral lapses and not to their contamination from too-close proximity
to science.

However, at this time science began to threaten belief in a world
with an antiquity of only a few thousand years, a world with one
global catastrophe in the past and one yet to be fulfilled, a world
unique because of its single creation and its occupancy by humans
who were degenerate creatures. As researchers in the developing fields
of astral and geological sciences were piously laboring to elucidate
the divine plan of nature, their efforts strained the credibility of
accepted traditions. The perfection of God's creation was questioned
when early telescopes revealed lunar craters and sun spots, and nature's
permanency could hardly be maintained when heavenly bodies were
recognized as having the properties of motion and physical alteration. As the concept of unlimited time emerged from the theories of
the formation of the universe, the concept of limited space appeared
incongruous beside it. Furthermore, while the astronomers and physicists of this period were gently ushering out the back door concepts
of immutable heavens and limited age of the earth, they were introducing through the front doors of their disciplines the notion of
cosmic evolution—an idea that was to be wed to the biological
sciences by the middle of the nineteenth century. At first, speculations on the nature of the *universe* did not seem pertinent to the
history of the *earth*, insofar as its creation and development are
recorded in Genesis. For while the scanners of the heavens were becoming progressively more concerned with discerning the laws of the
natural world, the religious philosophers of these times were intent
on demonstrating design in nature, and traditional doctrines seemed

unassailable. But questions about the origin of the earth and explanations of the Deluge could not exist independently of speculations already current in astronomical theory. The science of geology emerged from these late seventeenth century speculations. In the eighteenth century, the study of the earth introduced concepts of geological antiquity and change into the forefront of Western thought; in the century that followed, those concepts were recognized as having profound biological implications.

The Chain of Being

The Greeks believed that the Platonic World of Forms was an exhaustive replica of the World of Ideas, which had but a single creation. This was in harmony with the idea of an orderly cyclic system as the creation of a beneficent and intelligent Being. Hence the former world was fully stocked with all possible things since the Deity could not begrudge existence to anything that could conceivably exist. These *existants* were imperceptibly graded in their structures and properties so that there was a logical sequence of biotic phenomena—a unilinear graduation—based on each element's possessing certain qualities of "perfection" and "privation," according to Aristotle. Such a chain of being was composed of an indefinite number of links ranging in hierarchical order from the lowest sorts of existants through every possible grade of life up to the Absolute Being. Each element of the graduated series differed from the element above and below it in the least possible degree. Aristotle's classification of organic nature was actually a product of medieval scholasticism, for he did not formulate the *Scala Naturae*, or Ladder of Nature, beyond some eleven grades (*genos*) of animals originating with the zoophytes and terminating with humans. But he recognized the significance of grouping together animals that were interfertile and similar in their morphology as members of the same *eidos*—the category known to later naturalists as the *species*. All species were regarded as immutable entities. As to the place of humans in this system of nature, they clearly stood between those known infrahuman primates and legendary "near-men" of travelers' accounts, and the epic heroes and demigods—a place they maintained in every cycle.

The Neoplatonists introduced the concept of the chain of being into the biology of the Middle Ages. This concept gained the sanction of Augustine and Thomas Aquinas because of its relevance to their theological interpretations of inequality and evil in nature. The ideas of Aristotle became academic dogma, and instead of original research, scholars produced elaborate commentaries on the works of ancient philosophers.

The study of living things stagnated in Europe until the sixteenth century, when previously unknown flora and fauna were imported from the New World and from newly explored portions of Asia, Oceania, and Africa. "Natural history," the classification and description of biotic forms, was a less prestigious science than physics and astronomy. Its methodology seemed less reliable, and its research was neither dramatic nor utilitarian. But out of such humble beginnings came the first taxonomies. Jung devised a binomial system where a plant identified by a noun (its genus) was modified by an adjective (its species), which followed the noun in good Latin form. Jung's classification became influential in zoology, where his binomial system was introduced by the seventeenth century naturalist, John Ray. Linnaeus was in turn influenced by Ray in his efforts to arrive at a classification of all living things according to a system subject to a strict discipline of observation and description. Linnaeus prepared the first edition of his *Systema Naturae* in 1736. A natural classification had been devised—where life forms were grouped according to various criteria of form or configuration. The chain of being was now scientifically described.

The Nature of Fossils

To the thinkers of the ancient Greco-Roman world, the recognition of marine fossils on the tops of mountains and in the sediments of deposits far from the sea and the discovery of gigantic bones encased in rocks supported the cyclic concept. They thought that the oceans had once been considerably higher than they now were, and that they receded naturally as part of the great cycle. Fossils were interpreted as remains of organisms from a former cycle or from an earlier period of the present one. Human bones were the remains of epic heroes, and massive reptilian and mammal bones were the vestiges of Titans. Interest in finding fossil animals and plants continued into the Middle Ages, but it was an interest generated by the supposed magical and quasi-religious nature of the finds. To be sure, some early Christian writers believed that fossils were the vestiges of once-living things; but from this point they argued that the fossils had been transported to their present inaccessible reaches of the earth and to the peaks of high mountains by the waters of the Deluge. Other people believed that the fossils were not remnants of previously living organisms. They ascribed the origin of the findings to various occult causes. When prehistoric artifacts of early humans were encountered, they were lumped with the fossils of sea urchins, belemnites, and meteorites into a category called *ceraunia*, all of which were valued for their medicinal and auspicious qualities.

In the sixteenth century, da Vinci, Fracastoro, and Palissy rejected the notion that fossils were associated specifically with the Deluge; they considered fossils remains of organisms from different times and places. They did not, however, address the question of where the survivors of the fossilized organisms might be today. For in a world view that maintained the immutability of living things and precluded the extinction of any of God's creatures, the discovery of living examples of these strange animals and plants seemed imminent. In what regions of the world not yet explored were they to be found? Had some of them sought refuge in the mysterious depths of the sea? As new regions were opened up for discovery, however, students of nature became confounded by the multitude of unfamiliar organisms that had to be described and classified. Few of these new creatures resembled anything that could represent the descendant of familiar European fossil forms. Rather, the newly discovered regions yielded their own distinctive fossil specimens that were unmatched by known organisms, either living or fossil. This dilemma was further aggravated because neither the fossil record nor the collections of organisms from foreign parts served to fill the gaps between recognized forms in the chain of being. To admit that the fossils themselves were the missing links was only to beg the question of where these transitional forms might be today. Resistance to the idea of species extinction was strong. As late as the final half of the eighteenth century Thomas Jefferson claimed that the American and Siberian mammoths were extinct only in the minds of the unphilosophical: "Such is the economy of nature, that no instance can be produced, of her having permitted any one of her animals to become extinct; or her having formed any link in her great work so weak as to be broken."

While the growing fossil record was an incipient threat to the concept of everlasting species, the question of species *immutability*, later to become the refuge of providentialism in the latter part of the eighteenth century, seemed to be beyond the possibility of attack. To most naturalists of the seventeenth century, species were assumed to be the natural entities of the biotic world, the fixed representations of their Platonic types. Individual organisms might deviate from the ideally perfect morphological models representative of their species, but such variations were regarded as insignificant aberrations within the chain of being. Variations were considered useful in explaining the apparent gaps between adjacent species in the chain, for the variations were the bridges between distinct species. This view gained favor with the realization that the missing links were not to be found in the fossil record or among the unfamiliar organisms imported from afar. Common descent was considered the best criterion of an individual species, but morphology was also considered important. (Spontaneous generation was not completely disproved until the nineteenth century, but it had lost its biological respectability two centuries earlier through the experiments of Swammerdam, Redi, and Leeuwenhoek.) The idea of common descent strengthened the concepts of continuity and immutability of species, for comparative anatomists had yet to discover the evolutionary implications of their observations.

Of course, the concept of cosmic evolution was already widely present in the ideas of the sixteenth century cosmogonists. But when this idea was first widely applied to the origin and development of *living* things, it was viewed as a threat by conservative thinkers aware of the growing tendency of seventeenth century scholars to move divine supervision farther and farther from the phenomena of nature. If biotic forms were subject to evolution, then how could God's concern for his universe be demonstrated?

Providentialism in Natural History

By the year 1800, scholars were forced to admit something foreseen centuries earlier: The sketchy scriptural account of Adam and Eve and their immediate descendants could not resolve questions concerning the place of humans in nature, their precivilized condition, and their biological origin. In the eighteenth century there was a change in the orientation of natural philosophers. The term *science* appeared more frequently in the writings of the period, and it was applied to the study of the physical nature of the universe, a study that had become divorced from the theological focus that had characterized it earlier. This focus on the divine plan in science was called *Providentialism*. Research in astronomy, physics, and chemistry was now less spectacular, confined largely to refinement and demonstration of Newtonian principles. Providentialism, finding the physical sciences preoccupied, sought refuge in natural history. While similar to the physical sciences in its concern for *description* rather than the problems of origin, process, and development, natural history presented enigmas that Newtonian physics could not resolve and that seemed to involve supernatural intervention. To include both physical science and natural history, the term *natural theology* (or *divine theology*) came into use. The term had a broader meaning than the "natural philosophy" of the previous century. The natural theologian actively sought to integrate the data of physical science and natural history with current theology and scriptural interpretation. The earth and its creatures were held to have been immutable since the day of their creation, although *celestial* change could no longer be ruled out. Natural theologians believed that God was actively working in the world—the immanent manipulator of historical and natural processes, the initiator of revelations, and personally interested in the universe.

Within this philosophical matrix the earliest developments of geology, the "Theories of the Earth," had their inception. Some proposers of these theories, such as Burnet and Whiston, sought to keep within the traditional framework of theology; others, like de Maillet, Buffon, and von Holbach, were indifferent or antagonistic to theology. The latter emphasized geological antiquity and change. Both kinds of cosmogonists were operating outside any systematic method of direct field research, but the iconoclastic scholars de Maillet, Buffon, and von Holbach, with their interest in the roles of time and change, brought upon geology the stigma of heresy and atheism. Their position evoked further criticism for its materialistic connotations, particularly in France where intellectuals were markedly hostile to the established social order, then under considerable ecclesiastical domination. Those who were tradition-oriented reasoned that if the age of the earth could be strictly correlated with the biblical chronology, divergent opinions would be authoritatively silenced. Concern for a true understanding of natural geological processes became important to the supporters of Genesis, and scholars such as Hooke turned to first-hand examination of their planet for that support.

But to other observers, dissatisfied with traditional interpretations, the planet became the laboratory for nonscriptural explanations of its origin and history. The role of fire and flood, the causes of stratification, the presence of marine fossils on the tops of mountains far removed from the sea, and other puzzling geological phenomena outside the bounds of historical and religious records demanded investigation. Field geology began in earnest.

As geological theory began to move along the path trod earlier by astronomy in its emancipation from literal scriptural interpretation, the defenders of the "eternal hills" found themselves siding with Werner, a professor of mining at Freiberg whose theories could easily be correlated with Scripture. Werner thought that water was the prime agent of geological activity. A vast primal ocean covered the globe at the time of Creation, diminishing in volume coincidentally with the formation of the rocky strata from sedimentation. Werner's stages of geological formation could be synchronized with the Six Days of Creation, and his theory of periodic floods did not clash with the precepts of the champions of the Deluge, the so-called Diluvialists, Floodists, or "Mosaic geologists." Animal fossils were arranged in the strata that Werner described in a sequence that paralleled the order of mention of the fauna in Genesis. Nor was a lengthy time scale necessary for this theory, provided that the Six Days of Creation were interpreted allegorically as periods of geological development.

The geologists who were impressed *less* with the role of water than with that of fire and heat in the formation and history of the earth greatly offended established tradition by their insistence on the

great antiquity of the earth, their neglect of the geological importance of the Deluge, and their failure to hypothesize supernatural
intervention where direct geological evidence was not discernible. A
late champion of these Vulcanists—so called to mark their opposition
to the aqueous theories of the Wernerian Neptunists—was Scottish
geologist James Hutton. Hutton contributed the concept of *Uniformitarianism* to the science of geology. Given adequate time, the geological processes of deposition, uplift, and erosion, working gradually
and continuously on the earth today, would produce the kinds of
changes that the earlier Neptunists and Vulcanists attributed to
cataclysms. The Uniformitarianism that emerged from Hutton's
research did not become a contender with Neptunism for academic
respectability, for Werner's theories were already being superseded
during the first two decades of the nineteenth century by yet another
geological school.

    Catastrophism, championed by Cuvier, maintained that a series
of cataclysmic events had occurred on the earth with remarkable
periodicity, and that the last of these holocausts was the biblical
Deluge. A special creation was not necessarily coincident with the
termination of each catastrophe. But while admitting change, Catastrophists did not tolerate the suggestion of the mutability of living
species. The events that led to the destruction of life at the end of
each catastrophe were regarded as signs of God's beneficent intervention in his Creation, a process that was progressive since it was
directed toward preparing the world for human occupancy. It was a
cyclic process, but one not directed in its orientation to the maintenance of the *status quo*. In opposition to these views stood the
Uniformitarians, now marshalled behind Charles Lyell. They regarded
the Deluge as having played a negligible role in geology, and their
views concerning divine intervention were essentially agnostic. But
they also considered species immutable. Neither viewpoint was evolutionary, although both attributed a generous time span to earth's
history.

    By the close of the third decade of the nineteenth century
Catastrophism was losing its hold among intellectuals. The discovery
of the vestiges of an Ice Age, though perceived as a possible catastrophe, was interpreted in a Uniformitarian context as another geological process that had been far from sudden or unprecedented in
earth history. The Uniformitarians demonstrated that geology could
be self-sufficient outside the realm of theological interpretation, just
as the physical sciences had shown themselves to be a century earlier.
The "Mosaic geologists," deprived of the geological verification of
the Deluge and forced to surrender their hopes that the Six Days of
Creation would similarly receive literal confirmation, were now com-

pelled to find support for their premises outside geology. They took their next stand in the biological sciences.

Natural historians of the early eighteenth century had not reached any agreement on the questions of the possibility of the extinction of species, their mutability, and the origin of new species since the Fifth Day of Creation. Therefore, biology seemed a safe refuge for those who ridiculed such speculation. But their hopes were short-lived. The recognition that species could become extinct made its way into biology largely through the work of Cuvier, who regarded fossils as the inhabitants of a former world that was separated from the present one by a catastrophic episode. To Cuvier and his disciples, each species, extinct or extant, was the result of a special creation. The Catastrophists observed that there appeared throughout the succession of geological time, as revealed in the stratigraphic sequences, a "progression" of biotic forms of increasing complexity in morphological organization. Progressionism became the biological complement of the geological theory of Catastrophism, and so gave unity to the chaotic history of life that the Catastrophists preached. The chain of being had become temporalized, but its elements remained immutable. Catastrophism was popular as a reaction to the tenets of Uniformitarianism, which now responded with its own interpretation of life's history. Instead of asserting that biotic forms showed an increasing degree of complexity in anatomical organization through time, as the Catastrophists held, the Uniformitarians argued that complex organisms occupied ancient strata along with less complex ones, and that all forms of life came into existence simultaneously. The Uniformitarians thus substituted a single creation for the multiple divine interventions of the Catastrophists. Their non-Progressionist theory exempted humans, however, from original creation, since human arrival on earth seemed to postdate many fossil forms. Both the Catastrophist notion of progressive change and the Uniformitarian notion of continuity of progress lent support to the concept of organic evolution already forming in the minds of many naturalists.

Meanwhile, in the last decades of the eighteenth century, William Smith (a drainage engineer interested in locating geological deposits suited for the construction of canals and sumps) found that unique fossils in different deposits could be used as criteria for their stratigraphic identification. This led to the development of a descriptive methodology for stratigraphy and paleontology. But while paleontology forced conservative naturalists into admitting that some species had become extinct in the past, the question of species mutability appeared safe from attack. As early as the fourth decade of the nineteenth century, it became apparent that the role of Providentialism was to be judged by a biological question—the nature of species—rather than by a geological question—the origin and history of the earth. Each new theory of the earth and its living inhabitants came dangerously near to upsetting accepted concepts, but the feared crisis was consistently prevented by the assurance that the next step in the argument could not be taken.

The Concept of Organic Evolution

Gradually, there arose serious consideration of the thesis that products of a special creation might be vulnerable to relatively permanent morphological change. Many theorists contributed to this notion. The taxonomist Linnaeus suggested that new plant species might arise from fertile hybrids; thus, while genera were stable, species were potentially subject to change. Indeed, species were but the results of various crossings in the past of different members of a genus. Linnaeus regarded such a circumstance as accidental, but this did not deliver the great classifier of living nature from the disgrace of having some of his writings excluded from his church's sanction for a brief period: Such notions of mutability were not in accord with Biblical botany. Buffon later noted that when a species is forced to change its habitat because of changes in the environment to which it is adapted, alterations appear in its physical morphology. Such changes ensure its survival in the new habitat, and in time these changes become hereditary constituents of the species. Furthermore, if humans can alter a species through artificial selection, might not nature do more through long eons of time? Change, according to Buffon, depended on the circumstance of the environmental stimulus, the productivity of the species, and a sufficient amount of time for the mutability of species to occur. For Erasmus Darwin, grandfather of Charles, species mutability was a consequence of the progressive transformations organisms had to undergo to meet new internal and external environmental pressures. For Lamarck also, a changing environment seemed to be correlated with the mutability of the living things in it: The environment was not an incidental background to life, but rather life's determinant, since all living things must adapt to it.

The environmental theories of species mutability were incorporated in an anonymous work that appeared in 1844, *The Vestiges of the Natural History of Creation.* Its true author was the Scottish publisher Robert Chambers, whose interest in natural history led him to combine the Catastrophist notion of Progressionism, the Uniformitarian doctrine of the continuity of operation of natural processes, and the concept of the mutability of species, to form a theory of transformism, or organic evolution. Rejecting Lyell's non-Progressionism, Chambers argued that living things had ascended the chain of being through time from simple to more complex forms, fossils being the ancestors of organisms now living or the vestiges of extinct lines. Characteristics that organisms acquired in their adjustments to changing environments were passed on to future generations, which could also adapt to new environmental pressures.

Out of these heresies matured the concept of organic evolution, which would culminate in the middle of the nineteenth century in the works of Charles Darwin. The question facing pre-Darwinian evolutionists was this: If species are mutable, what are the mechanisms in nature that control mutability and determine which species shall become extinct and which shall pass on their traits to future generations? It seemed obvious to the early evolutionists that once an animal or plant had acquired a specific type of structure that would help it to survive, the new feature would become incorporated into the species through some hereditary process. The inheritance of such characteristics must somehow be under the control of nature. Lamarck hypothesized that they appeared as a consequence of the *felt needs* of the adapting animals: The animals would strive toward their own betterment. The result was a strongly directional "law of progress."

Charles Darwin's knowledge of Lamarck came from Lyell's treatment of his ideas in the *Principles of Geology*, a work that ridiculed evolutionism and Progressionism and espoused Uniformitarianism. But during his South American voyage, Darwin had noticed how species differed geographically and how, while the Galapagos Islands' fauna most closely resembled species from the mainland, they maintained their own characteristics. He hypothesized that the island species were parented by populations originally from the mainland, and that they were later modified slightly through time. The mode of modification might be a natural process analogous to artificial selection practiced by stock breeders. Darwin reasoned that such a process operating in nature over long periods should produce marked changes in organisms. Thus Darwin accepted both Lyell's Uniformitarianism and also evolutionism. Given the conditions of struggle for survival posed by Malthus, Darwin reasoned that favorable variations would tend to be preserved and unfavorable ones rejected, the result being the formation of a new species. Darwin had arrived at his theory of natural selection as early as 1838, but did not reveal his ideas formally until twenty years later, at which time they were presented in conjunction with a similar thesis by Alfred Russell Wallace. Darwin emphasized the importance of individual variation as an explanation for species change. Variations that had been considered aberrant defects of nature now became the crucial material of organic evolution. Darwin was fully aware of the formidable implications contained in his philosophy, for here indeed lay the most vital point of nineteenth century Providentialism: Surely humans, inheritors of the Kingdom of Heaven, were exempt from the normal processes of change in nature and were the focal interest of the Deity. That life in general should be modifiable by a natural selective process rather than fixed by a predetermined system regulated and periodically adjusted by its Creator was hardly the world view the devout might prefer; but that selection should also be capable of modifying humans was a suggestion as intolerable as it was impious. Characteristically, Darwin avoided controversy in the *Origin of Species* with the brief comment that by the pursuit of his theory of natural selection, "Light will be thrown on the origin of man and his history."

The Idea of Progress

Charles Darwin had amassed a large amount of data and had written a compelling argument in favor of evolution. A large number of scholars (including some, such as Lyell, who had rejected Lamarckian evolutionism) received Darwinian evolutionism enthusiastically. A critical factor was the development of the idea of progress in the social philosophy of the eighteenth and nineteenth centuries. Much of the Victorian intellectual world had already rejected the basic tenets of theological and social degenerationism. In a world of progressivism, the concept of biological evolution was easier to accept, and leading theologians began to incorporate biotic evolution into their world view. The doctrine of progress held that: (1) Progressive development is inherent in the psychical and social nature of humans and can operate independently of supernatural intervention; (2) this process will continue indefinitely for as long as humans exist; (3) happiness on earth is a goal of social progress and the end toward which individuals should strive; (4) humans may aspire to this goal since they are both morally and socially perfectable; and (5) knowledge and control of the social environment are the means by which progress can be realized. This doctrine was hardly compatible with the world view of the ancient and medieval periods, although Christianity had prepared the way by rejecting cyclic time and maintaining that human history was unique and significant. Christianity cut across circumscribed ethnic social units, and Christians felt themselves part of a universal world community. When the idea of progress was formulated during the late Renaissance, it was in part a reaction to the then popular belief among some nontheologically oriented intellectuals that the brightest period of human history—the Golden Age—was to be found only in antiquity, when minds were of a degree of excellence unequalled in subsequent times. But respect for the ancients was jarred by the recognition that many of their interpretations of nature were incorrect, as demonstrated by the substitution of Copernican for Ptolemaic astronomy and by the ascendency of Vesalius over Galen in the study of anatomy. As a result, natural philosophers began to speculate about a progressive acquisition of human knowledge. By the early part of the seventeenth century it became a truism that in the course of human history there had been advances in technology and that further improvements could be anticipated in the future. The human mind was conceived to be mechanistic and controlled by environmental determinants. If modified for good, the environment could impel the psychological betterment that was essential to social and moral progress. Direct divine intervention was excluded as a factor in the human condition. The Humanistic movement placed humans in the center of all speculative interests; what was good for humans was seen as abstractly and absolutely good or progressive. Since all minds were equal until molded for better or worse by the social environment, the task was to discover favorable environmental controls through rationalism, and thus hasten progress.

The quest was pursued along two related lines: (1) proposing various social controls, such as radical political reform, improved education, accelerated utilitarian and industrial projects in the economic sphere, or improved medical and hygienic measures; and (2) studying laws of society that, in the work of Comte, promised to elevate the concept of progress to a scientific discipline. The French Revolution exemplified the first approach, although both were inseparable in the minds of later champions of progress. In France the rational arguments for reform preached by Condorcet became manifest in the holocaust of the Revolution—a reign of terror that goes far to explain the subsequent retreat of proponents of the doctrine of progress into less activist pursuits. Thus Comte's positivism prevailed. The threat of the Revolution to the English reverence for the *status quo* precluded the liberals of that country from asserting a program of progress along French lines. The English (at least those in power), with their revolution well behind them, accepted the idea of progress during the eighteenth century but combined it with a well-entrenched Providentialism. They preferred to postpone their utopias until the distant future where they would not inconvenience the social order of this world, with which the middle and upper classes were rather satisfied. Thus, social reforms did not take place in England until well into the nineteenth century. By the time social utopias came into vogue in Britain, they were not revolutionary. Progress was the rationale for these utopias, whether closed systems where all members were assigned their proper functions by a powerful and enlightened system of political control, or less rigid societies where individuals were free to exploit their particular capacities for the betterment of neighbors. The concept of progress was introduced to Germany in the late eighteenth century writings of Herder; the interpretation was along French lines, but it included elements of Providentialism. Under the influence of Hegel, progressive theory justified a closed social system. Utopia, the final stage of human struggle, was supposed to be achieved in Hegel's contemporary Germany—following, of course, necessary political reforms. By 1850 the idea of progress permeated all levels of society in France, Britain, and Germany. Goals of progress varied, but the predominant theme was the achievement of human happiness, variously interpreted.

The most formidable opponents of the idea of progress were some Christian philosophers and the not-necessarily-Christian "philosophes." To the Christian, humanity had degenerated after the Fall, and the record of human immorality was evidence of this decline. To the philosophe—inheritor of Renaissance tradition—the Golden Age was not to be sought in the Garden of Eden, but in the classical world. Varying opinions about degeneration led to literary battles during the Renaissance over the question of whether ancient or contemporary scholars were superior. Renaissance Degenerationists argued that while their contemporaries might be superior to Europeans who had lived during the tenth century, how could the latter be conceived as superior to the classical thinkers of antiquity? The issue of intellectual stagnation in the Middle Ages became the focus of debate between the supporters and opponents of the theory of progress. As the concept of progress gained popularity, the problem was resolved by the gradual acceptance of a qualified concept of progress, according to which alternating periods of decline and ascent followed a gradually rising progressive trajectory. An unfavorable social environment could be blamed for the lack of progress in some periods, while positive social conditions were thought to foster human achievement. One philosophe, pessimistic about the course of human history but optimistic about humans as perfectible animals, was Rousseau. Rousseau believed humans could attain happiness through the practice of reason and application of reasoned rules of social action. But progress was far from inevitable. Both kinds of Degenerationists, the Christian and the philosophe, insisted that humans had been happier in the past than in their current circumstances.

Other attacks on the idea of progress came from those who saw the implications of Malthus's thesis on the nature of human population. Surely, if what he said was true, the unrestricted realization of Enlightenment ideals would lead to the extinction of the human species. The supporters of progress regarded increase in population as one of the anticipated improvements. Yet Malthus maintained that in the absence of those checks that were operating coincidentally with the tendency of populations to increase in a *geometric* ratio, their food supply, which increases only arithmetically, could not be sufficient to prevent the death by famine of vast numbers of individuals. The checks operating to prevent this condition were the very social evils that the upholders of progress were attempting to eliminate—vice, misery, and fear of want.

While the development of the idea of progress was independent of the growth of the natural sciences, by the nineteenth century "evidence" for progress was being sought in the research of physicists and biologists. When Spencer published his *Social Statics* in 1851, its readers found a social theory supporting progress and employing the tenets of Comte's positivism, to which was added as supportive evidence a theory of biological evolution. Spencer supplied his readers with a world view of such comprehensive scope that it could contain the entire gamut of phenomena in nature. As soon as Charles Darwin had enunciated the principle of natural selection, Spencer saw it as vindicating the theory of social selection that he had earlier conceived from a reading of Malthus. In effect, by making vice, misery, and fear of want the *vehicles* of progress, Spencer managed to nullify the Malthusian objection to the attainment of Enlightenment ideals. To Spencer all nature was evolving, and social progress was but an expected manifestation of this universal principle. By officiating as high priest at this unholy marriage of biological theory and social progress, Spencer facilitated the notion that the offspring of their union—biological progress—was legitimate. To the followers of Spencer, the emergence of a human fossil record in the latter half of the nineteenth century supported their claim of long-term progressive change and guaranteed its future continuation. Society could anticipate the eventual establishment of a perfect social order and a superior biological condition commensurate with it.

The philosophical position defined by Spencer, that society functions as an organism and is responsive to a deterministic mechanism analogous to natural selection, became known as Social Darwinism. Spencer maintained that the "free play of the fit" should be encouraged by political and legal sanctions. It was an inherent article of faith that Europeans and their descendants in various parts of the globe had succeeded to their state of political dominance because of natural selection, while those populations under their control were culturally and biologically less fit. This union of the doctrine of progress and organic evolution as natural corollaries contributed to racist theories and policies, especially with respect to justification of slavery and economic-military exploitation of non-Western peoples.

Just as the appeal of Social Darwinism to nineteenth century intellectuals influenced some of them to accept Darwinian evolution, disdain for Spencerian evolutionism influenced others to reject Darwinism. To many people, Spencerian and Darwinian evolution were interchangeable. Yet, curiously, in many ways, Darwin's *Origin of Species* challenged the Victorian doctrine of progress and laid the groundwork for much late twentieth century anti-Progressivism, especially in biological science. Darwin was greatly influenced by Lyell's Uniformitarianism; he rejected the major tenets of Progressionism, and railed against Lamarck's formulation of the law of inevitable progress. Most contemporary biologists disdain Social Darwinism, and many disavow any suggestion that evolutionary theory has ties with social doctrines. Some reject *any* notion of biological progress except in the sense of improved local adaptation, and virtually all modern biologists understand "progress" in terms very different from Spencer's. They often fail to understand the widespread popular perception of Darwinian evolution as wedded to a Spencerian world view.

Conclusion: People and Evolutionary Theory

As students of the universe, earth, and nature began to sever their dependence on scriptural authority and examine the world inductively, it became progressively more difficult for them to justify the concept of a static order of natural phenomena. Indeed, physicists, geologists, and biologists in turn came to question the very precepts on which their disciplines had been established. This intellectual crisis formed an hiatus that came to be filled by that complex body of data and theory called evolution. The genius of the concept of evolution was its apparent capacity to embrace the physical, natural, and social sciences in a way that earlier theories had been unable to do. By the end of the nineteenth century, natural science was no longer able to maintain the tenet of a static chain of being, and evolution became its integrating principle.

At the same time, humans became part of this dynamic evolving universe. The investigation of mankind's place in nature became the business of those natural historians who emerged in the middle of the last century and came to be known as anthropologists—students of human biological and cultural diversity and change. The accumulation of a hominid fossil record began at the very time that Darwinian evolution was gaining acceptance, although it was not until 1890, with the discovery of Middle Pleistocene fossil hominids in Java, that scientists completely abandoned the notion that humankind might be a rather special phenomenon with a recent evolutionary history. Earlier paleontological discoveries in Europe, beginning with the famous Neander Valley fossil recovered in 1856, were far more similar to modern humans, and most people now regard Neanderthals and their successors as members of our own species, *Homo sapiens*. As the hominid fossil record increased during the present century, and as both paleontological and geological evidence suggested a Miocene origin for members of the human family, the question of human evolution was resolved. However, the specific *course* of that evolution continues to be a source of exciting anthropological debate.

The recovery of the hominid fossil record has been basic to determining our place in nature. But it is important to stress that the major precepts of evolution surfaced without recourse to issues specifically involving the biological history of our human family. Rather, humankind has become more explicable through evolutionary models and propositions based on investigation of other living or fossil forms. This is the important fact overlooked by anti-evolutionists of many persuasions today: Humanity is not the critical piece in the thesis of evolutionary biology. The birth of evolution and its development as a concept during the past three centuries is as much an event of physics, geology, social philosophy, geography, and cosmology as it is the offspring of the biological and anthropological sciences.

Darwin laid the groundwork for the development of the science of evolutionary biology, a science that has changed and grown considerably in the present century. It has incorporated many non-Darwinian ideas. Still one can fairly attribute to Darwin a revolutionary role, not simply in writing the first treatise on biological evolution to receive wide intellectual acclaim, and not even because many of his ideas are still quite current. Darwinism has influenced practically every field of science; it has influenced social and political thought. In the century after Darwin, Darwinism has been everything but ignored.

NOTE

In the original work from which this reading is taken (McCown and Kennedy 1972), specific bibliographical references took the form of selected readings incorporated in the volume. This and other essays served as chapter introductions to the readings. In order that the reader of the present re-edited contribution may become familiar with some of the major published sources concerned with the history of evolutionary theory, a few references are added here.

For reference sources on geological sciences, see Adams 1938; Geikie 1905; Haber 1969; Hooykaas 1963; Stokes 1969. On paleontology, see Bowler 1976. On ideas as to mankind's place in nature, see Glacken 1967; Guthrie 1957; Woodbridge 1966. On general history of evolutionary biology, see Coleman 1971; Ritterbush 1964. On pre-Darwinian biologists, see Glass et al. 1958; Gundry 1946; Millhauser 1959. On Darwinian evolution, see Eiseley 1958, 1979; Ellegard 1957; Glick 1972; Gould 1977; Greene 1959; Himmelfarb 1959. On the concept of the chain of being, see Lovejoy 1936. On primitivism, see Lovejoy and Boas 1935. On the doctrine of progress, see Bury 1932; Pollard

1971. On Darwinism in social thought, see Gillispie 1959; Hofstadter 1955. And, on evolutionary theory in anthropology, see Hodgen 1964; Kennedy 1976; Teilhard de Chardin 1953.

SUGGESTED READINGS

Adams. Frank D. *The Birth and Development of the Geological Sciences.* Baltimore: Williams and Wilkins, 1938.

Bowler, Peter J. *Fossils and Progress: Paleontology and the Idea of Progressive Evolution in the Nineteenth Century.* New York: Science History Publications, 1976.

Bury, John B. *The Idea of Progress: An Inquiry into its Origin and Growth.* New York: Macmillan, 1932.

Coleman, W. *Biology in the Nineteenth Century.* New York: J. Wiley and Sons, 1971.

Eiseley, Loren. *Darwin's Century: Evolution and the Men who Discovered It.* Garden City: Doubleday, 1958.

———.*Darwin and the Mysterious Mr. X: New Light on the Evolutionists.* New York: E. P. Dutton, 1979.

Ellegard, Alvar. "Darwin's Theory and Nineteenth Century Philosophies of Science." In *Roots of Scientific Thought: A Cultural Perspective*, edited by Philip P. Wiener and Aaron Noland, pp. 537-568. New York: Basic Books, 1957.

Geikie, Archibald (Sir). *The Founders of Geology.* 2d ed. New York: Macmillan, 1905.

Gillispie, Charles C. *Genesis and Geology: A Study of the Relations of Scientific Thought, Natural Theology and Social Opinion in Great Britain 1790-1859.* New York: Harper and Brothers, 1959.

Glacken, Clarence J. *Traces on the Rhodian Shore: Nature and Culture in Western Thought from Ancient Times to the End of the Eighteenth Century.* Berkeley: University of California Press, 1967.

Glass, Bentley; Temkin, Owsei; and Strauss, William L., Jr., eds. *Forerunners of Darwin, 1745-1859.* Baltimore: Johns Hopkins, 1958.

Glick, Thomas F., ed. *The Comparative Reception of Darwinism.* Austin: University of Texas Press, 1972.

Gould, Stephen J. *Ever Since Darwin: Reflections in Natural History.* New York: W. W. Norton, 1977.

Greene, John C. *The Death of Adam: Evolution and its Impact on Western Thought.* Ames: Iowa State University, 1959.

Gundry, T. F. "The Bridgewater Treatises and Their Authors." *History* 31 (1946):140-152.

Guthrie, William K. C. *In the Beginning: Some Greek Views on the Origins of Life and the Early State of Man.* Ithaca: Cornell University, 1957.

Haber, Francis C. *The Age of the World: Moses to Darwin.* Baltimore: Johns Hopkins, 1959.

Himmelfarb, Gertrude. *Darwin and the Darwinian Revolution.* New York: Doubleday, 1959.

Hodgen, Margaret T. *Early Anthropology in the Sixteenth and Seventeenth Centuries.* Philadelphia: University of Pennsylvania, 1964.

Hofstadter, Richard. *Social Darwinism in American Thought*. Revised edition. Boston: Beacon, 1955.

Hooykaas, Reijer. *The Principle of Uniformity in Geology, Biology and Theology*. Leiden: Brill, 1963.

Kennedy, Kenneth A. R. *Human Variation in Space and Time*. Dubuque: W. C. Brown, 1976.

Lovejoy, Arthur O. *The Great Chain of Being: A Study of the History of an Idea*. Boston: Harvard University Press, 1936.

Lovejoy, Arthur O., and Boas, George. *Primitivism and Related Ideas in Antiquity: Contributions to the History of Primitivism*. A Documentary History of Primitivism and Related Ideas, vol. 1. Baltimore: Johns Hopkins, 1935.

McCown, Theodore D., and Kennedy, Kenneth A. R., eds. *Climbing Man's Family Tree: A Collection of Major Writings on Human Phylogeny, 1699-1971*. Englewood Cliffs, N.J.: Prentice-Hall, 1972.

Millhauser, Milton. *Just Before Darwin: Robert Chambers and Vestiges*. Middletown, Conn.: Wesleyan University Press, 1959.

Pollard, Sidney. *The Idea of Progress: History and Society*. Middlesex: Penguin, 1971.

Ritterbush, Philip C. *Overtures to Biology: The Speculations of Eighteenth Century Naturalists*. New Haven: Yale University, 1964.

Stokes, E. "The Six Days of the Deluge: Some Ideas on Earth History in the Royal Society, London, 1660-1775." *Earth Sciences Journal* 3 (1969): 13-39.

Teilhard de Chardin, Pierre, S. J. "The Idea of Fossil Man." In *Anthropology Today: An Encyclopedic Inventory*, edited by Alfred L. Kroeber, pp. 93-100. Chicago: University of Chicago, 1953.

Woodbridge, Frederick J. E. *Aristotle's Vision of Nature*. New York: Columbia University, 1966.

The Nature of Darwinian Explanation: Is Darwinian Evolutionary Theory Scientific?

ARTHUR L. CAPLAN

The Hastings Center

Introduction

If there is one philosophical spectre that has haunted Darwinian evolutionary theory—from the bilious initial assessments of various theologians and theologically minded scientists that greeted the publication of the *Origin of Species* in 1859 (Hull 1973; Glick 1974; Ruse 1979; Peckham 1959), down to the present-day caterwauls and polemics of pseudoscientific creationists and fundamentalists at school board meetings, legislative hearings, and public rallies (Godfrey 1981; Hadd 1979; Gurin 1981)—it is the charge that Darwinian evolutionary theory is not really scientific. During the 125 years since Darwin's famous abstract of his book first went to press, the theory he propounded has been variously disparaged as wrong, santanic, untestable, ridden with ideology, and tautologous. Occasionally those offering such criticisms have deigned to advance a view concerning the nature of science such that the alleged scientific failings of Darwinism might be plainly revealed. More frequently, however, critics of Darwinian evolutionary theory have been content to blast away at the theory's supposed failings qua legitimate science while leaving the bases for their assorted charges unstated and, thus, irrefutable. There is no doubt that in the battle of rhetoric over matters of methodology the critics of Darwinism have fared somewhat better than its defenders.

If evolutionary theory in its contemporary guise—the so-called modern synthetic theory of evolution (Mayr and Provine 1980)—is to be promulgated by teachers in the public schools to hordes of innocent and, supposedly, gullible and malleable minds, then surely, generations of critics have argued, the theory must pass the rigorous conceptual muster accorded all theories in science. Since few parties among the disputants have given any serious consideration to what

these rigorous conceptual standards might be, the critics seem to
have Darwinists over a methodological barrel. Unless the proponents
of Darwinism are able to say what distinguishes science from non-
science, they will find it difficult to defend the inclusion of the
modern synthetic theory of evolution as science in textbooks, class-
rooms, or even grant applications. Since the proponents of Darwinism
are usually biologists or social scientists, and not philosophers or
historians of science, they are often quite ill-prepared to articulate
the kinds of conceptual criteria and methodological attributes demanded by the critics. That many of the *critics* have no clue as to
the properties distinguishing science from nonscience, much less
nonsense, is not to the point. The inability of Darwinists to persuasively describe and defend their theory as scientific has, over the
years, done much to discredit the theory in the eyes both of other
scholars within the academy and among the general public.

Is Darwinian Theory Circular?

Probably the most serious charge that has been leveled at the Darwinian theory of evolution is that the theory is a tautology (Macbeth
1971, 1978; Bethell 1976; Peters 1976). What critics contend by
invoking this term is that Darwinian evolutionary theory is circular
and, thus, lacks empirical content. The most favored target for this
particular charge is the old saw that evolutionary theory ultimately
explains evolution as resulting from a "natural selection of the fittest"
(Rosen 1978; Simon 1976; Løvtrup 1976). The fittest, according to
this analysis of the empirical content of the theory, are defined solely
in terms of those organisms who do, as a matter of fact, survive. The
circular or tautological character of evolutionary theory, either *sensu*
Darwin or in its contemporary form, is said to be evident from the
fact that the key explanatory device utilized in the theory—natural
selection—is, by definitional sleight of hand, made synonymous with
both fitness and survival. If those creatures observed to survive on
earth today do so because they are fit, and if the only way available
for assessing their fitness is their survival, then natural selection, the
explanatory lynchpin of all Darwinian evolutionary accounts, is
nothing but an elaborate semantic obfuscation—a kind of conceptual
shell game where the shells are natural selection, fitness, and survival.

    The charge of tautology, if true, would be a devastating indict-
ment of the claim that evolutionary theory is acceptable as science.
Whatever else scientific theories or scientific propositions may be,
they surely must possess some empirical content. Tautologies have
no such content. If evolutionary theory did actually utilize a truism
to explain the phenomena of evolution in the organic world, there

would be little reason for attending to it seriously as an explanatory account, much less for teaching it to children and college freshmen.

However, the claim that evolutionary theory rests on the necessarily tautologous definition of natural selection is an utter straw man. The easiest way to see the total emptiness of this criticism is to examine exactly what the theory of evolution *claims* in attempting to explain the facts of evolution. By examining the version of evolutionary theory propounded by Darwin in his *Origin of Species* and its subsequent refinement and modification by later researchers in evolutionary biology, it is possible to see both the nontautological character of Darwinian theory and the truly scientific character of Darwinian explanations.

Evolution as Fact, Process, and Theory

In any attempt to access the scientific status of Darwinian evolutionary theory it is important to distinguish between the *fact* of evolution, the *process* of evolution, and *theories* of evolution. Few people, in Darwin's day or today, would deny the fact that evolution has occurred in the natural world. Evolution, in the factual sense of the term, simply refers to the observation that changes have occurred over time in the makeup of the organisms living on the earth (Stebbins 1971). It is a hard, observable, undeniable fact that such changes have occurred. As Darwin was well aware, human beings have themselves produced changes in the composition of creatures to be found over time living on the earth (Darwin, 1968; see also Ruse 1979). By selectively breeding various animals and plants, humans have been able to create new forms of organisms that certainly did not exist prior to human intervention. Human beings have also caused the extinction of many types of organisms, through pollution, pesticides, or as a consequence of hunting, habitat destruction, or medical intervention (Bajema 1971; Patterson 1978). The fact that smallpox appears to have been successfully eradicated from many nations through the sustained efforts of physicians and public health officials means that a type of organism once endemic in many parts of the world no longer exists. And this means that, within the past decade, a change has occurred in the organismic makeup of the world that is concrete, datable, and verifiable.

Human beings have certainly caused changes to occur in the composition of life on earth. Moreover, there are additional, equally certain evidences of change in the composition of nature as well. From Darwin's day to the present, it is an undeniable fact that organisms have evolved. It is known, for example, that in the past 125 years the number and variety of insects that can be found in various parts of the world have varied with time. In some years gypsy moths are very abundant in the American Northeast. In other years their numbers decline to less than one-half of that observed in periods of abundance. The same fluctuations can be observed in the numbers of fire ants, cicadas, ladybugs, grasshoppers, fruit flies, boll weevils, locusts, and termites in various locales around the globe. Similar shifts in numbers can be seen among populations of birds, plants, primates, fish, and amphibians (Savage 1969; Greenway 1967).

Not only do we know that the composition of living forms occupying the earth from year to year and month to month is constantly in flux, but we also know that different organisms have come to occupy new areas and habitats. The recent spread of the Med fly and the starling through portions of North America, rabbits throughout Australia, and African honeybees throughout South and Central America are matters of public record and, indeed, of public concern (Nitecki 1981). Scientists have been able to date the arrival and spread of new forms of life on small islands, in isolated ponds, and on barren mountain peaks (Frankel and Soule 1981). These changes are as factual as any facts can be. They are events that can be observed by anyone with the time, patience, and desire to do so. Evolution, understood as a claim about changes in the quantity and composition of life on earth, is an undeniable, irrefutable, puzzling, and marvelous fact. If this fact were not true, there would be nothing at all for Darwinians, creationists, Lamarckians, and others to argue about!

Once the fact of evolution is acknowledged, however, there is much to argue about. One central question is whether there are any patterns or directions to the kinds of changes that have occurred among the diverse organisms found on our planet. It is quite possible that there are no systematic alterations or shifts in organic evolution. The question of what types of changes are to be found in evolution—directional, patterned, or random—is an issue about the nature of the *process* of evolution.

In his *Origin of Species* Darwin devoted the bulk of his chapters to a demonstration that evolution in the factual sense was not a random, haphazard process. He argued that correlations existed between the features of organisms and their habitats; that the distribution of organisms was related to the distribution of natural resources; that organisms tended to produce offspring that closely resembled the parents in their external form; that the likelihood of any particular organism surviving appeared to be a function of its physical traits and behaviors; and that changes in the composition of life forms in various locales seemed to be related to prior changes in the physical or the organic environments of these areas (Caplan 1979).

Numerous biologists since Darwin's day have searched for other patterns and regularities among the variations and fluxes of organic evolution. They have found that warm-blooded organisms living in cold climates tend to be larger than similar forms living in warmer climes; that certain directional patterns of change can be observed in the fossil remnants of many types of organisms; that definite cycles of boom and bust exist in the numbers of organisms to be found in various regions of the globe; that definite patterns of inheritance are manifested in various families of organisms over time; and that evolutionary changes in the features of organisms rarely revert back to earlier forms displayed by the ancestors of such creatures. Some of these empirical generalizations have ascended to the status of low-level laws about the nature of evolutionary change—Bergmann's Law, Dollo's Law, Mendel's Laws, and so on.

Other scientists have argued that the process of evolutionary change reveals far more systematic order and alteration than is evident in the descriptive generalizations of a Darwin, Mendel, or Dollo. They argue that all of evolutionary change plainly reveals a steady, systematic march of organic progress. Historically, the most popular end point for this grand ascent in the flux of nature has been humans —variously instantiated by nineteenth century English aristocrats, twentieth century Aryan peoples, male members of the Prussian medical profession, and American industrialists (primarily oil and steel magnates) residing in large homes adjacent to large urban settings, depending on the idiosyncratic tastes of those doing the evaluation of the process (Gould 1977, 1980b).

Since Darwin's day a great deal of ink has been devoted to the question of evolutionary progress. Such diverse authors as Teilhard de Chardin, Leo Berg, Francis Galton, Henry F. Osborne, and Julian Huxley have all at one time or another argued that the sum total of changes constituting the facts of evolution reveal a steady march of progress, from the "lower" to the "higher," the simple to the complex, the stupid to the intelligent, the mindless to the mindful, the amoral to the moral, and/or the brutish to the civilized (Goudge 1961; Simpson 1967, 1975). Many of these authors believed that it was necessary to posit some sort of distinctive cause or law to explain the progressive pattern of change to be found in the facts of evolution. Some turned to mystical vitalistic forces or fields to explain the prevalence of progress. Others argued for the existence of distinctive laws governing evolutionary processes, whereby the final "best" outcome determined the kinds of changes that could previously occur—a kind of backward causation in which the effect determines the cause rather than the more mundane, converse sequence of affairs commonly found in the physical world.

The issue of whether any patterns are revealed in organic evolution, and, if so, what kinds of patterns and uniformities are to be found, has long been a source of contention among students of evolution. Suffice it to say that, in large measure, the determination of progressive patterns of change is a highly evaluative matter. What is not subject to dispute is that some patterns and uniformities do exist and can be found: That insects, bats, and birds all possess similar sorts of appendages enabling them to travel through the air is a pattern that cries out for some sort of explanation; that the cells of humans, primates, birds, bugs, and plants all possess common chemical substances is a uniformity (admittedly unknown in Darwin's day) that would seem to prove that at least some remarkable uniformities do exist (Dobzhansky et al. 1977, Chapter 2; Stebbins 1971, Chapter 7). Evolution is not merely a jumble of haphazard changes: The scope and range of the changes to be found reveal order and uniformity. It is this aspect of evolution—its nonrandomness—that, as much as the fact of organic change, demands scientific analysis and explanation.

The need to explain both the fact of evolution and the empirical fact that the *process* of evolution is nonrandom leads to the third and most controversial usage of the term "evolution": as a shorthand description for the various efforts that have been made to explain the verifiable existence of systematic patterns of change in nature.

Darwin's Explanatory Schema

Critics of Darwinian evolutionary theories have been manifestly schizophrenic over the years in their assessments of scientific efforts to explain the facts and patterns of evolution. On the one hand, some critics insist that evolutionary theories are not testable, and that the bog of circularity manifested by all the talk of fitness, survival, selection, and adaptation makes all discussion of tests, falsification, and verification absurd. On the other hand, other critics have been concerned to note that Darwinian evolutionary theories are simply not equal to the task of explaining the data of nature. No theory, in their opinion, can adequately explain the exquisite perfection of the human eye for seeing, or the delicate symbiotic relationships that exist between many creatures (Wysong 1976). Darwinian theories are, in the eyes of its critics, caught in a methodological bind between a rock and a very hard place—too circular and opaque to be tested, and yet too inadequate and simple-minded to be powerful enough to account for the facts. Fortunately neither of the horns of this supposed dilemma is very pointed because, as the historical development of evolutionary theory plainly shows, Darwinian theories have been both testable and quite powerful.

In order to see the amenability of Darwinian theories to test and proof, it is necessary that some attention be given over to the content of the theory. Nowhere in any of the writings of Darwin or his scientific legatees is anything even vaguely reminiscent of a truism or tautology advanced as a theory of evolution. It is true that the explanation of evolution (as fact and process) in terms of the "survival of the fittest" is tautological when the fittest are defined as "those that survive." Unfortunately, those who have over the decades railed against this hapless emasculation have never noticed that it bears no relationship whatsoever to any theory Darwin or subsequent generations of evolutionists ever propounded.

Darwin's *Origin of Species* is as good a place as any to locate the gist of Darwinian evolutionary theory. In this book Darwin begins by noting three facts: First, the process of evolution is nonrandom. This is exemplified by the limited nature of organic variation in all parts of the globe, relative to what might be empirically possible. Second and third, by utilizing certain time-tested breeding tricks and techniques, some human beings have been able both to duplicate the fact of evolution and to extend the constraints on variation to be found in nature (Darwin 1968, pp. 150–160). Surely, Darwin argues, if pigeon fanciers and sheep farmers have been able to produce systematic changes in the behavior and appearance of domestic animals, then analogous mechanisms may have been at work in producing the ordered pattern of changes to be found in the natural world.

In addition to these facts, Darwin offers a number of other observations about life on earth. A key observation is that there ought to be many more organisms alive on the planet than there in fact are. Organisms, Darwin remarks, from rabbits to humans have tremendous reproductive capacities. Even the elephant, which Darwin cites as an example of one of the slowest breeding of all known creatures, is, in principle, capable of reproducing 19 million of its own kind in a period of no more than 750 years (Darwin 1968, p. 117). Given the breeding inclinations and mighty reproductive capacities of insects, marine life, and many mammals, the entire earth ought to be full to the hilt with creatures. Yet this is not so. Moreover, Darwin notes, it is a matter of empirical fact that some varieties of creature are more abundant than others in patterns that do not always correlate with their reproductive abilities (Darwin 1968, Chapter III).

Darwin's hunch, fueled by his reading of Malthus on the dismal course of human history, is that limits on the gross numbers of creatures that can occupy the planet are set by the type and quantity of resources available for their use in various parts of the globe. These observations led Darwin, in the early chapters of the *Origin*, to propose a theoretical explanation for the empirically observable patterns of variation in the quantity and kinds of life on earth (Manier 1978). His analysis runs as follows:

The Argument for a Struggle for Existence

Empirically verified principles—

(P1) *Principle of Reproduction:* Nearly all organisms possess both the capacity and the drive to reproduce themselves at rapid rates.

(P2) *Principle of Dependence:* All organisms depend on natural resources such as air, water, and energy for life.

To these principles Darwin adds three factual observations:

Factual observations—

(F1) There are a limited number of places on the earth where natural resources exist.

(F2) The locations where natural resources can be found fluctuate over time.

(F3) A good deal of variation exists in the form and behavior of organisms.

Darwin then argues (Chapter IV) that the facts he has cited, when combined with the principles he has discerned to be operative in nature, lead directly to two important conclusions:

Logically necessary conclusions derived from principles and facts—

(C1) There must obtain a competition or a "struggle for existence" among organisms for natural resources (Chapter III).

(C2) The struggle for existence is a possible source for the patterns of quantity and variation found among the organisms dwelling on the earth.

The struggle for existence, so beloved of critics of evolutionary theory as the quintessential tautology, is not a tautology at all. Rather, competition or struggle is a logical consequence of certain principles and facts. Darwin argues that, if it is true that organisms can reproduce quickly and that resources are finite, struggle and competition are inevitable. This conclusion is generated from premises that say nothing about fitness, selection, or adaptation. The struggle for existence is as contingent a fact as one could ever hope for— diminish reproductive capacity or increase resources, and the struggle for existence disappears!

But Darwin knew that there were more puzzling uniformities in nature than the regulation of animal numbers. Some organisms simply fare better than others in certain habitats. Some organisms have fared so poorly, in fact, that all that remains of them are their bones! Darwin observed the great variety that exists among organisms and asked what the effect of such variation would be in the context of a struggle for existence. Furthermore, he observed a "strong tendency" for organisms to produce offspring that closely resemble their parents (Darwin 1968, Chapter IV; Bell 1977). If, Darwin reasoned, some traits or behaviors were more advantageous than others in terms of obtaining resources; and if it were true that organisms tended to pass along similar traits and behaviors to their offspring; then, in the context of a struggle for existence for scarce resources, a natural selection would occur tending to produce animals and plants with the traits and behaviors most likely to be advantageous in obtaining those scarce resources.

Schematically, the second part of Darwin's theory of evolution can be summarized as follows (Caplan 1979, pp. 346-347):

The Argument for Natural Selection

Empirically verified principles—

(P1) Certain traits and behaviors will allow organisms that possess them to obtain more resources than organisms that do not.

(P2) Organisms tend to reproduce similar organisms.

(P3) Organisms possessing advantageous traits and behaviors will tend to have higher survival and, thus, reproductive success than organisms possessing less advantageous traits and behaviors.

Factual observations—

(F1) A struggle for existence exists in nature.

(F2) A great deal of variation exists in the traits and behaviors possessed by organisms.

(F3) Some traits and behaviors, when assessed relative to other traits and behaviors, can be classified as advantageous, neutral, or disadvantageous in securing scarce natural resources.

Logically necessary conclusion deducible from principles and facts—

(C1) There will be a natural selection among the variegated traits and behaviors of organisms tending to favor an increase in organisms possessing the most advantageous traits and behaviors relative to those possessed by other organisms.

Natural selection, to put the matter succinctly, is a logical consequence of the combination of a struggle for existence with certain principles of inheritance and variation. This schematization of Darwin's theory, as presented in the *Origin*, makes plain the relationship between the struggle for existence and natural selection. The con cepts are not related via definitional fiat, as hordes of critics have erroneously maintained; rather, natural selection is the logical consequence of the struggle for existence when supplemented with other valid principles and facts. Thus, while it is true that a relationship does exist between the struggle for existence and natural selection, it is not of the circular sort so dear to the hearts of pseudoscientific creationists and other methodologically befuddled critics of Darwinian theory.

Darwin used this two-part theory to explain the innumerable facts and peculiar uniformities in nature. He argued against his fellow creationists, catastrophists, and Lamarckians that natural selection was the key causal mechanism driving the evolutionary process (Ruse 1979). One need not posit disasters of a Divine or natural sort to explain the fact that the number of animals and plants is not as large as it could be: The struggle for existence is a sufficient natural check on animal numbers. And one need not resort to Lamarckian influences in hereditary or Divine design to explain the regularities and patterns of variation found in nature, past or present. The interaction of a tendency toward reproductive constancy with differences in the utility of organic traits and behaviors in securing resources will produce a natural selection among organisms in which some organisms will fare better in the struggle for existence than will others.

Darwin's theory was, in its own time, recognized by many scientists as far preferable to its theoretical competitors—creationism, catastrophism, and Lamarckianism. All of Darwin's principles and alleged facts were susceptible to empirical verification and test. Indeed, the bulk of the *Origin of Species* is given over to just such an enterprise. The theoretical alternatives to Darwin's theory, by contrast, were truly untestable (as in the case of Biblical creationism), or relied on a steady stream of *ad hoc* events: catastrophes, upheavals, fortuitous environment/heredity interactions, and so on.

Nevertheless, despite the fact that Darwin's theory of evolution had far more empirical support than its available rivals, there were many problems and puzzles confronting the first version of the theory. Not the least of these was the question of how new variations could appear in nature once selection began to occur. Advantageous traits and behaviors would be favored, but once organisms lacking these had been eliminated, evolution would and should have come to a grinding halt (Olby 1966; Carter 1957). Moreover, as Darwin himself noted (1968, Chapter II), some organisms existed that did not reproduce at all, such as neuter insects and sterile hybrids. How could Darwin's theory, resting on principles of inheritance and advantage, explain the persistence of such creatures, which certainly were at a distinct reproductive disadvantage relative to their fertile peers? Darwin's theory was hardly untestable; indeed, Darwin was keenly

aware that a number of facts about evolution appeared to falsify
his theory.

The Unifying Power of Darwinism

The fact that certain puzzles and difficulties existed for Darwinian
theory, and that the theory nevertheless gained wide acceptance in
many scientific circles, reveals something of central importance for
understanding the scientific status of any theory. The Darwinism of
Darwin's day can be seen as scientific for a number of reasons. First,
it attempted to explain a number of facts and generalizations about
empirical events in the world. Second, it attempted to explain these
facts by means of a set of verifiable principles and assumptions.
Third, it attempted to explain a set of diverse facts and disparate
empirical generalizations by means of a single style or pattern of
explanation. Trends in the fossil record, limits on animal numbers,
regularities in the distribution of organisms around the globe, and
the adaptedness of organisms to their environments could all be
explained in Darwin's theory by the same rough set of principles,
assumptions, and conclusions. The struggle for existence and the
process of natural selection were utilized in every Darwinian account
of organic evolution. They provide the distinctive core or pattern
of Darwinian explanation; and, as such, they provide a means by
which apparently unrelated phenomena can be linked to a set of
common causes.

It is this unifying power of Darwinism (Kitcher 1981; Friedman
1974)—the ability to group what had previously been viewed as un-
connected and disparate aspects of evolution under a single explanatory framework—that guaranteed Darwinian evolutionary theory a
hearing as an exemplar of scientific theorizing. For theories, in order
to be scientific, need not only to be about empirical facts, and to
possess testable and confirmable premises and assumptions, but
should also allow for the unification of seemingly unrelated and
diverse facts. It is this unifying power of Darwin's explanatory schema
as first evidenced in his arguments in the *Origin of Species* that provides the vital psychological impact requisite in any good scientific
theory. Darwin's theory allows us to see the vast morass of facts and
patterns present in nature as the outcome of a few simple factors—
what scientists often refer to as the elegance and power of good
theories. As was the case with Newton's celestial mechanics and
Lyell's uniformitarian geology (Cohen 1980), Darwin's theory
allowed scientists to feel as if they understood something about the
world that they had not realized prior to the theory's formulation,
that the diverse facts of evolution were the by-products of a set of

simple common causes. Facticity, testability, and unificatory power are the hallmarks of sound scientific theories. While a theory possessing these attributes may be inadequate, flawed, or simply false, it is, nonetheless, still scientific. While Darwinism had its problems and flaws, it also had the central virtue of unificatory power—a virtue sadly lacking in many of Darwinism's theoretical competitors both in his time and today. Divine creation, whether of the sort depicted in Genesis or in the religious texts of other cultures, is not in any sense a testable theory. But just as important, the invocation of a deity to explain the facts and processual patterns of evolution provides no unification to the random facts and patterns of nature. Darwinism does. If some version of Darwin's argument is sound, then the seemingly disparate, inchoate, murky mass of phenomena we recognize as the facts and patterns of evolution become comprehensible as the related outcomes of a single set of principles and assumptions—a transformation that is characteristic of and distinctive to scientific theorizing (Cohen 1980, pp. 157-218). While critics of Darwinism have tended to focus solely on testability as the only criterion capable of distinguishing science from nonscience, they fail to realize that the unificatory power of a successful pattern of explanation is as important in attempting to draw such a distinction. When a theory manifests a unificatory pattern as powerful as that found in Darwinian theory's struggle for existence and natural selection, then scientists will go to great lengths (in the case of Darwinism a sustained effort of 125 years thus far) to preserve and defend the soundness of that basic pattern of explanation against apparent counter-examples, puzzles, and even empirical refutations.

Is Modern Evolutionary Theory Darwinian?

The issue of falsifiability has preoccupied critics of Darwinism since the inception of the theory. In part, this is a result of an undue attention in certain philosophy-of-science circles to matters of testability as the only means by which science can be distinguished from non-science and, by implication, sense from nonsense (Caplan 1978; Popper 1974). As I have tried to suggest in pointing to the unificatory power of Darwinism vis-à-vis empirical biological facts and low-level generalizations, testability is not all that matters in the determination of what will and ought to be counted as science. Nevertheless, testability is certainly a factor to be taken into account in assessing any proposition or theory that purports to be scientific. It is interesting to see how Darwinian theory has fared on this basis since Darwin's time, in light of the insistent claims of the theory's critics that it is not testable.

If we consider the version of the theory as I have reconstructed it from Darwin's presentation in the *Origin*, then strictly speaking it can be said that subsequent research and field investigations by many scientists have proved the theory *false* many times over.

Darwin's original theory claimed that all regularities in the distribution of organic variation could be totally explained by principles concerning (1) a tendency to constancy in inheritance; (2) the dependency of organisms on natural resources; and (3) some facts about scarcity, character variation, and relative advantage. It is not true that these factors suffice to explain all the regularities manifested in nature. Darwin offered no laws about patterns of inheritance resulting from the existence of genes and chromosomes. The laws governing these entities were rediscovered long after Darwin's death and were not made a part of his theory until well into the twentieth century. Indeed, for a short period at the turn of the century, many scientists saw Mendelism and its laws as a viable theoretical alternative to Darwinism for explaining all of the facts and processes of evolution (Provine 1971).

Mutation and recombination, key sources for the production of new variations in nature, were also not a part of Darwin's original views concerning inheritance. While the discovery of these processes solved one of the central problems confronting Darwin and his early supporters (the problem of where new varieties came from to replace those lost through natural selection), the fact that Darwinism makes no mention of them reveals the theory to be quite inaccurate—not only testable, but false!

Darwin's theory has proved to be inadequate in yet another way. In his theory, the bulk of organic evolution occurs as a result of *anagenesis*—evolution within a particular species lineage. But as later generations of field researchers have convincingly demonstrated (Lack 1947; Clausen 1951; Mayr 1963), it is *cladogenesis*—the splitting of an interbreeding population into groups via natural barriers (such as the formation of mountains or the rerouting of rivers), or via other processes (White 1978)—that is central to the phenomena of the diversity of organisms and their evolution. Darwin's theory assumed that most evolutionary change occurred as a result of the slow accumulation of advantageous traits by various populations of organisms (anagenesis). We now know that this process, while important, is not sufficient for explaining many important aspects of evolutionary change. Contemporary models of speciation (Stanley 1981; Bock 1970), with their emphasis on drift, isolation, and character displacement, hardly resemble the explanatory narratives derivable from the arguments given in Darwin's version of evolutionary theory.

Many other illustrations could be given of various ways in which Darwin's original outline of an explanatory theory has been found inadequate or simply erroneous. If the history of evolutionary theorizing since Darwin's day shows anything, it surely reveals that the theory has constantly been subject to modifications, alterations, refinements, and amplifications—hardly the characteristics one would expect of an untestable theory. Indeed, the changes that have been made to Darwin's theory since he first advanced it—the addition of a theory of genetics; the discovery of the importance of mutation and recombination; the realization that barriers to gene flow are key elements in understanding speciation; the refinement of Darwin's notions of competition, adaptation, species, and character traits; and so on—reveal that the real question that students of evolutionary theory must address is not whether the theory is testable, but whether the current modern synthetic theory of evolution retains enough commonality with Darwin's original theory to be still classified as Darwinian (Kitcher 1981; Cohen 1980; Lauden 1977; Gould 1980a).

Ultimately, the answer to this question will have to depend on the degree to which later theories preserve what I have termed the "pattern" of explanation present in Darwin's version of evolutionary theory, his arguments for the necessity of a struggle for existence, and the inevitability of the occurrence of natural selection. The issue of whether later theories are merely refinements and extensions of Darwin's basic theory, or are so different that they have evolved into an entirely new kind of evolutionary theory, cannot be settled in this reading.

What can, however, be settled is the issue of the scientific status of Darwinian evolutionary theories. As the history of the theory shows, Darwinism is eminently testable. As the analysis of Darwin's own arguments shows, there is nothing at all tautologous about the theory. As the analysis of the logic of Darwin's original arguments reveals, the theory possesses a robust, unifying, and elegant pattern of explanation that succeeds in linking a variety of puzzling facts and empirical generalizations. It may be true that Darwinian theory is, as some have argued, Satanic, ridden with ideology, and/or inadequate as an explanation of evolution. But, it is surely also true that Darwinian theory is scientific.

REFERENCES

Bajema, C. B. *Natural Selection in Human Populations*. New York: John Wiley & Sons, 1971.
Bell, E. A. "Heritability in Retrospect." *Journal of Heredity* 68 (1977):267-300.
Bethell, Thomas. "Darwin's Mistake." *Harper's Magazine* 252 (1976):70-75.
Bock, Walter J. "Microevolutionary Sequences as a Fundamental Concept in Macroevolutionary Models." *Evolution* 24 (1970):704-722.

Caplan, Arthur L. "Testability, Disreputability and the Structure of the Modern Synthetic Theory of Evolution." *Erkenntnis* 13 (1978):261-278.

——. "Darwinism and Deductivist Models of Theory Structure." *Studies in History and Philosophy of Science* 10, no. 4 (1979):341-353.

Carter, G. S. *A Hundred Years of Evolution.* New York: Macmillan, 1957.

Clausen, J. *Stages in the Evolution of Plant Species.* Ithaca: Cornell University Press, 1951.

Cohen, I. B. *The Newtonian Revolution.* Cambridge: Cambridge University Press, 1980.

Darwin, Charles. *The Origin of Species.* 1859. Edited by J. W. Burrow. Baltimore: Penguin, 1968.

Dobzhansky, Theodosius; Ayala, Francisco; Stebbins, G.; and Valentine, James. *Evolution.* San Francisco: W. H. Freeman, 1977.

Frankel, D. H., and Soule, M. E. *Conservation and Evolution.* New York: Cambridge University Press, 1981.

Friedman, M. "Explanation and Scientific Understanding." *Journal of Philosophy* 71 (1974):5-19.

Glick, T. F., ed. *The Comparative Reception of Darwinism.* Austin: University of Texas Press, 1974.

Godfrey, Laurie R. "The Flood of Antievolutionism." *Natural History* 90, no. 6 (1981):4-10.

Goudge, T. A. *The Ascent of Life.* Toronto: University of Toronto Press, 1961.

Gould, Stephen J. *Ever Since Darwin.* New York: W. W. Norton, 1977.

——. "Is a New and General Theory of Evolution Emerging?" *Paleobiology* 6 (1980a):119-130.

——. *The Panda's Thumb.* New York: W. W. Norton, 1980b.

Greenway, J. C., Jr. *Extinct and Vanishing Birds of the World.* 2d ed. New York: Dover, 1967.

Gurin, Joel. "The Creationist Revival." *The Sciences* 22, no. 4 (1981):22-26.

Hadd, J. R. *Evolution: Reconciling the Controversy.* Glassboro, N. J.: Kronos Press, 1979.

Hull, David L. *Darwin and His Critics.* Cambridge, Mass.: Harvard University Press, 1973.

Kitcher, P. "Explanatory Unification." *Philosophy of Science* 48, no. 4 (1981): 507-531.

Lack, David. *Darwin's Finches.* New York: Cambridge University Press, 1947.

Lauden, L. *Progress and Its Problems.* Berkeley: University of California Press, 1977.

Løvtrup, S. "On the Falsifiability of Neo-Darwinism." *Evolutionary Theory* 1 (1976):267-283.

Macbeth, Norman. *Darwin Retried.* Boston: Gambit Press, 1971.

——. "Book Review: Gould, S. J., *Ever Since Darwin.*" *Systematic Zoology* 27 (1978):264-266.

Manier, E. *The Young Darwin and His Cultural Circle.* Dordrecht: D. Reidel, 1978.

Mayr, E. *Animal Species and Evolution.* Cambridge, Mass.: Harvard University Press, 1963.

Mayr, Ernst, and Provine, W. B., eds. *The Evolutionary Synthesis.* Cambridge, Mass.: Harvard University Press, 1980.

Nitecki, M. H., ed. *Biotic Crisis in Ecological and Evolutionary Time*. New York: Academic Press, 1981.

Olby, R. C. *Origins of Mendelism*. New York: Schocken, 1966.

Patterson, Colin. *Evolution*. London: British Museum (Natural History), 1978.

Peckham, M. "Darwinism and Darwinisticism." *Victorian Studies* 3 (1959):3-40.

Peters, R. H. "Tautology in Evolution and Ecology." *American Naturalist* 110 (1976):1-12.

Popper, Karl R. "Darwinism as a Metaphysical Research Program." In *The Philosophy of Karl Popper*, edited by P. Schilpp, pp. 133-143. LaSalle, Ill.: Open Court, 1974.

Provine, W. B. *The Origins of Theoretical Population Genetics*. Chicago: University of Chicago Press, 1971.

Rosen, Donn E. "Book Review: Johnson, C., *Introduction to Natural Selection*." *Systematic Zoology* 27 (1978):370-373.

Ruse, Michael. *The Darwinian Revolution*. Chicago: The University of Chicago Press, 1979.

Savage, L. J. *Evolution*. 2d ed. New York: Holt, Rinehart and Winston, 1969.

Simon, M. A. *The Matter of Life*. New Haven: Yale University Press, 1976.

Simpson, George Gaylord. *The Meaning of Evolution*. Revised ed. New Haven: Yale University Press, 1967.

——. "The Concept of Progress in Organic Evolution." *Social Research* 41 (1975):51-64.

Stanley, Steven M. *The New Evolutionary Timetable*. New York: Basic Books, 1981.

Stebbins, G. L. *Processes of Organic Evolution*. Englewood Cliffs, N. J.: Prentice-Hall, 1971.

White, M. J. D. *Modes of Speciation*. San Francisco: W. H. Freeman, 1978.

Wysong, R. L. *The Creation-Evolution Controversy*. East Lansing, Mich.: Inquiry Press, 1976.

Darwinian, Spencerian, and Modern Perspectives on Progress in Biological Evolution

LAURIE GODFREY

The University of Massachusetts at Amherst

Introduction

It is currently in vogue in some circles to claim that Darwinian evolution violates a law of decreasing order in the universe, and therefore cannot have occurred. Proponents of this view define evolution as progressive change from simple to complex. Ironically, their view of the universe demands unidirectional change—in this case, degeneration—far more than neo-Darwinism demands progressive improvement.* In fact, the argument that evolution means progress from simple to complex is a straw man in a neo-Darwinian context. So it is odd to see an anti-evolutionary argument, however weak in its own right, trying to knock it down. The anti-evolutionists' definition of evolution belongs to the nineteenth century. But not, significantly, to Charles Darwin.

In fact this definition of evolution is largely Spencerian. Darwin's contemporary Herbert Spencer did indeed view evolution as progress from simple to complex. He also claimed to have preceded Darwin in the discovery of natural selection. He too had been reading Malthus; he too had derived from Malthus a principle of selection based on competition. (Indeed, everybody was reading Malthus, for Malthus had posed a supreme problem for those who would defend the Victorian ideal of progress.) But in reality, Spencer's selection differed from that of Darwin, as did his vision of evolutionary

---

*As numerous authors have shown (for example, Patterson 1983), this anti-evolutionary argument is based on a gross misinterpretation of the second law of thermodynamics. Its popularity stems not from its scientific validity but from the religious context in which it was formulated. Proponents believe that perfection existed at Creation, and that degeneration (decreasing perfection, increasing disorder brought about by the inauguration of the second law of thermodynamics) followed as a consequence of the original sin. In their world view, natural processes cannot reverse this manifestation of God's wrath. Perfection must be reinstated by God alone.

progress. In fact, Ernst Mayr, in his recent book on the history of evolutionary biology, refused to admit any role for Spencer in the development of evolutionary biology (Mayr 1982). Spencer was merely a contemporary of Darwin, who had misconstrued biology in general and misapplied Darwinism in particular to social evolutionary change. He was also a man who received misplaced praise during his own lifetime. In the late nineteenth century it was not unusual to find Spencer singled out as the scholar who had best "worked out . . . the theory of 'evolution,' or the gradual unfolding of nature . . . in all its details" (for example, Buckley 1892, p. 479). Yet even before his death in 1903 Spencer's reputation had considerably declined. Evolutionary biology was no longer Spencerian. In large part, it never was.

To be fair, I should point out that this negative assessment of Spencer's impact on evolutionary biology is not universally held (see Bury 1932; Harris 1968, 1974; Carneiro 1967, 1974; and Nisbet 1980; for contrary views). Some modern social historians, even those critical of Spencer's broader accomplishments, nevertheless credit Spencer with a central role in developing evolutionary theory—even with specifically anticipating Darwin's theory of natural selection (see especially Harris 1968, pp. 123-128). Spencer's most ardent defenders grant him, in addition, a better grasp than Darwin himself of the bearing of "Darwinian" principles of evolutionary progress on the nature of general evolutionary change. Obviously, they accept Spencer's definition of evolution as progressive change from simple to complex. So the straw-man argument of anti-evolutionists is not entirely of their own manufacture. It is a fact, however, that such a definition would strike most modern evolutionary biologists as misleading and simplistic.

Spencer (1904) claimed credit for formulating the theory of natural selection in an essay published in 1852, seven years before Darwin's *Origin* appeared. True, he acknowledged that in restricting his arguments to human populations he had failed to operationalize selection as a mechanism that could explain the origin of species. But he deemed his argument conceptually similar to Darwin's, and he made his case sufficiently convincing to others that he succeeded in gaining wide acceptance for it, even today—although not among biologists.

There is, of course, a marked disparity between the biologists' view that Spencer contributed little to the development of Darwinian evolutionary theory and the view, held by some social historians, that Spencer was a central figure in its development. At the core of these disparate evaluations are very different perceptions of Darwin's own contribution to evolutionary theory. One cannot fully understand Spencer's fall from grace in biological circles unless one understands twentieth century concepts of evolutionary progress. It is in his view of biological progress that Darwin departed most dramatically from Spencer. Darwin's vision departed from that of Spencer in a manner that foreshadowed twentieth century neo-Darwinian ambivalence toward the notion of general progress itself.

Spencer's Progress

Herbert Spencer was an evolutionary progressionist par excellence. Underlying his vision of evolutionary progress was a defense of individualism that was to emerge, under the label *Social Darwinism*, most clearly in the laissez-faire economics of the 1880s. Spencer opposed all forms of socialism as unwarranted political interference with individual freedom. Social and economic inequities should not be corrected by the State because individuals must accept the consequences of their own actions, Spencer wrote. His grandiose theory of social evolution (based, ultimately, on principles of physics), posited that the "right," or most "fit," people would survive and that order and perfection would be achieved through natural evolution.

Spencer's idea of fitness was imbued with nineteenth century notions of desirability and value, and it is impossible to read Spencer today without noticing the extent to which the social prejudices of his day affected his interpretation of progress. Eggs—the sex cells produced by women—could not play any role in the coordination of development; development must be directed instead by sperm, which must therefore figure more prominently in evolutionary progress! Australian aborigines must have body proportions that are less advanced—less "heterogeneous"—than those of Europeans! One biographer commented that we now approach Spencer as we might approach an "outmoded encyclopedia, . . . not expecting to find what is right, but rather to review errors that were plausible a century ago" (Kennedy 1978, p. 7). It was, however, precisely those errors that made him so attractive to his elite European contemporaries. He told them what they wanted to hear; he built a dream—a Victorian gentleman's vision of the best of all possible worlds. And then he assured his readers that this dream *had* to come true. In fact, his Utopia was very like that constructed by anti-evolutionists, except that the latter insisted that God must intervene, and Spencer insisted that progress was guaranteed by natural law.

From early on in his career, Spencer defended the inevitability of progress. Common features of diverse manifestations of progress must describe a law that could be used to predict the future. Since perfection, as Spencer imagined it, was not manifest in his own world, all of the successive steps leading to perfection and greatest happiness could not have occurred yet. They would in time, however, for "progress is not an accident, not a thing within human control, but a beneficient necessity" (1910, p. 60).

"Progress: Its Law and Cause" (1857) is sometimes cited as the essay in which Spencer's general doctrine of evolution first made its appearance. The concept of selection was not discussed, even though this essay was published five years after Spencer first introduced selection as a proximate cause of progress. One might even say that biological evolution was of little concern in this essay. It merely provided one, not terribly strong, example of evolution. Evolution comprised all change from simple to complex—all progress, in other words. Progress could be manifested in any of numerous forms: in the development of an individual; in the geological development of the earth; in the history of society, government, manufacture, commerce, language, literature, science, and art; and in the fossil record of biological life. Spencer sought a law that would guarantee the ultimate attainment of human happiness, and he thought he found it in von Baer's "law" of ontogenetic development. Organic progress comprised change from "homogeneous to heterogeneous," from simple to complex, from the uniform germ cell to the differentiated adult organism. "From the earliest traceable cosmical changes down to the latest results of civilization," Spencer wrote, "we shall find that the transformation of the homogeneous into the heterogeneous, is that in which progress essentially consists" (Spencer 1910, p. 10).

Once Spencer had formulated his law of all development, his only remaining task was to find the principle of change that produces heterogeneity from homogeneity. It would have to fit all of Spencer's proffered examples of progressive transformation. Since progress or evolution comprised more than biological transformation, its explanation could not be strictly biological. Furthermore, since it was widely held in the nineteenth century that general laws of development would be found that applied across all disciplines, there was no need to construct a biological explanation for biological change. This is why Spencer invoked physical forces to explain evolutionary change, and this is one of the reasons why natural selection was always, to Spencer, a secondary cause of evolutionary change. Spencer argued that increasing complexity was the necessary consequence of active forces, their persistence and cumulative effects. Thus, he thought, trees develop from seeds, animals develop from fertilized ova, European limb proportions develop from those of Australian aborigines, all because of "disturbing forces." Biological modifications are brought about by "mechanical conditions" or "muscular forces." Such modifications are transmitted to offspring through the inheritance of acquired characteristics—a notion compatible with the idea that the cumulative effects of force must persist.

Today this seems a naive and superficial argument, especially in light of the specific examples this law was supposed to explain. (Do "forces acting" really predict that Australian aborigines will have "less heterogeneous" body proportions—whatever that means—than

Europeans, or did Spencer simply contrive this example to fit his prior convictions about the physical superiority of Europeans?) But to Spencer, both the generalization that all progress consists of the transformation of the simple into the complex and the explanation that this is due to the persistence of force were central truths. From physical principles—the "indestructibility of matter," the "continuity of motion," the "integration of matter," and the "dissipation of motion"—Spencer attempted to derive all laws of change, and, in so doing, to prove the inevitability of human perfection.

Thus a set of physical principles became Spencer's *First Principles*; they predicted universal parallel transformations. Later, when it became evident that germ cells are not homogeneous in structure and chemical composition, Spencer was nevertheless reluctant to relinquish his law of universal development. His concept of the uniform, or homogeneous, germ cell affected not only his biology but also his cosmology, sociology, and history. This concept was the key to his First Principles—it was from the formulation of laws of the highest order of generality that he derived all other generalities. The doctrine of universal transformation was part and parcel with Spencer's definition of evolution. Matter tends to become integrated, Spencer wrote; motion to become dissipated. Put matter and motion together and you get greater coherence of individual parts, *and* more parts. Using such arguments Spencer could make the division of labor in society comparable to the multiplication of cells in an individual organism, or to the diversification of all biological life (each involved more "individual" parts!). To Spencer evolution was change in all orders of existence. He wrote, "Evolution is an integration of matter and concomitant dissipation of motion; during which the matter passes from a relatively indefinite, incoherent homogeneity to a relatively definite, coherent heterogeneity, and during which the retained motion undergoes a parallel transformation" (see Elliot 1970, p. 244). Notice that his definition of evolution is decidedly nonbiological. In Spencer's world, biological evolution was but one manifestation of a broader process of change. And selection was but one process that would aid the development of life on earth. Darwin constructed a theory of change by natural selection, according to which general progress was one possible consequence; Spencer constructed a theory of progress according to which selection, and indeed, biological evolution, were possible consequences.

Spencer's Selection

Use inheritance, Spencer's preferred mechanism of biological evolutionary change, was not rejected by most biologists until after the publication of Weismann's germ theory in 1883. Darwin accepted use inheritance, although he defended natural selection as the primary mechanism of evolutionary change. Spencer, on the other hand, was never an ardent defender of natural selection; and after the publication of Weismann's germ theory threatened to destroy the foundation of his own preferred mechanism of evolutionary change, he intensified his critique of selection and elevated use inheritance to a primacy that even he had not advocated before (Kennedy 1978). So it is perhaps surprising that rather late in his life he wanted to claim credit for discovering natural selection in *human* populations. He lamented having overlooked the "obvious corollary" that selection must be a "universally-operative factor in the development of [*all*] species" (1904, p. 451):

> *It seems strange that, having long entertained a belief in the development of species through the operation of natural causes, I should have failed to see that the truth [I] indicated [in some passages of "Theory of Population"] . . . must hold, not of mankind only, but of all animals; and must everywhere be working changes among them. If when human beings are subjected by pressure of population to a competition for the means of subsistence, it results that on the average the tendency is for the select of their generation to survive, so, little by little, producing a better-adapted type; then the like must happen with every other kind of living thing similarly subjected to the "struggle for existence." And if so, this must in all cases cause a modification.*

He excused his narrow focus on the grounds that he had considered use inheritance to be a sufficient explanation for general biological evolutionary change.

It was in the following passage from "A Theory of Population, Deduced from the General Law of Animal Fertility" that Spencer claimed to have found natural selection (1852, pp. 266–267):

> *The effect of pressure of population, in increasing the ability to maintain life, and decreasing the ability to multiply, is not a uniform effect, but an average one. . . . All mankind in turn subject themselves more or less to the discipline described; they either may or may not advance under it; but, in the nature of things, only those that do advance under it eventually survive. . . . Families and races whom this increasing difficulty of getting a living which excess of fertility entails, does not stimulate to improvements in production—that is, to greater mental activity—are on the high road to extinction; and must ultimately be supplanted by those whom the pressure does so stimulate. . . . And here, indeed, without further illustration, it will be seen that premature death under all its forms, and from all its causes, cannot fail to work in the same direction. For as those prematurely carried off must, in the average of cases, be those in whom the power of self-preservation is the least, it unavoidably follows that those left behind to continue the race, are those in whom the power of self-preservation is the greatest—are the select of their generation.*

"Theory of Population" was one of several early Spencerian statements about the nature of progress. It concerned the implications for human progress of the so-called law of animal fertility. Rather than failing to generalize or to consider organisms in general, this essay begins with the simplest organisms and attempts to generalize *to* humans. Darwin's theory of natural selection is not there, not because of an oversight, not because the focus was too narrow, not because Spencer believed the inheritance of acquired characteristics sufficient to explain organic evolution; but because, conceptually, Spencer's selection was different from that of Darwin. It would be impossible to derive Darwinian selection from it.

That is not to say that there are no parallels between Darwin's theory of natural selection and the argument Spencer developed in "Theory of Population." As mentioned earlier, both Darwin and Spencer developed a principle of selection based on Malthus. Both were members of a community of scholars writing about the so-called population problem—Malthus's supreme dilemma and "justification" for social injustice (Chase 1980). The phrases *struggle for life, self-preservation, competition,* and *overproduction* were not concerns of Darwin alone, but of an entire academic world to which both Darwin and Spencer belonged. Like Darwin, Spencer used competition and overproduction to make an argument *for* rather than *against* evolutionary change. Both Spencer and Darwin reversed the prevailing view that the struggle for life preserved the integrity of species by eliminating the unfit (contrast Darwin and Spencer with William Kirby, John Crawfurd, and, indeed, Malthus himself; see Jones 1980).*
But the similarities between Spencer's and Darwin's original formulations of selection end here.

Spencer's law of animal fertility was, like many other Spencerian laws, a loose empirical generalization based on a limited and carefully selected sample of observations. Specifically, it was based on the observation that simple organisms, such as bacteria, reproduce very rapidly and in great quantities but produce short-lived offspring; whereas more complex organisms, such as mammals, tend to produce few offspring, each of which has greatly enhanced powers of self-

---

*Jones (1980) points out that Spencer actually agreed with Kirby and Crawfurd that the struggle for existence preserved the type of species. But he argued that the struggle would lead to constantly improving that type, and in this sense to "evolutionary" change. John Crawfurd's view of the struggle for existence was more typical. Witness this statement made in an address to the Ethnological Society of London ten years after the publication of Darwin's *Origin:* "As to 'the struggle for life,' there is no doubt that, through all living beings, it is the weak that perish and the vigorous that survive. Nature, in some cases, takes some pains for preserving the integrity of the species but never for its improvement by mutation."

preservation and therefore greatly enhanced chances of surviving for a long period of time. From this Spencer derived a law that he took as characterizing the Great Chain of Being—that there is an inherent necessary opposition between *individuation* (that is, self-preservation, complexity, coordination, capacity for self-regulation) and *reproduction* (that is, fertility). In order to advance along the ladder of life, Spencer thought, there must be some sacrifice in the realm of reproduction. Thus, Spencer believed that it was not possible to advance in the realm of individuation without simultaneously experiencing a decline in fertility. (A similar though not identical argument was advanced in his *Principles of Biology*, Vol. II, 1867.)

Spencer liberally applied his law to a variety of very specific biological and social phenomena. For example, sperm cells provided Spencer with one arena for his battle between individuation and reproduction. Since, Spencer thought, eggs could contain only material "to be coordinated," sperm must be responsible for coordinating the growth of the nervous system and thus must possess remarkable powers of individuation. Such powers could be enhanced only at the expense of reproduction—that is, decreased production of sperm cells. Spencer argued that in sustaining this natural antagonism between reproduction and individuation, sperm cells must strike a delicate balance, sacrificing fertility for greater efficiency in individuation.

Another application of the law of animal fertility was to the problem of perfection in human social and economic life. It was in this section of his essay that Spencer erected selection as a proximate cause of progress.

Spencer argued here that humans clearly had not yet achieved ultimate perfection since human populations were still plagued by excess fertility. As long as excess fertility existed, there was room for its reduction; and as long as there was room for reduced fertility, increased individuation could occur. It was in this sense that Spencer posed excess fertility as a problem for human populations, and it was in this sense that he viewed population pressure as a "proximate cause of progress" (or of individuation). Stated in this way, Spencer's early formulation of selection looks very non-Darwinian, and also very nineteenth century. And as might be anticipated, Spencer envisioned that this increased individuation would be manifested in human anatomy as well as in social behavior.

The argument went like this: Population pressure poses a problem whose solution necessitates technological or industrial advance—that is, improvements in the skills of self-preservation. One improves one's own and one's family's chance of survival (self-preservation) by increasing industrial or agricultural production (most definitely not by increasing fertility). Premature death comes to those who fail to contend *in this way* with the problem of population pressure. Thus, the proximate cause of progress is excess fertility. Given excess fertility, there is necessarily competition, and given competition, there is necessarily improvement in skill by selection. Those males "in whom the power of self-preservation is the greatest" will be "the select of their generation." In other words, they will exhibit a prescribed and predictable set of improvements—prescribed and predictable not because selection is operating under specific environmental conditions, but because of a law that requires all improvement to be unidirectional.

It was only after Spencer had carefully described all of the presumed manifestations and ramifications of individuation that he felt ready to predict future change. The "select of their generation" would have bigger brains, would have heightened senses of morality, and would be less fertile than those in whom the "power of self-preservation" was the least. "So long as there is pressure on the means of subsistence," Spencer wrote (1852, p. 267), "further mental development must go on, and further diminution of fertility must result."

This rather startling conclusion is but a short step from the next, and perhaps least Darwinian, of Spencer's deductions—that selection generated by population pressure or the struggle for life would be the vehicle of its own eradication. Selection, as originally formulated by Herbert Spencer, was a self-destructive process!

Spencer reasoned that intellectual, moral, and physical improvement could not accrue forever, just as fertility cannot decrease ad infinitum, since such a decrease would threaten the extinction of the population. But according to Spencer's law, without a concomitant decrease in fertility there could be no progress in the realm of individuation. "For a cessation in the decrease of fertility implies a cessation in the development of the nervous system." Spencer did not see this as a problem, however, since "this implies that the nervous system has become fully equal to all that is demanded of it— has not to do more than is natural to it. . . . In the end the obtainment of subsistence will require just that kind and that amount of action needful to perfect health and happiness" (Spencer 1852, p. 267).

When the operation of the natural law of animal fertility had continued to the point where the population produced only enough offspring to sustain itself, Utopia would have emerged. There would be no further suffering, no further evil. Virtually no youth would succumb to disease or to accident, and the powers of self-preservation of those born into this world would be as perfect as possible. The population would have increased to the maximum possible to comfortably people the globe. There would continue to be only enough offspring to sustain the population. The inferior, lazy people (and,

Spencer believed, races) would have disappeared, entirely via natural processes. Perfect individuals having been obtained, no further evolution would be possible. Here was the making of the perfect human type—one that satisfied the prejudices of the Victorian world.

Interestingly, Spencer's conclusion that decreased fertility would solve Malthus's population problem was not unique. Indeed, as Nisbet (1980) has shown, Malthus himself had come to this conclusion in late versions of his famous essay. Perhaps Spencer's most striking distinction was that he couched his argument in terms of a biological *law*—of necessity rather than opportunity. This was in part why Spencer was so esteemed in the nineteenth century, when every scholar's goal was to discover those few laws from which, presumably, everything could be logically derived. But it did not make Spencer's essay strikingly Darwinian; Darwin did not hang selection on a law of necessary antagonism between individuation and reproduction.

It is only when selection is allowed to mean differential survival of any context-specific superior trait, rather than differential survival of a specific quality called individuation at the expense of another specific quality called reproduction, that Spencer's "Theory of Population" seems to read like Darwin. The wide acceptance of Spencer's argument of scholarly precedence is most curious, especially since twentieth century definitions of Darwinian selection have tended to emphasize its synonymy with differential reproduction, including fertility and fecundity. Spencer's early selection was in some ways antithetical to Darwinian selection as currently understood.

Of course Spencer's selection did involve differential *survival*—the differential survival of *acquired traits*. There was no question in Spencer's mind that greater industriousness, larger brains, and less inclination to reproduce, would be inherited. The conscious choice to work hard in the face of population pressure would effect behavioral and physical changes that would be passed on through use inheritance to offspring. On the other hand, the conscious choice to flaunt opportunity would not be passed on because of premature death. Spencer never considered it possible that people who devoted energy to reproducing would be the "select of their generation," since to him this meant dullness, stupidity, premature death. The "select" must be disinclined toward the physical act of reproduction itself. To them, normal and pleasurable activities would be those of the mind.

In sum, when Spencer wrote that population pressure is the cause of progress, he meant, first, that it is the problem that humans must strive to overcome; and second, that it is the physical or mechanical cause of a competitive struggle that must result in differential survival. The difficulty of getting a living stimulates improvements in industrial and agricultural production. Individuals strive toward self-preservation. Those who seek to solve the population problem by improving their own lot through hard work will succeed, and their success will be manifested in biological changes that are inherited. Their offspring will exhibit larger brains, lower fertility, greater skill, intelligence, self-regulation, and self-satisfaction!

Spencer's scenario was Lamarckian in more than its reliance on use inheritance: It was tied to a vision of an end point beyond which no further change was possible. It was also tied to a concept of unidirectionality—not that individuals have no choice (to the contrary, their own fate in the scheme of things is entirely up to them), but that their options are dictated by law, and their probable success, given their particular chosen behavior, is preordained by law.

Spencer's law meant that there could be only one successful solution to the problem of excess fertility. Selection was posited merely as a vehicle of its own demise—a vehicle through which Utopia, the goal of progressive evolution, would be attained. Spencer's selection was far more deterministic than that Darwin was to propose seven years later. How could Spencer's selection apply to change in pigmentation or lactose intolerance in humans, let alone the shape of the beak of finches? Spencer did not frame selection as a vehicle of pluralistic or variable change. A concept of selection effecting local adaptation and adaptive differentiation fit nowhere in Spencer's scheme. Spencer had not merely failed to extend his concept beyond humans; he had also failed to apply it to human adaptive diversity as well.

Even later, after Spencer had incorporated a more Darwinian concept of selection into his work (a selection that allowed him to talk about adaptive diversity), he clung to his vision of unilinear progress. Selection was always a means to achieve ultimate order, ultimate stability in human society. It was always a means toward perfecting the human type.

To his credit, in his *Autobiography*, Spencer acknowledged his failure to incorporate variation into his scheme; he realized that here lay the key to Darwin's interpretation of the population problem and particular formulation of selection. The fact remains, however, that in 1852, Spencer was nowhere near formulating a concept that could account for adaptive diversity—human or otherwise. This was, of course, Darwin's central concern in his *Origin of Species*.

Darwin's Genius

It may seem odd to say that one can recognize genius in ambivalence. Yet skepticism is the stuff of scientific advance, and it is all the more impressive when it challenges a belief that has become entrenched in the scholarly literature. Such was the belief in progress. When Darwin wrote *The Origin of Species*, the belief in progress dominated far more than the discipline of biology; it dominated all fields of natural, social, and physical science, as well as the humanities. The second half of the nineteenth century was the heyday of the idea of progress (Bury 1932; Nisbet 1980). Charles Darwin was a product of that age. He was certainly an evolutionary progressionist, but he was also one of the most severe critics of the "law" of progressive development. This is why Gould (1977, p. 13) has maintained that "an explicit denial of innate progression is the most characteristic feature separating Darwin's theory of natural selection from other nineteenth century evolutionary theories." Darwin only weakly defended the best accepted standards of overall advance in organization. He found problematic both von Baer's criterion of increased complexity and Milne Edwards's criterion of increased specialization in function of organs.

The difficulty Darwin experienced in accepting any single standard of progress in the biological world stemmed from his acute sense that the pattern of diversification does not describe a simple pattern of increase in any one thing, and also from his awareness that the theory he had developed did not require it. Natural selection was Darwin's agent of progress; yet he had defined it in such a way that progress could not be a necessary consequence. Natural selection was a mechanism whereby fitness—an organism's adaptation to a particular environment—is enhanced. In other words, natural selection was, to Darwin, an agent of local adaptation. Furthermore, although Darwin left the causes of variation undefined, he was explicit in his belief that natural selection must work with variation produced by some process independent of selection itself. If beneficial variants are not somehow a priori produced; or if there is no modification in the physical or biotic environment providing an incentive (or pressure) for improvement; or, finally, if certain existing complex adaptations are no longer needed in a changed or newly occupied environment; then it follows that progress may not occur. It is even possible that *retrogression* in the scale of organization will occur. In a nutshell, if different environments require different adaptations, Darwin's theory provided no clear standard by which an organism from one environment could be judged superior to an organism from another. Indeed, it provided no clear standard by which they could be compared.

"We can see," Darwin wrote, "bearing in mind that all organic beings are striving to increase at a high ratio and to seize on every unoccupied or less well occupied place in the economy of nature, that it is quite possible for natural selection gradually to fit a being to a situation in which several organs would be superfluous or useless: in such cases there would be retrogression in the scale of organisation. . . " (Darwin 1963, p. 105). Also: "On our theory the continued existence of lowly forms offers no difficulty; for natural selection, or the survival of the fittest, does not necessarily include progressive development—it only takes advantage of such variations as arise and are beneficial to each creature under its complex relations of life" (1963, p. 105).

By asking how much the level of organization had actually tended to advance, Darwin converted the general truth of progress into a hypothesis demanding more data for verification. He acknowledged that his hypothesis that organization on the whole should advance under natural selection had not yet been adequately tested, and he admitted practical difficulties in testing it. There were, for example, difficulties in ranking "high" and "low" when comparing biota from different areas or from different times, or in comparing organisms exhibiting very different organizational plans. "Who will decide," wrote Darwin (p. 337), "whether a cuttle fish be higher than a bee?" In their own worlds, barnacles, parasites, and earthworms are as perfect as are horses, falcons, and people. What's more, Darwin marshalled evidence to show that general progress had not, indeed, universally occurred, and that the pattern of diversification produced by natural selection was hard to interpret in terms of a simple polarity between low and high or simple and complex. Darwin went so far as to say that if one insists that his theory demands that progress must occur, one is then forced to consider his theory falsified! Progress (in the sense of overall advance in organization) is a prediction, but not a necessary consequence, of natural selection. Perfection in a local context and overall advance in organization are not the same thing. Under specific environmental conditions, overall advance in organization could not be expected to occur.

Darwin's theory was an optimization theory based on context-specific competition. He talked about natural selection producing increasingly complex organisms, or increasingly reproductively successful organisms, or organisms with increasingly bigger brains. But he left only one criterion for judging overall fitness—competitive success within specific environmental contexts. The metaphors he used, including those he borrowed from Spencer (most notably "survival of the fittest"), reflected his concern for competitive success as the criterion whereby fitness could be ranked. As modern non-Darwinian biologists are quick to point out (for example, Ho and Saunders 1979), ordering by fitness, thus conceived, breaks down whenever competition cannot be an issue. Suppose, for instance, that a species moves into a new niche or a new environment in order to avoid competition, and that this move is the basis of a new success. When two organisms do not compete it is difficult if not impossible to evaluate their relative fitness.

Of course, species are also affected by the abiotic conditions of life. If an organism is known to do poorly in a particular environment, it can be said to be poorly adapted to that environment, whether or not other species with which it might compete are present. Any assessment of relative fitness depends on the specific abiotic as well as biotic environment. A species that has a clear competitive advantage over another species may lose that advantage completely in a different environment. It follows that no single quantity increases as a result of natural selection, and that one cannot even apply Darwin's theory to make predictions without first specifying a complex set of conditions (see Maynard Smith 1978; Bock 1979).

So Darwin's theory allows one to define and predict relative fitness under specific local conditions, but not to define fitness in a global sense as a quantity tending to increase during evolution. It is possible that there simply is no one quantity that increases in such a manner—at least not as a consequence of Darwin's mechanism of natural selection. Still, based on the premise that modern organisms have beaten their predecessors in the game of survival, and on the assumption that time's arrow will be reflected in improvements representing the cumulative effects of competition, numerous scholars have tried to define such a quantity. The results have been equivocal, as we shall see.

What is remarkable about Darwin is that he was willing to defend evolution without simultaneously defending a progress-dependent vectorial view of the universe. The reluctance of many modern biologists to define evolution as anything more than constant adjustment of lineages to changing environmental conditions, their unwillingness to recognize more than net progress of different sorts in different evolutionary lineages, and their general refusal to equate evolution with progress of any sort, are direct consequences of the Darwinian paradigm. Modern neo-Darwinists do not depart radically from Darwin's ambivalence toward the concept of overall evolutionary progress.

Modern Interpretations of Progress: Neo-Darwinism

Progress does have an interpretation in the neo-Darwinian paradigm. Most neo-Darwinists agree that there is no standard by which *uniform* progress can be said to have taken place (Simpson 1974; Ayala 1974, 1977). Evolution is too erratic. But neo-Darwinists also believe that net progress has occurred, and that progress can only be understood in a Darwinian context. Progress is not possible without selection, although selection does not necessarily result in progress. Selection, while not directed, gives direction to evolution. That direction results either in adjustment to local conditions (perfection only in the sense of better local adaptation), or in improved capacity to compete under a variety of circumstances (perfection in a more general sense). Directional evolution is said to occur without progress if, despite long sustained directional change, terminal members of a lineage are not "better off" in some general sense than early members of the same lineage. Spatial clines may exhibit adaptive fine-tuning whereby individuals at opposite ends of a geographic range are adapted to entirely different environments, but individuals at neither end are more progressive than the others. Similarly, temporal gradients may exhibit the same kind of directional change without general improvement. General progress is said to occur when later members of a lineage acquire true improvements. There have been repeated attempts to find simple quantities that may improve in such a manner as a result of natural selection. Such a quantity may be defined as a function of optimization processes or as a consequence of long-term competition. Fitness will be optimized during natural selection; therefore, one has to discover the properties of greater fitness. What has emerged is a multifocal definition of general progress. There are many standards of progress, and all of them are believed to accrue as a function of natural selection. Competition will result in broader ranges of adaptive response to adversity; it will result in increased homeostasis, improved potential for reproductive success, increased complexity, increased efficiency in the utilization of limited resources, and so on. Even adaptive diversification has been attributed to natural selection (although clearly other factors are also involved, at least in the multiplication of lineages).

What has also emerged in the neo-Darwinian literature is the sense that none of these standards is entirely satisfactory as a criterion for general progress, because increases in a given direction will not always give species a competitive advantage. Take, for example, increases in the range of adaptive response. Generalists display tremendous adaptive flexibility; yet when resource diversity is low, a generalist adaptive strategy is not successful—specialists are better able to utilize the ubiquitous, if monotonous, available foods. Similarly, complexity is not always beneficial. Simple parasites do quite well by taking advantage of the vital life services provided by their hosts. Greater metabolic efficiency may not be a good standard under all conditions; one can easily envision circumstances under which new metabolically expensive adaptations will be selected in order to attain some other advantage. It seems that even general criteria of progress cannot be applied universally. Modern Darwinism recognizes, just as Darwin did, that the context-specific nature of the theory prohibits a single best criterion for progressive change from being formulated. Standards of progress appear ad hoc or axiological.

G. G. Simpson has stated this eloquently. Simpson concluded his review article on "The Concept of Progress in Organic Evolution" with the following observations (1974, pp. 50–51):

> *Some organisms are better than their ancestors or than some of their relatives at doing certain things in certain ways. Some oysters are better at being oysters than their ancestors. Some trees are better at living on mountain tops than others. We are doubtless better at being men than Australopithecus was, although I go along with Haldane far enough to believe that monkeys are better at being monkeys than we would be even if we tried. It is also true that sometimes whole groups have been carried by selection to a point where their great expansion into various adaptive zones became possible, a progressive feature of evolution. . . . That is the explanation, in unduly broad terms, of the spread of dominant groups from time to time.*
>
> *With such examples it is perfectly reasonable to say that improvement has factually occurred and that there is therefore evolutionary progress. The progress is, however, ad hoc in every case. Our ancestors' progress was not the oysters', the trees', or the monkeys', nor was theirs ours. Since we are humans, after all, the most interesting and important progress is progress toward us, but let us not mistake this for a general phenomenon.*
>
> *Probably the most important result of this somewhat dispersive inquiry is negative: there is no innate tendency toward evolutionary progress and no one, overall sort of such progress. We cannot sit back and assume that natural selection will lead to progress for us, or for anything else. We cannot even assume that prolongation of past progress would continue to be progress.*

Francisco Ayala (1977, p. 516) draws a similar conclusion: "Needless to say, organisms are more or less progressive depending on what criterion of progress is used. By certain criteria, flowering plants are more progressive than many animals." *Homo* is only the "most perfect" of organisms if one chooses one's standard of progress accordingly. But such a standard as "the ability to perceive the environment, and to integrate, coordinate and react flexibly to what is perceived . . . is not necessarily better or worse than other criteria of progress" (Ayala 1977, p. 516).

So progress is ambiguous in a neo-Darwinian context, and neo-Darwinism simultaneously claims and disavows it. Neo-Darwinists certainly do not equate progress with evolution, as some anti-evolutionists have claimed. Even if we could find some one quantity that increases with time as a result of natural selection, we would have to assess the relative importance of that increase as opposed to other kinds of evolutionary change before evolution could be equated in any sense with progressive change.

Recently the adequacy of neo-Darwinism to explain different

forms of progress has been challenged on other grounds. Progress has not only different meanings, but also different potential causal mechanisms.

Modern Interpretations of Progress: Non-Darwinian Frameworks

Perhaps the least radical of the challenges comes from proponents of the theory of punctuated equilibria (Eldredge, this volume; Eldredge and Gould 1972; Gould and Eldredge 1977; Gould 1980; Stanley 1975, 1979). Their argument is less a challenge to selection as formulated by Darwin than it is a challenge to selection as mathematized and reformulated by the authors of the Modern Synthesis in the 1940s. The emphasis on population genetics in the 1940s led to the reformulation of natural selection as "the differential reproduction of individual members of the same species." This seems to exclude selection operating at a higher level (for example, according to the relative success of whole species). Darwin did not exclude higher than species-level competition when he described the operation of natural selection. So the new focus on individuals developed not from Darwin directly but from a new emphasis on genes. Neo-Darwinism developed as a theory of genes, and the survival of genes was believed to depend on the survival of their individual hosts. One can also justify an emphasis on individuals using a more clearly Darwinian argument. If competition is the fundamental component of natural selection or the struggle for existence, then in order to discover the level at which natural selection operates we should ask where we would expect to find the most severe competition. Logically the intensity of the "struggle" should depend on the similarity of the individuals and their overlapping requirements. Because members of the same genus tend to resemble each other more than members of different genera, congeneric competition should be more severe than competition between species of different genera. Competition between individual members of the same species should be the most severe.

Proponents of the theory of punctuated equilibria argue that long-term macroevolutionary trends are less a product of differential success of individuals than of differential success of whole species. They claim competition between individuals within species, at least during the vast majority of the existence of most species, will lead to fine adaptive adjustments but rarely to long-term directional trends of the sort that may be identified as progressive.

Punctuationalists base this claim on the postulate that rapid phenotypic evolution most often occurs under conditions that are also, incidentally, conducive to the generation of new lineages.

Speciation (the multiplication of lineages) generally occurs because small populations have become geographically or genetically separated (due to karyotypic changes that initiate reproductive isolation) from their parent populations (White 1978). Furthermore, small populations facilitate the fixation and spread of evolutionary novelties generated either by selection or by stochastic processes. Thus, punctuationalists argue, it is the process of speciation per se, and not the intensity of competition between individuals, that predicts rapid morphological evolution. Indeed, it has been suggested that periods of relaxed (rather than intense) competition may occur in association with speciation, and that such relaxed selection may allow the survival of novelties that would not ordinarily survive. Finally, punctuationalists argue that if the factors affecting evolutionary change during speciation differ from the factors affecting evolutionary change in whole lineages, we cannot predict evolutionary trends as products of the constant adjustment of individuals to their changing environments. Speciation trends (associated with the differential survival of species) may have little in common with trends associated with the differential survival of individuals belonging to single species (Stanley 1979). The relative competitive success of a species may ultimately depend on events that occur in a short period of time during its origination. This of course leaves wide open the question of whether selection as used by neo-Darwinists drives "progressive" evolution! It seems we must build a hierarchical model of evolution, in which selection can act at multiple levels and independent directional trends can be produced at those different levels (Gould 1980).

A more basic challenge to the tenets of neo-Darwinism has come from evolutionists who reject the notion that directional trends are the product of selection operating at any level (see, for example, Saunders and Ho 1976, 1981; Ho and Saunders 1979). They argue that classic examples of evolutionary progress driven by selection (especially increase in complexity) can be understood without reference to either optimization theory or competition. Instead they offer a theory that examines the properties of biological systems and the internal developmental constraints on the direction of evolutionary change. An optimization model that predicts merely that "advantageous" changes will occur is, at the very least, incomplete.

It is the link between genes and phenotypes that so fascinates these investigators. The phenotype emerges from the genes through development or so-called epigenetic pathways. Ho and Saunders maintain that we cannot understand the pattern or directionality of evolutionary change unless we pay more attention to how the epigenetic system works. It's like trying to understand or predict patterns of change in computer programs without trying to understand the language in which the programs are written. If we want to understand modifications of a computer program, they say, it is far more useful to understand the language than to build expectations based on an optimization model. We should ask, What sorts of changes are possible? What sorts of changes are *easily* made? What sorts of changes are *not* possible? By analogy, Ho and Saunders want to discover the loops, subroutines, built-in functions, and mathematical identities of biological developmental systems (see especially Saunders and Ho 1981).

Using a Darwinian predictive framework alone, one might imagine that changes in all directions are generated by "random" mutation, and that the actual direction of change is limited by competitive advantage alone. One assumes nearly constant competition and enough variation generated by accident to make natural selection a viable force, generation by generation. However, recent field studies have demonstrated that competition may not be as important as Darwin and his contemporaries believed (for example, Wiens 1983). Perhaps competition only matters during resource crunches and selection operates intermittently in populations in general. Furthermore, it is abundantly clear that the variations on which natural selection works are not random. To the extent that they are themselves patterned and predictable, they will impart some directionality to evolutionary change (Bonner 1982; Ho and Saunders 1979; Saunders and Ho 1981). Finally, there is the (alas! neo-Lamarckian) suggestion that cytoplasmic inheritance may be involved, at least in the initial stages of fixing new epigenetic pathways (Ho and Saunders 1979; see also Saunders, this volume). If so (and the evidence for this is far from conclusive), we have yet another agent of directional and progressive change.

So progress has changed considerably from its nineteenth century Spencerian formulation. To Spencer, progress was a law of all evolutionary change—a law of increasing complexity that was also strongly associated with "fitness for the conditions of life" and with the attainment of the ideal type. Natural selection was a consequence of progress, although not its sole cause. To Darwin, progress was a consequence of natural selection, although not a necessary consequence. Neo-Darwinists treat progress essentially as Darwin did, although it has become more openly multifocal and, to some leading neo-Darwinists, ad hoc. Some non-Darwinian evolutionists now argue that the notion of increasing complexity must be divorced from the notion of selection or fitness. Increases in complexity, long believed to be a major indicator of progressive or advantageous change, may follow automatically from the way in which the epigenetic system operates. Complexity is probably not best conceived as a measure of fitness, but as a measure of the information content of developmental building instructions. It will not necessarily increase as a function of optimization. Phenotypic changes will not occur randomly, but will depend on the existence of alternative developmental pathways that can accommodate them. At issue is the probability of the occurrence of changes in different directions.

What has been called progress, then, is quite probably the product of a host of factors, only one of which is the natural selection of individuals belonging to single lineages. And evolution is not merely progressive change!

REFERENCES

Ayala, Francisco J. "The Concept of Biological Progress." In *Studies in the Philosophy of Biology*, edited by F. J. Ayala and T. Dobzhansky, pp. 339-355. London: Macmillan, 1974.

———. "Philosophical Issues." In *Evolution*, edited by T. Dobzhansky, F. J. Ayala, G. Ledyard Stebbins, and J. W. Valentine, pp. 474-516. San Fransisco: W. H. Freeman, 1977.

Bock, Walter J. "The Synthetic Explanation of Macroevolutionary Change—a Reductionistic Approach." In *Models and Methodologies in Evolutionary Theory*, edited by J. H. Schwartz and H. R. Rollins, pp. 20-69. *Bulletin of Carnegie Museum of Natural History*, No. 13, 1979.

Bonner, J. T., ed. *Evolution and Development*. Berlin, Heidelberg, New York: Springer-Verlag, 1982.

Buckley, Arabella B. *A Short History of Natural Science*. 2d edition. New York: D. Appleton, 1892.

Bury, J. B. *The Idea of Progress: An Inquiry into its Origin and Growth*. London: Macmillan, 1932.

Carneiro, Robert L. "Introduction." In *The Evolution of Society: Selections from Herbert Spencer's Principles of Sociology*, edited by R. L. Carneiro, pp. ix-lvii. Chicago: University of Chicago Press, 1967.

———. "CA* Comment on 'The Evolutionary Theories of Charles Darwin and Herbert Spencer' by Derek Freeman." *Current Anthropology* 15 (1974): 222-223.

Chase, Allan. *The Legacy of Malthus. The Social Costs of the New Scientific Racism*. Urbana: University of Illinois Press, 1980.

Crawfurd, John. "On the Theory of the Origin of Species by Natural Selection." *Transactions of the Ethnological Society of London* VII (1869):29.

Darwin, Charles. *The Origin of Species*. 1859. New York: Washington Square Press, 1963.

Eldredge, Niles, and Gould, Stephen J. "Punctuated Equilibria: An Alternative to Phyletic Gradualism." In *Models in Paleobiology*, edited by T. J. M. Schopf, pp. 82-115. San Francisco: Freeman, Cooper, 1972.

Elliot, H. S. R. *Herbert Spencer*. 1917. Freeport, New York: Books for Libraries Press, 1970.

Gould, Stephen J. "Eternal Metaphors of Paleontology." In *Patterns of Evolution as Illustrated by the Fossil Record*, edited by A. Hallam, pp. 1-26. Amsterdam and New York: Elsevier, 1977.

——. "Is a New and General Theory of Evolution Emerging?" *Paleobiology* 6, no. 1 (1980):119-130.

Gould, Stephen J., and Eldredge, Niles. "Punctuated Equilibria: The Tempo and Mode of Evolution Reconsidered." *Paleobiology* 3 (1977):115-151.

Harris, Marvin. *The Rise of Anthropological Theory*. New York: Thomas Y. Crowell, 1968.

——. "CA* Comment on 'The Evolutionary Theories of Charles Darwin and Herbert Spencer' by Derek Freeman." *Current Anthropology* 15 (1974):225-226.

Ho, M. W., and Saunders, P. T. "Beyond Neo-Darwinism. An Epigenetic Approach to Evolution." *Journal of Theoretical Biology* 78 (1979):573-591.

Jones, Greta. *Social Darwinism and English Thought. The Interaction between Biological and Social Theory*. Atlantic Highlands, N.J.: Humanities Press, 1980.

Kennedy, James G. *Herbert Spencer*. Boston: Twayne Publishers, a division of G. K. Hall, 1978.

Maynard Smith, John. "Optimization Theory in Evolution." *Annual Review of Ecology and Systematics* 9 (1978):31-56.

Mayr, Ernst. *The Growth of Biological Thought. Diversity, Evolution, and Inheritance*. Cambridge, Mass.: Harvard University Press, Belknap Press, 1982.

Nisbet, Robert. *History of the Idea of Progress*. New York: Basic Books, 1980.

Patterson, John W. "Thermodynamics and Evolution." In *Scientists Confront Creationism*, edited by L. R. Godfrey, pp. 99-116. New York: W. W. Norton, 1983.

Saunders, P. T., and Ho, M. W. "On the Increase in Complexity in Evolution." *Journal of Theoretical Biology* 63 (1976):375-384.

——. "On the Increase in Complexity in Evolution II. The Relativity of Complexity and the Principle of Minimum Increase." *Journal of Theoretical Biology* 90 (1981):515-530.

Simpson, George Gaylord. "The Concept of Progress in Organic Evolution." *Social Research* 41, no. 1 (1974):28-51.

Spencer, Herbert. "A Theory of Population, Deduced from the General Law of Animal Fertility." *Westminster Review* 57 (1852):250-268. (American ed.)

——. "Progress: Its Law and Cause." 1857. Reprinted in *Essays. Scientific, Political, and Speculative*. Vol. 1, pp. 8-62. New York and London: D. Appleton, 1910.

——. *First Principles*. London: Williams & Norgate, 1862.

——. *Principles of Biology*. Vol. II. London: Williams & Norgate, 1867.

——. *An Autobiography*. New York and London: D. Appleton, 1904.

Stanley, Steven M. "A Theory of Evolution above the Species Level." *Proceedings of the National Academy of Sciences USA* 72 (1975):646-650.

——. *Macroevolution. Pattern and Process*. San Francisco: W. H. Freeman, 1979.

White, M. J. D. *Modes of Speciation*. San Francisco: W. H. Freeman, 1978.

Wiens, John A. "Competition or Peaceful Coexistence?" *Natural History* 93, no. 3 (1983):30-34.

Wallace's Fatal Flaw

STEPHEN JAY GOULD
Museum of Comparative Zoology
Harvard University

> *"I hope," wrote Darwin, "you have not*
> *murdered . . . your own and my child."*

In the south transept of Chartres cathedral, the most stunning of all medieval windows depicts the four evangelists as dwarfs sitting upon the shoulders of four Old Testament prophets—Isaiah, Jeremiah, Ezekiel, and Daniel. When I first saw this window as a cocky undergraduate in 1961, I immediately thought of Newton's famous aphorism—"If I have seen further it is by standing on the shoulders of Giants"—and imagined that I had made a major discovery in unearthing his lack of originality.

Years later, and properly humbled for many reasons, I learned that Robert K. Merton, the celebrated sociologist of science from Columbia University, had devoted an entire book to pre-Newtonian usages of the metaphor (*On the Shoulders of Giants*, Harcourt, Brace & World, 1965). In fact, Merton traces it back to Bernard of Chartres in 1126 and cites several scholars who believe that the windows of the great south transept, installed after Bernard's death, represent an explicit attempt to capture his metaphor in glass.

Although Merton wisely constructs his book as a delightful romp through the intellectual life of medieval and Renaissance Europe, he does have a serious point to make. Merton has devoted much of his work to the study of multiple discoveries in science. He has shown that almost all major ideas arise many times, usually independently and virtually at the same time. Thus, great scientists are embedded in their cultures, not uniquely divorced from them. Most great ideas are "in the air," and several scholars simultaneously wave their nets.

One of the most famous of Merton's "multiples" resides in my own field of evolutionary biology. Charles Darwin, to recount the famous tale briefly, developed his theory of natural selection in 1838 and set it forth in two unpublished sketches of 1842 and 1844. Then,

---

Reprinted with permission from *Natural History*, vol. 89, no. 1, copyright the American Museum of Natural History, 1980.

never doubting his theory for a moment, but afraid to expose its revolutionary implications, he proceeded to stew, dither, wait, ponder, and collect data for another fifteen years. Finally, at the virtual insistence of his closest friends, he began to work on his notes, intending to publish a massive tome that would have been four times as long as the *Origin of Species*.

But in 1858 Darwin received a letter and manuscript from a young naturalist, Alfred Russel Wallace, who had independently constructed the theory of natural selection while lying ill with malaria on an island in the Malay Archipelago. Darwin was stunned by the detailed similarity. Wallace even claimed inspiration from the same nonbiological source—Malthus's essay on population. Darwin, in great anxiety, made the expected gesture of magnanimity but devoutly hoped that some way might be found to preserve his legitimate priority. He wrote to Lyell: "I would far rather burn my whole book, than that he or any other man should think that I have behaved in a paltry spirit." But he added a suggestion: "If I could honorably publish, I would state that I was induced now to publish a sketch . . . from Wallace having sent me an outline of my general conclusions."

Lyell and Hooker took the bait and came to Darwin's rescue. While Darwin stayed home, mourning the death of his daughter from scarlet fever, they presented a joint paper to the Linnaean Society containing an excerpt from Darwin's 1844 essay, together with Wallace's manuscript. A year later, Darwin published his feverishly compiled "abstract" of the longer work—the *Origin of Species*. Wallace had been eclipsed.

Wallace has come down through history as Darwin's shadow. In public and private, Darwin was infallibly decent and generous to his younger colleague. He wrote to Wallace in 1870:

> *I hope it is a satisfaction to you to reflect—and very few things in my life have been more satisfactory to me—that we have never felt any jealousy towards each other, though in one sense rivals.*

Wallace, in return, was consistently deferential. In 1864, he wrote to Darwin:

> *As to the theory of Natural Selection itself, I shall always maintain it to be actually yours and yours only. You had worked it out in details I had never thought of, years before I had a ray of light on the subject, and my paper would never have convinced anybody or been noticed as more than an ingenious speculation, whereas your book has revolutionized the study of Natural History, and carried away captive the best men of the present age.*

This genuine affection and mutual support masked a serious disagreement on what may be the fundamental question in evolutionary theory—both then and today. How exclusive is natural selection as an agent of evolutionary change? Must all features of organisms be viewed as adaptations? Yet Wallace's role as Darwin's subordinate alter ego is so firmly fixed in popular accounts that few students of evolution are even aware that the two men ever differed on theoretical questions. Moreover, in the one specific area where their public disagreement is a matter of record—the origin of human intellect— many writers have told the story backward because they failed to locate this debate in the context of a more general disagreement on the power of natural selection.

All subtle ideas can be trivialized, even vulgarized, by portrayal in uncompromising and absolute terms. Marx felt compelled to deny that he was a Marxist, while Einstein contended with the serious misstatement that he meant to say "all is relative." Darwin lived to see his name appropriated for an extreme view that he never held— for Darwinism has often been defined, both in his day and in our own, as the belief that virtually all evolutionary change is the product of natural selection.

Darwin often complained, with uncharacteristic bitterness, about this misappropriation of his name. He wrote in the last edition of the *Origin* (1872):

> As my conclusions have lately been much misrepresented, and it has been stated that I attribute the modification of species exclusively to natural selection, I may be permitted to remark that in the first edition of this work, and subsequently, I placed in a most conspicuous position—namely, at the close of the Introduction—the following words: "I am convinced that natural selection has been the main but not the exclusive means of modification." This has been of no avail. Great is the power of steady misrepresentation.

England did house a small group of strict selectionists—"Darwinians" in the misappropriated sense—and Alfred Russel Wallace was their leader. These biologists attributed all evolutionary change to natural selection. They viewed each bit of morphology, each function of an organ, each behavior as a product of selection leading to a "better" organism. They held a deep belief in nature's "rightness," in the exquisite fit of all creatures to their environments. In a curious sense, they almost reintroduced the creationist notion of natural harmony by substituting an omnipotent force of natural selection for a benevolent deity.

Darwin, on the other hand, was a consistent pluralist gazing upon a messier universe. He saw much fit and harmony, for he believed that natural selection holds pride of place among evolutionary forces. But other processes work as well, and organisms display an array of features that are not adaptations and do not promote survival directly. Darwin took particular interest in two principles leading to nonadaptive change: (1) Organisms are integrated systems and adaptive change in one part can lead to nonadaptive modifications of other features ("correlations of growth" in Darwin's phrase); (2) An organ built under the influence of selection for a specific role may be able, as a consequence of its structure, to perform many other, unselected functions as well.

Wallace stated the hard, hyperselectionist line—"pure Darwinism" in his terms—in an early article of 1867, calling it "a necessary deduction from the theory of natural selection."

> *None of the definite facts of organic selection, no special organ, no characteristic form or marking, no peculiarities of instinct or of habit, no relations between species or between groups of species, can exist but which must now be, or once have been, useful to the individuals or races which possess them.*

Indeed, he argued later, any apparent nonutility must only reflect our faulty knowledge—a remarkable argument since it renders the principle of utility impervious to disproof *a priori*:

> *The assertion of "inutility" in the case of any organ . . . is not, and can never be, the statement of a fact, but merely an expression of our ignorance of its purpose or origin.*

All the public and private arguments that Darwin pursued with Wallace centered upon their differing assessments of the power of natural selection. They first crossed swords on the issue of "sexual selection," the subsidiary process that Darwin had proposed to explain the origin of features that appeared to be irrelevant or even harmful in the usual "struggle for existence" (expressed primarily in feeding and defense), but that could be interpreted as devices for increasing success in mating—elaborate antlers of deer, or tail feathers of peacocks, for example. Darwin proposed two kinds of sexual selection: competition among males for access to females and choice exercised by females themselves. He attributed much of the racial differentiation among modern humans to sexual selection, based upon the different criteria of beauty that arose among various peoples. (His book—*The Descent of Man and Selection in Relation to Sex* [1871]—is an amalgam of two works: a long treatise on sexual selection throughout the animal kingdom and a shorter speculative account of human origins, relying heavily upon sexual selection.)

The notion of sexual selection is not really contrary to natural selection, for it is just another route to the Darwinian imperative of differential reproductive success. But Wallace disliked sexual selection for three reasons: it compromised the generality of that peculiarly nineteenth century view of natural selection as a battle for life itself, not merely for copulation; it placed altogether too much emphasis upon the "volition" of animals, particularly in the concept of female choice; and most importantly, it permitted the development of numerous, important features that are irrelevant, if not actually harmful, to the operation of an organism as a well-designed machine. Thus, Wallace viewed sexual selection as a threat to his vision of animals as works of exquisite craftsmanship, wrought by the purely material force of natural selection. (Indeed, Darwin had developed the concept largely to explain why so many differences among human groups are irrelevant to survival based upon good design, but merely reflect the variety of capricious criteria for beauty that arose for no adaptive reason among various races. In the end, Wallace did accept sexual selection based upon male combat as close enough to the metaphor of battle that controlled his concept of natural selection. But he firmly rejected the notion of female choice and distressed Darwin with his speculative attempts to attribute all features based upon it to the adaptive action of natural selection.)

As he prepared the *Descent of Man*, Darwin wrote to Wallace in 1870: "I grieve to differ from you, and it actually terrifies me and makes me constantly distrust myself. I fear we shall never quite understand each other." He struggled to understand Wallace's reluctance and even to accept his friend's faith in unalloyed natural selection: "You will be pleased to hear," he wrote to Wallace,

> *that I am undergoing severe distress about protection and sexual selection; this morning I oscillated with joy towards you; this evening I have swung back to [my] old position, out of which I fear I shall never get.*

But the debate on sexual selection was merely a prelude to a much more serious and famous disagreement on that most emotional and contentious subject of all—human origins. In short, Wallace, the hyperselectionist, the man who had twitted Darwin for his unwillingness to see the action of natural selection in every nuance of organic form, halted abruptly before the human brain. Our intellect and morality, Wallace argued, could not be the product of natural selection; therefore, since natural selection is evolution's only way, some higher power—God, to put it directly—must have intervened to construct this latest and greatest of organic innovations.

If Darwin had been distressed by his failure to impress Wallace with sexual selection, he was positively aghast at Wallace's abrupt about-face at the finish line itself. He wrote to Wallace in 1869: "I hope you have not murdered too completely your own and my child." A month later, he remonstrated: "If you had not told me, I should have thought that [your remarks on Man] had been added by some one else. As you expected, I differ grievously from you, and

I am very sorry for it." Wallace, sensitive to the rebuke, thereafter referred to his theory of human intellect as "my special heresy."

The conventional account of Wallace's apostasy at the brink of complete consistency cites a failure of courage to take the last step and admit man fully into the natural system—a step that Darwin took with commendable fortitude in two books, the *Descent of Man* and *The Expression of the Emotions in Man and Animals* (1872). Thus, Wallace emerges from most historical accounts as a lesser man than Darwin for one (or more) of three reasons, all related to his position on the origins of human intellect: for simple cowardice; for inability to transcend the constraints of culture and traditional views of human uniqueness; and for inconsistency in advocating natural selection so strongly (in the debate on sexual selection), yet abandoning it at the most crucial moment of all.

I cannot analyze Wallace's psyche and will not comment on his deeper motives for hewing to the unbridgeable gap between human intellect and the behavior of mere animals. But I can assess the logic of his argument and recognize that the traditional account is not only incorrect, but precisely backward. Wallace did not abandon natural selection at the human threshold. Rather, it was his peculiarly rigid view of natural selection that led him, quite consistently, to reject it for the human mind. His position never varied—natural selection is the only cause of major evolutionary change. His two major debates with Darwin—sexual selection and the origin of human intellect—represent the same argument, not an inconsistent Wallace championing selection in one case and running from it in the other. Wallace's error on human intellect arose from the inadequacy of his rigid selectionism, not from a failure to apply it. And his argument repays our study today, since its flaw remains as the weak link in many of the most "modern" evolutionary speculations of our current literature. For Wallace's rigid selectionism is much closer than Darwin's pluralism to the attitude embodied in our favored theory today, which, ironically in this context, goes by the name of Neo-Darwinism.

Wallace advanced several arguments for the uniqueness of human intellect, but his central claim begins with an extremely uncommon position for his time, one that commands our highest praise in retrospect. Wallace was one of the few nonracists of the nineteenth century. He really believed that all human groups had innately equal capacities of intellect. Wallace defended his decidedly unconventional egalitarianism with two arguments, anatomical and cultural. He claimed, first of all, that the brains of "savages" are neither much smaller nor more poorly organized than our own:

> In the brain of the lowest savages, and, as far as we know, of the prehistoric races, we have an organ . . . little inferior in size in complexity to that of the highest type.

Moreover, since cultural conditioning can integrate the rudest savage into our most courtly life, the rudeness itself must arise from a failure to use existing capacities, not from their absence:

> *It is latent in the lower races, since under European training native military bands have been formed in many parts of the world, which have been able to perform creditably the best modern music.*

Of course, in calling Wallace a nonracist, I do not mean to imply that he regarded the cultural practices of all peoples as equal in intrinsic worth. Quite the contrary. Wallace, like most of his contemporaries, was an ardent cultural chauvinist who never doubted the evident superiority of European ways. He may have been bullish on the capability of savages, but he certainly had a low opinion of their life, as he mistook it:

> *Our law, our government, and our science continually require us to reason through a variety of complicated phenomena to the expected result. Even our games, such as chess, compel us to exercise all these faculties in a remarkable degree. Compare this with the savage languages, which contain no words for abstract conceptions; the utter want of foresight of the savage man beyond his simplest necessities; his inability to combine, or to compare, or to reason on any general subject that does not immediately appeal to his senses.*

Hence, Wallace's dilemma: all savages, from our actual ancestors to modern survivors, had brains fully capable of developing and appreciating all the finest subtleties of European art, morality and philosophy; yet they used, in the state of nature, only the tiniest fraction of that capacity in constructing their rudimentary cultures, with impoverished languages and repugnant morality.

But natural selection can only fashion a feature for immediate use. The brain is vastly overdesigned for what is accomplished in primitive society; thus, natural selection could not have built it:

> *A brain one-half larger than that of the gorilla would . . . fully have sufficed for the limited mental development of the savage; and we must therefore admit that the large brain he actually possesses could never have been solely developed by any of those laws of evolution, whose essence is, that they lead to a degree of organization exactly proportionate to the wants of each species, never beyond those wants . . . . Natural selection could only have endowed savage man with a brain a few degrees superior to that of an ape, whereas, he actually possesses one very little inferior to that of a philosopher.*

Wallace did not confine this general argument to abstract intellect, but extended it to all aspects of European "refinement," to language and music in particular. Consider his views on "the wonderful power, range, flexibility, and sweetness of the musical sounds producible by the human larynx, especially in the female sex."

> *The habits of savages give no indication of how this faculty could have been developed by natural selection, because it is never required or used by them. The singing of savages is a more or less monotonous howling, and the females seldom sing at all. Savages certainly never choose their wives for fine voices, but for rude health, and strength, and physical beauty. Sexual selection could not therefore have developed this wonderful power, which only comes into play among civilized people. It seems as if the organ had been prepared in anticipation of the future progress in man, since it contains latent capacities which are useless to him in his earlier condition.*

Finally, if our higher capacities arose before we used or needed them, then they cannot be the product of natural selection. And if they originated in anticipation of a future need, then they must be the direct creation of a higher intelligence: "The inference I would draw from this class of phenomena is, that a superior intelligence has guided the development of man in a definite direction, and for a special purpose." Wallace had rejoined the camp of natural theology. Darwin remonstrated, but failed to budge his partner.

The fallacy of Wallace's argument is not a simple unwillingness to extend evolution to humans, but rather the hyperselectionism that permeated all his evolutionary thought. For if hyperselectionism is valid—if every part of every creature is fashioned for and only for its immediate use—then Wallace cannot be gainsaid. The earliest Cro-Magnon people, with brains bigger than our own, produced stunning paintings in their caves, but did not write symphonies or build computers. All that we have accomplished since then is the product of cultural evolution based on a brain of unvarying capacity. In Wallace's view, that brain could not be the product of natural selection, since it could always do so much more than it did in its original state.

But hyperselectionism is not valid. It is a caricature of Darwin's subtler view, and it both ignores and misunderstands the nature of organic form and function. Natural selection may build an organ "for" a specific function or group of functions. But this purpose need not fully specify the capacity of a structure. Objects designed for definite purposes can, as a result of their structural complexity, perform many other tasks as well. A factory may install a computer only to issue the monthly pay checks, but such a machine can also analyze the election returns or whip anyone (or at least perpetually tie them) in tick-tack-toe. Our large brains may have originated for some set of necessary skills in gathering food, socializing, or whatever; but these skills do not exhaust the limits of what such a complex machine can do. Fortunately for us, those limits include, among other things, an ability to write—from shopping lists for all of us to grand opera for a few. And our larynx may have arisen for a limited range of articulated sound needed to coordinate social life. But its physical design permits us to do more with it—from singing in the shower for all to the occasional diva.

Hyperselectionism has been with us for a long time in various guises, for it represents the late nineteenth century's scientific version of the myth of natural harmony—all structures well designed for a definite purpose. It is, indeed, the vision of foolish Dr. Pangloss, so vividly satirized by Voltaire in *Candide*—"all is for the best in the best of all possible worlds." As the good doctor said in a famous passage, which predated Wallace by a century, but captures the essence of what is so deeply wrong with his argument:

> *Things cannot be other than they are. . . . Everything is made for the best purpose. Our noses were made to carry spectacles, so we have spectacles. Legs were clearly intended for breeches, and we wear them.*

Nor is Panglossianism dead today—not when so many books in the pop literature on human behavior state that we evolved our big brain for hunting, then trace all our current ills to limits of thought and emotion supposedly imposed by such a mode of life.

Ironically then, Wallace's hyperselectionism led right back to the basic belief of an earlier creationism that it meant to replace—a faith in the rightness of things, a definite place for each object in an integrated whole. As Wallace wrote, quite unfairly, of Darwin:

> *He whose teachings were at first stigmatized as degrading or even atheisti-cal, by devoting to the varied phenomena of living things the loving, patient, and reverent study of one who really had faith in the beauty and harmony and perfection of creation, was enabled to bring to light innumerable adaptations and to prove that the most insignificant parts of the meanest living things had a use and a purpose.*

I do not deny that nature has its harmonies. But structure also has its latent capacities. Built for one thing, it can do others—and in this flexibility lies both the messiness and the hope of our lives.

SECTION TWO

Modern Challenges to Neo-Darwinism

Natural Selection
and Neutral Evolution

MOTOO KIMURA
National Institute of Genetics
Mishima, 411 Japan

Introduction

Darwin's theory of evolution by natural selection has been a great unifying principle of biology. After the rise of Mendelian genetics in this century, the Darwinian theory was fused with genetics, leading to the formation of the neo-Darwinian (or *synthetic*) theory of evolution. According to this theory, almost all genetic changes in evolution are adaptive and have accumulated in the species by positive natural selection. At one time it seemed that the mechanism of evolution could be understood exclusively in neo-Darwinian terms.

With the advent of molecular genetics, it became possible to study evolution and variation at the molecular level (that is, at the level of the internal structure of the gene), and this study has brought many puzzling as well as enlightening observations. The neutral mutation–random drift hypothesis (or the *neutral theory*, for short) that I proposed in 1968 was an attempt to explain these observations based on the mathematical theory of population genetics. Unlike the traditional Darwinian view, the neutral theory claims that the majority of evolutionary mutant substitutions are caused by random fixation of selectively neutral or nearly neutral mutations (Kimura 1968a; see Kimura 1979 for a review).

For a long time, evolution has been treated qualitatively, dominated by facile adaptive explanations or even by nonscientific arguments. With molecular data in conjunction with the stochastic (or probabilistic) theory of gene frequencies, however, quantitative treatments of evolution became feasible. The neutral theory, I hope, is the first step in this new quantitative direction. As a paradigm, it leads to many interpretations that contrast sharply with those that might be derived from the neo-Darwinian theory.

I thank Drs. J. F. Crow and K. Aoki for carefully reading the first draft of this reading and for giving many useful suggestions for improving its presentation.

The Neutralist-Selectionist Controversy

Soon after I proposed the neutral theory, King and Jukes (1969) provided strong support by presenting essentially the same idea backed by a wealth of cogent molecular data. They published their paper under the provocative title "Non-Darwinian Evolution." On the whole, however, the neutral theory has met strong opposition and severe criticism from those who believed that the new molecular observations could be better understood from the orthodox neo-Darwinian standpoint.

This has led to the neutralist-selectionist controversy. Although the debate still continues, the neutral theory has survived for over a decade, and I believe that there is now more supporting evidence for it. It is particularly supported by the recent finding that, in evolution, nucleotide substitutions within protein-coding DNA regions that cause no amino acid changes (called *synonymous* changes) occur at much higher rates than do amino-acid–altering substitutions (Kimura 1977; Jukes 1978, 1980; Jukes and King 1979; Nichols and Yanofsky 1979). Since natural selection acts through phenotypes of the organism for which the structure and function of proteins play a decisive role, one should expect that the mutations that do not cause amino acid changes in proteins, other things being equal, will be much less subject to natural selection than those that do cause amino acid changes. Yet, undeniable facts have emerged in the last few years suggesting that synonymous changes and "silent" nucleotide changes in the noncoding regions of DNA that do not participate in protein formation are the most prevalent evolutionary changes at the molecular level (Miyata, Yasunaga, and Nishida 1980). It has also been discovered that most genes of eukaryotes (higher organisms with a true nucleus) contain regions called *intervening sequences*, or *introns*, that do not participate in protein formation because they are not included in the mature messenger RNA. There is evidence that evolutionary nucleotide substitutions occur very rapidly in introns (van Ooyen et al. 1979; Miyata, Yasunaga, and Nishida 1980; Kimura 1980). Still more remarkable is the new finding that "dead" globin genes evolve very rapidly (in terms of nucleotide substitutions), and that their rates of change are not very different from synonymous substitution rates (Kimura 1980; Miyata and Yasunaga 1981).

A general rule has emerged from these observations: *Molecular evolution proceeds more rapidly when changes are less likely to be subjected to natural selection.* In retrospect, it seems evident that King and Jukes (1969) had remarkable insight when they wrote, "if DNA divergence in evolution includes the random fixation of neutral mutations, then the third-position nucleotides should change more rapidly." They reasoned that since most nucleotide changes at the third position of the codon are synonymous, these changes will be more likely to be neutral, while a majority of changes that produce amino acid substitutions will most likely be harmful and, therefore, weeded out by natural selection. This prediction has now been fully substantiated.

In this connection, my early comment regarding the neutral theory (Kimura 1968b) was more conservative. I wrote, "The recent findings of 'degeneracy' of DNA code, that is, existence of two or more base triplets coding for the same amino acid, seem to suggest that neutral mutations may not be as rare as previously considered." Furthermore, I added a cautious qualifier that "probably not all synonymous mutations are neutral, even if most of them are nearly so." In light of the recent finding that synonymous codons are often used in nonrandom or unequal fashion (Ikemura 1980, 1981; Grantham et al. 1980), it appears this note of caution may be correct.

Contrasting Claims

The contrast between the claims of neutralists and selectionists may best be shown by considering an evolutionary process in which mutant genes are substituted one after another within the species. Each such substitution is made up of a sequence of events in which a rare mutant form appearing, usually singly represented, in the population, finally spreads through the whole population reaching fixation, that is, frequency of 100 percent (Figure 1). In this figure, paths of change in the frequencies of mutants destined to fixation are shown by thick lines. Neutralists and selectionists make diametrically opposed claims regarding the mechanism by which a mutant form of the gene (mutant allele) spreads through the population.

The selectionists claim that for a mutant allele to spread through the species it must have some selective advantage, although they admit that occasionally a selectively neutral mutant may be carried along by linkage to a favored gene ("hitchhiking") to reach a high

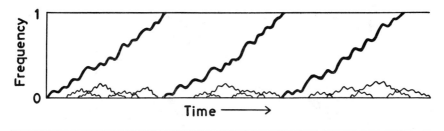

FIGURE 1. The behavior of mutant alleles in a finite population. Paths of change in the frequency of mutant alleles destined to fixation are shown by thick lines.

frequency or even fixation. On the other hand, the neutralists claim that mutants do not *need* a selective advantage to spread through the population. If mutants are selectively equivalent to the preexisting forms, their fate is left to chance and their frequencies increase or decrease fortuitously as time goes on. Such a fluctuation occurs because of the finite size of populations. In each generation a relatively small number of gametes are sampled out of a vast number of male and female gametes to produce individuals of the next generation. Figure 2 illustrates this process, assuming a population consisting of four breeding individuals. In this example, the frequency of the "black" allele changes by chance from 4/8, or 50 percent, to 3/8, or 37.5 percent, in one generation. In natural populations the number of breeding individuals is much larger, and therefore the process proceeds much more slowly.

Although the overwhelming majority of mutants are lost by chance, the remaining minority will eventually become fixed in the population. If neutral mutations are common at the molecular level,

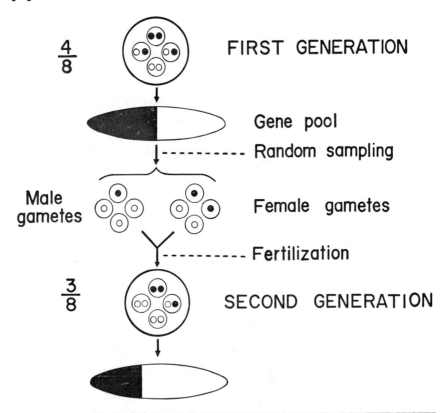

FIGURE 2. The process of random genetic drift, assuming a hypothetical population consisting of four diploid breeding individuals.

and if such a random process goes on incessantly for a long time, say tens of millions of generations, the genetic composition of the population will change tremendously.

This random process is known as *random genetic drift* (or *random drift*) in population genetics. A fundamental concept involved here is the *effective population size*, usually denoted by N_e. This is roughly equal to the number of breeding individuals in one generation, and is usually considerably smaller than the total number of individuals making up the species (for details, see, for example, Kimura and Ohta 1971b, pp. 33-43). For a neutral mutant that has appeared in the population, the probability of its eventual fixation is equal to its initial frequency. The average length of time until fixation, excluding cases of eventual loss, is four times the effective population size of N_e. (This was first shown by Kimura and Ohta (1969).)

The neutralist-selectionist controversy is also concerned with the mechanism by which genetic variability is maintained within a species, particularly in the form of protein polymorphisms. Here *polymorphism* means coexistence of two or more allelic forms at a gene locus in a species, usually excluding the situation where the frequency of the most prevalent allele is higher than 99 percent (in which case the population is called *monomorphic*). Neutralists claim that the majority of polymorphisms detectable by refined molecular techniques (such as electrophoretic methods) are selectively neutral or nearly neutral. They further argue that these polymorphisms are maintained in the population through mutational input and random extinction (Kimura 1968a, 1968b; Kimura and Ohta 1971a). A number of such mutants arise in the population in each generation, and they will eventually be either lost from the population or fixed in it. In the process, they contribute to genetic variability in the form of polymorphism. Thus, polymorphism is a phase of molecular evolution (Kimura and Ohta 1971a).

On the other hand, selectionists claim that polymorphisms are actively maintained by some form of *balancing* selection. The detailed mechanism involved is usually not specified, and selectionists' claims are sometimes vague and elusive, but two of the most popular explanations of selection are *overdominance*—that is, heterozygote advantage—and *frequency-dependent selection* that favors the minority. Of these two, many selectionists once enthusiastically proposed overdominance as the main cause. However, it has become unpopular since Milkman (1973) discovered that protein polymorphism is abundant in the bacterium *Escherichia coli*. Since *E. coli* is a haploid organism, heterozygotes do not exist, and therefore an explanation based on heterozygote advantage is untenable. Nowadays many selectionists resort to frequency-dependent selections as

the most likely mechanism for the maintenance of protein polymorphism.

A large number of papers have been published claiming that
selection has been detected experimentally between enzyme alleles
derived from natural populations of fruit flies (*Drosophila*) and other
organisms. In most cases, however, it is not clear whether selection
occurs directly at the enzyme locus in question, or at surrounding
linked loci. In fact, unambiguous cases of selection are rare. So far,
the strongest case appears to be in the alcohol dehydrogenase (ADH)
locus in *Drosophila melanogaster*. In natural populations, two alleles
denoted by F ("fast") and S ("slow") are segregating; and Clark
(1975) claims that in his laboratory, frequency-dependent selection
was confirmed for these alleles. In order to check Clarke's claim,
Yoshimaru and Mukai (1979) have done very careful, large-scale
experiments, but they have not obtained any evidence for frequency-
dependent selection at the ADH locus in *D. melanogaster*. Thus, the
existence of marked frequency-dependent selection at the ADH
locus is now much in doubt. It is likely that selection involved in
protein polymorphism, if any, is very weak—with an intensity per
locus of the order of 10^{-4} or less, as shown by Mukai and his colleagues (Mukai, Tachida, and Ichinose 1980).

Note that, in any large population, the probable change in frequencies of polymorphic neutral alleles per generation due to random
drift must be very small. Such changes are likely to be of the order
of 10^{-3} at most. So these alleles will look "balanced" to casual
observers. Several years ago I estimated that at each cistron (gene)
in mammalian species, mutant genes will be substituted at intervals
of roughly ten million years, and each substitution will take, on
average, some two million years (Kimura 1973).

Some Misunderstandings

The neutral theory has been the target of a number of criticisms based
on misunderstanding. I shall try to discuss some of them in this
section.

First of all, I must emphasize that the essence of the neutral
theory is not that molecular mutants are selectively neutral in the
strict sense, but that their fate is largely determined by random
genetic drift. In other words, the selection intensity involved in the
process is so weak that random drift predominates.

The neutral theory by no means claims that the genes involved
are functionless, as mistakenly asserted by some critics. What the
neutral theory assumes is that mutant forms of each evolving gene
are selectively *nearly equivalent*—that is, they can do the job equally

well in terms of survival and reproduction of the individual. Sometimes neutral changes are called evolutionary "noise," but I think this is a misnomer. Just as synonyms are not noise in language, it is not proper to regard the substitution of neutral alleles simply as noise or loss of genetic information. If the variants represent amino acid changes in a protein, this means that such changes are equally acceptable for the working of the protein in the body. Furthermore, this equality need not be exact. All that is required is that the resulting difference in fitness be small—say, for example, less than 10 percent of the reciprocal of the effective population size. It is of course possible, and indeed likely, that the latitude for interchangeability without loss of Darwinian fitness will increase as the functional importance of the molecule or portion of the molecule decreases. But this does not mean that the neutral alleles are necessarily functionless.

I also would like to point out that in organisms, particularly in higher forms, physiological homeostasis is a well-developed buffer against internal and external environmental disturbances. So, fluctuation of environmental conditions by no means automatically implies fluctuation of Darwinian fitness of mutants. This very important point is often overlooked by mathematical population geneticists. Some criticisms of the neutral theory come from the wrong definition of natural selection. The term *natural selection* should be used strictly in the Darwinian sense. Natural selection acts through survival and reproduction of the individual. Very often, existence of detectable functional differences between two molecular forms is taken as evidence for the existence of natural selection. To prove that natural selection is involved, the survival and fecundity must be investigated. It is unfortunate that the term *selection* is often used in quite a meaningless way without taking this into account.

It is also important that a clear distinction be made between positive and negative selection. The latter, which is concerned with the elimination of deleterious mutants (unless the deleterious effect is extremely small), has little to do with gene substitution in evolution. Since the great work of Muller in the early days of *Drosophila* genetics, it has been known that negative selection is the most common form of natural selection (Muller 1962). *Stabilizing* or *centripetal* selection reflects negative selection, whereas *directional* selection usually involves positive selection. The existence of negative selection by no means contradicts the neutral theory. Finally, the distinction between gene mutations at the individual level and substitution of mutant forms at the population level must be made clear. Only the substitutions of the mutant forms in the population are directly related to molecular evolution. As a population geneticist, I would like to emphasize that for advantageous mutations, the rate of mutant substitutions in evolution is greatly influenced by the population size and the degree of selective advantage, as well as by the mutation rate.

Some authors, such as Zuckerkandl (1976) and Gillespie (1977) claim that they have produced selectionist theories whose consequences are indistinguishable from the neutral theory. As far as I know, these claims are all based on mistaken theories; some, such as Zuckerkandl, forget the contribution of the population size to the rate of gene substitution by advantageous mutants; others, such as Gillespie, intentionally omit the contribution of mutations. In short, they assume (rather unnecessarily, I think) that natural selection acts in such a way that its consequences are indistinguishable from no selection!

On the other hand, it is sometimes remarked that neutral alleles are by definition not relevant to adaptation, and therefore biologically not very important. I believe that this is too short-sighted a view. Even if the neutral alleles are functionally equivalent under a prevailing set of environmental conditions of a species, it is possible that selection can begin to act on some of them when new environmental conditions are imposed. As Dykhuizen and Hartl (1980) succinctly put it, neutral genes have a "latent potential for selection." Therefore, I believe that neutral mutants can be the raw material for adaptive evolution.

Two Outstanding Features of Molecular Evolution

Among the features revealed by recent studies of molecular evolution, the following two are particularly noteworthy, and help to show that the *patterns* of molecular evolution are quite different from those of phenotypic evolution. They also suggest that the *mechanism* of molecular evolution is different from that of phenotypic evolution.

1. For each protein, the rate of evolution (that is, rate of amino acid substitutions) is approximately constant per amino acid site per year for various lineages.

2. Molecules or portions of molecules that are subject to less functional constraint evolve faster (in terms of mutant substitutions) than those that are subject to stronger constraint.

As to the first feature, the constancy (or uniformity) of the evolutionary rate is most apparent in hemoglobin. The hemoglobin molecule in bony fishes and higher vertebrates is a tetramer, consisting of two identical α chains and two identical β chains. In mammals, amino acid substitutions in the α chain, consisting of 141 amino acids, occur roughly at the rate of one substitution per seven million years in diverse lineages. This corresponds to about 10^{-9} substitutions per year per amino acid site, and, surprisingly, does not seem to depend on such factors as generation time, living conditions, and population size. In Figure 3 the number of amino acid differences between the α chains of the human, and a few other vertebrates, are given together with their phylogenetic tree and a list of geological epochs to show the times of their divergence. Note that the numbers in each row are roughly equal to each other; they represent the amino acid differences that occurred during the same length of time (in years) since divergence.

This constancy of the molecular evolutionary rate is a striking and now well-substantiated phenomenon. I once pointed out (Kimura 1969) that, should hemoglobins and other molecules of "living fossils" be shown to have undergone as many DNA base (and therefore amino acid) substitutions as corresponding genes (proteins) in

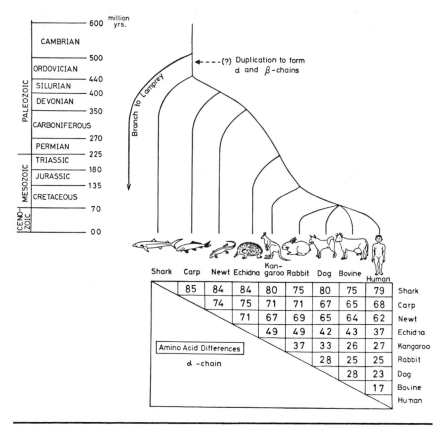

FIGURE 3. A phylogenetic tree of vertebrates together with their times of divergence. Also shown are the number of amino acid differences when their hemoglobin α chains are compared to each other.

more rapidly evolving species, my neutral theory would be supported. The amino acid sequences of the β chain and the α chain of the principal hemoglobin of the Port Jackson shark have recently been determined (Fisher, Nash, and Thompson, 1977). According to Romer (1968), this shark is a relict survivor of a type of ancestral shark with numerous representatives in the late Paleozoic days, notably in the Carboniferous period (270–350 million years ago); so this shark is well entitled to be called a living fossil. In Table 1 I present a comparison of the α and β chains of the Port Jackson shark, together with a similar comparison of α and β chains of humans. Each comparison lists the numbers of amino acid sites that can be interpreted from the code table as due to a minimum of 0, 1, 2, and 3 nucleotide substitutions. From the two sets of comparisons it is clear that genes coding for the α and β chains of hemoglobin in the shark have diverged to roughly the same extent as (or slightly more than) the corresponding two genes in humans. This had to have occurred by accumulation of random mutations since the origin by duplication of the α and β globin genes, possibly during the early Ordovician period (after the late Cambrian period when the agnatha, the jawless fish, probably originated).

Selectionists have questioned and disputed the rate-constancy hypothesis of molecular evolution (also called the "molecular evolutionary clock" concept). An especially strong claim of nonconstancy was made by Goodman and his associates in their study of globin evolution (Goodman et al. 1974; Goodman, Moore, and Matsuda 1975). They maintain that mutant substitutions occurred at a very high rate in the early stage of globin evolution soon after the duplications producing myoglobin and α and β hemoglobins occurred, and that this was followed by a markedly reduced rate of change during the 300 million years from the ancestral amniote to the present.

TYPE OF CHANGE	HUMAN α vs β	SHARK α vs β
0	62	50
1	55	56
2	21	32
3	0	1
Gap	9	11
Total	147	150

TABLE 1. Comparison of differences between the α and β chains of human and shark hemoglobins. For each species, this table gives the number of amino acid sites that can be interpreted as exhibiting a minimum of 0, 1, 2, and 3 nucleotide substitutions, together with the number of gaps (expressed as equivalents of the number of amino acid sites).

According to Goodman, Moore, and Matsuda (1975), between 500 and 400 million years ago the genes descending from the basal vertebrate ancestor through the hemoglobin-myoglobin and β-α ancestors to the teleost-tetrapod α ancestor evolved at the rate of 109 NR percent (NR percent means the number of nucleotide replacements per 100 codons per 10^8 years). This corresponds to a replacement rate of 10.9×10^{-9} per amino acid per year (in my terminology, $k_{aa} = 10.9 \times 10^{-9}$, where k_{aa} represents the mutant substitution rate: Kimura 1969), and it is some ten times as high as my estimate of about 10^{-9} per amino acid site per year. On the other hand, for the last 300 million years their estimated rate is only 15 NR percent (that is, $k_{aa} = 1.5 \times 10^{-9}$), which is not very different from mine. Goodman, Moore, and Matsuda (1975) made use of an extensive series of computer programs to analyze the globin sequence data, and, together with their plausible Darwinian adaptive explanations of the postulated change in rate, their work has been widely cited as evidence against the neutral theory.

Recently I pointed out that the claim that globin evolution was accelerated in its early stages is based on an erroneous assignment of the time of divergence of vertebrate myoglobin and hemoglobin (Kimura 1981a). When this is corrected, there is no basis for the claim. The data are much more consistent with the nearly constant rate expected from the neutral theory than with the uneven rates expected if most amino acid changes were caused by substitutions of definitely favorable mutants through Darwinian selection. Furthermore, I have shown that the overwhelming majority of codons determined by Goodman et al. (1974) by their *maximum parsimony* method are either wrong or ambiguously presented when compared to the actual nucleotide sequences of rabbit α and human β hemoglobins determined by direct sequencing. I have also pointed out that both the maximum parsimony method of codon assignment and the augmentation procedure used by Goodman and his associates are liable to serious errors, and should not be used for studying molecular evolution in general and globin evolution in particular (Kimura 1981b).

The second feature of molecular evolution is even more remarkable than the first. It has become increasingly clear that the weaker the functional constraint on a molecule or a part of a molecule, the higher the rate at which mutant substitutions occur.

Before we proceed, I would like to remark that the mutant substitution rate (or rate of molecular evolution, often denoted by k) is not the same as the rate at which individual mutant alleles increase or decrease within a population (usually denoted by Δp). In the former case, the rate is the long-term average of the number of mutant substitutions. Although it is expressed as change *per year*, k is usually

estimated by counting the number of mutant substitutions during a
span of several tens of millions of years at least. What is relevant is
the average interval between two consecutive fixations, not the time
required for an individual fixation. Thus, in two cases, A and B, as
illustrated in Figure 4, individual mutants increase much more rapidly
in the population in A than in B, yet the rate of evolution (k) is the
same in both cases.

Of the proteins so far investigated, the fastest evolving are the
fibrinopeptides. They have an evolutionary rate 9×10^{-9} per amino
acid site per year (although a lower estimate 4.5×10^{-9} has also been
reported). On the other hand, the slowest evolving protein is histone
H4, which changes at a rate of 0.008×10^{-9} per amino acid site per
year. Indeed, the histone H4 molecule of pea plants differs from that
of calf thymus by only two amino acid replacements from a total of
about 100 amino acids (Isenberg 1979); this implies that plants and
animals diverged some 1.2 billion years ago. It is interesting to note
that the quickly evolving fibrinopeptides have little known function
after they become separated from fibrinogen during the clotting of
blood. A similar situation exists in the middle segment (C) of the
proinsulin molecule. This part is removed when the active insulin is
formed, and it is known that this part evolves at the rate 2.4×10^{-9}
per amino acid site per year. This rate is several times as fast as that

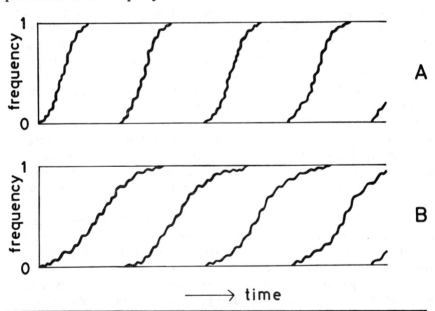

FIGURE 4. The process of mutant substitutions in the population. Of the two
cases illustrated, A and B, individual mutant alleles increase much more rapidly
within a population in case A than in case B, but the rate of evolution in terms
of mutant substitutions is the same in both cases.

of insulin. More examples of this sort should be forthcoming, because it appears that tailoring of a precursor molecule to produce a functionally active form is a common phenomenon. As pointed out by Dickerson (1971), hemoglobins have a definite function in carrying oxygen and therefore their specifications are more restrictive than those of fibrinopeptides. Thus, they have a lower evolutionary rate. Cytochrome c interacts with both cytochrome oxidase and reductase, and is smaller than either. It is likely that there are even more functional constraints on cytochrome c than on hemoglobin; indeed, it has a lower evolutionary rate: roughly 1/3 of that of hemoglobin.

A similar relationship between functional constraint and evolutionary rate holds among different *parts* of hemoglobin molecules. It is known that the surface of hemoglobins is less vital to maintaining the structure and function of the molecule than is the heme pocket. It is therefore, generally, under many fewer constraints. A colleague and I found that in both α and β hemoglobins the surface portion evolves about ten times as fast as the heme pocket (Kimura and Ohta 1973). These examples suggest that natural selection (mostly in the form of negative selection) acts to maintain functionally important folded protein structures rather than particular amino acid sequences *per se*.

As mentioned already, histone H4 is by far the most conservative of proteins, with only one percent change per 1.2 billion years. However, a report by Grunstein, Schedl, and Kedes (1976) shows that even in *this* protein synonymous nucleotide substitutions have occurred at a very high rate. These authors compared histone H4 messenger RNA sequences between two sea urchin species, *Strongylocentrotus purpuratus* and *Lytechinus pictus*. Using their data, together with paleontological knowledge on the time of divergence of these two species, I estimated that the rate of nucleotide substitution is $(3.7 \pm 1.4) \times 10^{-9}$ per year at the third position of the codon (Kimura 1977). This is a very high rate, since the amino acid substitution rate of fibrinopeptides, when converted into the corresponding nucleotide substitution rate, amounts to roughly 4.0×10^{-9}. It is remarkable that synonymous mutant substitutions have occurred in this gene at nearly the highest known rate, despite the fact that amino acid substitutions have occurred in the corresponding protein at the lowest known rate.

In addition, we now have evidence that, even when two genes code for proteins that exhibit very different amino acid substitution rates, their synonymous substitution rates will be roughly equal. In other words, synonymous substitution rates are not only high but also nearly equal for different genes, when expressed per nucleotide site (Kimura 1980; Miyata, Yasunada, and Nishida, 1980).

These observations can easily and consistently be interpreted within the framework of the neutral theory. As the functional constraint diminishes, a larger and larger fraction of mutations becomes selectively neutral (not deleterious), and therefore the mutation rate for neutral alleles approaches the total mutation rate. It is known (Kimura 1968a; see also Crow and Kimura 1970, p. 369) that, if mutations are selectively neutral, the rate of evolution (in terms of mutant substitutions) in the population is equal to the mutation rate per gamete, independent of population size. Therefore, as I predicted before, there must be a maximum evolutionary rate set directly by the mutation rate (Kimura 1977).

Here I must emphasize that the existence of negative selection due to functional constraint by no means contradicts the neutral theory. At the time of their occurrence, a significant fraction of mutations may be definitely deleterious (particularly when they occur in the coding region of a gene). However, they are eliminated before they reach any appreciable frequencies in the population. Only those mutations whose deleterious effects are so small as to be regarded as practically neutral can spread through the species by random drift (when chance favors them). The probability of a mutation being selectively neutral (not harmful) must be larger, the more the mutation permits retention of the existing (normal) conformation of the protein. This is why evolutionary amino acid substitutions are mostly conservative. It is a pity that so many criticisms of the neutral theory have been based on misunderstanding of such a simple fact.

The second feature of molecular evolution, which we have just discussed, could be paraphrased as follows (Kimura and Ohta 1974):

Functionally less important molecules or portions of molecules evolve (in terms of mutant substitutions) faster than more important ones.

Although this statement is less exact than the corresponding one given at the beginning of this section, it may be more useful as a guide in treating molecular data. Certainly this justifies the practice of searching for various DNA signals, such as "splicing" signals (see Ohno 1980), by comparing a relevant region of homologous sequences of diverse organisms and picking out a constant (consensus) pattern, but disregarding variable ones as unimportant.

All the above generalizations concerning the relationship between functional importance and evolutionary rate will not make sense to selectionists. They claim that rapidly evolving molecules or parts of molecules have some unknown but important function and that they are undergoing rapid adaptive change by accumulating advantageous mutations. In this view, "dead" globin genes are not dead but are very much alive, probably doing some important jobs such as controlling the expression of other normal globin genes.

Which of these two opposing views is nearer to the truth, and therefore more useful, will become clear as more and more DNA data accumulate.

Discussion and Conclusions

There is little doubt that positive Darwinian selection is the major cause of evolutionary change at the phenotypic level, that is, at the level of form and function. If we call *pan-selectionism* the view that ascribes every facet of biological characters to environmental adaptation, this has been a very successful view in treating evolution at the phenotypic level.

Pan-selectionism has flourished within the framework of the neo-Darwinian or synthetic theory of evolution. It has been pushed to its limit by workers in ecological genetics trying to demonstrate the natural prevalence of balancing selection in protein polymorphisms (Clarke 1975).

However, in order to treat evolution and variation at the molecular level, we need a new viewpoint; and I believe that the neutral theory fulfills this function. It emphasizes the importance of chance (random frequency drift), claiming that, at the level of the molecular constitution of genes, evolutionary changes are mainly caused by random fixation of selectively equivalent or nearly equivalent mutant alleles. In other words, mutation pressure and random genetic drift prevail at the molecular level. More and more, as data on nucleotide sequences accumulate, I believe that this is a very useful way of interpreting the data.

One final question remains: How can these apparently conflicting viewpoints be reconciled? We should like to know why natural selection prevails at the phenotypic level and yet random fixation of selectively neutral alleles prevails at the molecular level.

The answer to this question, I believe, comes from the fact that the most common type of natural selection at the phenotypic level is stabilizing selection. Here it is important to note that natural selection acts directly on phenotypes, but only secondarily on the molecular constitution of genes; the latter are subject to selection only through their effect on phenotypes.

Unlike the type of natural selection Darwin had in mind when he tried to explain evolution, stabilizing selection eliminates phenotypically extreme individuals and preserves those near the population mean. It acts to keep the *status quo*, rather than to produce a directional change. Stabilizing selection is also called normalizing or centripetal selection, and many examples have been reported. Probably the best example in human populations is the relationship between the birth weights of babies and their neonatal mortality, as studied by Karn and Penrose (1951). These authors found that babies whose weight is very near the mean have the lowest mortality. The optimum weight is slightly heavier than the mean, and mortality increases progressively as the weight deviates from this optimum.

Let us consider a quantitative character such as height, weight, concentration of some chemical substance, or a more abstract quantity that underlies fitness in a significant way. Let us assume that the character is determined by a large number of gene loci (or sites), each with a small effect, in addition to being subject to environmental effects. Let us also assume that, under the continued action of stabilizing selection, the mean has been brought very near the optimum, or even to coincide with it. Under such conditions, it can be shown mathematically that the intensity of natural selection involved between alleles at an individual locus or site can be extremely minute, and that every mutation will be slightly deleterious but nearly neutral (see the Appendix to this reading for details; also see Kimura 1981c). It can also be shown that, when the mean is shifting under the process of directional selection, a shifting of gene frequencies should also quickly occur; but this will seldom lead to gene substitutions (see Appendix).

We are thus led to a general picture of evolution, as follows: From time to time, the position of the optimum shifts due to change of environment, and the species tracks such a change rapidly by altering its mean. Most of the time, however, stabilizing selection predominates. Under this selection, neutral evolution through random fixation of mutant alleles occurs extensively, transforming all genes (including those of living fossils) profoundly at the molecular level. Thus we see that neutral molecular evolution is an inevitable process under stabilizing phenotypic selection.

APPENDIX

Let us assume that the measured character (X) follows a normal distribution with the mean M and variance σ^2, and that the fitness of individuals whose measured character is X is given by $W(X) = \exp\{-K(X - X_{op})^2\}$, where X_{op} stands for the optimum phenotypic value. This is illustrated in Figure 5.

Consider a particular locus in which a pair of alleles A_1 and A_2 are segregating with respective frequencies $1 - p$ and p, and let A be the effect of substituting A_2 for A_1 on the quantitative character. Then it can be shown, under the assumption of additive effects of genes on X, that the selection coefficient s that gives the selective advantage of A_2 over A_1 is

$$s = -\lambda ma + (\lambda m^2 - 1)(1 - 2p)\lambda a^2/2,$$

where $\lambda = 2K\sigma^2/(2K\sigma^2 + 1)$ is a parameter relating phenotype to selection inten-

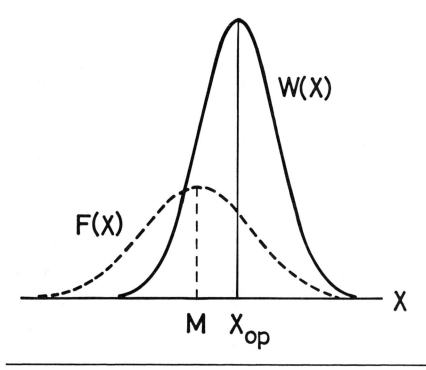

FIGURE 5. Stabilizing selection on a quantitative character X. The fitness function $W(X)$ is shown by a solid curve and the frequency function $F(X)$ by a broken curve.

sity; $m = (M - X_{op})/\sigma$ is the deviation of the mean from the optimum in standard units; and $a = A/\sigma$ is the effect of allelic substitution on X also measured with the phenotypic standard deviation as the unit. With this selection coefficient s, the change of gene frequency in one generation is given by $\Delta p = sp(1 - p)$.

From the above formula for s, we can see that if the deviation of the mean from the optimum is much larger than the effect of an allele substitution (that is, $|m| \gg |a|$), the term involving a^2 is negligible, and the situation is similar to truncation selection (see Milkman 1978; Crow and Kimura 1979). Then, natural selection acts very efficiently to change the mean toward the optimum. Under this process of directional selection, shifting of gene frequencies should occur, but this will seldom lead to gene substitutions.

If, on the other hand, the mean is at the optimum ($m = 0$), we have $s = -\lambda(1 - 2p)a^2/2$. In this case alleles behave as if negatively overdominant (that is, equivalent to the case of heterozygote disadvantage), and every mutation is deleterious, since $s < 0$ for $p < 0.5$. Let us pursue this case further. Although we considered a single quantitative character, in reality there must be a very large number of quantitative characters that are subject to natural selection and that determine the Darwinian fitness of individuals. Many of them are mutually correlated, so let us suppose that we can choose a certain number of independent characters that collectively represent, as a first approximation, the total pattern of selection in the lifetime of an individual. This collection may be called the total phenotype.

Under a simplifying assumption that the component quantitative characters are equivalent, we can estimate the average selection intensity per segregrating nucleotide site. We shall use a symbol s_s (meaning selection coefficient for stabilizing selection) to stand for $\lambda a^2/2$ so that $s = -s_s(1 - 2p)$. Then it can be shown that $s_s = L\rho^2/n_{\text{HET}}$, where L is the intensity of natural selection (or the genetic load) acting on the total phenotype; ρ^2 is the fraction of the phenotypic variance that is due to genetic variability (or broad sense heritability), and n_{HET} is the average number of heterozygous nucleotide sites per individual. For mammals, a typical set of values of these parameters is roughly $L = 0.5$, $\rho^2 = 0.5$, and $n_{\text{HET}} = 10^6$. These give $s_s = 2.5 \times 10^{-7}$, which is an exceedingly small selection coefficient. This means that the great majority of mutations at the molecular level are nearly neutral but very slightly deleterious, in accordance with Ohta's claim (Ohta 1973, 1974). Of course, some sites produce larger phenotypic effects and therefore are subject to stronger selection than the average, while others are much less so. Furthermore, it is possible, and indeed likely, that a certain fraction of sites produce no phenotypic effects at all and therefore are completely free from natural selection. Mutational changes in such sites are selectively neutral in the strict sense of the word. In addition it can be shown, based on the mathematical theory of population genetics, that negatively overdominant alleles are far more susceptible to random genetic drift than unconditionally deleterious alleles with the same magnitude of selection coefficient.

REFERENCES

Clarke, B. "The Contribution of Ecological Genetics to Evolutionary Theory: Detecting the Direct Effects of Natural Selection on Particular Polymorphic Loci." *Proceedings XIII International Congress in Genetics, Part II*, pp. 101–113. *Genetics* 79, Supplement (1975).

Crow, James F., and Kimura, Motoo. *An introduction to Population Genetics Theory.* New York: Harper and Row. Reprint by Minneapolis: Burgess, 1970.

———. "Efficiency of Truncation Selection." *Proceedings of the National Academy of Sciences USA* 76 (1979):396–399.

Dickerson, R. E. "The Structure of Cytochrome c and the Rates of Molecular Evolution." *Journal of Molecular Evolution* 1 (1971):26–45.

Dykhuizen, D., and Hartl, D. L. "Selective Neutrality of 6PGD Allozymes in *E. coli* and the Effects of Genetic Background." *Genetics* 96, no. 4 (1980):801–817.

Fisher, W. K.; Nash, A. R.; and Thompson, E. O. P. "Haemoglobins of the Shark, *Heterodontus portusjacksoni* III. Amino Acid Sequence of the β-chain." *Australian Journal of Biological Sciences* 30 (1977):487–506.

Gillespie, J. H. "Sampling Theory for Alleles in a Random Environment." *Nature* 266 (1977):433–445.

Goodman, Morris; Moore, G. W.; Barnabas, J.; and Matsuda, G. "The Phylogeny of Human Globin Genes Investigated by the Maximum Parsimony Method." *Journal of Molecular Evolution* 3 (1974):1–48.

Goodman, Morris; Moore, G. W.; and Matsuda, G. "Darwinian Evolution in the Genealogy of Hemoglobin." *Nature* 253 (1975):603-608.

Grantham, R.; Gauthier, C.; Gouy, M.; Mercier, R.; and Pave, A. "Codon Catalog Usage and the Genome Hypothesis." *Nucleic Acids Research* 8 (1980): r49-r62.

Grunstein, M.; Schedl, P.; and Kedes, L. "Sequence Analysis and Evolution of Sea Urchin (*Lytechinus pictus* and *Strongylocentrotus purpuratus*) Histone H4 Messenger RNAs." *Journal of Molecular Biology* 104 (1976):351-369.

Ikemura, T. "The Frequency of Codon Usage in *E. coli* Genes: Correlation with Abundance of Cognate tRNA." In *Genetics and Evolution of RNA Polymerase, tRNA and Ribosomes,* edited by S. Osawa, H. Ozeki, H. Uchida, and T. Yura, pp. 519-523. Tokyo: University of Tokyo Press, 1980.

———. "Correlation Between the Abundance of *Escherichia coli* tRNAs and the Occurrence of the Respective Codons in its Protein Genes." *Journal of Molecular Biology* 146 (1981):1-21.

Isenberg, I. "Histones." *Annual Review of Biochemistry* 48 (1979):159-191.

Jukes, Thomas H. "Neutral Changes During Divergent Evolution of Hemoglobins." *Journal of Molecular Evolution* 11 (1978): 267-269.

———. "Silent Nucleotide Substitutions and the Molecular Evolutionary Clock." *Science* 210, no. 4473 (1980):973-978.

Jukes, Thomas H., and King, J. L. "Evolutionary Nucleotide Replacement in DNA." *Nature* 281 (1979):605-606.

Karn, M. N., and Penrose, L. S. "Birth Weight and Gestation Time in Relation to Maternal Age, Parity, and Infant Survival." *Annals of Eugenics* 16 (1951):147-164.

Kimura, Motoo. "Evolutionary Rate at the Molecular Level." *Nature* 217 (1968a):624-626.

———. "Genetic Variability Maintained in a Finite Population Due to Mutational Production of Neutral and Nearly Neutral Isoalleles." *Genetical Research* 11 (1968b):247-269.

———. "The Rate of Molecular Evolution Considered from the Standpoint of Population Genetics." *Proceedings of the National Academy of Sciences USA* 63 (1969):1181-1188.

———. "Gene Pool of Higher Organisms as a Product of Evolution." *Cold Spring Harbor Symposia on Quantitative Biology* 38 (1973):515-524.

———. "Preponderance of Synonymous Changes as Evidence for the Neutral Theory of Molecular Evolution." *Nature* 267 (1977):275-276.

———. "The Neutral Theory of Molecular Evolution." *Scientific American* 241, no. 5 (1979):94-104.

———. "A Simple Method for Estimating Evolutionary Rates of Base Substitutions Through Comparative Studies of Nucleotide Sequences." *Journal of Molecular Evolution* 16 (1980):111-120.

———. "Was Globin Evolution Very Rapid in Its Early Stages—A Dubious Case Against the Rate-Constancy Hypothesis." (letter) *Journal of Molecular Evolution* 17, no. 2 (1981a):110-113.

———. "Doubt about Studies of Globin Evolution Based on Maximum Parsimony Codons and the Augmentation Procedure." *Journal of Molecular Evolution* 17, no. 2 (1981b):121-122.

———. "Possibility of Extensive Neutral Evolution under Stabilizing Selection with Special Reference to Nonrandom Usage of Synonymous Codons." *Proceedings of the National Academy of Sciences USA* 78, no. 9 (1981c):5773-5777.

Kimura, Motoo, and Ohta, Tomoko. "The Average Number of Generations until Fixation of a Mutant Gene in a Finite Population." *Genetics* 61 (1969):763-771.

———. "Protein Polymorphism as a Phase of Molecular Evolution." *Nature* 229 (1971a):467-469.

———. *Theoretical Aspects of Population Genetics.* Princeton: Princeton University Press, 1971b.

———. "Mutation and Evolution at the Molecular Level." *Genetics* 73, Supplement (1973):19-35.

———. "On Some Principles Governing Molecular Evolution." *Proceedings of the National Academy of Sciences USA* 71 (1974):2848-2852.

King, J. L., and Jukes, Thomas H. "Non-Darwinian Evolution." *Science* 164 (1969):788-798.

Milkman, R. "Electrophoretic Variation in *E. coli* from Natural Sources." *Science* 182 (1973):1024-1026.

———. "Selection Differentials and Selection Coefficients." *Genetics* 88 (1978): 391-403.

Miyata, T., and Yasunaga, T. "Rapidly Evolving Mouse αGlobin-Related Pseudo Gene and Its Evolutionary History." *Proceedings of the National Academy of Sciences USA* 78 (1981):450-453.

Miyata, T.; Yasunaga, T.; and Nishida, T. "Nucleotide Sequence Divergence and Functional Constraint in mRNA Evolution." *Proceedings of the National Academy of Sciences USA* 77 (1980):7328-7332.

Mukai, T.; Tachida, H.; and Ichinose, M. "Selection for Viability at Loci Controlling Protein Polymorphisms in *Drosophila melanogaster* is Very Weak at Most." *Proceedings of the National Academy of Sciences USA* 77 (1980):4857-4860.

Muller, Hermann J. *Studies in Genetics.* Bloomington: Indiana University Press, 1962.

Nichols, B. P., and Yanofsky, C. "Nucleotide Sequences of *trpA* of *Salmonella typhimurium* and *Escherichia coli*: An Evolutionary Comparison." *Proceedings of the National Academy of Sciences USA* 76 (1979):5244-5248.

Ohno, S. "Origin of Intervening Sequences within Mammalian Genes and the Universal Signal for Their Removal." *Differentiation* 17 (1980):1-15.

Ohta, Tomoko. "Slightly Deleterious Mutant Substitutions in Evolution." *Nature* 246 (1973): 96-98.

———. "Mutational Pressure as the Main Cause of Molecular Evolution and Polymorphism." *Nature* 252 (1974):351-354.

Romer, Alfred, S. *The Procession of Life.* London: Weidenfeld and Nicolson, 1968.

van Ooyen, A.; van den Berg, J.; Mantel, N.; and Weissman, C. "Comparison of Total Sequence of a Cloned Rabbit β-Globin Gene and Its Flanking Regions with a Homologous Mouse Sequence." *Science* 206 (1979): 337-344.

Yoshimaru, H., and Mukai, T. "Lack of Experimental Evidence for Frequency-Dependent Selection at the Alcohol Dehydrogenase Locus in *Drosophila melanogaster.*" *Proceedings of the National Academy of Sciences USA* 76 (1979):876–878.

Zuckerkandl, E. "Evolutionary Processes and Evolutionary Noise at the Molecular Level. II. A Selectionist Model for Random Fixations in Proteins." *Journal of Molecular Evolution* 7 (1976):269–311.

SUGGESTED READINGS

Calder, N. *The Life Game.* London: British Broadcasting Company, 1973.

Crow, J. F. "The Dilemma of Nearly Neutral Mutations: How Important are They for Evolution and Human Welfare?" *Journal of Heredity* 63 (1972):306–316.

——. "The Neutralist-Selectionist Controversy: An Overview." In *Population and Biological Aspects of Human Mutation,* edited by E. B. Hook and I. H. Porter, pp. 3–14. New York: Academic Press, 1981.

Kimura, Motoo. "How Genes Evolve; A Population Geneticist's View." *Annales de Génétiques* 19 (1976):153–168.

Lewontin, Richard C. *The Genetic Basis of Evolutionary Change.* New York and London: Columbia University Press, 1974.

Ohno, S. *Evolution by Gene Duplication.* Berlin: Springer-Verlag, 1970.

Ohta, T. *Evolution and Variation of Multigene Families.* Lecture Notes in Biomathematics, No. 37. New York: Springer-Verlag, 1980.

Ruffié, J. *De la Biologie à la Culture.* Paris: Flammarion, 1976.

The Role of Chance in Evolution

DAVID M. RAUP

Department of Geophysical Sciences
University of Chicago

Introduction

Most interpretation of the fossil record has centered around finding specific causes for specific evolutionary events. Why was there a sudden diversification of life in the late Precambrian? Why did one group of corals replace another? Why did the dinosaurs go extinct? Why did the human species evolve when it did? And so on. The approach has been highly deterministic; each event has been treated as unique, and although generalizations have been made there have been few attempts to look at groups of events in a probabilistic way.

Out of all the paleontological work, there has developed a strong consensus on a couple of major generalizations: First, there has been a marked and broad increase in number of species over the last 600 million years, interrupted only by a few periods of mass extinction; and second, it is generally agreed that the fossil record shows steady improvement or progressive optimization of fitness of biologic structures. Optimal structures are common, but well-documented examples of the steps leading to the optima are hard to find.

Let me say a bit more about the first generalization—that of increased species diversity. Approximately 200,000 fossil species have been described since Linnaeus (Raup 1976); the vast majority are invertebrate animals, and most are marine. Plants and terrestrial vertebrates make up a small fraction.

Figure 1 shows the distribution of invertebrate fossils through geologic time—based on a tabulation of about half of the 140,000 species described since 1900. It shows a Paleozoic peak in the Devonian and a post-Paleozoic rise to a maximum in the Cenozoic. The latter is not nearly as great as has been previously estimated and much of it may be an artifact of sampling. Younger rocks are much better exposed than older ones and inevitably yield more species.

This article is a revision of David M. Raup, "Probabilistic Models in Evolutionary Paleobiology," *American Scientist* 65 (1977):50–57.

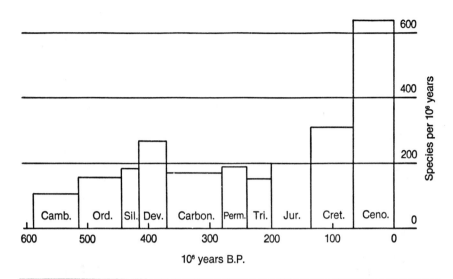

FIGURE 1. The variation in apparent numbers of fossil invertebrate species during the Phanerozoic (the past 600 million years) can be seen from this chart, which is based on published citations to about 70,000 of the species described between 1900 and 1970. (David M. Raup, "Species Diversity in the Phanerozoic: A Tabulation," *Paleobiology* 2, no. 4, 1976, p. 286. © The Paleontological Society.

Figure 2 shows variation in the exposed area and volume of sedimentary rocks. These plots—particularly the one for area—are very similar to the species plot. The raw data for diversity are statistically correlated with both area and volume, and the correlations are significant at the 99 percent level. Ironically, area and volume are correlated with each other only at the 95 percent level! Recent work on this problem by Bambach (1977) and Sepkoski (1978, 1979) indicates that although there has been some net increase in diversity, there have been substantial periods during which the number of taxa has been relatively constant. That is, during these periods, origination and extinction of species have been in some sort of dynamic equilibrium.

Figure 3 shows the changes over time in the percentage composition of the invertebrate fossil record—again based on a sample of 70,000 species. Some of the changes are striking: The domination of the early Paleozoic by trilobites was followed by the virtual takeover of the invertebrate world by molluscs and protozoans after the Permian. (Keep in mind that insects do not play a large role here because of lack of preservation.) Must we find specific causes for all these changes? Because so much time is involved, it may be that small random fluctuations in numbers of taxa can accumulate as a Markov chain—a sequence in which future states of a system are influenced by preceding states—to produce changes of this magnitude.

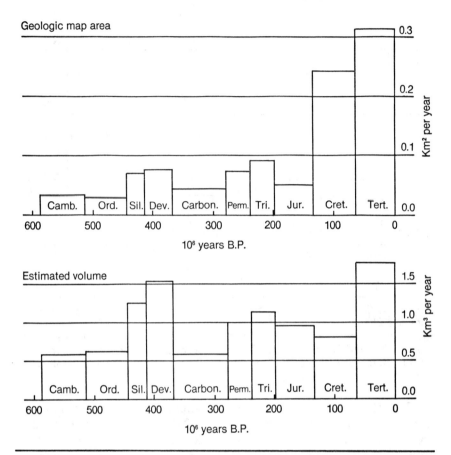

FIGURE 2. These charts show the surviving areas and volumes of sedimentary rocks (for Cambrian-Tertiary). *Top,* geologic map area. (H. Blatt and R. L. Jones, "Proportions of Exposed Igneous, Metamorphic, and Sedimentary Rocks," *Geological Society of America Bulletin* 86, 1975; personal communication with H. Blatt, 1975.) *Bottom,* sedimentary volume. (C. B. Gregor, "Denudation of the Continents," reprinted by permission from *Nature* 228, p. 274, copyright © 1970 Macmillan Journals Limited; (modified) deep-sea deposits have been excluded from Gregor's data.)

Probabilistic Approaches

The fossil record as a whole provides many possibilities for probabilistic models, with ample opportunity for making predictions and testing them. Although we have only one historical record, it is a large one and it contains many reasonably independent histories— those of biologic groups that have occupied widely separated continents and have had little interaction. Above all, we have very long time series—so long that events with small probabilities become likely, including rare physical events that have biological impact.

It may be that the length of time involved is such that changes in the adaptive relationships among species and in the relationships between species and their environment are so complex and multifactorial that natural selection may behave (mathematically) as a random variable. To be sure, there have been monotonic trends of environmental change, and these have had evolutionary consequences; but such trends reverse and go forward and back in an apparently unpredictable fashion. To describe such changes as "random" does not deny cause and effect; it just means that the sequence of events can be predicted only in a statistical sense. Each event has a cause, but the distribution of these causes in geologic time may be essentially random.

Recently, several frankly probabilistic models have been proposed for application to the fossil record of evolution. One is Steven

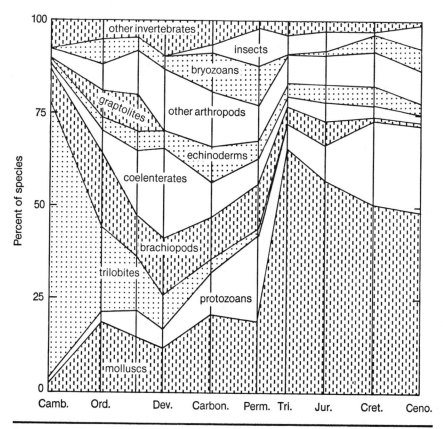

FIGURE 3. Considerable variation is evident in the taxonomic composition of the invertebrate fossil record through the Phanerozoic. (David M. Raup, "Species Diversity in the Phanerozoic: A Tabulation," *Paleobiology* 2, no. 4, 1976, p. 287. © The Paleontological Society.)

Stanley's (1975) idea of *species selection*. This model proposes that speciation may be a largely random process, with characteristics of the founder individuals in small populations being very important; and that a lot of selection actually takes place between species—in other words, selection within genera or families rather than within populations.

Another model of current interest is Leigh Van Valen's (1973) Red Queen Hypothesis, which he uses to explain fossil data that he contends show the probability of extinction to be stochastically constant within a taxonomic group. Van Valen thinks it possible to talk about species as having a "half-life"—descriptively analogous to the half-life of a radioactive isotope.

Let me return to Markov chains. Evolution certainly should be viewed in a Markovian framework, at least as far as time series are concerned. Figure 4 presents three simple random walks—time series characterized by small steps, showing values of, say, a morphologic character or a genetic frequency as it changes over time. There is uncertainty about whether the line will go up or down at a given point, but its position after the move is heavily constrained by where it was before the move: It can only be a small distance from the previous position. The analogy to evolution is that each species owes more to its phylogenetic legacy than to the genetic changes that took place during its speciation event. It need not concern us now *why* the line goes up or down; suffice it to say that such patterns of change are very common in the fossil record.

Imagine for a moment that we were to look at only the 500 points on each of these plots, ignoring the lines connecting them, and think of a scatter diagram of time versus some attribute (the vertical coordinate). If conventional correlation coefficients are calculated, it turns out that the majority are statistically significant at the 99 percent level. In a sense, therefore, we can say that the attribute is significantly correlated with time in most cases even though we *know* that we are dealing with a totally random process. This is an important warning for those who are quick to describe evolutionary trends and interpret them in terms of single causes. Thanks to mathematicians such as William Feller, it is possible to test these trends using the random walk as a null hypothesis. None of these three shows significant departures from statistical expectations (see Feller 1968 for methodology).

Figure 5 shows two fossil time series from a paper by Hayami and Ozawa (1975), who used them as examples of orthoselection— that is, long-term response to single selective factors. Although the top one does depart significantly from expectations, and thus is a candidate for biological interpretation, tests using the Markov chain model on the bottom example demonstrate that the change could

Time ⟶

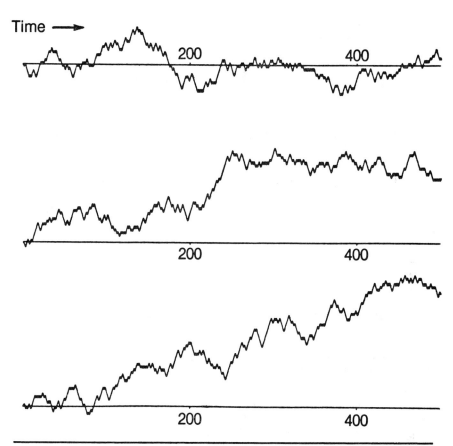

FIGURE 4. Three computer-generated random walks show the evolution of a morphological character or a genetic frequency. The three random walks, each 500 steps long, were selected from twenty that were constructed. The upper one comes closest to the normal idea of a random walk, yet is a relatively uncommon type; the two lower ones are actually more typical because of the Markov property of random walks. In random walks that are reasonably long, the line of steps will cross the starting point (horizontal axis) in the second half of the walk in only 50 percent of the cases; in 20 percent of random walks, the line will stay on one side 97.6 percent of the time; in 10 percent of random walks, there will be no crossing after the first 3 percent of the walk. (David M. Raup, "Stochastic Models in Evolutionary Paleontology," in *Patterns of Evolution*, A. Hallam, ed., Amsterdam: Elsevier, 1977.)

easily have occurred by chance, so the orthoselection explanation model is not justified (Raup 1977). The obvious trend here could have resulted either from genetic drift or from a chance combination of independent selection events.

To summarize, the first question for the paleobiologist faced with an evolutionary trend should be: Does the trend represent a

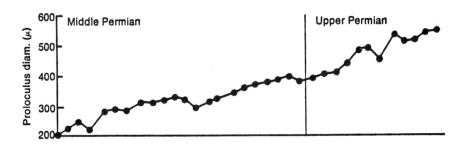

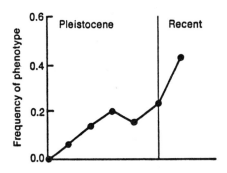

FIGURE 5. Fossil time series expressed in the format of a random walk. *Top:*
This size variation through time for a Permian protozoan departs significantly
from chance expectations, and is thus a candidate for biological interpretation.
Bottom: Variation in frequency of one phenotype in a Pleistocene and recent
scallop could easily have resulted from chance. (After I. Hayami and T. Ozawa,
"Evolutionary Models of Lineage-Zones," *Lethaia* 8, 1975.)

statistically significant departure from chance expectations? Only
if the answer is positive is there justification for proceeding to look
for a specific biologic or geologic cause for the trend. In evolutionary
time series, the random walk model (as a kind of Markov chain) is
the appropriate null hypothesis.

A Monte Carlo Model

Let me now turn to a much more ambitious attempt at probabilistic
modeling. It is based on my recent collaboration with Stephen Gould,
Thomas Schopf, and Daniel Simberloff, and involves an application
of branching processes to phylogenetic patterns, and as such represents a somewhat more complex version of the Markov model (Raup
et al. 1973; Raup and Gould 1974; Gould et al. 1977). The work
uses computer simulation and Monte Carlo methods to generate
imaginary evolutionary trees. As shown in Figure 6, a branching
pattern of lineages is built up using random numbers. In effect, we

are asking: What would evolution have looked like if it were a completely random process, without natural selection and adaptation and without predictable environmental change? The simulations are thus a giant null hypothesis for comparison with the real world.

Figure 6 illustrates the basic framework of the program. It operates in an arbitrary time scale, and it deals with a series of computer-generated evolutionary lines or lineages. The program is written in such a way that, at each time interval, the evolving lineage may go extinct or persist to the next time interval; if it persists, it may branch to form a second lineage. These choices are based entirely on preset probabilities of one outcome or the other. Once a second lineage has been produced by the branching process, it too is subject to the same set of choices for extinction or survival or

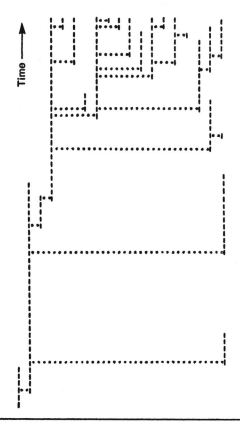

FIGURE 6. This simulated evolutionary pattern starts on the lower left with a lineage that lasted a half dozen time units. Each vertical dash is a time unit in the computer system, and each series of vertical dashes is a lineage; branching (*dots*) and extinction are signaled by machine-generated random numbers. (David M. Raup and Stephen J. Gould, "Stochastic Simulation and Evolution of Morphology Towards a Nomothetic Paleontology," *Systematic Zoology* 23, 1974.)

branching. In the case shown in Figure 6, the starting lineage branched after three time intervals but became extinct after six. The newly formed branch lasted considerably longer and before it became extinct gave rise either directly or indirectly to all the other lineages shown. The average length of a lineage will, of course, be a function of the probability assigned to extinction.

The resulting output is an evolutionary tree of the sort most paleontologists spend much of their time developing or trying to decipher. As the program is written, several hundreds of these evolutionary lineages are generated in the course of a single run, so the output of a single run is several times larger and more complex than the one illustrated in Figure 6.

Now, if the probabilities of branching and extinction are the same and constant throughout the run, the number of coexisting lineages will wander up and down as a random walk. If, on the other hand, the probability of branching is higher than the probability of extinction, the number of coexisting lineages will increase geometrically. In most runs, we elected to compromise between these two strategies. We established, in advance, an equilibrium number of lineages and had probabilities of extinction and branching continuously monitored on the basis of the number of lineages present, so that the number of lineages rises to the equilibrium value and then fluctuates around it in dynamic equilibrium.

What we have established, therefore, is a kind of evolution machine that is an extremely stylized expression of one evolutionary model. It is deterministic in that the branching continues until the equilibrium is reached, then fluctuates about that equilibrium. It is stochastic in the sense that the fate of any lineage is determined only in a probabilistic sense.

We were not really attempting to simulate the real world; in fact, we did not expect very close correspondence with the real world. Rather, we wished to use this means to separate those kinds of events that are readily amenable to a stochastic explanation from those that require a more deterministic explanation. In short, we were looking at the differences rather than the similarities between our simulations and the real world.

Figure 7 shows the basic format we used for the computer simulations. In order to make the results more applicable to paleontology as it is practiced, we wrote into the program routines for grouping the lineages into higher taxa, such as families, orders, or phyla. This was done by purely mechanical means based on the size and persistence of groups of lineages. Figure 8, a simplified form of the output of four computer runs, shows one level of computer-generated classification grouping. The patterns bear remarkable resemblance to

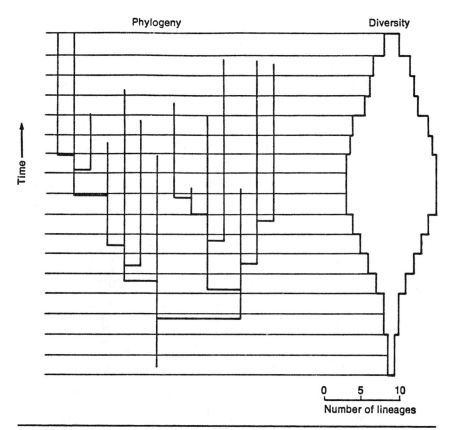

FIGURE 7. The hypothetical evolutionary pattern (*left*) is similar to what the computer produces: The lineages are all interrelated in the sense that they are derived from a single ancestor. Its summary (*right*) is a paleontologically common means of expressing the change in abundance of forms within an evolving group; the width of the pattern reflects the number of coexisting lineages through time. (D. M. Raup, S. J. Gould, T. J. M. Schopf, and D. S. Simberloff, "Stochastic Models of Phylogeny and Evolution of Diversity," *Journal of Geology* 81, 1973.)

many in the paleontological literature. It is a very easy matter indeed to pick out well-known groups in this array; for example, you can find patterns that resemble that of the trilobites, like group 16 in row C, where there is a very rapid radiation and diversification early in the history of the group followed by a gradual decline toward extinction. At the opposite extreme is group 6 in row B, which might simulate the insects: diversification over quite a long period of time so that the current diversity is extremely high.

In the computer output it is very common for several groups of lineages to go extinct at the same time—just as a matter of chance.

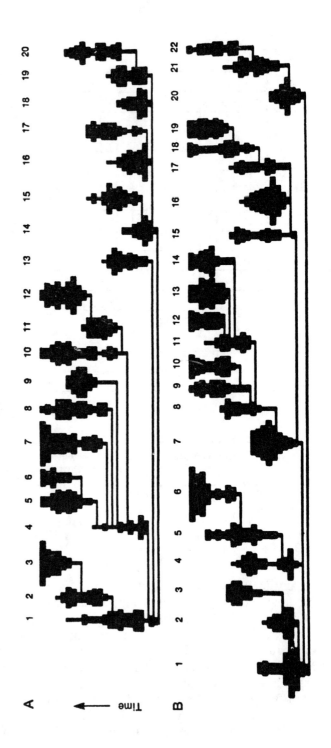

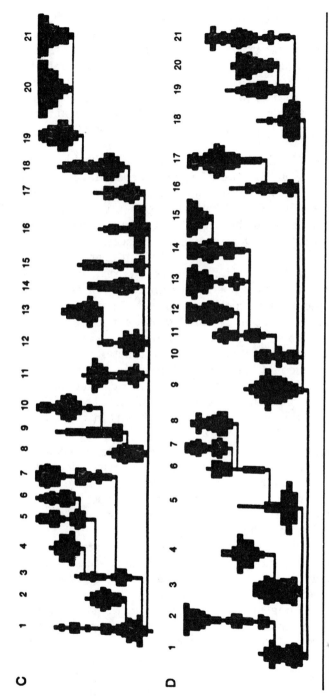

FIGURE 8. All runs of the simulation program, from which these samples were taken, used the same input constants (that is, probabilities of branching and extinction); the differences in pattern are therefore due to chance. Each color area shows the diversity history of a monophyletic group of lineages. The ancestry of the groups relative to one another is shown by horizontal lines. In each run, there were up to 500 lineages segregated into about twenty larger groups. The groups at the top tend to be very flat-topped: This does not indicate extinction; it is simply where the computer run ended and is analogous to the present-day end of the fossil record. (D. M. Raup, S. J. Gould, T. J. M. Schopf, and D. S. Simberloff, "Stochastic Models of Phylogeny and Evolution of Diversity," *Journal of Geology* 81, 1973.)

In row B of Figure 8, for example, groups 4, 15, and 17 "die out" at precisely the same time (the 73rd time interval). These three groups represent 20 percent of the groups existing at that time, and thus the extinction event is a significant one. Also, there are several other groups in row B that become extinct either shortly before or shortly after the 73rd time interval. In the real world, it is usually assumed that extinctions that coincide in time (actually or approximately) have a common cause. In the simulations, we know there is no common cause!

Before we jump to the conclusion that the diversity histories of trilobites and insects were a matter of chance or that the mass extinctions were coincidences, we must examine the important element of *scale* (Stanley et al. 1981). Consider group 16 in row C of Figure 8, which was earlier likened to the trilobites. In the computer simulation, group 16 consists of twenty separate lineages, each of which persists or dies out as a matter of chance. The entire group becomes extinct fairly early in the computer run. This is a reasonably improbable event, but not a startling one in view of the small numbers involved. Now consider real trilobites. Many thousands of species existed in the Paleozoic, and it is estimated that as many as six thousand may have coexisted at any one time in the early Paleozoic. Knowing the half-life of the species we can estimate the probability that the entire group could have "drifted" to extinction by a chance excess of extinctions over originations. It turns out that this probability is vanishingly small (about 10^{-82}), suggesting that a biological explanation for the demise of the trilobites is in order (Raup 1981).

Does the foregoing reasoning invalidate the analogy between the computer simulations and the real world? The answer depends on scaling and on what we consider to be the basic unit of evolutionary origination and extinction. If the basic unit is the species, then the simulations are improperly scaled for the trilobite example. But suppose the basic evolutionary unit is the family or superfamily; that is, suppose that all species in a family or superfamily are sufficiently similar that if one goes extinct they all do. In such a case, the trilobite case is properly scaled and extinction of the group by a random process becomes credible.

The same reasoning applies to mass extinctions, because the probability of coincidental extinction of several groups depends on the absolute numbers of subgroups involved. Paleobiologists are only beginning to look at these problems in a mathematically rigorous fashion, and the results to date are tentative. It does appear, however, that the major mass extinctions seen in the fossil record are indeed real in the sense that they are "off-scale" with respect to a random model, and thus they require a deterministic explanation.

Morphological Change

So far I have not said anything about the morphology of the "organisms" produced by the computer simulations. Partly for the fun of it, we introduced morphology into the system in a completely random manner. That is, as an independent part of the program, we assigned to the starting lineage a morphology based on ten to twenty completely arbitrary characters. Character states were expressed on integer scales starting at 0. At each branch point, each trait or character could change by one unit in either direction—that is, from 0 to +1 or from 0 to −1, or if already at +1 it could go back to 0 or up to +2—so that as the program developed the complex branching network, it also allowed the several traits to wander independently or drift as a random walk.

We expected to find complete chaos because we were modeling the evolution of morphology without benefit of natural selection, and it is conventional wisdom to credit adaptation through natural selection with most of the order we observe in the biological world. But to our surprise we found a very high degree of order in the morphological results, and we found examples of a great many of the trends and patterns that we are used to seeing in the evolutionary record.

Figure 9, which shows some of the results, reveals that although there is quite a bit of variation in shape among these imaginary animals we call triloboids, departing in several directions from the starting configuration, there is also considerable order. Those in group A, for example, are characterized by a relatively wide head and a long, narrow tail, in contrast to those in group D, which tend to have long, narrow heads and wide, short tails. The groups in Figure 9 are quite consistent internally: The groups of lineages appear to be "natural" collections of like shapes. This has been confirmed by applying conventional numerical taxonomy to the morphological data and comparing the resulting classification with the known branching pattern of the simulation (Schopf et al. 1975).

As mentioned above, we can see in the computer output many trends and patterns that are common in the fossil record and that carry with them a host of purely deterministic explanations. It is often claimed, for example, that there is an inevitable increase in specialization with time, and certainly the more specialized or bizarre forms occur late in the computer sequence—that is, near the top of the diagram. They are either very large or very small, and have other peculiarities with respect to the average. In the simulations, we know that this is not caused by biological processes. Rather, random drift away from the starting point practically insures that the bizarre forms will be concentrated at the greatest distance from the starting point.

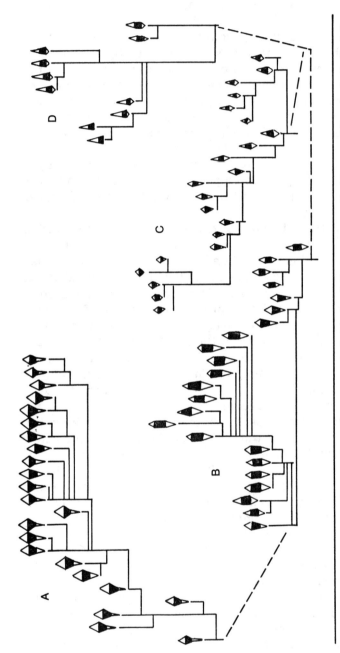

FIGURE 9. In this part of the morphologic output of the simulation program, the shapes of the glyphs reflect the states of five of the independently evolving morphologic characters. (Two define the shape of the head, one the length of the midsection, and two the shape of the tail.) The five traits are expressed as dimensions of these fictitious animals (which we call triloboids). The four regions are higher taxonomic groupings generated by the program on the basis of lineage branching patterns. The morphologic data did not contribute to the classification, yet the groupings are clearly reasonable ones. (David M. Raup, "Stochastic Models in Evolutionary Paleontology," in *Patterns of Evolution*, A. Hallam, ed., Amsterdam: Elsevier, 1977.)

Figure 10 illustrates slightly more rigorously one of the kinds of results we got from the morphological modeling—a simple plot of the values of two characters for the 200 lineages in one of the runs. The two are highly correlated—overwhelmingly significant at the 99 percent level. It clearly suggests that the two characters here are corre-

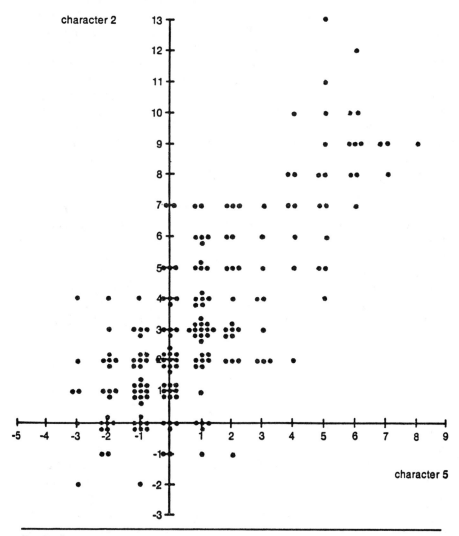

FIGURE 10. There is a considerable correlation between two morphologic characters from the 200 lineages of one computer run. Each point represents one lineage. The correlation is high, and though this might be interpreted in the real world as having a genetic or adaptive cause, the two characters developed independently, both starting at 0, 0. (D. M. Raup and Stephen J. Gould, "Stochastic Simulation and Evolution of Morphology—Towards a Nomothetic Paleontology," *Systematic Zoology* 23, 1974.)

lated with each other, so that, as one changes, a predictable change occurs in the other. But we know that this is not causal from the way in which the computer program was designed: The two characters here were generated in a completely independent fashion. This sort of correlation in the real world is automatically interpreted as indicating either genetic linkage or a functional or adaptive coordination.

The high degree of correlation observed in Figure 10 is not an exception. In fact, in approximately 75 percent of the possible combinations between characters a statistically significant correlation was found. The reasons for this have to do with the branching pattern of evolution, and although in hindsight it is easy to see that such correlations are in fact inevitable, we did not anticipate them (see Raup and Gould 1974 for further discussion). It is in this sense that the computer simulation has been extremely valuable as an exploratory tool. We were able to see, for example, that a selection-free model will inevitably produce certain patterns that we have always assumed were possible only as a result of natural selection.

This does not of course mean that we can argue persuasively against natural selection. It does mean that some of the patterns that are interpreted as resulting from selection cannot *in themselves* be used as evidence for selection: Natural selection is only one way in which orderly patterns can be developed. The main difference between the integrated morphology seen in the real world and that found in the simulated world is that, in the real world, the collections of traits "make sense" in terms of the functioning of the organism. It is thus the functional analysis of morphology rather than the simple fact of correlation between characters that provides the basic evidence for adaptive evolution.

Perspective

The fossil record of evolution is amenable to a wide variety of models ranging from completely deterministic to totally stochastic. The computer program described here is crude and stylized and is most useful as an exploratory tool. It provides a source of hunches and works well as a test of one's own logic by showing what is possible and what is impossible under a given set of circumstances. The next step is to devise more rigorous tests for random variables in the fossil record. Some of these may employ Monte Carlo techniques using large samples. Others may make use of direct, analytical solutions based on probability arguments.

The approaches discussed here are controversial. The real world of the fossil record probably contains a mixture of two types of events (or sequences of events): those caused by specific, nonrecurring phenomena, and those so complex and unpredictable that they are best treated probabilistically in groups. We do not yet know the proportions of the two types, let alone the behavior of the second. It may turn out that the second type shows more order and predictability than is now apparent.

The concepts of *chance* and *randomness* are anathema to many scholars. To paleobiologists in particular, these concepts often seem unscientific and unmanageable and imply a defiance of cause and effect. Nothing could be farther from the truth, as has been demonstrated so often in other fields. It is perhaps ironic that some of the most effective applications of probabilistic models have been in fields traditionally close to paleobiology: geology (especially geomorphology) and evolutionary biology.

REFERENCES

Bamback, R. K. "Species Richness in Marine Benthic Habitats through the Phanerozoic." *Paleobiology* 3 (1977):152-167.

Blatt, H., and Jones, R. L. "Proportions of Exposed Igneous, Metamorphic, and Sedimentary Rocks." *Bulletin of the Geological Society of America* 86 (1975):1085-1088.

Feller, William, ed. *An Introduction to Probability Theory and Its Applications.* New York: J. Wiley & Sons, 1968.

Gould, S. J.; Raup, D. M; Sepkoski, J. J., Jr.; Schopf, T. J. M.; and Simberloff, D. S. "The Shape of Evolution: A Comparison of Real and Random Clades." *Paleobiology* 3 (1977):23-40.

Gregor, C. B. "Denudation of the Continents." *Nature* 228 (1970):273-275.

Hayami, I., and Ozawa, T. "Evolutionary Models of Lineage-Zones." *Lethaia* 8 (1975):1-14.

Raup, David M. "Species Diversity in the Phanerozoic: A Tabulation." *Paleobiology* 2, no. 4 (1976):279-288.

——. "Stochastic Models in Evolutionary Paleontology." In *Patterns of Evolution*, edited by A. Hallam, pp. 59-78. Amsterdam: Elsevier, 1977.

——. "Extinction: Bad Genes or Bad Luck?" *Acta Geologica Hispanica* 16 (1981):25-33.

Raup, David M., and Gould, Stephen J. "Stochastic Simulation and Evolution of Morphology—Towards a Nomothetic Paleontology." *Systematic Zoology* 23 (1974):305-322.

Raup, D. M.; Gould, S. J.; Schopf, T. J. M.; and Simberloff, D. S. "Stochastic Models of Phylogeny and Evolution of Diversity." *Journal of Geology* 81 (1973):525-542.

Schopf, T. J. M.; Raup, D. M.; Gould, S. J.; and Simberloff, D. S. "Genomic Versus Morphologic Rates of Evolution: Influence of Morphologic Complexity." *Paleobiology* 1 (1975):63-70.

Sepkoski, J. J., Jr. "A Kinetic Model of Phanerozoic Taxonomic Diversity: I. Analysis of Marine Orders." *Paleobiology* 4 (1978):233-251.

——. "A Kinetic Model of Phanerozoic Taxonomic Diversity: II. Early Phanerozoic Families and Multiple Equilibria." *Paleobiology* 5 (1979):222-251.

Stanley, Steven M. "A Theory of Evolution Above the Species Level." *Proceedings of the National Academy of Sciences USA* 72 (1975):646-650.

Stanley, S. M.; Signor, P. W.; Ligard, S.; and Karr, A. F. "Natural Clades Differ from 'Random' Clades: Simulations and Analyses." *Paleobiology* 7 (1981):115-127.

Van Valen, Leigh. "A New Evolutionary Law." *Evolutionary Theory* 1 (1973):1-30.

Evolutionary Tempos and Modes: A Paleontological Perspective

NILES ELDREDGE

Curator, Department of Invertebrates
The American Museum of Natural History

Introduction

Charles Darwin saw organic evolution as a process of "descent with modification": All organisms are interrelated, and as the chain of ancestry and descent is forged, anatomical features are transformed into newer guises, to be passed on to future descendants until they are again modified. Evolutionary theory seeks to understand how both aspects of evolution occur: How are physical and behavioral properties of organisms, and their underlying genetic controls, modified in the course of evolution? What processes are involved in the development of descendants from ancestors?

Evolutionary biology, like any other field of science, has as its core a body of observations about the nature of the world. These perceptions fall into patterns: the pattern of similarity interconnecting all forms of life (produced by life's genealogical history), as well as patterns of distribution of plants and animals over the earth's surface up through the 3.4 billion years of geologic time in the fossil record. These patterns are crucial for two reasons. Without them, of course, there would be nothing to explain, and thus no need for an evolutionary theory. But our observations of nature also serve a more practical purpose, as all scientific theories must constantly be checked against hard information drawn from the real world. All evolutionary theory must be compatible with what we know about patterns of ancestry and descent, and the patterns of anatomical, behavioral, and genetic change we find in nature. This is the fundamental requirement of all scientific investigation.

George Gaylord Simpson, the most influential twentieth century paleontologist to consider the evolutionary process, characterized evolutionary patterns in terms of tempos and modes (the very title of his first book on evolution, *Tempo and Mode in Evolution*, 1944). By tempo, Simpson simply meant rates: How fast

I thank Dr. S. N. Salthe of Brooklyn College for direct inspiration for the style, if not content, of Table 1, and Dr. E. S. Vrba, Transvaal Museum, Pretoria, for comments on the manuscript.

does evolutionary change occur? How quickly and often do descendants arise from ancestors? Are the rates constant, or do they vary? By mode, Simpson was thinking of other elements of patterns. When descendants follow ancestors in a smoothly unbroken array, and when evolutionary modification itself occurs within such unbroken lineages, Simpson spoke of the *phyletic* mode. *Speciation* (later called simply "splitting": Simpson 1953) is another mode, where an ancestral species divides to form two or more species. Simpson's third evolutionary mode was *quantum evolution*, a special case he postulated to explain the rapid origin of major new groups of organisms with distinctively different anatomical features—the orders, classes, and phyla of the upper echelons of the Linnaean hierarchy. Although in 1953 Simpson called quantum evolution a "special, more or less extreme and limiting case of phyletic evolution" (p. 389), quantum evolution also originally embodied the notion of a small population splitting off from an ancestral species and undergoing rapid adaptive change. As we shall see, quantum evolution shares some similarities with the hypothesis of *punctuated equilibria* subsequently advanced by some paleontologists.

Simpson's notions of tempo and mode both ably characterized the basic ingredients of evolutionary patterns of the fossil record, and set the tone and standard for further paleontological discussions of evolutionary theory to the present day. Current controversies about the evolutionary process are debates about tempo and mode. They also deal with both descent (origin of new species from old) *and* modification (morphological change). As we shall see, much of the confusion in evolutionary theory is a direct result of confounding questions of rate with questions of mode. And much of the debate about evolutionary modes reflects a confusion of the notion of descent with the notion of modification.

Darwin and Afterwards: Evolutionary Theory and the Fossil Record

Darwin's (1859) *Origin of Species* put paleontologists in a difficult position. Claiming that his theory would ultimately stand or fall on the testimony of the fossils (1967, p. 342), Darwin devoted two entire chapters to explaining why the fossil record as known in his day was so far proving more of an embarrassment than a source of corroboration of his ideas. Darwin clearly saw a conflict between his predictions about what the fossil record *should* look like, and what it did, in fact, appear to show. Darwin explained the discrepancies as stemming from two main sources: The fossil record, as of the 1850s, was incompletely explored; and, more importantly, the record was so poor, so fraught with gaps and other sorts of preservational biases, that the patterns paleontologists saw must be mere vestiges of what they would look like *if* the record were perfect.

What did Darwin expect to see if the fossil record had been more complete? Darwin's notions of evolutionary change were steeped in the more general idea of gradualism—the idea that when change of any sort (say, in economic systems) occurs, it is usually gradual and "for the better." The ideas of progress and gradualism were inseparable from the notion of change in nineteenth century England, and Darwin's particular views of the evolutionary process were typical of general views of the nature of change current in his day. He saw evolutionary change as slow, steady, and progressive in nature. He expected to find a pattern of gradual yet persistent change as the history of a lineage was traced up through successive layers of sedimentary rock. Though in later editions of the *Origin* Darwin conceded that many species found in the fossil record exhibit little or no change throughout their history, he maintained his basic prediction that evolutionary change is inevitable and inexorable, gradual and progressive—and that species can be expected to change, slowly but steadily, as time goes by.

The history of paleontological thinking on evolution since Darwin is labyrinthine. Paleontologists as a group accepted evolution, but many, in the years 1880–1930, were more attuned to Lamarckian notions (centering around the inheritance of acquired characters) than the pure Darwinian notion of natural selection acting on variation to modify and perfect adaptations. Others were *vitalists*—seeing evolution as a function of some sort of internal drive within organisms themselves. But only one aspect of the history of paleontological evolutionary thought need concern us here: From 1859 right on up to the present day, most paleontologists have simply ignored the entire subject of evolution! Paleontologists, it is true, are often involved with the more geological aspects of their subject (such as the use of fossils to establish a general chronology of events in earth history); yet the lack of concern with evolution shown by the vast majority of paleontologists still demands explanation.

Why, since 1859, have most paleontologists looked the other way whenever the subject of evolution has been raised? After intensive exploration and analysis, the fossil record is far better known now than in the 1850s; and yet good examples of gradual, progressive change in the fossil record are still hard to come by. And the old stand-by explanation—that the fossil record is too poor, too "gappy" to preserve the expected pattern—seems less and less plausible. But rather than point directly to the conflict between the pattern we see and our expectations of what ought to be there, paleontologists for the most part have simply turned to other pursuits.

Of course, some paleontologists *have* noted the discrepancy and attempted to explain why it was that the fossil record did not agree with Darwin's predictions. Noting the lack of many examples of smooth transitions between groups of closely related organisms, the German paleontologist Otto Schindewolf (for example, 1936) talked of *typostrophism*—the sudden appearance of new kinds of organisms, produced in abrupt jumps from their ancestors. Schindewolf's views were broadly similar to those of the geneticist Richard Goldschmidt (1940) who spoke of "hopeful monsters" as means whereby new groups could suddenly evolve. Schindewolf and Goldschmidt were saltationists—biologists who invoke an evolutionary process in which both descent *and* modification occur in exceedingly rapid spurts.

Saltationist views collide head-on not only with Darwin's gradualistic notions, but also with the central ideas of the *evolutionary synthesis*, the view of evolution paramount today that was developed in the 1930s and 1940s. The synthesis sees evolution as a gradual, adaptive process. The basic mechanism of evolution envisioned by the synthesis is sometimes called the *neo-Darwinian paradigm*. (The *neo* refers to the development of genetics: Darwin himself knew nothing of the mechanisms underlying the heritable variations he discussed). The neo-Darwinian paradigm says that, within a population or species, organisms vary, the variation is heritable (offspring resemble their parents), and more offspring are produced each generation than can possibly survive. Thus a pattern of differential reproductive success is automatically produced: Those organisms best suited to their environment tend to flourish and produce more offspring than other, less fit individuals. Such differential reproductive success of individuals within populations is called *natural selection*. The variation on which natural selection works is maintained by such normal genetic processes as recombination, but the ultimate source of variation (hence of new behaviors and anatomical structures) is mutation—the spontaneous change of genetic material without regard to the possible advantages or disadvantages the mutation might offer to the individual in which it occurs. As natural selection constantly favors those organisms best suited to the environment at the moment, adaptations (structures or behaviors that match organisms with their environments, thus permitting survival) are either improved (in an unchanging environment) or modified as a response to environmental change. Such evolutionary change, in the synthesis every bit as much as in Darwin's original exposition, is gradual. It is important to realize that the neo-Darwinian paradigm is a theory about how *modification* occurs. Its relation to the *descent* (in the phrase "descent with modification") is far less clear, and provides much of the fuel to the fires of evolutionary controversy these days.

The modern synthesis is a fusion of the data of genetics, systematics, paleontology, and other biological disciplines. It states, simply, that all evolutionary patterns can be explained by the neo-Darwinian paradigm: "The proponents of the synthetic theory maintain that all evolution is due to the accumulation of small genetic changes, guided by natural selection, and that transpecific evolution (Rensch 1947) is nothing but an extrapolation and magnification of the events that take place within populations and species" (Mayr 1963, p. 586). Put another way, the synthesis sees the neo-Darwinian model of adaptive change through natural selection as both necessary and sufficient to explain all evolutionary phenomena.

G. G. Simpson, whose views on evolutionary tempos and modes opened this chapter, played the central role in showing that the data of paleontology were consistent with the views of the emerging synthesis. His ideas on gaps in the fossil record are therefore particularly important. In *Tempo and Mode in Evolution* (1944), Simpson concluded that some 90 percent of the data of paleontology fell within the phyletic mode (p. 203): that ancestral species become transformed into descendant species in a linear fashion consistent with the notion of gradual adaptive change. The process, he felt, typically proceeded for sufficiently long intervals of time to produce new genera. The lack of examples of gradual phyletic change in the fossil record, according to Simpson, is due to the gaps that permeate the geologic column and plague paleontologists. However, in an important departure from typical complaints on the inadequacy of the fossil record, Simpson felt that the gaps between major taxa (those classified rather high in the Linnaean hierarchy—orders, classes, and so on) involved too much anatomical change in too little time to be explicable in terms of gaps in the fossil record. Hence his notion of quantum evolution: New taxa—major departures from the ancestral condition—arise when relatively small populations split off from an ancestral species, lose the ancestral adaptations, and rapidly attain a new, rather different set of adaptations. The rapidity of change, the small number of individuals involved, plus additional factors, he felt, could sufficiently explain the relative scarcity of intermediate fossils between the higher taxa. In contrast to the saltationists, Simpson believed that the intermediates *did* exist, but that their chances of fossilization were vanishingly small. Consequently we seldom see them, though the primitive Jurassic bird *Archaeopteryx*, in Simpson's view, served to show that intermediates in fact existed.

More recently, some paleontologists have suggested that the fossil record should be taken even more literally than Simpson urged. Never denying that the vast majority of organisms will not be fossilized, discovered, collected, and studied by a professional, nonetheless paleontologists in the 1980s now acknowledge the possibility that their data may be more accurate indicators of actual evolutionary patterns than Darwin and most neo-Darwinians have supposed.

One critical observation about the fossil record prompted this change in attitude. Each new generation, it seems, produces a few young paleontologists eager to document examples of evolutionary change in their fossils. The changes they have always looked for have, of course, been of the gradual, progressive sort. More often than not their efforts have gone unrewarded—their fossils, rather than exhibiting the expected pattern, just seem to persist virtually unchanged. Marine invertebrates (such as clams, snails, arthropods, and other groups), which make up the bulk of the fossil record, frequently persist unchanged for five or ten *million* years—and sometimes even longer. This extraordinary conservatism looked, to the paleontologist keen on finding evolutionary change, as if no evolution had occurred. Thus studies documenting conservative persistence rather than gradual evolutionary change were considered failures, and, more often than not, were not even published. Most paleontologists were aware of the stability, the lack of change we call *stasis*. Darwin noted it briefly in later editions of the *Origin*, and the stability of species has proved useful to paleontologists who attempt to correlate rocks in different regions on the basis of the similarities in their fossil content. But insofar as evolution itself is concerned, paleontologists usually saw stasis as "no results" rather than as a contradiction of the prediction of gradual, progressive evolutionary change. Gaps in the record continue (to this day) to be invoked as the prime reason why so few cases of gradual change are found.

But evolutionary change *can* be found in the fossil record. Working with the *Phacops rana* trilobite species group, whose approximately eight-million-year history began around 370 million years ago, Eldredge (1971) found few anatomical changes. Extreme conservatism was the rule: yet another example where an evolutionary study in paleontology seemed doomed to "failure." The compound eyes of these trilobites, however, did exhibit some changes. During the eight-million-year history of this group of trilobites, the number of vertical columns of lenses in the eye was reduced from eighteen to fifteen. But then change seems to have occurred in two discrete events, producing descendant forms in at most a few tens of thousands of years, which subsequently persisted without further change for millions of years. In this case at least, the evolutionary modifications that allow descendants to be told apart from ancestors occurred in periods of rapid change followed by far longer periods of evolutionary quiescence.

Evolution in the *P. rana* lineage also showed a strong geographic pattern. The relatively rapid bursts of change seem to have been concentrated in small local areas. The first event, for example (see Figure 1), apparently occurred in the seas at the continental margin (in what is now the Appalachian Mountains); only one quarry sample, in New York, has so far been found that produces intermedi-

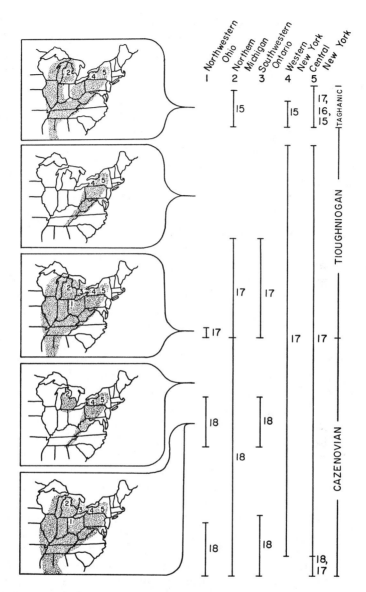

FIGURE 1. Five maps illustrating the spread of Devonian seaways (stippling) during the history of the *Phacops rana* species group. The vertical distributions of the different taxa at each of five localities are shown to the right of the maps. The numbers 18–15, symbolizing the taxa, represent the number of columns of lenses in the eye; 18 is the most primitive, 15 the most advanced. (From Niles Eldredge and Joel Cracraft, *Phylogenetic Patterns and the Evolutionary Process: Method and Theory in Comparative Biology*, New York: Columbia University Press, 1980, p. 142, figure 4.12. © 1980, Columbia University Press. Reprinted by permission.

ates between the more primitive and the descendant forms. The pattern of occurrence of these trilobites in typical exposures in Ohio, Michigan, and southwestern Ontario, however, shows a long history of the primitive form, its sudden disappearance, and the equally sudden appearance of the descendant. A saltationist, noting the lack of any detectable change within the older, ancestral form leading in the direction of the descendant, would be tempted to claim such a pattern as evidence of sudden, abrupt transitions. A more Darwinian-minded paleontologist would probably cite the independent evidence that the sea had dried up, producing a time gap at precisely the point where the ancestor disappears from the rock record. The conclusion: A chunk of time during which the transition from ancestor to descendant occurred is missing, and we can assume that the transition occurred by normal Darwinian processes during this missing interval of time of unspecified length. Both paleontologists would be drawing incorrect inferences from correct observations. In not examining the entire (known) geographic pattern, neither would see that the descendant had evolved fully two million years earlier elsewhere, that the transition was rapid but did involve intermediates, and that the descendant evidently was unable to colonize the central regions of the North American continent until, in a major event that destroyed the marine environment there, the ancestral form became extinct. When the seas again invaded the continental interior, it was populated by the descendant form that had survived in the seas of the continental margin.

Eldredge (1971) likened the evolutionary history of the *Phacops rana* group to the patterns typically produced by geographic (or *allopatric*) speciation, a notion championed in the United States primarily by the systematist Ernst Mayr (especially 1942, 1963). The only unexpected addition was the evidence that each species, once evolved, tended to persist unchanged for truly prodigious intervals of time. Eldredge and Gould (1972) generalized the *P. rana* story and, adding further examples, claimed that the pattern of stasis interrupted by brief periods of rapid change is the general picture of evolutionary change presented by the fossil record as a whole. They also argued even more strongly that the pattern was most consistent with expectations drawn from allopatric speciation theory. They called the pattern of stasis interrupted by episodes of rapid change, followed by more stasis, *punctuated equilibria*. Though they stopped short of rejecting the traditional prediction of what evolutionary change should look like in the fossil record (a pattern they called *phyletic gradualism*), they did maintain that stasis is an empirical reality and extremely common. Hence, *punctuated equilibria* seemed to them both a more accurate description of normal evolutionary events and a better explanation of how evolution actually occurs in geologic time, than the usual interpretations afforded by the evolutionary synthesis.

It is important to note that, from the outset, the notion of punctuated equilibria was both (1) a generalization about rates of morphological change, and (2) a hypothesis about evolutionary modes. Punctuated equilibria postulated abrupt periods of rapid change followed by far longer periods of stasis. But it also stated that speciation—the origin of new species from old by a process of splitting—is a far more prevalent mode of evolution than phyletic evolution. Put another way, morphological change (Darwin's "modification") occurs sluggishly if at all in the phyletic mode. Modification seems to occur mainly in conjunction with descent—specifically, the origin of new species from old by some sort of process of fission.

The notion of punctuated equilibria provoked a good deal of reaction, if for no other reason than nearly all paleontologists had data of their own that shed light on the evolutionary questions raised. Debate was intense in the mid-1970s, and sometimes heated. The current status of the notion of punctuated equilibria is best understood if we consider its two components (tempo and mode) separately. To date, the discussion of punctuated equilibria has been confused because the original authors and subsequent discussants did not fully realize that punctuated equilibria involves two separate hypotheses, one concerning tempos, the other modes.

Insofar as tempos are concerned, the assertion of punctuated equilibria that modification as a rule is sporadic, with rapid change briefly and only occasionally interrupting long periods of nonchange, has stood the test of time rather well. Many paleontologists have supplied examples of this pattern of rates of evolutionary change from their data (see the reviews in Gould and Eldredge 1977 and Stanley 1979). But the pattern is by no means universal. In particular, change in absolute size (a common occurrence in evolution) seems quite frequently to be a gradual affair within lineages. Examples from the fossil records of mammals (see, for example, Gingerich 1976) and from protistan (unicellular) microfossils (for example, Hays 1970; Ozawa 1975) quite clearly document cases of gradual, progressive size increase. However, anatomical changes in shape that are not mere correlates of size change do not, as a rule, exhibit a pattern of gradual progressive change in the fossil record.

The most positive contribution of the notion of punctuated equilibria insofar as rates of phenotypic evolution are concerned appears to be simply bringing the prevalence of stasis—truly formidable *lack* of change—to the attention of geneticists and developmental biologists. Such stability of the phenotype, as an empirical generality drawn from the fossil record, could not have been anticipated by students of the recent biota (and, as we have seen, has even been habitually ignored or denied by paleontologists, the only ones with data that bear on distributions of rates of change through geologic time). Now that stasis has become established as a problem deserving attention, both geneticists and developmental biologists can examine the bearing of this information on their own theories of how the evolutionary process works. An explanation of stasis in geologic time in terms of genetics will greatly improve evolutionary theory.

But it is the contribution of punctuated equilibria to the debate over evolutionary modes that, confused as it has been, perhaps holds the greatest promise of progress in evolutionary biology. How do new species evolve? Punctuationalists, borrowing openly from modern speciation theory and noting the temporal overlap between ancestors and descendants in the fossil record, favor the notion that new species arise by fission. Opponents (those who favor gradual transformation within lineages) acknowledge that splitting of lineages occurs, but, inasmuch as most evolutionary change accrues through the gradual transformation of features through time (in their view), most new species arise by the wholesale transformation of ancestors into descendants. Change goes on to the point where the paleontologist is forced to give a new name because the ancestor and descendant come to differ about as much from each other as two closely related contemporary species do (see Gingerich 1979 for an excellent discussion developing this point of view).

This aspect of the debate has been particularly hard fought. And until recently, few if any of the more vocal participants have realized that the two sides have been arguing from different premises. In a nutshell, the punctuationalists and gradualists have two radically different concepts of *species* in mind. Small wonder, then, that the two sides cannot agree on the mechanisms that produce new species! Though the modal aspect of the debate has resulted in some needless wheelspinning, clarification of the different premises on each side sheds much light on the internal anatomy of evolutionary theory and indicates possible new directions that the theory can take.

Species

Species is the Latin word for "kind." Biologists today still use the word in that sense: Species are the smallest divisions of the organic realm, the kinds of organisms we see around us. (Though some biologists recognize *subspecies*, the tendency today is to regard the species as the lowest formal category of the Linnaean hierarchy). Particular species, genera, families, and so forth are all taxa—groups of individual organisms defined and recognized according to a set of criteria. The categories of the Linnaean hierarchy (species, genera, and so on) assign a rank to each taxon; each genus contains one or more species within it, each family contains one or more genera, and so on.

Early biologists seeking to classify the diverse biota of the earth generally thought of species as fixed entities. Darwin, faced with the formidable task of convincing not only his colleagues but also a doubting public, that evolution had occurred, had to attack the idea that species are fixed. And in assaulting the fixity of species, he called into question the very existence of species—beyond their being the lowest ranked category of the Linnaean hierarchy. Darwin argued that, whereas most species alive today seem rather different from one another, in the past they were *less* different as they diverged from a common ancestor, and in the future they will be (on average) more different from one another than they are now. Far from being fixed, species are constantly changing. It then becomes the role of the paleontologist to set arbitrary limits, chopping up these slowly changing lineages to recognize a succession of ancestral-descendant species. Viewing species in this manner, Darwin saw species' origins largely as a simple byproduct of accumulated change. Thus the problem of the "origin of species" is none other than the problem of how modification occurs. To Darwin, a discussion of adaptation by natural selection as an agent of evolutionary change was the same as a discussion of the origin of species. Descent springs from modification, and involves nothing more than change accumulating as the process of generation by generation parentage goes on. Darwin saw no irony in his title *On the Origin of Species*, though it has become commonplace (see, for example, Mayr 1942, p. 147) for biologists to note that nowhere in his epochal book does Darwin actually discuss the origin of species!

Clearly, the claim that Darwin never addressed himself to the problem of species' origins when in fact he thought that species' origins was precisely what his entire book was about, implies a difference in viewpoint about what a species actually is. The problem is this: When one speaks about the origin of anything (such as a star, or a new business venture) one is speaking about a more-or-less concrete, recognizable, and definable entity. In making this point, the biologist Michael Ghiselin (1974) and the philosopher David Hull (1976; 1978) call species *individuals*. To speak of the origin of something, it follows that that "something" must exist, or have a reality. Species in this view are individuals *in addition* to being categories. This notion restores some of the meaning that the word *species* had in pre-Darwinian days—although because species can be re-

garded as individuals is no reason to suppose they cannot change
(that is, must remain fixed). After all, individual *Homo sapiens* are
born, grow up, age, and die—changing quite a bit in the process. So,
too, species can theoretically be expected to change quite a lot in the
course of their individual histories (although, according to the hypothesis of punctuated equilibria, few species change appreciably in
the course of their lifetimes).

Naturalists have been discussing species' origins at least since the
mid-nineteenth century. The prevailing view is that new species arise
when an ancestral species becomes fragmented, usually because some
segments have become geographically isolated from one another. In
his *Systematics and the Origin of Species* (1942), Mayr reviewed and
extended this work. Mayr saw the dilemma posed by discussing the
origin of species if species are viewed merely as arbitrary segments of
an evolving continuum. He likened speciation to the fission of an
individual *Paramecium:* starting with one, there is a brief period
when the number of individuals is moot, but in due course we end up
with two discrete *Paramecium* individuals where once we had but
one. All naturalists who have discussed the origins of species have implied that species are individuals. But even Mayr, in his book, saw
species as inevitably changing entities in geologic time, destined to
evolve into new forms and hence be transformed into "new" species.
His view of species was, to some extent, equivocal.

But anatomical discreteness in space and time is not the most
telling property that makes species individuals. Mayr (1942, p. 120)
defined species as collections of individual organisms actually or
potentially interbreeding and reproductively isolated from other such
groups. Eldredge and Cracraft (1980, p. 92) put it in just slightly different form: "A species is a diagnosable cluster of individuals within
which there is a parental pattern of ancestry and descent, beyond
which there is not, and which exhibits a pattern of phylogenetic ancestry and descent among units of like kind." Species, in other
words, are reproductive communities; the plexus of parental ancestry
and descent simultaneously binds together the individual organisms
within a species, and separates that species from other species.
From time to time, a species may bud off one or more descendant
species. Finally, the fate of all species is extinction. In other words,
in its fullest form, the view that species are individuals sees species as
having origins, histories, and terminations. It sees them, in short, as
spatiotemporally discrete entities.

There is evidence that such a view of the nature of species is
both apt and appropriate. Though Mayr's definition of species as
reproductive communities has been questioned, criticism usually
focuses on the utility of the concept: How, in most instances (and
all cases involving fossils), are we to demonstrate that we are dealing

with a reproductive community? Yet, to my knowledge, no one has denied that discrete reproductive communities exist in nature. And inasmuch as there are millions of species, past and present, and most are extinct (with a number currently disappearing each year), no biologist doubts that species originate, have histories, and eventually succumb to extinction.

This view of species as spatiotemporally discrete individuals underlies all punctuationalist discussions of speciation. The static anatomical packages paleontologists see surviving for prodigious intervals of time in the fossil record are *assumed* to be discrete species. Is this assumption warranted? A biologist today, sampling a field or a stream bottom, collects some number of different organisms. In nearly all cases, all of the organisms are easily sorted into piles of similar individuals. Sometimes variation (for example, black and gray squirrels within the same species) will be misleading, as will the presence of marked sexual dimorphism. There is a slight tendency, in other words, to overestimate the true number of species present. Closer scrutiny, however, shows that nearly all the piles of organisms sorted according to anatomical similarities are also reproductive communities.

Paleontologists follow the same procedure. At any one place and time in the fossil record, a number of discrete piles of specimens can be assembled. The inference is that these are discrete species just as they most likely would prove to be if sampled from a sea bottom today. Punctuationalists, seeing these same anatomical groups persist for millions of years, infer that they *are* species, and that species consequently have longevities numbering in the millions of years. Though they failed to say so explicitly, this is the view of species and their nature espoused by Eldredge and Gould (1972).

If the view that species are spatiotemporally discrete individuals is *wrong*, then there is nothing overtly incorrect with Darwin's belief that new species arise as the simple consequence of anatomical change accumulating over the millenia, regardless of whether splitting has occurred or not. If the view is *correct*, however, the origin of new reproductive communities is *not* the same thing as the modification of anatomical and genetic properties. In fact, some punctuationalists have claimed that Darwin's modification is the *effect*, not the *cause*, of descent (speciation). (This view, theoretically not necessary, is supported by the observation that anatomical differences between closely related species appear to evolve as descendant species bud off from ancestors). Each view has its adherents today: The sorts of evolutionary theories entailed by the two different views of the nature of species are themselves rather different. We shall now compare two contrasting evolutionary theories, each based on a different view of the nature of species.

The Modern Synthesis and the Adaptive Landscape

We have already noted the central theme of the evolutionary synthesis: Natural selection tracks the environment, working to modify adaptations in response to changing external conditions. The mostly slow, gradual evolutionary change that accrues within lineages allows paleontologists to recognize "new" species. Diversity—numbers of different species living at the same time—represents the splitting of ecological niches, with natural selection dividing the lineage into two groups, each tracking the diverging niches.

Scientists, like everyone else, love to use graphic images to illustrate their ideas. The biologists who created the modern synthesis were no exception, and today virtually every textbook in evolution uses the pictorial metaphor of the *adaptive landscape*. First introduced in 1932 by the geneticist Sewall Wright, the adaptive landscape itself has undergone a fascinating evolution of its own. Wright's conception was the essence of simplicity: He asked his readers to imagine populations of individuals within a species, with a number of genetic loci, each with several variant gene forms (alleles). The many possible combinations of alleles were bound to produce some individuals whose gene combinations were more "harmonious" and some whose gene combinations were somewhat less salutary. Wright drew a crude topographic map and suggested that if the thriving individuals with the better gene combinations were symbolized as the occupants of the upper slopes and hilltops, the less fortunate individuals would be found further down the slopes and in the valleys. The problem of evolution, as Wright saw it, "is that of a mechanism by which the species may continually find its way from lower to higher peaks in such a field" (Wright 1932, p. 358). Wright's imagery pertained to a within-species problem: How does a species concentrate its individuals on the peaks, and how are higher peaks found and occupied?

The adaptive landscape imagery was soon applied far more broadly. In *Tempo and Mode in Evolution*, Simpson wrote (1944, pp. 89–90):

> *Wright (1931) [sic] has suggested a figure of speech and a pictorial representation that graphically portray the relationship between selection, structure, and adaptation. The field of possible structural variation is pictured as a landscape with hills and valleys, and the extent and directions of variation in a population can be represented by outlining an area and a shape on the field. Each elevation represents some particular adaptive optimum for the characters and groups under consideration, sharper and higher or broader and lower, according as the adaptation is more or less specific. The direction of positive selection is uphill, of negative selection downhill, and its intensity is proportional to the gradient. The surface may be represented in two dimensions by using contour lines as in topographic*

maps. . . . The model of centripetal selection is a symmetrical, pointed peak and of centrifugal selection, a complementary negative feature, a basin. Positions on uniform slopes or dip-surfaces have purely linear selection. The whole landscape is a complex of the three elements, none in entirely pure form. To complete the representation of nature, all these elements must be pictured as in almost constant motion—rising, falling, merging, separating, and moving laterally, at times more like a choppy sea than like a static landscape—but the motion is slow and might, after all, be compared with a landscape that is being eroded, rejuvenated, and so forth, rather than with a fluid surface.

Simpson simply took Wright's imagery of within-species gene combinations and used it as a metaphor to explain the adaptive differentiation of all life. (Though Simpson's was apparently the earliest complete discussion of the landscape in such expanded terms, casual use of Wright's imagery to explain life's diversity occurs even earlier—see Mayr 1942). But perhaps the most beguiling use of an extended version of the adaptive landscape comes from Theodosius Dobzhansky, in the third edition of his famous *Genetics and the Origin of Species.* Though he discussed Wright's original pictorial formulation in both the first and second editions of this book (1937; 1941), it was not until the third edition (1951) that Dobzhansky explained the entire diversity of life in terms of the adaptive landscape (pp. 9–10):

The enormous diversity of organisms may be envisaged as correlated with the immense variety of environments and of ecological niches which exist on earth. But the variety of ecological niches is not only immense, it is also discontinuous. One species of insect may feed on, for example, oak leaves, and another species on pine needles; an insect that would require food intermediate between oak and pine would probably starve to death. Hence, the living world is not a formless mass of randomly combining genes and traits, but a great array of families of related gene combinations, which are clustered on a large but finite number of adaptive peaks. Each living species may be thought of as occupying one of the available peaks in the field of gene combinations. The adaptive valleys are deserted and empty.

Furthermore, the adaptive peaks and valleys are not interspersed at random. "Adjacent" adaptive peaks are arranged in groups, which may be likened to mountain ranges in which the separate pinnacles are divided by relatively shallow notches. Thus, the ecological niche occupied by the species "lion" is relatively much closer to those occupied by wolf, coyote, and jackal. The feline adaptive peaks form a group different from the group of the canine "peaks." But the feline, canine, ursine, musteline, and certain other groups of peaks form together the adaptive "range" of carnivores, which is separated by deep adaptive valleys from the "ranges" of rodents, bats, ungulates, primates, and others. In turn, these "ranges" are again members of the adaptive system of mammals, which are ecologically

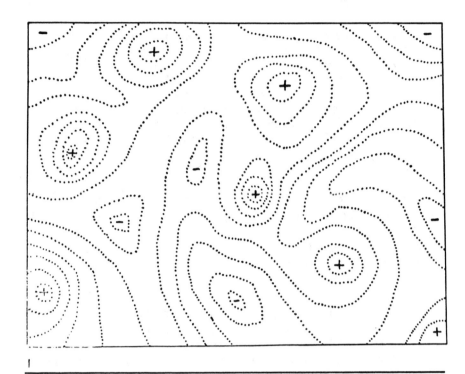

FIGURE 2. Two versions of the adaptive landscape. (a) Sewall Wright's original sketch of the adaptive landscape. His original caption follows: "Diagrammatic representation of the field of gene combinations in two dimensions instead of many thousands. Dotted lines represent contours with respect to adaptiveness." (Sewall Wright, "The Roles of Mutation, Inbreeding, Crossbreeding and Selection in Evolution," *Proceedings of VIth International Congress of Genetics* 1, 1932, p. 358, fig. 2). (b) (facing page) A recent use of the adaptive landscape, from Lewontin. The original caption follows: "Species track environment through niche space, according to one view of adaptation. The niche, visualized as an "adaptive peak," keeps changing (moving to the right); a slowly changing species population (dots) just manages to keep up with the niche, always a bit short of the peak. As the environment changes, the single peak becomes two distinct peaks, and two populations diverge to form distinct species. One species cannot keep up with its rapidly changing environment, becomes less fit (lags farther behind changing peak) and extinct. Here niche space and actual-species space have only two dimensions; both of them are actually multidimensional." (From "Adaptation" by R. Lewontin. Copyright © 1978 by Scientific American, Inc. All rights reserved.)

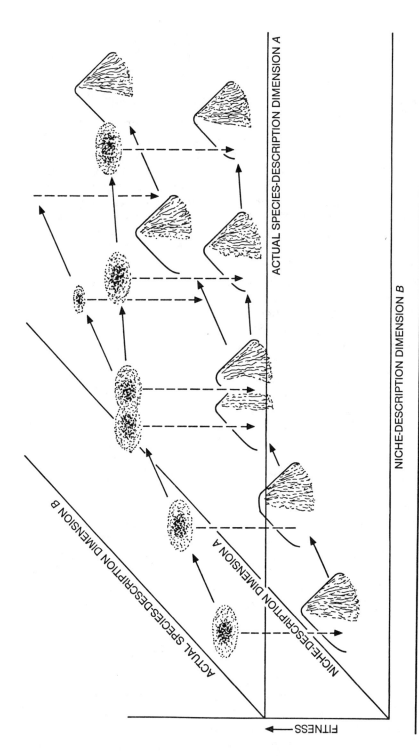

FIGURE 2. Continued.

129

and biologically segregated, as a group, from the adaptive systems of birds, reptiles, etc. The hierarchic nature of the biological classification reflects the objectively ascertainable discontinuity of adaptive niches, in other words the discontinuity of ways and means by which organisms that inhabit the world derive their livelihood from the environment.

This, in a nutshell, *is* the synthetic theory of evolution. Couched in Dobzhansky's gentle but compelling prose, it makes abundant sense. The notion is simple, and perhaps therein lies the secret to much of its appeal: To have all of life, in its exuberant anatomical and behavioral diversity, explained essentially as natural selection monitoring environmental change is simplicity itself. All evolutionary patterns in life's history are reduced to a single maxim: Natural selection modifies adaptations in response to environmental change.

As we have already noted, this, the central message of the evolutionary synthesis, remains the predominant view of the evolutionary process in biology today. The imagery of the adaptive landscape envisions a direct continuity between generation-by-generation change within species, up through the progressive change that produces new species, genera, and so on. Episodes of splitting—by the fission of the environmental hilltops themselves—increase the number of different species alive at any one time. The whole process of progressive modification and niche splitting combines to produce all the phyla, with their subordinate classes, orders, and lower taxa. The evolution of life is one grand adaptive continuum.

Such simple imagery seems eminently reasonable. But from a paleontological perspective, there seem to be substantial problems with the landscape metaphor as an explanation for the evolution of life. Patterns of change in the fossil record do not jibe with the contention that change within an ancestral species is directional and accumulates smoothly to produce the morphology of an eventual descendant species. And, on a theoretical level, the continuity theme of adaptive change flies squarely in the face of the notion that species are spatiotemporally discrete individuals. To work at all, the synthesis requires that species be only arbitrarily delineated classes: Species cannot be discrete individuals (Bock 1979).

An Alternative to the Synthesis

All theories in science have underlying axioms and assumptions. *If,* we say, we assume such and such to be true, what are the consequences? Here we ask: *If* we assume that species are individuals, what are the consequences for evolutionary theory?

The most striking consequence, perhaps, is the observation that morphological and genetic change, whatever their causes, are not synonymous with the origin of new species. Species are reproductive communities; while there is always at least some small measure of difference between even the most closely related species, the magnitude of such difference varies enormously in nature. Immediately, we see that the origin of species cannot be reduced simply to a theory of genetic and morphologic change, be it an adaptive conception, as in the synthesis, or some other notion of change.

The overlapping ranges of morphologically stable species that many paleontologists now see as the main pattern of evolution in the fossil record seems to imply that anatomical change occurs only at speciation *events*. Thus Stanley (1979), for example, discusses *quantum speciation* at length. The notion of quantum speciation involves rapid morphological change occurring during speciation. Though the fossil record does seem to show that quantum speciation is more common than previously suspected, it must be remembered that some speciation events result in very little morphological differences between ancestral and descendant species. By no means does speciation inevitably yield major spurts of morphological change.

There is another factor coloring our perception of rates of speciation and morphological change: Paleontologists can assert that species arise quickly with respect to their subsequent durations of millions of years, but how quick is quick? The sudden jumps that the fossil record, taken at face value, frequently shows, may occupy periods of 50,000 years or more—so hard is it to tell time in such "brief" increments in the vastness of geologic time. To paleontologists and geologists, even 100,000 years may seem hardly more than an instant. To a geneticist, such a block of time seems more like an eternity. Thus paleontological data ordinarily do not allow a choice between, for example, rapid natural selection acting over 50,000 years or a "hopeful monster" appearing in a single generation, as an explanation for the sporadic pattern of change in the fossil record. The data are too coarse to preclude one in favor of the other.

If, as punctuationalists claim, there is no evidence that within-species change leads inevitably to the sorts of changes we see between ancestors and descendants, another view of the evolutionary process emerges. This alternative sees a distinction between evolutionary changes *within* species and changes *between* species. If species are discrete individuals, each with its own origin, history, and (eventual) end, what goes on within each species through time is seen as, to some considerable degree, independent of what is going on within other species. Thus larger-scale evolutionary patterns may be imagined to result from a simple shuffling of the composition of species within lineages through time. Stanley (1975; 1979) has proposed the useful term *decoupling*, referring to the disruption of within-species change caused by the process of speciation. We therefore hypothesize that within-species change (*microevolution*) is to a certain extent divorced from among-species change (*macroevolution*). The evolutionary synthesis, in contrast, sees all evolutionary patterns as the direct outgrowth of microevolutionary processes, specifically the mechanisms of the neo-Darwinian paradigm.

This alternative, somewhat more complex, view of the evolutionary process thus recognizes at least two different *levels* of phenomena: within-species and among-species. (Genetic processes governing individual development constitute another, third, distinct level of evolutionary phenomena.) (See my book, *Approaching Complexity* (Eldredge 1985), for a detailed and somewhat different discussion of hierarchically structured evolutionary theory.) This view claims that the various levels are complexly interrelated, but are not reducible down to the lowest common denominator. In general, for each level, there are evolutionary patterns produced by a combination of deterministic and stochastic elements (see Table 1). For example, if one accepts the neo-Darwinian paradigm for microevolution (as I am inclined to do), patterns of genetic and morphological change from generation to generation (P, for pattern) are attributable to natural selection (the deterministic component—D) and genetic drift (S—the stochastic, or chance, component) plus the inherent uncertainty (E for error) that the pattern has been correctly perceived in the first place. This particular version of the *multiphe-*

LEVEL:	1	2	3	4
P	individual development	microevolution	macroevolution	ecosystem evolution
D		natural selection	species selection	
S		genetic drift	random factors governing speciation and extinction	
E				

TABLE 1. The general structure of a multiphenomenological-level view of evolutionary theory. Each level has its own pattern (P) produced by a combination of deterministic (D) and stochastic (S) processes; E signifies perceptual error of the pattern itself. For each level, $P = D + S + E$. Four levels are indicated; there could be more. One set of the several possible values for D and S are indicated for level 2 (microevolution: change in gene content and frequency within populations) and level 3 (macroevolution: change in species composition within single lineages); other values could have been specified. Values for levels 1 and 4 are not specified. Level 4, ecosystem evolution, is coordinate change among lineages in geologic time.

nomenological-levels theory of evolution differs from the synthesis only in its insistence that the neo-Darwinian paradigm cannot be extrapolated to the higher, among-species level. Put another way, among-species patterns cannot be reduced completely to within-species processes. There are, of course, other microevolutionary theories that could be plugged into the equation and structure shown in Table 1.

Eldredge and Gould (1972) saw a paradox in the notion of punctuated equilibria. If species show little or no evidence of progressive change during their long histories, how do we explain trends—persistent, directional change—in evolution? After admitting that many apparent trends really represent E (that is, perceptual error—they are not real patterns after all), Eldredge and Gould were forced to admit that many trends (such as an increase in brain size in human evolution) were real evolutionary phenomena begging for an explanation. Punctuated equilibria effectively removed the usual explanation of cumulative adaptive change. In its stead, they suggested a process of differential species survival (Eldredge and Gould 1972). Stanley (1975) discussed the evidence for such a process, calling it *species selection*. A direct analogue to true natural selection (differential reproductive success of individuals within populations), species selection is envisioned to work as a culling process, where some species within a lineage will tend to survive longer and produce more descendants than others by virtue of their superior adaptations. This would be the D (deterministic) component of macroevolution.

The idea that selective processes can operate on different levels has had a long history. The subtitle of *On the Origin of Species By Means of Natural Selection* was *Or the Preservation of Favoured Races in the Struggle for Life*—though Darwin did little to develop the notion of differential survival of "races" or other groups. Notions of group selection—usually populations within species—have been developed and argued extensively since the early 1930s. And some biologists (such as the geneticists Wright and Lewontin and the botanist-geneticist V. Grant) from time to time have discussed *levels* of selection. The particular view of species-level selection proposed by Eldredge and Gould (1972) stemmed from some specific suggestions by Mayr (1963, p. 621) and particularly by Wright (1967). Especially persuasive is Wright's now oft-quoted remark (1967, p. 120):

> With respect to the long term aspects of the evolution of higher categories, the stochastic process is speciation. This was treated as directed above but may be essentially random with respect to the subsequent course of macro-evolution. The directing process here is selection between competing species often belonging to different higher categories.

Gould and Eldredge (1977) and Stanley (1979) have refined the notion of species selection and its measure. (Vrba and Eldredge (1984) provide a recent summary comparison and analysis of the various competing versions of species selection.) And Eldredge and Cracraft (1980, Chapter 6), Gould (1980), and Eldredge (1982) have recently summarized the arguments for a multilevel approach to evolutionary theory. Meanwhile, the search for the controls of differential rates of speciation and extinction that produce the various macroevolutionary patterns (such as trends, radiations, and arrested evolution—extremely low rates) has turned to ecological theory (Eldredge 1975; 1979; Eldredge and Cracraft 1980; Vrba 1980). To these authors, species selection appears to be a function of ecologic niche occupation: Groups composed of broadly niched species evolve (behaviorally and anatomically) at characteristically slower rates because they speciate less frequently; groups composed of narrow-niched species appear to speciate more frequently and accrue morphological change much more rapidly. Indeed, to Vrba (1980), trends are a simple, almost automatic, function of the rapid proliferation of species in the narrow-niched lineages; this is a view that calls the notion of interspecific competition into question as a deterministic culling device. We may not need the notion of species selection after all.

The Outlook for Evolutionary Theory

Evolutionary theory is currently in a state of flux. There is far less agreement on basic elements of evolutionary theory now than there was ten years ago. One reason for this state of affairs is that paleontologists have seen that their data are best interpreted as a refutation of the most extreme formulation of the evolutionary synthesis: that evolution is nothing more than the accumulation of adaptive change through time. If that view had been fundamentally correct, the fossil record should have provided ample corroboration. But it doesn't, and the basic assertion that evolution is simply a matter of gradual adaptive change—a view we have from Darwin—must be abandoned.

In the ensuing uproar in recent years, a great diversity of ideas has been put forward. Most will not stand the test of time. But paleontologists have at least come back to an active consideration of evolutionary theory. Under the synthesis, paleontologists were limited to the claim that their data were consistent with the theories of genetics. They could do no more. But *if* we explore the possibility that species are discrete, and that many evolutionary patterns reflect alterations in species compositions within lineages through time, then it is the paleontologists, systematists, and ecologists who, it turns out, have the data suitable for testing specific evolutionary hypotheses of macroevolution. In so doing, they do not supplant the efforts of population geneticists. A multiphenomenological-level evolutionary theory, whatever its specific form, sees the need for deterministic and stochastic components underlying morphologic change within species. It merely also adds that these components may be necessary but not sufficient to explain evolutionary change at the next higher level—macroevolution. Though some biologists may long for the halcyon days when nearly everyone agreed on the essentials of a single, simple, and quite elegant evolutionary theory, the zest for renewed explorations in evolutionary theory is more than adequate compensation. The fervor of argument in evolutionary biology these days is the surest sign of its intellectual health: Evolutionary theory, perhaps now more than ever before, is an active, vital, and truly scientific endeavor.

REFERENCES

Bock, Walter J. "The Synthetic Explanation of Macroevolutionary Change—A Reductionistic Approach." In *Models and Methodologies in Evolutionary Theory*, edited by Jeffrey H. Schwartz and Harold B. Rollins, *Bulletin of Carnegie Museum of Natural History* 13 (1979):20-69.
Darwin, Charles. *On the Origin of Species.* 1859. Facsimile ed. New York: Atheneum, 1967.
Dobzhansky, Theodosius. *Genetics and the Origin of Species.* 1st ed. New York: Columbia University Press, 1937.
——. *Genetics and the Origin of Species.* 2d ed. New York: Columbia University Press, 1941.
——. *Genetics and the Origin of Species.* 3d ed. New York: Columbia University Press, 1951.
Eldredge, Niles. "The Allopatric Model and Phylogeny in Paleozoic Invertebrates." *Evolution* 25 (1971):156-167.
——. "Survivors from the Good Old, Old, Old Days." *Natural History* 84, no. 2 (1975):60-69.
——. "Alternative Approaches to Evolutionary Theory." In *Models and Methodologies in Evolutionary Theory*, edited by Jeffrey H. Schwartz and Harold B. Rollins, *Bulletin of Carnegie Museum of Natural History* 13 (1979):7-19.
——. "Phenomenological Levels and Evolutionary Rates." *Systematic Zoology* 31 (1982):338-347.
——. *Approaching Complexity.* New York: Oxford University Press, 1985.
Eldredge, Niles, and Cracraft, Joel. *Phylogenetic Patterns and the Evolutionary Process: Method and Theory in Comparative Biology.* New York: Columbia University Press, 1980.

Eldredge, Niles, and Gould, Stephen J. "Punctuated Equilibria: An Alternative to Phyletic Gradualism." In *Models in Paleobiology*, edited by T. J. M. Schopf, pp. 82-115. San Francisco: Freeman, Cooper, 1972.

Ghiselin, Michael. "A Radical Solution to the Species Problem." *Systematic Zoology* 23 (1974):536-544.

Gingerich, Philip. "Paleontology and Phylogeny: Patterns of Evolution at the Species Level in Early Tertiary Mammals." *American Journal of Science* 276 (1976):1-28.

——. "The Stratophenetic Approach to Phylogeny Reconstruction in Vertebrate Paleontology." In *Phylogenetic Analysis and Paleontology*, edited by Joel Cracraft and Niles Eldredge, pp. 41-77. New York: Columbia University Press, 1979.

Goldschmidt, Richard. *The Material Basis of Evolution*. New Haven: Yale University Press, 1940.

Gould, Stephen J. "Is a New and General Theory of Evolution Emerging?" *Paleobiology* 6 (1980):119-130.

Gould, Stephen J., and Eldredge, Niles. "Punctuated Equilibria: The Tempo and Mode of Evolution Reconsidered." *Paleobiology* 3 (1977):115-151.

Hays, J. D. "Stratigraphy and Evolutionary Trends of Radiolaria in North Pacific Deep-Sea Sediments." *Geological Society of American Memoirs* 126 (1970):185-218.

Hull, David. "Are Species Really Individuals?" *Systematic Zoology* 25 (1976):174-191.

——. "A Matter of Individuality," *Philosophy of Science* 45 (1978):335-360.

Lewontin, Richard C. "Adaptation." *Scientific American* 239, no. 3 (1978): 212-230.

Mayr, Ernst. *Systematics and the Origin of Species*. New York: Columbia University Press, 1942.

——. *Animal Species and Evolution*. Cambridge: Harvard University Press, 1963.

Ozawa, T. "Evolution of *Lepidolina multiseptata* (Permian foraminifer) in East Asia." *Memoirs Faculty of Science Kyushu University (Series D) Geology* 23 (1975):117-164.

Rensch, Bernhard. *Neuere Probleme des Abstammungslehre, die transspezifische Evolution*. Stuttgart: Enke, 1947. (Translated into English: *Evolution Above the Species Level*. Revised and translated by Dr. Altevogt. New York: Columbia University Press, 1960.)

Schindewolf, Otto H. *Paläontologie, Entwicklungslehre und Genetik*. Berlin: Borntraeger, 1936.

Simpson, George Gaylord. *Tempo and Mode in Evolution*. New York: Columbia University Press, 1944.

——. *The Major Features of Evolution*. New York: Columbia University Press, 1953.

Stanley, Steven M. "A Theory of Evolution Above the Species Level." *Proceedings of the National Academy of Sciences* 72 (1975):646-650.

——. *Macroevolution: Pattern and Process*. San Francisco: Freeman, Cooper, 1979.

Vrba, E. "Evolution, Species and Fossils: How Does Life Evolve?" *South African Journal of Science* 76 (1980):61-84.

Vrba, E., and Eldredge, N. "Individuals, Hierarchies and Processes: Towards a More Complete Evolutionary Theory." *Paleobiology* 10, no. 2 (1984): 146-171.

Wright, Sewall. "The Roles of Mutation, Inbreeding, Crossbreeding and Selection in Evolution." *Proceedings of VIth International Congress of Genetics* 1 (1932):356-366.

Wright, Sewall. "Comments on the Preliminary Working Papers of Eden and Waddington." In *Mathematical Challenges to the Neo-Darwinian Interpretation of Evolution*, edited by Paul S. Moorehead and Martin M. Kaplan, pp. 117-120. Philadelphia: Wistar Institute Press, 1967.

Some Thoughts on the History and Future of Punctuationalism

JEFFREY H. SCHWARTZ and HAROLD B. ROLLINS
Department of Anthropology and Department of
Geology and Planetary Science
University of Pittsburgh

The Current Polarization of Evolutionary Biology

Evolutionary biology is currently in the midst of one of those sudden bursts of vigorous secondary growth that at one time or another come to virtually every branch of science. Not since the late nineteenth and early twentieth centuries have there been such controversy and polarization in this field. At the center of the controversy sit the punctuationalists and the gradualists.

In the first half of this century, the most eminent of American paleontologists, neontologists, and geneticists synthesized their particular evolutionary insights and produced a modern statement of Darwinian theory and natural selection. Some have referred to this statement as the *synthetic theory of evolution.* The synthetic theory found an explanation of how species originate or multiply in the relatively new study of genetics. Species multiplication (or origin) was a subject with which Darwin could not adequately deal, even though he called his most famous work *On the Origin of Species by Natural Selection.* The founders of the New Synthesis reasoned that since genetic continuity between generations maintains the continuity of a species, genetic isolation should produce new species. The most obvious way to start the process—to produce genetic isolation and, eventually, speciation—would be to separate populations of a species physically or geographically. Natural selection acting on these populations would produce genetic incompatibility between successive generations of these isolates. Eventually the accumulation of small changes would be great enough to produce evolutionary divergence. The tempo of evolutionary change was thought to be slow and gradual, dependent on this gradual accumulation of micromutations. Indeed, organisms in our present-day world do appear to change slowly, at times not at all. Perhaps this was one reason why

Darwin felt compelled to tie his theory of natural selection to a model of gradual evolution. Now there appeared to be a genetic model to support Darwin's earlier suggestion.

Just prior to the rise of the synthetic theory of evolution in the 1930s, two Germans, Goldschmidt and Schindewolf, also brought together paleontological, neontological, and genetic insights, and came to a conclusion diametrically opposed to the model of gradualism. Rather than by the accumulation of a series of micromutations, they hypothesized, evolutionary change was rapid, caused by relatively sudden, major genetic changes (macromutations). Evolution proceeded not gradually, but by leaps, saltations. Unfortunately, such profound macromutations had not been observed in laboratories. Equally unfortunate for the consideration of the model, Goldschmidt referred to the inheritors of these macromutations as "hopeful monsters"—unexpected recipients of what could be evolutionarily significant. The hypotheses of Goldschmidt and Schindewolf fell prey to the proponents of a more easily intuited view. Retorts from those of the Synthetic/Gradualistic School, though not proper scientific falsification of an alternative theory, had their impact.

> *It should . . . be possible to find true evolutionary series illustrating the origin of species of mammals. The chief difficulties arise from the rarity of cases in which we have a series of successive forms representing the same econiche. (Watson 1963, p. 47)*

> *There is . . . no positive reason to believe that in animals there is here any phenomenon in the nature of a "saltation" . . . In rapid evolutionary changes in animal lines the process may have been a typically Neo-Darwinian one of the accumulation of numerous small adaptive mutations, but an accumulation at an unusually rapid rate. Unfortunately, there is in general little evidence on this point in the fossil record, for intermediate evolutionary forms representative of this phenomenon are extremely rare (a situation bringing smug satisfaction to the anti-evolutionist). (Romer 1963, p. 114)*

When, in 1972, Niles Eldredge and Stephen Jay Gould published their first paper on punctuated equilibria, they in fact resurrected an old debate. Faced with a history of paleontologists not finding the intermediate fossil forms predicted by gradualism and taking these gaps in the fossil record as nonbiological (that is, as nondepositional, or as erosional), Eldredge and Gould asked whether the fossil record is really as poor as proponents of the New Synthesis had thought. Are these gaps really holes in our knowledge of morphologic intermediates that nevertheless existed over long spans of time, or are they biologically real? In other words, could the gaps represent speciation events occupying relatively short spans of time and involving small numbers of individuals? In such populations the chance that individuals would be preserved and discovered would be greatly reduced, and we would be left with gaps that have a *biological*, not a geological, basis.

The other major postulate of Eldredge and Gould's model was that the kinds of changes one observes in known evolutionary lineages—from the first time one sees a particular species in the fossil record until its last known occurrence—are not those that produce a new species. In other words, after the genetic and morphologic re-organization accompanying speciation, organisms change (by comparison) relatively little. Therefore, in contrast to a gradual model in which there is constant evolutionary motion, the punctuational model posits relative stasis with evolutionary change occurring basically during speciation.

How can individuals, all of whom agree that the evidence of evolution is indisputable, and working with presumably the same data sets, come to such disparate conclusions about the nature of evolutionary change? It is in large part due to a difference in observational philosophy. Those who adhere to the doctrine that the "present is the key to the past" (= uniformitarianism) take present-day observations as indicative of what occurred—and how it occurred—earlier. This is not necessarily wrong nor inappropriate, nor is this a recently derived procedure or approach. In pre-Darwinian days, this was a major approach used in attempts to unravel the earth's history. Since it appears to an observer that such processes as mountain building are slow and gradual, this interpretation was extrapolated backward over geological time. This view of a serenely changing earth was espoused by, among others, the nineteenth century British geologist, Charles Lyell, whom many acknowledge as the father of modern geology. Lyell had no little influence on Charles Darwin. Thus it was in part by way of the geological sciences of the time that Darwin was exposed to gradualism—a belief Gould (1977) has suggested was sociologically and politically important for the British aristocracy amid revolution-ridden nineteenth century western Europe.

For whatever reasons, Darwin incorporated a model of gradual change into his theory of evolution by way of natural selection. Interestingly, Thomas Huxley, the eminent British anatomist who was Darwin's public defender, admonished Darwin for embracing a gradual model of evolutionary change. Perhaps Huxley's reaction was due, as Gould has pointed out, to his being a saltationist—an evolutionist with a different view of the nature of evolutionary change. Regardless, this disagreement serves to illustrate how more than one model or theory comprises what many consider evolution by way of natural selection, and how the same basic theory can be espoused by those who disagree on some of the details (for example, rapid versus gradual change by way of natural selection; rapid or gradual speciation via allopatry). With regard to a fundamental component of the widely held belief in the nature of evolutionary change, it is interesting to note that the hypothesis of gradual morphologic transformation was derived not from the study of organisms over evolutionary time, but from the geologists' uniformitarian world-view. If the earth changed slowly, the organisms inhabiting it must do so as well.

The late nineteenth and early twentieth centuries saw an explosion in paleontological activity. Fossils had been given scientific credibility. Natural history museums flourished, and there were the equivalents of range wars among curators and their museum crews for fossil-bearing localities and the best, the biggest, and the most specimens. But with each succeeding field season and increasing documentation of the diversity of now-extinct organisms, the predicted series or chain of morphologic intermediates between discrete taxa did not emerge. Missing links were viewed in a manner similar to geologic discontinuities, which had been interpreted as due to erosion or local depositional "by-pass" of what would otherwise be a depositional continuum.

The failure of paleontology to provide the documentation for gradual evolutionary change almost led to its own demise. However, developmental phases of organisms studied by contemporary embryologists and those in the fledgling field of genetics were viewed as proof of gradual evolutionary change. Although Ernst Haeckel's specific view that "ontogeny recapitulates phylogeny" had been rejected (he postulated that the developmental phases of an embryo and fetus reflected the adult stages of less advanced, or less evolved, organisms), embryology still provided a continuum of morphologic transformation. Population genetics provided the capstone for Darwin's model. Thus neontological, not paleontological, studies were the twentieth century bases of the synthetic theory of evolution. Uniformitarianism once again permitted the extrapolation from short-term studies in an ecologic slice of time to an evolutionary time scale. As one of its consequences, interest and merit in paleontological pursuits revived.

Although here we can only highlight aspects of the historical development of the prevailing view of the nature of evolutionary change, it is important to re-emphasize that in the biological and geological fields there have been, and continue to be, alternative models and hypotheses. Thus, while there was a school of gradualism among certain nineteenth century geologists, there were, alternatively, those who used such phenomena as volcanoes and earthquakes as the basis for a disruptive, episodic model of geomorphologic earth change. Similarly in the twentieth century, as a result of Eldredge and Gould's model of punctuated equilibria, we have seen a remarkable polarization of evolutionary biologists and paleontologists into two camps: the gradualists and the punctuationalists (for want of better names).

Pattern and Process: Biological Explanations
for a Punctuational Pattern

Eldredge and Gould (1972) formulated the punctuated equilibria model in terms of a particular mode of speciation involving the geographic separation of segments of a species, rapid genetic change in the more isolated segments, and, eventually, the production of genetic incompatibility between the peripheral isolates and the parent populations. Punctuated equilibria thus became identified with this particular *allopatric* mode of speciation. This was true despite the later claim of Gould and Eldredge (1977, p. 117) that their model works "equally well for sympatric speciation" under certain conditions. Yet the *pattern* of punctuated equilibria exists quite independently of any mechanism of speciation. The only prerequisites are rapid genetic change and small population size. Documenting a punctuational pattern in the fossil record is quite distinct from testing a particular mode of speciation. Does failure to document speciation in a peripheral isolate constitute refutation of a punctuational pattern? We think not.

The punctuational pattern should be the object of close scrutiny by evolutionary biologists and paleontologists alike, and we should decouple the pattern from any particular mode of speciation so we will not overlook other potential causes of stasis in the fossil record. For if the punctuational pattern is biologically "real," and not an artifact of an incomplete fossil record, there are a number of possible causative processes. Allopatric speciation is certainly plausible and consistent with the current thinking of evolutionary biologists. But it is not the only possible cause. Also to be considered are balanced polymorphism, polyploidy, competitive interaction, genetic drift, and epigenesis.

1. *Balanced polymorphism.* Balanced polymorphism is the genetic maintenance of discrete nonintergrading segments within a species. It is common enough in extant animal species to suggest that it may have been responsible for certain patterns of stasis with discrete gaps in morphology in the past as well. Hayami and Ozawa (1975) discussed this process at some length and considered it complementary, rather than contradictory, to the Eldredge and Gould model. Certainly it does not conflict with the assessment of pattern in the punctuational model even though it does not assume speciation. Furthermore, the two processes may not be readily separable through even moderately close scrutiny of the fossil record. It is often difficult to distinguish real species in the fossil record: How many fossil species represent examples of intraspecific polymorphism?

2. *Polyploidy.* The phenomenon of polyploidy, which involves the spontaneous multiplication of chromosome number, is common within certain groups of plants and can be assumed to have played an important role in determining the major features of plant evolution. Polyploidy would probably cause a punctuational pattern of evolution; thus we might predict that the paleofloral record should be more generously endowed with discrete morphological gaps than the paleofaunal record. In fact, we wonder to what extent polyploidy might explain the relative paucity of documented phyletic lineages in plant evolution.

3. *Competitive interaction.* Perhaps the most underrated causes of punctuational patterns are intraspecific and interspecific competition for space, food, and so on. Such competition sometimes leads to morphological shifts known as *character displacements*. To be sure, these morphological shifts operate over ecological, not geological, spans of time. Nevertheless, they do create gaps in morphology that can be amplified into speciation events if changing environmental conditions render them more permanent. For example, sea level transgression in terrestrial habitats and regression in marine habitats may lead to an abundance of enduring morphological shifts. Under these circumstances, speciation would result from biotope narrowing and fragmentation rather than from founder populations. Thus, clearly, diverse models of speciation would predict a punctuational pattern (see Dodson and Hallam 1977). Competitive interaction and character displacement are difficult but not impossible to demonstrate in the fossil record (see Eldredge 1974 and Alexander 1976). Changes in sea level, for example, are geologically recognizable and form the background against which the pattern of morphological change can be tested.

4. *Genetic drift.* Genetic drift refers to random changes of gene frequency in populations. Its efficacy in small isolated populations--especially its role in leading such populations to exploit new adaptive zones--is still debatable (but see Lande 1976). If genetic drift is a significant evolutionary process, then it certainly could result in discrete morphological gaps in the fossil record. Under these circumstances a speciation model such as *contiguous allopatry* or *parapatry* might be important. Such a model involves the origin of species on the margins of closely-knit species but does not require the long-term physical isolation of a founder population.

5. *Epigenesis.* Finally, we suggest that *developmental epigenesis* represents another potential cause of a punctuational pattern. This phenomenon involves the action of extrinsic factors on the early growth stages of an organism to the extent of influencing what would otherwise be the silent components of the genome.

The Future of Punctuationalism

Inevitably, a controversy such as that between gradualists and punctuationalists can be resolved only by proper testing. Gould and Eldredge (1977, pp. 147-148) set forth five guidelines for testing punctuated equilibria:

1. "Study the geographic variability of species over their entire preserved range."

2. "Study the distribution of evolutionary tempos for *all* members of an ecosystem or community," thus paying proper attention to the less attractive incidence of stasis—or lack of noticeable evolutionary change.

3. "Study phyletic gradualism not from the point of view of universal acceptance but rather with the question—where and how often."

4. "Study general patterns in the history of diversity, whenever possible, at the species level." Thus Gould and Eldredge emphasize—correctly, we believe—that the species is a "basic and stable evolutionary unit, not merely an intermediate rank in a hierarchy from individual to kingdom, defined as an arbitrary segment of a continuously changing lineage."

5. "Test Wright's Rule as a precondition for species selection." (Gould and Eldredge (1977, p. 139) state Wright's Rule as "the proposition that a set of morphologies produced by speciation events is essentially random with respect to the direction of evolutionary trends within a clade").

These guidelines certainly provide a viable mechanism for testing punctuated equilibria, but they are inadequate for objective assessment of the causes of a general punctuational pattern. For this reason, and to afford other possible species-level phenomena their due attention, we advocate that additional guidelines be added to those of Gould and Eldredge. First, situations involving potential intraspecific and interspecific interaction should be studied with the aim of recognizing punctuational morphologies that might represent character displacements due to competitive interaction. This will require a holistic community approach—that is, a consideration of all elements of ecosystems rather than only certain faunal elements (see Kauffman and Scott 1976)—and careful attention to the reconstruction of community structure and trophic levels. Next, paleontologists should gather evidence for conditions of rapid environmental stress, because such situations might have played major roles in causing the final breakdown in genetic transfer throughout populations experiencing the effects of intraspecific and interspecific interaction. Particular attention should be directed toward sea level transgressions and regressions, because these phenomena might commonly result in restriction and breakdown of habitat in the terrestrial environments and isolation in the marine environments. This in turn might result in speciation among contiguous populations. Thus, we believe that the study of fossil communities represents one of the most rewarding frontiers of paleobiological research; it will play an important role in bridging the gaps between natural selection at the populational level and the species level (species selection).

A predictable consequence of the unraveling history of controversy between the gradualists and punctuationalists has been renewed interest in evolutionary phenomena at the species level. Eldredge and Gould (1972) and especially Stanley (1975) advocated, in fact, the decoupling of natural selection from species selection. This seems justified if natural selection is to be construed as a predominantly populational phenomenon and if species selection is assumed to be prefaced by allopatric speciation. Under such conditions, natural selection and species selection could be viewed as having separate controlling mechanisms—natural selection in part dependent on mutation, recombination, differential reproduction, and differential mortality, and species selection involving varying rates of allopatric speciation in peripheral isolates followed by differential species survival.

If, however, we acknowledge the potential of other models of speciation, we can easily envision the existence of gray zones between natural selection and species selection. A large amount of variability seems to result from intraspecific and interspecific competition, via niche narrowing, character displacement, and so on; and these phenomena seem to amalgamate the commonly held views of natural selection and species selection. Certainly they depend on interaction at both levels. We suspect that such interaction is often a prerequisite of speciation and, as stated previously, that other models of speciation apply. Although we agree that the recognition of the importance of species selection will be enhanced by decoupling it, at least in name, from natural selection, we fear that such action will cause the transitional phenomena outlined above to be even more slighted by future workers than they have been in the past.

Fundamental to the demonstration of any particular instance of gradual or punctuational evolution is the means of adequate taxa recognition. Debates have often centered upon the model(s) of evolution of taxa, but usually the manner by which these taxa were initially identified and delineated has been left unspoken. There are two prominent and significantly different approaches. One is steeped in the geological tradition of biochronology and classifies the stratigraphy first, allowing the fossils to passively align with the rock units. The other utilizes, initially at least, morphological features of the fossil organisms divorced from any taxonomic role of time and space.

Surely, we believe, no matter how refined our collecting techniques or our philosophy of science may be, the conflicts of evolutionary biologists regarding tempo and mode will persist as long as these disparate fundamental methodologies persist.

Very recently, in some portions of this arena, there has been a return to the idea that most gaps in the fossil record are of nonbiological (taphonomic, erosional, and so on) origin. This view, in combination with presumed conservatism in fossil species recognition, has led Schopf (1981) to suggest that the fossil record (and our glimpse of it) has an intrinsic bias toward a punctuational pattern (stasis). Recognizing gaps in the fossil record of some organisms, certain workers have tended to focus on those organisms with the more complete records in the hope of finding the most fertile testing ground for punctuational and gradualistic hypotheses (see Prothero and Lazarus 1980).

Undoubtedly the controversy between gradualists and punctuationalists will rage for many more years and will take many currently unpredictable twists and turns. We predict a resurgence of interest in a whole host of phenomena, many of which have been tucked away in some corner or another as unimportant, untestable, or even unapproachable, utilizing data from fossils.

We are certain that we will see more rigorously objective approaches in the future and we eagerly await the next shift of momentum in the punctuationalist/gradualist conflict . . . and the next.

REFERENCES

Alexander, R. R. "Intraspecific Variability in Rhynchonellid Brachiopods: Test of a Competition Hypothesis." *Lethaia* 9 (1976):235-244.

Dodson, M. M., and Hallam, A. "Allopatric Speciation and the Fold Catastrophe." *American Naturalist* 111 (1977):415-433.

Eldredge, Niles. "Character Displacement in Evolutionary Time." *American Zoologist* 14 (1974):1083-1097.

Eldredge, Niles, and Gould, Stephen Jay. "Punctuated Equilibria: An Alternative to Phyletic Gradualism." In *Models in Paleobiology*, edited by T. J. M. Schopf, pp. 82-115. San Francisco: Freeman and Cooper, 1972.

Gould, Stephen Jay. "Earth's Erratic Pace." *Natural History* 86 (1977):12-16.

Gould, Stephen Jay, and Eldredge, Niles. "Punctuated Equilibria: The Tempo and Mode of Evolution Reconsidered." *Paleobiology* 3 (1977):115-151.

Hayami, I., and Ozawa, T. "Evolutionary Models of Lineage-Zones." *Lethaia* 8 (1975):1-14.

Kauffman, E. G., and Scott, R. W. "Basic Concepts of Community Ecology and Paleoecology." In *Structure and Classification of Paleocommunities*, edited by R. W. Scott and R. R. West, pp. 1-28. Stroudsburg, Penn.: Dowden, Hutchinson and Ross, 1976.

Lande, R. "Natural Selection and Random Genetic Drift in Phenotypic Evolution." *Evolution* 30 (1976):314-334.

Prothero, D. R., and Lazarus, D. B. "Planktonic Microfossils and the Recognition of Ancestors." *Systematic Zoology* 29 (1980):119-129.

Romer, Alfred S. "Time Series and Trends in Animal Evolution." In *Genetics, Paleontology and Evolution*, edited by G. L. Jepsen, G. G. Simpson, and E. Mayr. 1949. New York: Atheneum, 1963.

Schopf, T. J. M. "Current Item 3. Punctuated Equilibrium and Evolutionary Stasis." *Paleobiology* 7 (1981):156-166.

Stanley, Steven. "A Theory of Evolution Above the Species Level." *Proceedings of the National Academy of Sciences USA* 72 (1975):646-650.

Watson, D. M. S. "The Evidence Afforded by Fossil Vertebrates on the Nature of Evolution." In *Genetics, Paleontology and Evolution*, edited by G. L. Jepsen, G. G. Simpson and E. Mayr. 1949. New York: Atheneum, 1963.

The Inheritance of Acquired Characteristics: A Concept That Will Not Die

SHELLEY R. SAUNDERS
Department of Anthropology
McMaster University

Most evolutionary biologists today would accept the dictum that Lamarckism—the inheritance of acquired characteristics—is a dead theory. The rumblings of disagreement in evolutionary theory still center around the relative importance of Darwinian natural selection—not whether it occurs but how rapidly it occurs, and how responsible it is (as opposed to random processes) for the genetic variability we can document. Recently, however, there have been whisperings from the grave of Lamarckism that have an air of plausibility to them. It is worthwhile to have a look at these to see what they have to contribute to our understanding of the processes of evolution. But first let us examine the historical development of Lamarckism and what Lamarckism means to the current generation of scientists.

Students of the history of biology have discovered that Lamarck, the man, is mistakenly associated with the theory of Lamarckism. Jean Baptiste de Lamarck, born in 1744, is usually not remembered for being the father of modern biology, for his contributions to taxonomy, or for being the first scholar to formulate a general theory of evolution and uniformitarianism in sharp contrast to his catastrophist and essentialist contemporaries (Fine 1979). Instead Lamarck is remembered for his acceptance of the inheritance of acquired characteristics and of the effects of use and disuse, concepts not original with him but representing widely held beliefs during Lamarck's time and earlier (Mayr 1972; Boesiger 1974; Burkhardt 1980). Through the ages people have observed that physical traits are transmitted from generation to generation. They have also seen that physical traits can be modified by influences of the environment. It is therefore not unreasonable to assume these modifications may also be inherited, and many people have believed just that.

Despite some recent serious treatments of Lamarck's broader contributions to evolutionary theory, it is still common practice to caricature Lamarck's failure and Darwin's triumph through a series of cartoons depicting giraffes feeding on the leaves of trees. Darwin's giraffes become long-necked through natural selection. Some inherit random variations that allow them to reach the leaves more easily. These then survive better and are "selected" to pass on their inherited characteristics to subsequent generations. Lamarck's giraffes, in contrast, stretch their necks willfully to reach higher leaves, compelled by their inner wants or wishes. But *want* and *wish* are mistranslations of Lamarck's original word *besoins*; they suggest that Lamarck thought adaptation occurs by volition. Indeed, it has been asserted that Lamarck saw organisms as driven to improve themselves by "metaphysical inner necessity" (Lasker and Tyzzer 1980). But Lamarck was not a vitalist (Boesiger 1974), and he never claimed that adaptation takes place in this manner. He rejected the notion of a vital principle, or soul, in organisms.

A second major misinterpretation of Lamarck concerns the effect direct physical or external events have on organisms. Contrary to popular belief, Lamarck emphatically denied that the environment "works any direction modification whatever in the shape and organization of animals" (Elliot 1914). He did recognize that the form or morphology of an organism is neither accidental nor the result of direct creation; rather, it is the product of an analyzable interaction between structure and environment (Boesiger 1974). I suspect (as did Hardy 1965) that Lamarck had, to some extent, perceived the importance of somatic or phenotypic flexibility in evolutionary change, although, of course, he did not appreciate the distinction between genotype and phenotype.

Phenotypic flexibility results when an organism possesses an adaptive range of phenotypic reactions to environmental change. A parent plant of a single genotype, subdivided and grown under different climatic conditions, will produce good growth in some environments and poor growth in others. A person's blood pressure will acclimatize to a wide range of atmospheric conditions. Phenotypic flexibilty protects the individual organism against environmental stress, thus buffering against selection. Theoretically, a population composed of genotypes with a *complete* range of adaptive phenotypic reactions would not respond to natural selection at all, and every organism in the population would be equally biologically fit.

In modern terms, Lamarckian inheritance refers to the transfer from parent to offspring of genetic material that was *newly acquired* in the parent's lifetime. This avoids any confusion with phenotypic flexibility, which we assume would be inherited from the parent. Lamarck himself never proposed a mechanism for how acquired characteristics might become transferred to offspring. Ironically, Darwin did propose such a mechanism, the theory of pangenesis. An organ altered by use or disuse during an organism's lifetime will release similarly altered *pangenes* that circulate around the body, reach the gonads, and register a change in the germ cells. This was not a new idea either. Maupertuis wrote of particles that could be modified under the influence of external conditions, circulate in the blood, and pass through the germinal tract into the sex cells (Grant 1977). Hippocrates first expressed the later common classical belief that germinal seed comes from all parts of the body—healthy seed from healthy parts and diseased seed from diseased parts.

The idea of the inheritance of acquired characteristics came to be known as Lamarckism by historical accident (Burkhardt 1980). The neo-Lamarckian school in America in the late 1800s adopted Lamarck as its "patron saint," but it believed in the inheritance of *direct* environmental modifications and generally embraced vitalism. Lamarckism in the early twentieth century drew its support from such a diversity of sources that there was no single scientific understanding of what Lamarckism meant. Most generally, early twentieth century Lamarckism invoked what Mayr (1980) terms a belief in "soft inheritance." Mayr (1980) claims that this universal Lamarckism stemmed from the failure to distinguish between genotype and phenotype that afflicted most natural scientists until the 1930s. All theories of soft inheritance denied the complete constancy of the genetic material, and ranged from an acceptance of some immediate direct influence of the environment on the germ plasm to a belief in the gradual inheritance of acquired characteristics over a long period of time (somewhat reminiscent of a modern explanation of selection of genotypes controlling somatic flexibility). Most twentieth century Lamarckians were simply responding to unanswered problems of classical Darwinism, and many rejected the primacy of natural selection as the mechanism of evolution. The argument for creativity was a common one; many Lamarckians found it difficult to understand how natural selection might produce or select the fit. Selection was seen as the destroyer, eliminating the unfit. Lamarckians could not understand how the apparently perfect adaptations of the natural world could be produced from an essentially random process. It is essential under Darwinian theory that the production of variation be undirected. If, on the other hand, new environments elicited adaptive, heritable variation, then creativity would lie in the production of variation itself, not merely in the selection of randomly produced variation via the mechanism of differential reproduction.*

Lamarckism today contrasts with Darwinism in two basic ways. First, Lamarckism requires that the environment have an effect on

---

*Modern critics of the Darwinian synthesis have turned this argument around to claim that (1) many structures now important to survival may have arisen for totally nonfunctional reasons, and (2) constraints of development and form may channel evolutionary pathways more than selection does (Waddington 1975; Gould and Lewontin 1979; Gould 1982).

the classes of mutations that occur. That is, it calls for the production of *directed* or *favorable* variations. This is denied by modern Darwinism, which considers production of all mutations to be random.

Second, Lamarckism calls for these directed variations to be passed on to first-generation offspring by the transfer of information from changed somatic cells into germ cells. Darwin had embraced this notion, and had tried to explain it with his theory of pangenesis. This is the Lamarckian principle discredited by Weismann's doctrine of the continuity of the germ plasm. Weismann (1889) had proposed a complete separation between the germ cell line and the somatic cells at an early stage of development. His was an anatomical (cellular) distinction. Later the chromosomal theory of heredity made a developmental distinction between the set of genes on the chromosomes in the nuclei of cells and the physical traits they determine. Here, finally is the distinction between genotype and phenotype that was later confirmed by the central dogma of molecular genetics—that genetic information is transmitted from DNA to RNA to protein and not in reverse order.

It is defamatory to call a colleague a Lamarckian today. This is not really due to the biology of Lamarckism but to the social and political events associated with it. The Soviet communist brand of Lamarckism (Lysenkoism) was official government policy into the 1960s, much to the disgust of the western scientific world. The Kammerer affair (see Koestler 1971) did much to destroy the credibility of Lamarckism in the western world, and suspicions arose that other experimentalists in addition to Kammerer might have made fraudulent claims about environmentally induced genetic changes. Experimental tests for acquired genetic changes conducted in the early twentieth century in Europe and North America had also weakened Lamarckism; while they did not disprove it, they did fail to support it. Thus the Lamarckians were unable to provide themselves with unassailable support for their claims. At the same time, most tests of Mendelian inheritance were positive. Lamarckism was not so much falsified by experiment as simply rejected as unnecessary.

In 1979 E. J. Steele published *Somatic Selection and Adaptive Evolution: On the Inheritance of Acquired Characters*. Steele now proposes that Lamarckism lives, at least in the immune system.

His theory is based on certain properties of the antibody-producing immune system. Steele begins with the fact that, at a few days' notice, lymphocytes are able to produce antibodies that will recognize almost any foreign organism or molecule that might infect or be injected into an animal. The mechanism of such antibody production has been long debated. As Medawar (1980) has put it, how can a rabbit not yet born react specifically to a chemical not yet synthesized? The potential diversity of antibodies is really quite staggering: Antibodies can recognize an apparently limitless array of foreign antigens, and in turn each antigen can stimulate the production of hundreds of different antibodies.

Most scientists explained antibody diversity by invoking the germ line theory, which assumed a huge library of genes coding for all possible antibodies. The library, they thought, would be passed from one generation to the next in the genomes of eggs and sperm. But others, such as Steele, subscribed instead to the somatic mutation theory—the notion that mutational events occurring in the cells of the somatic immune system during an organism's ontogeny produce much of the diversity. The antigens entering an animal during its lifetime would select those somatic mutations that code for the antibodies giving the best fit to those particular antigens. This is a type of intraorganismic Darwinian natural selection that does not involve the germ cells. The presence of the antigen would then trigger a clonal expansion of the cells producing the selected antibody; these cells would proliferate and produce numerous antibody-secreting progeny.

Based on work done in the past several years, it is now known that the structure of an antibody molecule (and more particularly, its variable regions) is assembled from a collection of minigenes located on different chromosomes shuffled during development in the somatic cells called B lymphocytes. This is called somatic *recombination*. Studies of the structure of many vertebrate genes have established that some of the DNA of vertebrate cells is highly mobile, moving about in the course of cell differentiation. Somatic recombination provides for an exceptional amount of antibody diversity. Immunoglobin genes are highly unstable, however, and somatic mutation still seems to be an essential contributor to antibody diversity (Bothwell et al. 1982; Leder 1982).

The Lamarckian aspect of Steele's hypothesis comes next. Steele proposes that a cloned somatic gene mutation of an immunoglobin gene can be transferred to an endogenous RNA viral vector (the C-type RNA tumor virus, or *retrovirus*). The mutated gene is captured in the form of *m*RNA. This RNA virus crosses the tissue barrier partitioning the gametes in the gonads, infects the ova or sperm (either in the chromosomes or traveling as extrachromosomal particles), and then synthesizes a copy of germline DNA by a process involving reverse transcriptase (RNA-dependent DNA polymerase).*

---

*RNA tumor viruses carry a gene coding the enzyme reverse transcriptase that catalyzes the synthesis of a DNA copy from an RNA template. This DNA copy is then converted into a double stranded form by a DNA-dependent DNA polymerase. The discovery of reverse transcriptase (Temin 1971) eroded the central dogma of genetics by showing that *m*RNA can be transcribed back into DNA. However, this does not mean that proteins can be reversely *translated* into RNA, although such a possibility has been discussed (Cook 1977).

Thus, in the first part of his hypothesis Steele is still relying on randomly produced variation via the Darwinian mechanism of natural selection. This second part of the hypothesis breaks the Weismann barrier by proposing that random somatic mutations can become incorporated into the germ cells via the retroviral vector. This process could be adaptive, for example, as an antibody response to a new disease. Steele's mechanism might provide the next generation with an inherited immunity to the disease.

Academic response to Steele's book was prompt and vigorous. Some reviewers reacted with anger or disdain, while others, among them respected geneticists and immunologists, applauded Steele for stretching his neck out (metaphor intended) and carrying clonal selection and reverse transcription to their most extreme implications (Medawar 1980; Crow 1980). The major value of Steele's hypothesis is that, like proper scientific hypotheses, it is testable and falsifiable.

Subsequent experiments by Gorczynski and Steele seemed to confirm the hypothesis (1980, 1981). Gorczynski and Steele induced neonatal tolerance to foreign tissue in infant male mice of the CBA strain by repeated injections of large numbers of cells from hybrid mice bearing a foreign tissue-type marker. (Interestingly, this immunological phenomenon is not the same as antibody production and its mechanism is uncertain.) They then mated the mature tolerant males with normal, intolerant females and tested the immune response of the progeny. Males were used to avoid the complications of placental transfer and cytoplasmic inheritance expected if females were the treated parents. Gorczynski and Steele reported that approximately one-half of the offspring showed evidence of tolerance, and some mice (though fewer) showed evidence of tolerance in the second generation. In a second experiment they indicated that individual male mice made tolerant to two different histocompatibility antigens can transmit the tolerant state of each independently, yet often simultaneously, at a high frequency to both first- and second-generation progeny. This was further support for the somatic selection hypothesis.

Interest in this work was sufficient to stimulate independent laboratories to attempt to repeat Gorczynski and Steele's results. Brent et al. (1981) failed to confirm the findings, but their experimental protocol was not the same as that of Gorczynski and Steele. Steele (1981) claimed that Brent and his coworkers had simply failed to induce the same *degree* of tolerance in their infant male mice, and he criticized some aspects of Brent's experimental methodology. Gorczynski and Steele were in turn criticized for not using skin grafts in testing the tolerance of offspring mice (although they have since done so).

Two more very different kinds of experiments were undertaken to test the Steele hypothesis. McLaren et al. (1981) and Nisbet-

Brown and Wegmann (1981) produced chimaeric mice by fusing embryos of two different strains. These mice thus grew up exhibiting a mixture of tissues from two strains. In both experiments the chimaeras, when mated with pure-bred animals of the parental strains, produced progeny of one strain or the other who were intolerant of cells of the opposite strain. Thus these experiments also did not confirm Steele's hypothesis. Nisbet-Brown and Wegmann, however, ventured that the passively acquired tolerance of the chimaeric mice may be incapable of being fixed in the germ line, while the active tolerance induced by environmental pressure (repeated injections of antigenic cells during early development) in the Gorczynski and Steele experiments might favor genetic transfer.

The current arguments over the somatic selection hypothesis thus center around experimental methodology and the nature of the tolerance response. The major defect of all of these experiments is that they are conducted at the phenotypic level; none of them directly tests for the mechanism of the hypothesis, the retroviral vector that supposedly picks up mutated somatic genes and inserts them into germ cells.

Recent experimental work in molecular genetics and virology does, however, have some positive implications for the plausibility of a Lamarckian hypothesis of the sort Steele posited. This work informs us that genomes can be very fluid and that some genes may be able to move about at will within them. Furthermore, endogenous retroviruses are ubiquitous in vertebrate somatic and germ cells, and some genes and most retroviruses resemble extrachromosomal elements, structures that can move about in the cytoplasm of the cell.

It is well known that most higher vertebrates are natural and frequent hosts to retroviruses. The RNA of a retrovirus carries the gene for reverse transcriptase, which catalyzes the synthesis of a DNA copy from the RNA template. Retroviruses replicate themselves by integrating a double-stranded form of this DNA into the chromosomal DNA of one of the host's cells. This integrated DNA is called a *provirus* (Temin 1976). To complete viral replication, viral proteins and the *m*RNA coded from the DNA provirus assemble near the cell surface, and virus particles are budded off from the cell membrane (Figure 1).

Thus an endogenous provirus can produce exogenous viral particles. DNA provirus sequences are widespread in the chromosomal DNA of normal vertebrate cells, including humans. At least 1 percent of DNA mice is made up of retrovirus proviruses. These proviruses are then passed from one generation to the next by *vertical genetic transmission* (Weiss 1975). They may remain "silent" for many generations, they may be partially expressed, or they may give rise to virus particles that subsequently propagate by infection. Other types

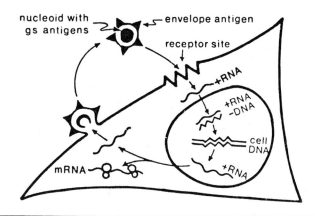

FIGURE 1. Replication of a C-type virus. (After R. A. Weiss, "Genetic Transmission of RNA Tumor Viruses," *Perspectives in Virology* 9, 1975. © 1975, Raven Press, New York.)

of retroviruses are transmitted across generations only by *vertical congenital infection*, where the infectious virus particles are passed from the mother to the offspring via the placenta or milk.

Virologists have naturally asked the question, Where did retrovirus proviruses come from and how did they get into the chromosomal DNA of cells of healthy organisms? In 1971 Temin proposed the *protovirus hypothesis*, suggesting that there is a continual evolution of viral forms from cellular elements called protoviruses. Protoviruses appear to be escaped cellular genetic elements. Temin postulated that these elements might act as vectors of genetic exchange between somatic cells during normal development (such as the somatic recombination phenomenon of immunology) by helping to create and distribute new DNA sequences. In doing so they would depend on the use of reverse transcriptase. Thus Temin proposed that reverse transcriptase activity exists in normally functioning cells (including mammalian cells, for which such activity has *not* been confirmed), and that it plays a role in normal cellular processes such as differentiation. According to this model, retroviruses (or tumor viruses) are aberrations or abnormal products of this normal genetic exchange process. Therefore the DNA proviruses found in genomes are normal structures and the retroviruses produced from them are not. To have a provirus, an organism or species would not have had to acquire a retrovirus by infection in the past. It would simply have had to produce it from the normal, mobile activity of genes in its developing cells.

Temin draws support for his protovirus hypothesis from the activities of the movable genetic elements found in prokaryotes and eukaryotes and the resemblance of these elements to DNA proviruses

(Temin 1980; Flavell 1981). The process of genetic *transduction*—the transfer of genetic material by phage from one bacterial cell to another under natural conditions—is massively documented in a number of bacterial species (Reanney 1976); this process occurs via movable genetic elements. Furthermore, there are a number of eukaryotic genes that are now known to resemble the movable genetic elements of bacteria. These are called *transposable* elements, and they include the copia-like sequences and foldback elements of *Drosophila melanogaster* and the V130 gene family of mice (Flavell 1981; Finnegan 1982). Also, control of mating type in yeast, the alteration in surface antigens in trypanosomes, and the generation of antibody diversity in mammals (discussed above) all occur via DNA rearrangements that share features in common with transposable elements. Both eukaryotic transposable elements and retrovirus proviruses possess direct DNA sequence repeats at their ends, bounded by short inverted repeats. The Alu family of genes is the most prominent of short, dispersed DNA repeat families in primates and rodents. Schmid and Jelinek (1982) suggest that Alu genes *are* transposable elements that have been inserted into chromosomal DNA via reversely transcribed intermediates. The human haploid genome consists of about 3-percent Alu sequences.

Certain recently studied mammalian genes have been found to have features characteristic of messenger RNA; that is, they lack introns or intervening sequences normally spliced out during the processing of *m*RNA from DNA. The genes studied so far include three for human tubulin, one for rat tubulin, two for the enzyme dihydrofolate reductase, and two for immunoglobulin (Marx 1982). Most of these intronless or processed genes are also flanked by short, direct repeats of DNA, so they also resemble transposable elements. Thus there is strong support for the notion that RNA is copied back into DNA in mammalian cells, and we can suggest that retrovirus protoviruses (as transposable cellular elements) may conduct much of the exchange between developing and differentiating cells.*

Temin argues that endogenous proviruses mark an evolutionary intermediate stage between protoviruses and infectious retroviruses. Steele is postulating a reversal of this model: Rather than incidental byproducts of the normal activity of proviruses, retroviruses are, Steele believes, the agents of the primary introduction of proviruses into the organism. Steele suggests that infecting viruses entered the germ cells of a potential host in the past, became incorporated into the genome, and were then passed on for generations as DNA proviruses in the normal chromosomal DNA, displaying features of classical Mendelian inheritance.

---

*Recently it has been shown that reverse transcription is central to the life cycle of hepatitis B viruses and thus not restricted to retroviruses (Varmus 1982).

There is some evidence to suggest that proviruses could indeed have derived from exogenous infections in the past. Jähner and Jaenisch (1980) cultured four to eight cell embryos with Moloney leukaemia virus cells *in vitro*; the developing blastocysts were then transferred into the uterus of a pseudopregnant female. They found that a viraemic male was able to transmit virus to a fraction of his offspring. The male was found to be mosaic for the Moloney leukaemia virus in both his somatic cells and germ cells. The viraemic sons of this father mouse transmitted viraemia to their offspring in classical Mendelian fashion, indicating that the exogenous virus had been converted to an endogenous one.

In 1975 Weiss suggested that retrovirus proviruses, derived from exogenous infection, could become integrated into the chromosomal DNA of host germ cells and give rise to inherited germinal proviruses. In one example he points to the substantial similarity between endogenous feline virus and a C-type virus of baboons. The virus is detectable only in domestic cats and Old World monkeys, suggesting that the cat virus could have been acquired from some primate prior to domestication (Weiss 1975). Others have suggested, based on gene sequence comparisons, that *genes* jump from one species to another through the medium of endogenous viruses incorporating themselves into the germ-line DNA—a form of interspecific acquired inheritance (Hyldig-Nielson et al. 1982). Such a phenomenon is normal for prokaryotes (Reanney 1976) but, until recently, unexpected for sexually reproducing organisms.

In 1977 Grant cited various experimental examples of apparent genetic transduction in higher organisms where information seems to have been inherited via cytoplasmic viruses or cytoplasmic DNA. He argues, however, that the chromosomal genotype is too well integrated and protected from external influences to allow genetic transduction to become a major evolutionary mechanism. Grant says that the evolution of sexual reproduction in eukaryotes has channeled and ordered the mechanism of genetic exchange between lineages by producing a chromosomal gene headquarters that directs the development of a complex organism. But the most recent scientific picture of the nuclear genome suggests that it may not be as autonomous as previously thought.

Critics of Steele have argued that germ cell bombardment by somatic viruses would lead to genetic chaos and disruption of predictable Mendelian patterns of inheritance. But Steele argues in response that once acquired somatic states enter the germ-line they can be passed on to future generations in a Mendelian manner, displaying stable transmission in the absence of environmental stimuli and segregating in expected Mendelian ratios. Other critics of Steele (Crow 1980; Dawkins 1982) have asked how an organism that transmits the effects of somatic selection would be able to distinguish between good and bad somatic changes. Crow (1980), for example, points out that the most extreme example of somatic mutation is malignancy, which is not linked to evolutionary progress. Steele (1981) has responded to this by claiming that tumors may well be the "price of progress" paid by flexible adaptive somatic systems in multicellular eukaryotes.

The most cogent and valid argument against the somatic selection hypothesis is that of Bateson (1979), published before the appearance of Steele's book. Bateson argues that if Lamarckian inheritance were the rule, the whole process of evolution would become tied up in the rigidities of genetic determination. His argument centers around the importance of somatic flexibility. Somatic change, Bateson says, is simply bodily change brought about during the lifetime of the individual. Somatic change is hierarchic in structure; it deals with immediate adjustments at the superficial (most concrete) level, and more general adjustments at deeper (more abstract) levels. A person traveling from sea level to 12,000 feet experiences immediate somatic changes, such as panting and tachycardia. An extended visit to the mountains results in long-term acclimation (respiratory changes, expanded rib cage, higher hemoglobin levels, and so on). Populations living in mountainous areas may perhaps pass on some of these characteristics to their offspring, but a shift from somatic flexibility to genetic stability would only occur if the environmental stresses (high altitude) are constant. In that case the population does not need the reversibility that is the hallmark of somatic change. Genetic change is the highest, most abstract component in the hierarchy of adaptive adjustment, and should therefore be the least reversible. Lamarckian inheritance without selection would eat up somatic flexibility because *all* acquired change would enter the genome.*

Applying Bateson's hierarchy, one can see here that it is really useless to speak of organisms "determined" by their genes. Bateson stresses that somatic change may, in fact, precede the genetic, so that it would be more appropriate to regard any genetic change as the result or copy of somatic change. In other words, somatic changes may partly determine the pathways of evolution, and "at the population level, with appropriate selection of phenotypes, environment and experience will generate better-adapted individuals on which selection can work" (Bateson 1979, p. 160).

There is no doubt that the biological world *looks like* a product of Lamarckian evolution. Even so, evolutionary biologists have generally ignored the laments of some of the earlier Lamarckians and the

---

*I should note here that Steele admits that it is imperative that his system possess inbuilt rules governing organ specificity of endogenous viruses (or other vectors) and integrational specificity for the incoming genes (1981).

more recent integrationists who point out that environmental change and organisms, by their own life activities, determine which aspects of the outer world make up their environment (Lewontin 1981). The rigidity of a genetic change is avoided and delayed until environmental circumstances or stresses previously handled by the soma are themselves permanent. Waddington (1975) proposed genetic assimilation as the mechanism for such genetic change.

Genetic assimilation takes place either by recombinational events in the genome, making a genocopy of the phenotypic response, or by selection of random mutations. Thus we again introduce the random element into the process of genetic change—what Bateson calls the great stochastic process (1979). In his terms, *stochastic* combines a random component of change with a selective process so that only certain outcomes are allowed to endure.

An unwillingness to accept a random component of evolution (chance versus necessity) is pervasive in the writings of many who criticize the neo-Darwinian synthesis. They argue that it is difficult to see how complex biological organisms and systems could have been built up from random statistical events. The answer probably lies in the mechanism of hierarchical control, which is the universal system of organization in the biological world. The subunit structures of a hierarchy, such as DNA or individual cells, do not exert control on biological development in isolation (there is no intrinsic chemical property of DNA that determines it to be the "master molecule of life"); but the control value of these structures is established in collective hierarchical organizations requiring the whole organism (Pattee 1973). Very little is known about the integrated control mechanisms operating between the realms of structure and of development of form. This is why a "Lamarckian" (this term is used for want of a better word) interpretation of adaptation has been so attractive to many scholars, and why today we see published pleas for research into directed mutations (Rosen and Buth 1980).

The recent molecular evidence for infinite genetic variation may mean that the flexibility of the genome is sufficient to provide for almost any outcome, and therefore true Lamarckian inheritance is simply unnecessary. But it is at the collective levels of hierarchical control of phenotypic development that we must understand the constraints and integrated ordering of the developmental process.

REFERENCES

Bateson, G. *Mind and Nature.* New York: E. P. Dutton, 1979.
Boesiger, Ernest. "Evolutionary Theories after Lamarck and Darwin." In *Studies in the Philosophy of Biology*, edited by Francisco J. Ayala and Theodosius Dobzhansky, pp. 21-44. London: MacMillan, 1974.

Bothwell, A. L. M., Paskind, M., Reth, M., Imanishi-Kari, T., Rajewsky, K., and Baltimore, D. "Somatic Variants of Murine Immunoglobin λ Light Chains." *Nature* 298 (1982):380-382.

Brent, L., Rayfield, L. S., Chandler, P., Fierz, W., Medawar, P. B., and Simpson, E. "Supposed Lamarckian Inheritance of Immunological Tolerance." *Nature* 290 (1981):508-512.

Burkhardt, Richard W., Jr. "Lamarckism in Britain and the United States." In *The Evolutionary Synthesis*, edited by E. Mayr and W. B. Provine, pp. 343-351. Cambridge, Mass.: Harvard University Press, 1980.

Cook, N. D. "The Case for Reverse Translation." *Journal of Theoretical Biology* 64 (1977):113-135.

Crow, James F. "Can Lamarck be Resurrected?" *Cell* 19 (1980):807-808.

Dawkins, R. "The Necessity of Darwinism." *New Scientist* 94 (1982):130-132.

Elliot, H. Introduction to English translation of *Zoological Philosophy*, by J. B. Lamarck. London: MacMillan, 1914.

Fine, Paul E. M. "Lamarckian Ironies in Contemporary Biology." *The Lancet* (2 June 1979):1181-1182.

Finnegan, D. J. "The 'Fold-Back' Elements of *Drosophila*." *Nature* 297 (1982): 181-182.

Flavell, Andrew. "Did Retroviruses Evolve from Transposable Elements?" *Nature* 289 (1981):10-11.

Gorczynski, R. M., and Steele, E. J. "Inheritance of Acquired Immunological Tolerance to Foreign History Compatibility Antigens in Mice." *Proceedings of the National Academy of Sciences U.S.A.* 77 (1980):2871-2875.

――――. "Simultaneous yet Independent Inheritance of Somatically Acquired Tolerance to Two Distinct H-2 Antigenic Haplotype Determinants in Mice." *Nature* 289 (1981):678-681.

Gould, Stephen J. "Change in Developmental Timing as a Mechanism of Macroevolution." In *Evolution and Development*, edited by J. T. Bonner, pp. 333-346. Dahlem Konferenzen, Life Sciences Research Report #22. New York: Springer-Verlag, 1982.

Gould, S. J., and Lewontin, R. C. "The Spandrels of San Marco and the Panglossian Paradigm: A Critique of the Adaptationist Programme." *Proceedings of the Royal Society London B* 205 (1979):581-598.

Grant, Verne. *Organismic Evolution*. San Francisco: W. H. Freeman, 1977.

Hardy, Sir Alister. *The Living Stream*. London: Collins Press, 1965.

Hyldig-Nielson, J. J.; Jensen, E. O.; Paludan, K.; Wiborg, O.; Garrett, R.; Jorgensen, P.; and Marcker, K. A. "The Primary Structures of Two Leghemoglobin Genes from Soybean." *Nucleic Acids Research* 10 (1982):689.

Jähner, D., and Jaenisch, R. "Integration of Moloney Leukaemia Virus into the Germ Line of Mice: Correlation between Site of Integration and Virus Activation." *Nature* 289 (1980):456-458.

Koestler, Arthur. *The Case of the Midwife Toad*. London: Pan Books, 1971.

Lasker, G., and Tyzzer, R. N. *Introduction to Physical Anthropology*. New York: Holt, Rinehart and Winston, 1980.

Leder, P. "The Genetics of Antibody Diversity." *Scientific American* 246 (1982): 102-115.

Lewontin, Richard C. "On Constraints and Adaptation." *The Behavioral and Brain Sciences* 4 (1981):224-245.

Marx, J. L. "Is RNA Copied into DNA by Mammalian Cells?" *Science* 216 (1982):969-970.

Mayr, Ernst. "Lamarck Revisited." *Journal of the History of Biology* 5 (1972): 55-94.

———. "Prologue: Some Thoughts on the History of the Evolutionary Synthesis." In *The Evolutionary Synthesis*, edited by E. Mayr and W. B. Provine, pp. 1-48. Cambridge, Mass.: Harvard University Press, 1980.

McLaren, A.; Chandler, P.; Buehr, M.; Fierz, W.; and Simpson, E. "Immune Reactivity of Progeny of Tetraparental Male Mice." *Nature* 290 (1981): 513-514.

Medawar, Sir Peter B. "Lamarckian Approach to Immunology." *Trends in Biochemical Science* 5 (1980): XV.

Nisbet-Brown, E., and Wegmann, T. G. "Is Acquired Immunological Tolerance Genetically Transmissible?" *Proceedings of the National Academy of Sciences U.S.A.* 78 (1981):5826-5828.

Pattee, H. *Hierarchy Theory: The Challenge of Complex Systems.* New York: George Braziller, 1973.

Reanney, D. "Extrachromosomal Elements as Possible Agents of Adaptation and Development." *Bacteriological Reviews* 40 (1976):552-590.

Rosen, D. E., and Buth, D. G. "Empirical Evolutionary Research Versus Neo-Darwinian Speculation." *Systematic Zoology* 29, No. 3 (1980):300-308.

Schmid, C. W., and Jelinek, W. R. "The Alu Family of Dispersed Repetitive Sequences." *Science* 216 (1982):1065-1070.

Steele, E. J. *Somatic Selection and Adaptive Evolution: On the Inheritance of Acquired Characters.* 2d edition. Chicago: University of Chicago Press, 1981.

Temin, H. M. "The Protovirus Hypothesis: Speculations on the Significance of RNA-directed DNA Synthesis for Normal Development and for Carcinogenesis." *Journal of the National Cancer Institute* 46 (February 1971):3-7.

———. "The DNA Provirus Hypothesis." *Science* 192 (1976):1075-1080.

———. "Origin of Retroviruses from Cellular Moveable Genetic Elements." *Cell* 21 (1980):599-600.

Varmus, H. E. "A Growing Role for Reverse Transcription." *Nature* 299 (1982): 204-205.

Waddington, C. H. *The Evolution of an Evolutionist.* Ithaca, N.Y.: Cornell University Press, 1975.

Weismann, A. *Essays Upon Heredity and Kindred Biological Problems.* Oxford: Clarendon, 1889.

Weiss, R. A. "Genetic Transmission of RNA Tumor Viruses." *Perspectives in Virology* 9 (1975):165-205.

SECTION THREE

Evolution
and the Public

Modern Antievolutionism: The Scientific Creationists

ALICE B. KEHOE
Department of Sociology and Anthropology
Marquette University

> *When the plain sense makes common sense, we seek no other sense.*
> —Pastor Robert Brien,
> Greendale Baptist Church

> *For a scientist, the solution of a difficult conceptual or instrumental puzzle is a principal goal.*
> —Thomas S. Kuhn, philosopher of science
> (1970, p. 21)

Introduction

The speakers quoted above inhabit two different universes. Pastor Brien lives in a world of real objects, external to him and to his God, a world he and his fellow men can know through their God-given senses. Dr. Kuhn lives in a universe of flux where humans construct an apparent order through the artifices of languages. Pastor Brien's world is well and accurately described in the King James and New American Standard or New International Bibles. Dr. Kuhn's world is imperfectly known, a never-ending challenge to the most creative thinkers. As in science fiction, Pastor Brien and Dr. Kuhn might live out their lives in their parallel worlds like matter and anti-matter, except for a devil in Pastor Brien's world—*the* Devil, Satan, the Ad-

I am grateful to Robert Brien, Mr. Czeszynski, and Mr. Eigenfeldt of the Milwaukee Public Schools biology curriculum, Dean Fowler of Marquette University's Theology Department, Mr. and Mrs. Tony Kaminski of Greendale Baptist Church, David Lewycky of Winnipeg Bible College, David O. Moberg, Lamar Modert of Greendale Baptist Church, Marian Olson of the Milwaukee Public Museum, Charles Roessger, Arthur Rumpf of the Milwaukee Public Schools social studies curriculum, and Claude E. Stipe of Marquette University for their generosity and patience in interviews and critiques. I am particularly grateful to Pastor Brien and Professor Moberg for their unstinting help in the preparation of this reading.

versary. According to some contemporary leaders of Pastor Brien's world, Satan has been seducing mankind into damnation by persuading millions to accept an evil doctrine of Dr. Kuhn's world, the theory of evolution. Evolutionism is the root of many of society's horrors, these men claim, and it must be fought relentlessly. It is generally assumed that the war between Biblical creationists and adherents of evolution was won by the evolutionists in 1925 at the Tennessee trial of John Thomas Scopes, during which an aged William Jennings Bryan orated ineffectively against the brilliant Clarence Darrow. Bryan lost the battle, but the war continued; and since the 1960s it has escalated, pulling in hundreds of educated, shrewd men and many hundreds of thousands of dollars to deliver mankind from the Satanic sedition of evolutionisn.

Scientific Creationism

On every continent at least one organization is now putting much energy and a steady flow of money into presenting to the public the idea that the theory of evolution is a mistaken conclusion from clear facts. These organizations espouse the concept of scientific creationism—that science, correctly pursued, will lend credence to the position that the Book of Genesis exactly describes a series of prehistorical events. About ten thousand years ago, according to the scientific creationists, our Creator brought into being our world and its various kinds of organisms, including its first humans, Adam and Eve. Somewhat later a universal deluge occurred, causing the extinction of some organisms, massive deposition of sediments, and erosion of rocks. Scientific creationists marshall an array of facts—geological observations, statistical probabilities, the laws of thermodynamics— to support this explanatory model of the origin and early history of Earth. Underlying their expositions is the premise, "When the plain sense makes common sense, we seek no other sense."

The roots of scientific creationism lie in late eighteenth century lowland Scotland, where Thomas Reid and Dugald Stewart developed the philosophy known as Scottish Realism. Reid and Stewart reacted against the ideas of John Locke and the eighteenth century Enlightenment, which questioned received knowledge. It disturbed Reid that Locke could dismantle the apparent certainty of examples of reasoned knowledge, and that Locke's own reasoning could be attacked by Hume. Reid determined to seek a stronger mode of reasoning, one that might restore certainty. He thought he discovered what he required in the works of the seventeenth century philosopher Francis Bacon. Bacon has been considered one of the founders of modern science, presenting an inductive mode of reasoning from carefully controlled or tested observations. Reid, a close friend of several of the important scientists of his day, touted Bacon's scientific method as the answer to the quest for certainty. The basis of the method, as Reid read it, was empirical, or *realist*—the commonsense assumption that there is an objective world external to the human observer and that the observer can perceive consistently and manipulate the phenomena of this world. Reid gleaned from Bacon a straightforward practical procedure for discovering and testing the first principles on which our world is constructed. Once someone has made a discovery, anyone else can confirm it by replicating the discoverer's procedures. Certainty seemed possible.

Early nineteenth century American Presbyterians were receptive to Reid and Stewart's philosophy. Many came from a similar Scottish background and shared the same middle-class, or bourgeois, status as the Scottish thinkers. This was a comfortable status, one that gave a pleasant measure of prestige and financial power. In America, the rapidly expanding European-descended population was a rewarding market for entrepreneurs who could tailor manufactured goods or even social organizations to satisfy the market's requirements with minimal elaboration. Indeed, Europeans of this period spoke of the "American system" of turning out products stripped to their bare essentials for the mass market. Reid and Stewart's Baconian method of discovering knowledge was highly compatible with the American emphasis on utilitarian values, the positivist spirit, and distrust of high-flown abstract theories. An engineer's science, a doer's science, Scottish Realism promised solid understanding as the prize of disciplined work. Far from the ivory tower, it was accessible to every earnest seeker, provided he kept his eyes open and his goal clear. Metaphysical games were eschewed, and so was revolution. This was a philosophy for the bourgeoisie.

An unbroken line connects the early nineteenth century American enthusiasts for Scottish Realism to late twentieth century scientific creationists. Presbyterians dominated among leaders of the United States, especially south of New England, through much of the nineteenth century. In 1837, conservatives won control of the Presbyterian General Assembly. Princeton's prestigious seminary was Presbyterian. Presbyterian lecturers and writers in influential periodicals promoted an uncompromising empiricism coupled with firm Christian faith, a pairing that seemed paradoxical to some of their opponents. Defending these twin faiths in plain reality and in the miracle of Christ, the conservative Presbyterians asserted that God laid out the world and then gave men the senses to learn about it: The more we know about nature, the more obvious is God's plan and the Bible's truth. Proper science—science conducted according to Reid and Stewart's Baconian methodology—cannot fail to support the Bible. Empirical confirmation of biblical statements may then serve to justify confidence in those Scriptures that cannot be empirically confirmed by living humans: the statements on Redemption. Miracles are proof that divine power transcends natural law, and eternal happiness is bestowed as God chooses. Through God's goodness He reveals to mankind that He has chosen to offer salvation through Christ. There need be no conflict between science and religion: One must only realize that science is contained within the religious domain. God is the final Answer. In 1874, Charles Hodge, the most prominent orthodox Presbyterian thinker in America, published an essay on Darwinism that judged it "tantamount to atheism." The conservative Realists of his generation, like scientific creationists today, contrasted "facts" with "hypotheses" and "theories." The Bible demands faith, but that faith is corroborated by empirical facts, rightly interpreted.

Modern scientific creationists claim there are two principal models currently available to explain the origin of the earth and of life. In one model life arises spontaneously from nonliving organic molecules, then changes over millions of years into all the extinct and living organisms, including, eventually, humans. This is the evolution model. The other model, the creation model, posits the making of the world and the kinds, or organisms, by a Creator. Tied to the scientific creationist model is the claim that the earth has been in existence only about ten thousand years, and that it suffered one universal deluge after its creation and the creation of its organisms. Scientific creationists usually insist that only these two competing models are available to explain the origin of earthly life.

The Public Controversy

Scientific creationists believe that their creation model makes better sense of the facts of earthly phenomena than does the evolution model. From this position many scientific creationists have been lobbying for the presentation of both models in school science classes. They argue that not only does the creation model appear truer to observed facts, in the opinion of many parents, than does its competitor, but also that teaching by comparing and contrasting two models gives students a better understanding of the logic and methodology of science. Comparing the two models is said to awaken student interest and enthusiasm. Thus, teaching the two models is presented as more honest, truer to science, and pedagogically more valuable than teaching only evolution. If school boards protest that the creation model is religious and therefore does not belong in public school science classes, scientific creationists reply that nowhere in their creation model is God or any biblical personage mentioned, and further, that evolution is a doctrine of the religion of secular humanism. They conclude that the creation model is a more suitable choice for presentation in American public schools.

Scientific creationists have adapted their strategy to the laws and general public opinion of the United States. The legal ramifications of the position promoting the two-model pedagogy are discussed in detail in two articles by a young Georgia lawyer, Wendell R. Bird. Bird's first article (1978) argued that forcing children of creationist households to listen to exclusively evolutionist teaching abridges their constitutionally protected right to the free exercise of their religion; he suggested that the two-model presentation is a reasonable compromise between those who would practice secular humanism and those who would not. Bird's second article (1979) claims that the exclusive teaching of evolution in public schools contravenes the constitutional prohibition against the establishment of a state-supported religion—specifically, "nontheistic, Humanist, and secular faiths" (Bird 1979, p. 178). Through these articles the scientific creationists deny the possibility of any truly nonreligious discussion on the origin of the earth and of its organisms. They then appear to advocate religious tolerance by asking for a balanced presentation of the two (as they see it) competing models.

The 1925 Scopes trial focused on different issues. The trial itself addressed the question of a citizen's (Scopes's) right to refuse to obey an unjust law. Clarence Darrow, defending the young biology teacher, brought together a formidable roster of scientists and theologians to testify that the law was unjust because the doctrine it preserved, creationism, was in error. Judge Raulston of the Rhea County Circuit Court, who happened to be a Fundamentalist evangelist, correctly instructed the jury that they were not charged to examine the propriety of the law forbidding the teaching of evolution, but only whether Scopes was guilty of disobeying the law. Darrow's experts were ruled irrelevant and not allowed to testify. Scopes was found guilty and fined $100. Popular opinion, fed by newspaper stories filed for the most part by liberal Northern urban reporters, stereotyped Raulston and the Rhea County jurors as ignorant Southern rednecks who could not comprehend modern science. William Jennings Bryan, the prosecution's star speaker, was excoriated as a has-been who belonged in the past century—he did, in fact, die five days after the trial.

After the urban press blasted creationism, fundamentalists long avoided national confrontations. Few liberals realized that Darrow had not won anything in 1925. As recently as 1967, a Tennessee high school teacher, Gary Scott, was dismissed for disobeying a state law prohibiting the teaching of evolution. The National Science Teachers

Association assisted Scott's case, as the American Civil Liberties Union had assisted Scopes. This time the ballyhoo was absent but the evolutionists won, for Tennessee repealed the statute. The next year, 1968, in a similar case in Arkansas, the United States Supreme Court found the Arkansas law unconstitutional, after which Mississippi rescinded a parallel statute. The Supreme Court's ruling on the Arkansas case indicated to many conservative Protestants that the strategy of instituting state laws to prohibit the teaching of evolution must be abandoned, and a strategy more defensible under the Constitution developed. Hence the shift from the either/or stance of the Scopes trial era to the present muted anti-evolutionism, with attention drawn to the alleged validity of a competing scientific model rather than a simple attack on evolution as ungodly.

The year 1963 was a watershed year for creationism. In that year, the Biological Sciences Curriculum Study Project, financed by the National Science Foundation, published basic textbooks frankly presenting evolution as the core of biology. Before this, biology textbooks even on the high-school level had treated evolution very gingerly, if at all; for textbook publishers knew, as the general public did not, that considerable segments of the textbook market remained controlled by conservatives who either rejected evolution themselves or felt vulnerable to the demands of citizens who rejected it. Fundamentalists in 1963 saw for the first time the open promotion of reinvigorated evolution in textbooks aimed at nationwide markets; worse, these textbooks had been developed with public tax monies!

In 1963 ten men founded the Creation Research Society. These men were attending a meeting of the American Scientific Affiliation, begun in 1941 as an association of people who had committed themselves to "Jesus Christ as Lord and Savior" and "to a scientific description of the world"—scientists who believed that the "Holy Scriptures are the inspired Word of God." The founders of the Creation Research Society agreed that these statements of the American Scientific Affiliation were too weak. Those who join the Creation Research Society must subscribe to the belief that "the Bible is the written Word of God, and . . . all of its assertions are historically and scientifically true in all of the original autographs. . . . This means that the account of origins in Genesis is a factual presentation of simple historical truths. All basic types of living things, including man, were made by direct creative acts of God during Creation Week as described in Genesis. . . . The great Flood described in Genesis . . . the Noachian Deluge, was an historical event, worldwide. . . . Finally, we are an organization of Christian men of science, who accept . . . salvation can come only thru accepting Jesus Christ as our Savior." By 1981, 693 voting members, each of whom had earned at least a master's degree in some recognized area of science, 1172 sustaining members who lacked such a degree, and 378 student members had signed adherence to the society's Statement of Belief.

Such an unequivocal commitment to the inerrancy of Scripture—particularly the King James or American Standard translations—is shared by other active national scientific creationist groups: The Bible-Science Association, with its office in Minneapolis; Students for Origins Research, in Goleta, California; Creation-Science Research Center in San Diego; Creation Social Science and Humanities Society, Wichita, Kansas; Geoscience Research Institute, Loma Linda, California; Museum of Creation Publications, Lincoln, Nebraska; Creation-Science Associations in Canada (Edmonton, Alberta), and Australia (Adelaide); North American Creation Movement, Victoria, B.C., an arm of the British Evolution Protest Movement; and Creation Scientists' Forum of India, Kottayam, Kerala, modeled on the Creation Research Society. Many fundamentalist colleges, particularly Bob Jones University of Greenville, South Carolina, promote scientific creationism with traveling lecturers as well as in their own campus programs. Christian Heritage College of San Diego, California, describes itself as stressing "the foundational importance of special creationism in every subject," not only in its science majors in geophysics, physics/math, and biological sciences; and it has a research division in its Institute for Creation Research, headed by Dr. Henry M. Morris, the College's president until 1980. Most of these organizations publish quarterly journals and monthly or weekly newsletters, biology or general science textbooks or topic readers for school use, teachers' guides and charts, and pamphlets.

Within the scientific creationist ranks there is some difference of opinion on the best strategy for converting the public schools to the two-model concept, though there seems a consensus that teaching the two models is the most feasible way to get the teaching of creationism, and the questioning of the validity of evolution, into mainstream education. Paul Ellwanger of Anderson, South Carolina, coordinates a national campaign to persuade state legislatures to make the teaching of scientific creationism compulsory in the public schools of their states. For one dollar Ellwanger will mail a copy of a suggested draft bill, "Law for the Teaching of Scientific Creationism," said to be compatible with federal and all state constitutions. Two states, Arkansas and Louisiana, passed versions of Ellwanger's model bill in 1981. Still the Institute for Creation Research, probably the best organized and effective of the scientific creationist groups, considers such legislation too remote from teachers themselves to be the most suitable medium for curriculum changes. The Institute urges creationists to pressure local school boards to endorse teaching the two models, and citizens can obtain from the Institute a sample "Resolution for Balanced Presentation of Evolution and

Scientific Creationism," drawn up by Wendell Bird. By working on the local or district level, proponents of scientific creationism can follow up the introduction of resolutions by arranging public lectures and debates and by contacting teachers personally or through sessions and exhibits at teachers' conventions. By targeting their campaigns at this level, creationists may be most successful in raising public support and persuading teachers to actually use their materials. The theme of the local-level efforts is that the public, teachers, and students have been brainwashed into blind acceptance of the less valid model of the origin of life. We do not need legislation compelling the teaching of creationism, say the Institute and its supporters: We ask only the opportunity to introduce our scientific model into the free market of ideas where open-minded persons can examine it.

Nonpublic Aspects of Scientific Creationism

The Institute for Creation Research sponsors a textbook (Morris 1974) written by its founder, Dr. Morris, and a popular book (Gish 1978) by a staff scientist, Duane Gish, discrediting evolution. Both books are published in public and general editions. The public editions carefully avoid any mention of God or Christianity, while the general editions add chapters tying in the public chapters to the Bible and Fundamentalist Christianity. The public is told that scientific creationism is purely scientific and has no necessary tie to any religion (whereas commitment to evolution, the public is informed, is a faith). Students in Christian schools, such as the growing number of Christian Academies associated with fundamentalist churches, read Henry Morris's introduction to the general edition of his text and learn that "It is precisely because Biblical revelation is absolutely authoritative and perspicuous that the scientific facts, rightly interpreted, will give the same testimony as that of Scripture. There is not the slightest possibility that the *facts* of science can contradict the Bible" (Morris 1974, p. 15, his italics). In another of Morris's books, published the year after his textbook, readers discover that scientific creationism's model of origins is built on four Biblical events (Morris 1975, p. 109):

1. *Special creation of all things in six days. . . .*
2. *The curse upon all things, by which the entire cosmos was brought into a state of gradual deterioration ["entropy"]. . . .*
3. *The universal Flood, which drastically changed the rates of most earth processes. . . .*
4. *The dispersion at Babel, which resulted from the sudden proliferation of languages and other cultural distinctives.*

At Babel, Morris deduced, "the entire monstrous complex . . . Pantheism, polytheism, astrology, idolatry, mysteries, spiritism, materialism . . . was revealed to Nimrod . . . by demonic influences, perhaps by Satan himself" (Morris 1975, pp. 72, 74-75).

"Satan himself is the originator of the concept of evolution," says Morris (1975, p. 75). Tim LaHaye, pastor of Scott Memorial Baptist Church in San Diego and former president of Christian Heritage College, explains in his Introduction to Morris's book (1975, p. 5), "The theory of evolution is the philosophical foundation for all secular thought today, from education to biology and from psychology through the social sciences. It is the platform from which socialism, communism, humanism, determinism, and one-worldism have been launched. . . . Accepting man as animal, its advocates endorse animalistic behavior such as free love, situation ethics, drugs, divorce, abortion, and a host of other ideas that contribute to man's present futility and despair. . . . It has wrought havoc in the home, devastated morals, destroyed man's hope for a better world, and contributed to the political enslavement of a billion or more people."

Creationists see themselves called upon to save mankind from this evil. Dr. Vernon L. Grose, an engineer trained in physics, spoke out in 1969 to urge California to adopt textbooks teaching the creationist model. He told an interviewer, "The forces of evil [are] being met in these last days [before the Second Coming of Christ] with an aggressive, explosive reaction of men who are led and filled by the Spirit of God . . . not simply to withstand their attack, but to attack them. . . . As C. S. Lewis has put it, we who believe in Jesus Christ are little Christs. Just as Jesus 'directly interfered in the affairs of men' by His coming to earth, so we believers today must continue to interfere with Satan's well-laid plans" (Bredesen 1971, pp. 148-149).

The lesson of the Scopes trial was clear: Soft-pedal Satan when speaking to his dupes, play within the rules of *their* game. The public face of scientific creationism is sophisticated; it talks of models and probabilities. Within its own circle, it reveals its basic fundamentalism, the total inclusion of its science inside a traditional orthodox Christian framework.

Scientific Creationists' Position Among Christians

Most scientific creationists are Fundamentalist Christians, though not all fundamentalists are scientific creationists. Certainly a very large proportion of Christians are not fundamentalists. A Gallup Poll conducted in 1978 found that only 16 percent of a nationwide sample of adults fit its definition of orthodox Christians. This definition is not precisely the same as that for fundamentalist Christian, but it should have included most Christian fundamentalists (Christianity Today 1980). It is a tenet of fundamentalism that the only *true* Christians are those who subscribe to their beliefs, but obviously this position is disputable.

Among Christians—broadly defined—today, the majority viewpoint is that evolution is the process through which life developed, and is developing, on earth. God may have instituted the process, or God may be actively working within the process. Several prominent Catholic and Protestant theologians consider evolution central to understanding the mystery of God and Christ. Pierre Teilhard de Chardin, a Jesuit, developed the thesis that evolution is teleological, leading to the fulfillment of God's purpose for mankind. Karl Rahner, a contemporary German Jesuit, argues that evolution is the Incarnation of God's Word, essential to a comprehension of the meaning of Christ. More conservative Catholics accept evolution as the description of the history of physical organisms, including the bodily aspect of humans, though not the soul. Two papal encyclicals, *Providentissimus Deus* and *Divino Afflante Spiritu*, are cited in support of this acceptance of evolution among Catholics. Protestants who have expounded the view that evolution is a prime manifestation of God the Creator include: Charles E. Raven of Cambridge; A. R. Peacocke of Oxford; E. L. Mascall of London; Arthur F. Smethurst, a canon of Salisbury Cathedral; Americans such as Kenneth Cauthen and Errol E. Harris; and theologically sophisticated scientists such as the Oxford biologist W. H. Thorpe; Ian Barbour; and Richard Bube, former president of the American Scientific Affiliation. The profound compatibility between Christianity and a science recognizing evolution was well discussed by eminent scientists and theologians during the decade of the Scopes trial, as the books by the British Broadcasting Corporation and by Edward Cotton attest. Subsequent discoveries and modifications of the theory of evolution have confirmed this compatibility to most Christians.

Against this broad and varied aggregation stand the scientific creationists. They begin, as fundamentalists, with the "Five Fundamentals" listed in 1910 by the Presbyterian General Assembly as the *sine qua non* of orthodox Protestant Christianity: The miracles of Christ; the virgin birth; the bodily resurrection; the sacrifice on the cross, constituting atonement for mankind's sins; and the Bible as the directly inspired Word of God. None of these ideas seems to fit ordinary commonsense expectations; therefore acceptance of them becomes a test of faith, or of God's grace. The last tenet, the inerrancy of Scripture, is perhaps the most difficult to use as a criterion. Clearly, some Biblical statements are metaphors, allegories, or parables. There are also variations of interpretation due to choosing among differences between the texts of the several early manuscripts of the Bible, and among two or more English terms equally justifiable as the translations of the Hebrew or Greek words in these early texts. Members of the Dean Burgon Society follow their nineteenth century eponym in insisting the King James version, and it alone, is the true Word of God. More fundamentalists accept the New American Standard and New International Bibles as well. Fundamentalists are not likely to accept the Revised Standard Version and the New English Bible, which reflect the "higher criticism" analyses of biblical texts that Bishop Burgon railed against. To steer between the occasional necessity of reading a scriptural term as metaphor or allegory and the danger of always reading Scripture critically, a fundamentalist can rely on the adage, "When the plain sense makes common sense, we seek no other sense"—modified by the fundamental position that the miracles of God and Christ were indeed miracles. Scientific creationists go a little farther than many other fundamentalists in rejecting alternative usages of a scriptural term whenever a narrow literal interpretation seems also to make sense—for example, in insisting that the six days of Creation were six twenty-four-hour days, not more extended periods of time.

For many fundamentalists, insistence on a literal reading of the more traditional versions of the English Bible is both a test of faith and the sole basis for faith. The crucial question, they say, is, How can we know that Jesus is the Redeemer, that we can be saved through Him? They see the Bible as the answer to their query, and the authority for accepting the biblical answer as true is the conviction that the Bible is wholly and without qualification true. Any doubt of the certain truth of any portion of the Bible is to them the seed of all doubt, the pitfall prepared by Satan. Damnation lurks before the man or woman who in the sin of pride is so arrogant as to pick and choose in Scripture, fitting the Word of God into modern human ideas instead of human ideas to God's Word. Underlying the insistence on total faith, and the assertion that anything less equals no faith, is a strong tendency among creationists to structure concepts as opposing pairs, antitheses. Scholars of the Judaic literary tradition note that it frequently develops concepts through this oppositional dualism; the Old Testament has innumerable examples, including the initial verses of Genesis contrasting form and the void, the waters and the air, water and land, day and night, man and woman, obedience to God and sin. A popular creationist writer, Francis A. Schaeffer, states, "The basic [presupposition] was that there really are such things as absolutes ... in the area of Being (or knowledge), and in the area of morals.... Absolutes imply antithesis ... right and wrong, ... true and false.... Historic Christianity stands on the basis of antithesis" (Schaeffer 1968, pp. 14-15). Thus the creationist's commitment to Scripture molds his thinking toward a disposition to perceive everything in terms of opposing absolutes, an opposition in which God must have an Adversary and creationism its antithesis—evolution.

Scientific Creationism and Science

The essential and overwhelming difference between scientific creationists and evolutionists is the difference between the basic postulates of the two positions. The creationist accepts the accuracy of the Bible *a priori*. Observations must be wrestled with until they can be fitted to the biblical statements. Geological phenomena such as rock strata and fossils *must* be evidence of the Noachian flood, since evidence *should* be out there and the Bible describes no other event so likely to leave such massive deposits. New species cannot have arisen by mutation and natural selection, because the Bible states that God created each kind of organism. The Bible describes human lifespans of hundreds of years, which add up to several thousand years, but nowhere does the Bible state that there have been ages of millions or billions of years. The Bible tells us of degeneration from a primeval Eden and promises us the possibility of eventual redemption, but present circumstances prove the world is still within the degenerative phase, though the Second Coming may well be nigh. In each case, the creationist has argued *deductively* from his postulate that the biblical statement is true. Bacon is famous for promoting the superiority of *inductive* reasoning as the mode of science, and the Scottish Realists championed induction of general principles from observational data, but the scientific creationists cannot be said to proceed inductively.

It is generally held that the foundational principle of science, including evolutionary theories and in contrast to creationism, is independence from any conscious *a priori* commitment. Ideally, the scientist should make observations on what are postulated to be related phenomena and then should construct an explanation solely from the observations. Of course, scientists' minds are not blanks, so in fact they shift between hypotheses (*if* statements), observations, refined hypotheses, more observations, and progressively more satisfying explanations, endeavoring throughout to recognize and scrupulously examine *a priori* assumptions. One test of good scientific work is the care with which *a priori* constraints have been excluded from the gathering of observational data and the formulation of explanatory hypotheses. Scientific creationists may appear to follow Baconian scientific methodology—they make observations, they organize the data, they offer explanations for them—but they deny themselves the possibility of working in the *spirit* of science when they insist that their conclusions cannot validly contradict their reading of Scripture.

More broadly, science today differs from scientific creationism in its philosophy of knowledge. For half a century scientists have acknowledged that our formulations of patterns and categories are heavily influenced by the conventions of our languages and cultural traditions. It is impossible for any human to think free of such conventional molding, though great minds may break through to a degree and shift boundaries and links of concepts.

In 1929 the philosopher Alfred North Whitehead published an exposition of the arbitrariness of our descriptions of the world. Whitehead saw that what we categorize as discrete events or objects are part of a process, a flux, that we break up by our nouns and verb tenses in order to grasp what, to our purposes, may be significant aspects. We impose gaps on the continuity of reality by labeling this segment of experience a tree, that a sparrow, this a birthday cake, that an electron impulse. In 1962 Thomas Kuhn demonstrated that not only is experience artificially broken up into these categories, but the categories are conventionally patterned into, as he termed it, paradigms. Classical astronomers categorized experiential observation into stars, planets, sun, moon, and so on, and then constructed a pattern of relationships of these concepts whereby the earth was the stable center of the universe. Copernicus and his followers accepted the classical categories but shifted the pattern so that the sun was seen as the center of the universe. Modern astronomers have invented new categories with their quasars and black holes, and have further shifted the pattern so that our sun is a minor star in a universe with no center at all. Kuhn's particular contribution was to argue that none of the earlier theories of relationships was wrong, but rather that the accumulation of new observations (experiences) strained the conventional categories and patterns until they no longer seemed to contain the data satisfactorily. During the period of strain, a powerful thinker such as Copernicus or Einstein reconstructs a paradigm.

The lesson we should learn from the history of science, according to Kuhn and other philosophers of science such as Stephen Toulmin or Imre Lakatos, is that our knowledge is partial, biased by conventions, and likely to be severely readjusted in the generations to come. Kuhn and his fellows do not see this as cause for despair, but as an exciting challenge, an infinite set of wonderful puzzles. Many of the most satisfying puzzles concern the nature of life and its history on earth: Evolution.

Scientific creationists are disturbed by the view of reality as flux, of experience as process, of proof as conditional upon time and culture, of truth as an abstract ideal, and of certainty as beyond human grasp. They can only feel comfortable in a world of absolutes. Dr. Gary Parker, a biologist on the staff of the Institute for Creation Research, testified that he had accepted evolution until he published a programmed instruction textbook on biology. "I knew what went into it, all the doubts and last minute changes; the whole thing was a collection of uncertainties and incomplete knowledge. Beforehand, I thought that if something was printed, some scholar had written it, but now I was suddenly struck by the reality that 'people who write books don't know any more about the world than I do!' . . . 'Where, then, do I put my trust?' . . . Science can't be trusted, but God can. . . . Scientific data is [sic] so permanently incomplete that it's hardly a good place to sink an anchor for anything having to do with eternity" (Parker 1978). Francis Schaeffer had the answer to Parker's crisis, "The Christian world view . . . [has] the certainty of something 'there'—an objective reality—for science to examine. What we seem to observe is . . . a real world which is there to study objectively. Another result of the Christian base was that the world was worth finding out about, for in doing so one was investigating God's creation. And people were free to investigate nature. . . . God himself had told mankind to have dominion over nature" (Schaeffer 1976, p. 140). Parker could not accept a world of flux; he needed to see stability, a world of fixed authority. "That's what the whole evolution-creation controversy boils down to: Whom are you going to trust?" he concluded (Parker 1978).

Conditioned to think in antitheses and absolutes, scientific creationists like to debate evolutionists. They make the points that (1) the fossil record shows no transitional forms between kinds of organisms; (2) geologic strata and fossils are tautologically dated by means of each other; (3) the statistical probability of life arising from non-living matter, or of more complex forms mutating viably from less complex, is extremely low; and (4) modern experiments and observations have failed to document the evolution of one kind of organism into another.

Evolutionists who agree to debate creationists find that the first point rests on creationists' rejection of the term *species* as imprecise and the substitution for it of the King James Bible word *kind*, which by creationists' definition is a group of organisms that do not mutate or vary into another group: Creationists recognize variation *within* kind in adaptation to environment, but evolution *from* one kind into another is made impossible by their interpretation of Genesis—and, of course, by their definition of kind. Biostratigraphers have countered the second point by noting that it is based on a common misunderstanding of the methods of their discipline. Furthermore, chronometric dating methods provide independent support of age estimates based on rock or fossil order. Creationists reply that chronometric datings are based on false assumptions of uniformity in natural processes. In fact, while uniformity was the initial working hypothesis for the development of chronometric methods, the methods are constantly being refined to account for variations in rate through time of the processes studied. For the third point, evolutionists reply that statistically low probabilities are not impossibilities, especially considering the billions of years and uncountable plentitude of molecules and organisms in earth's history. The fourth point is merely a restatement of the first, and like it rests entirely on the creationists' usage of the colloquial term *kind*, which incidentally comes from the same Indo-European root as the Latin word *genus*. Biologists recognize hundreds of well-documented observations and experiments of evolutionary change between species, but creationists insist these are only instances of variation within kind, the interpretation required by their *a priori* postulate that evolution of one kind into another cannot occur.

A final creationist point is seldom taken seriously by evolutionists: The usual stratification in rock series—nonreptilian or mammalian marine life in the lower strata, reptiles above, and mammals (the most intelligent forms of life) highest—represents the presence of fish in the sea of the Noachian flood, slow-moving reptiles caught first by the rising waters, and the most intelligent organisms taking refuge, futilely, on the highest peaks and ridges.

On a more general plane, scientific creationists argue that the Second Law of Thermodynamics invalidates evolution. Nineteenth century physics describes thermodynamics, or heat energy, as having three important properties: the capability of converting heat energy into mechanical work, the tendency of heat energy to transfer from hotter to colder bodies, and the availability of energy for work. Because in our universe the thermal energy of hot bodies such as stars is dissipated into their surrounding cold interstellar space, the amount of thermal energy available for conversion into work tends to lessen, although the total amount of thermodynamic energy in the universe (converted and nonconverted) is constant. Description of thermodynamics under three universal laws was typical of mid-nineteenth century physics: strongly Realist, searching for First Principles, naive about language conventions such as the ancient predilection for the magic number three. Scientific creationists insist that the Second Law's descriptive (and probabilistic) statement that energy *tends* to be dissipated is an authoritative rule stating that all energy *is* dissipated. Thus the harnessing of energy by increasingly complex organisms (their definition of evolution) is impossible because it is contrary to this universal law. Most evolutionists simply dismiss the Second Law of Thermodynamics as irrelevant to the central questions of their field because it deals with closed systems and does not preclude local build-ups of more highly organized energy in open systems; but both Teilhard de Chardin and the respected American anthropologist Leslie White focussed on the Second Law as a *proof* of the validity of evolution. White believed that this law expressed the conditions in which evolution occurred, with evolution as a powerful cumulative force reversing the otherwise general tendency for energy to be dissipated. The way in which creationists invoke the Second Law of Thermodynamics is consistent with their mid-nineteenth century version of science, in contrast to contemporary science.

Scientific creationists' fondness for debate is disconcerting to evolutionists, who are unaccustomed to a world of such absolutes and antitheses. Most scientists today consider forensic debate an improper forum for discussing scientific matters, polarizing opinion rather than resolving differences. Evolutionists who do overcome their reluctance to debate speak from their world of puzzles, flux, and uncertainty; they speak of hypotheses rather than Truth, of validity rather than proof. As the philosophers put it, creationists and evolutionists are in different universes of discourse. Scientific creationists talk of facts and physical laws as if the former were objective entities and the latter authoritative, while evolutionists consider facts to be data of experience and scientific laws to be descriptions of probability. Most basically, creationists argue deductively from Scripture while scientists attempt to draw conclusions inductively from observations.

Scientific creationists are living fossils from a bygone era of science. Their postulates and terminology are archaic, which befits thinking rooted in a seventeenth century literature and an eighteenth century philosophy. They can claim to be scientists today only because the public allows those who practice the methodology of science to use the title, regardless of whether they accept the impropriety of *a priori* axioms. In the final analysis, the claim of scientific creationists to science is a red herring insofar as they insist that the real issue is that both creationism and evolutionism are faiths. Their debates are designed to cause hearers to doubt the foundations of one faith, evolutionism, and thereby become receptive to another, their narrowly orthodox Protestant Christianity. They are really attempting to prepare the way for the apocalyptic advent of the returned Messiah. Their business is more properly with theologians, and they engage scientists only through their own reasoning that apparent confirmation of scriptural statements on creation is confirmation of God's promise of redemption through Christ.

The Appeal of Scientific Creationism

Scientific creationists do not form a single sect, but they tend to be found among the most conservative Baptists, Lutherans, Presbyterians, Episcopalians, Methodists, and Seventh-Day Adventists, as well as in the more strongly fundamentalist churches. Many are engineers or scientists employed by business. While scientific creationism is prominent in the South and in southern California, it is also strong in the Midwest and has been active in some eastern states, such as New York, and in Canada. As the membership of the Creation Research Society and concurring churches indicates, the movement is attractive to college-educated, middle-class professional men deeply concerned about their families and country and disturbed by the threats they see to these institutions. America must be strong, the family must be strong, the men—college-trained, middle-class—on whose shoulders these institutions are borne must be strong. Where can they find the strength?

Pastor Brien of the independent Greendale Baptist Church in Milwaukee finds his fundamentalist congregation attracting people "needing a sense of direction. People feel their lives are going nowhere; people realize that they're flubbing. . . . They really have a sense of needing God in their lives, they can't make it alone." David O. Moberg, a sociologist of religion at Marquette University and an active, widely-traveled evangelical Baptist, like Brien, sees the search for "an aid in solving life's problems" to be a basic human need through which many have been converted to fundamentalist beliefs. These seekers for guidance are not materially impoverished or alienated; they do not want to change the external circumstances of their lives. What they have had has been good: They want to conserve it, deepen it, strengthen it, confirm its goodness. They want to protect their wives and children so that these loved ones will receive the rewarding life. Change can be threatening.

Evolution is change, adaptation to new circumstances. Evolutionists see a world of process, of flux, incomplete, imperfectly known. This is a world in which free-thinkers, nonconformists, adventurers can feel at home; it is not a world designed to comfort the bourgeoisie. A middle-class man from a strict Christian background may recognize the world of evolution as degenerate, not a world in which a good husband and father would place his family. If such a man has been educated, he has been shown how to reason from facts. He has perceived a world dominated by evolutionary ideas to be a world where sexual immorality, divorce, crime, and American defeat have been visibly increasing. These are problems that beset the bourgeoisie. The good man looks for help, for support. He will not find his support in late twentieth century evolutionary theory, negating, as it seems, the security of an infallible Book and rejecting the pre-Darwinian opposition of degeneration and Utopia.

Scientific creationism does offer support to the sincere, hardworking, disciplined head of a family. It works in conjunction with the local congregational community and its pastor, who provide a sheltering social environment and fraternal counsel. The rightness of this way of life is upheld by the authority of God and the document of revelations, the Bible. Anxiety is stilled once a man has turned the direction of his life over to God speaking through Scripture and appearing in Jesus. Doubt disappears before the vigor and beatitude of the spokesmen for creationism (Charles Roessger, a Milwaukee creationist, describes Henry Morris of the Institute for Creation Research as "the most loving, most kind, a walking saint"). Against the nebulousness of modern process philosophy and situational ethics, these fundamentalists declare "God has created a real, external world" (Schaeffer 1968, p. 28) "and it has form and order" (Schaeffer 1972, p. 5). Absolutes, black-and-white antitheses, truth, certainty, the strength that comes with freedom from nagging doubt and indecision, these are the rewards of the concerned citizen who makes the one leap of faith, that of receiving Jesus into his heart and plain sense as his guide.

Creationism is a beacon into a protected harbor. However naive and irrational it may appear to persons who enjoy confidence in their own judgment of morality and worth, who relish the intellectual puzzles of relativity, creationism can be an integral part of a doctrine of hope for many anxious citizens. Unhappily for nonbelievers, its proponents are determined to guard their children and hold out salvation to others by demanding that the creationist conceptualization of the world and man's nature be taught as a scientifically valid model in tax-supported public schools and museums. A small but energetic, well-organized, and politically sophisticated set of Christians who have found at least mundane redemption from anxiety are seeking to purge the world of every belief except their own rigid scriptural fundamentalism.

NOTE

The use of "men" rather than "persons" is deliberate in this paper. Men appear as the leaders and proselytizers of scientific creationism. This dominance of men conforms to fundamentalist interpretation of scriptural statements on the proper roles of the sexes, and is also a byproduct of the Creation Research Society's requirement that voting members have earned an advanced degree in a science—far fewer women than men can meet this requirement. The Institute for Creation Research did appoint a woman, Dr. Jean Sloat Morton, to its Technical Advisory Board in 1979.

REFERENCES

Bird, Wendell R. "Freedom of Religion and Science Instruction in Public Schools." *Yale Law Journal* 87 (1978):515-570.
———. "Freedom from Establishment and Unneutrality in Public School Instruction and Religious School Regulation." *Harvard Journal of Law and Public Policy* 2 (1979):125-205.

Bredesen, Harald. "Anatomy of a Confrontation." *Journal of the American Scientific Affiliation* 23 (1971):146-149.

Christianity Today. "Evangelical Christianity in the United States—National Parallel Surveys of General Public and Clergy." Manuscript report of poll by the Gallup Organization, Inc., and the Princeton Religion Research Center for *Christianity Today*, 1980.

Gish, Duane T. *Evolution: The Fossils Say NO!* 3rd ed. San Diego: Creation-Life Publishers, 1978.

Kuhn, Thomas S. *The Structure of Scientific Revolutions.* Chicago: University of Chicago Press, 1962.

——. "Reflections on my Critics." In *Criticism and the Growth of Knowledge,* edited by Imre Lakatos and Alan Musgrave, pp. 2-27. Cambridge: Cambridge University Press, 1970.

Morris, Henry M. *Scientific Creationism.* San Diego: Creation-Life Publishers, 1974.

——. *The Troubled Waters of Evolution.* San Diego: Creation-Life Publishers, 1975.

Parker, Gary. "Evolution: My Religion." *Today's Student* (Ames, Iowa) 2, no. 11 (1978):n.p.

Schaeffer, Francis A. *The God Who Is There.* Downers Grove, Ill.: Inter-Varsity Press, 1968.

——. *He Is There and He Is Not Silent.* Wheaton, Ill.: Tyndale House Publishers, 1972.

——. *How Shall We Then Live?* Old Tappan, N.J.: Fleming H. Revell, 1976.

Whitehead, Alfred N. *Process and Reality.* London: Allen and Unwin and Macmillan, 1929.

SUGGESTED READINGS

Acts and Facts. Institute for Creation Research, El Cajon, California.

Barbour, Ian G. *Christianity and the Scientist.* New York: Association Press, 1960.

——, ed. *Science and Religion.* New York: Harper and Row, 1968.

——. *Myths, Models and Paradigms.* New York: Harper and Row, 1974.

Bible-Science Newsletter. Bible-Science Association, Minneapolis, Minnesota.

Bozeman, Theodore D. *Protestants in an Age of Science.* Chapel Hill: University of North Carolina Press, 1977.

British Broadcasting Corporation. *Science and Religion.* Reprint. Freeport, N.Y.: Books for Libraries Press, 1969.

Bube, Richard H., ed. *The Encounter Between Christianity and Science.* Grand Rapids, Mich.: William B. Eerdmans, 1968.

Cauthen, Kenneth. *Science, Secularization and God.* Nashville: Abingdon Press, 1969.

Coffin, Harold G. *Creation: Accident or Design?* Washington, D.C.: Review and Herald Publishing Association, 1969.

Cotton, Edward H., ed. *Has Science Discovered God?* Reprint. Freeport, New York: Books for Libraries Press, 1968.

Creation Research Society Quarterly. Creation Research Society, Ann Arbor, Michigan.

Darrow, Floyd L. *Through Science to God*. Indianapolis: The Bobbs-Merrill Company, 1925.

Davidheiser, Bolton. *Evolution and Christian Faith*. Nutley, N.J.: Presbyterian and Reformed Publishing Company, 1969.

Gatewood, Willard B., Jr. *Preachers, Pedagogues and Politicians*. Chapel Hill: University of North Carolina Press, 1966.

Gerstner, John H. "Theological Boundaries: The Reformed Perspective." In *The Evangelicals*, edited by David F. Wells and John D. Woodbridge, pp. 21–37. Grand Rapids, Mich.: Baker Book House, 1977.

Harris, Errol E. *Revelation Through Reason*. New Haven: Yale University Press, 1958.

Hovenkamp, Herbert. *Science and Religion in America 1800–1860*. Philadelphia: University of Pennsylvania Press, 1978.

Jeeves, Malcolm A., ed. *The Scientific Enterprise and Christian Faith*. Downers Grove, Ill.: Inter-Varsity Press, 1969.

Journal of the American Scientific Affiliation. Elgin, Ill.: American Scientific Affiliation.

Keen, William W. *I Believe in God and in Evolution*. Philadelphia: J. B. Lippincott Company, 1922.

Klotz, John W. *Genes, Genesis and Evolution*. 2d ed. St. Louis: Concordia Publishing House, 1970.

Kuhn, Thomas S. "Reflections on my Critics." In *Criticism and the Growth of Knowledge*, edited by Imre Lakaros and Alan Musgrave, pp. 231–278. Cambridge: Cambridge University Press, 1970.

Lammerts, Walter E., ed. *Why Not Creation?* Nutley, N.J.: Presbyterian and Reformed Publishing Company, 1970.

Layton, Edwin T., Jr., ed. *Technology and Social Change in America*. New York: Harper and Row, Publishers, 1973.

Lakatos, Imre, and Musgrave, Alan. *Criticism and the Growth of Knowledge*. Cambridge: Cambridge University Press, 1970.

Lee, Harold N. *Percepts, Concepts and Theoretic Knowledge*. Memphis: Memphis State University Press, 1973.

Marsh, Frank L. *Evolution, Creation and Science*. Washington, D.C.: Review and Herald Publishing Association, 1947.

Mascall, E. L. *Christian Theology and Natural Science*. London: Longmans, Green and Company, Limited, 1956.

Moore, John N. *Questions and Answers on Creation/Evolution*. Grand Rapids: Baker Book House, 1976.

Nelkin, Dorothy. *Science Textbook Controversies and the Politics of Equal Time*. Cambridge: M.I.T. Press, 1977.

Noble, David F. *America by Design*. New York: Alfred A. Knopf, 1979.

Nogar, Raymond J., O.P. *The Wisdom of Evolution*. Garden City, N.Y.: Doubleday and Company, 1963.

O'Brien, John A. *God and Evolution*. Notre Dame, Ind.: University of Notre Dame Press, 1961.

O'Connell, Patrick, B. D. *Science of Today and the Problems of Genesis*. Hawthorne, Calif.: Christian Book Club of America, 1969.

Ong, Walter J., S.J. *Darwin's Vision and Christian Perspectives*. New York: Macmillan, 1960.

Origins Research. Students for Origins Research, Goleta, California.

Patten, Donald W., ed. *Symposium on Creation II.* Grand Rapids, Mich.: Baker Book House, 1970.

Peacocke, A. R. *Science and the Christian Experiment.* London: Oxford University Press, 1971.

——. *Creation and the World of Science.* Oxford: Clarendon Press, 1979.

Rahner, Karl, S. J. "Die Christologie Innerhalb Einer Evolutiven Weltanschauung." *Schriften zur Theologie* 5 (1962):183-221.

Raven, Charles E. *Science, Religion and the Future.* Cambridge: Cambridge University Press, 1943.

Ryan, Bernard, F. S. C. *The Evolution of Man.* London: Sands and Company, Publishers, Limited, 1965.

Shipley, Maynard. *The War on Modern Science.* New York: Alfred A. Knopf, 1927.

Smethurst, Arthur F. *Modern Science and Christian Beliefs.* New York: Abingdon Press, 1955.

Teilhard de Chardin, Pierre, S. J. *The Phenomenon of Man.* New York: Harper and Brothers, 1959.

Thorpe, W. H. *Purpose in a World of Chance.* Oxford: Oxford University Press, 1978.

Toulmin, Stephen E. *Human Understanding.* Princeton: Princeton University Press, 1972.

White, Leslie A. *The Evolution of Culture.* New York: McGraw-Hill, 1959.

Zimmerman, Paul A. *Rock Strata and the Bible Record.* St. Louis: Concordia, 1970.

Anatomy of a Controversy: Halstead vs. the British Museum (Natural History)

STEVEN D. SCHAFERSMAN
Texas Council for Science Education
Houston, Texas

Introduction

"Science is a human enterprise." This statement can serve as a rallying cry for those scientists who maintain that a scientist's job is just as exciting and fulfilling as that of an artist, a senator, or any other professional. It is sometimes used to justify the view that human cultural and social factors external to both scientific method and empirical evidence are very important in scientific discovery and in the initiation and success of new scientific theories. And it helps us to understand and excuse the intense competition and bitter controversy that periodically erupts among scientists (whom a large segment of the public falsely perceives as individuals quietly doing their work in a spirit of cooperation and unity of purpose). This reading examines a particular scientific controversy that involves all of the above. To anyone working in the disciplines of evolutionary paleontology and biosystematics, this controversy is fascinating and deserves the attention of a wide audience. The issues involved in this controversy bear not merely on our understanding of evolutionary science, but also on the history and philosophy of science, and the relationship between science and society.

In 1972, the Trustees of the British Museum (Natural History) responded to a report criticizing the existing natural history displays as static and uninformative by proposing that major changes be made (Miles 1978a). By 1973 the various scientific departments of the Museum had prepared documents outlining plans for new exhibits that would more clearly present the notion that life is dynamic and changing. These new displays would emphasize evolution and evolutionary relationships. The primary goal was to diffuse knowledge to the general public, since it had been found that few people visiting the Museum had actually learned anything from the visit. The Public Services Department, headed by R. S. Miles, was created in 1975 to implement the new exhibition scheme. Its efforts led to one of the most bitter controversies in the history of the British Museum.

186

The person who led the attack on the new exhibits was L. B. Halstead of the Departments of Zoology and Geology, University of Reading. In 1978 he published a short note criticizing the new policies and new exhibits on a number of points (Halstead 1978a). First, he claimed that the Public Services Department seemed anxious to go ahead with the exhibits "in spite of serious opposition from the scientific side of the Museum." Halstead provided no evidence to support this assertion, and in a brief reply, Miles (1978b) simply denied such a dichotomy of purpose. But Halstead objected to the displays on other grounds, although at that time he did not spell them out in detail. He simply wondered whether "it is an appropriate role for a national museum to be concerned with aspects of social engineering by promoting concepts that happen to be current in the present climate of opinion," claiming that such a role would contribute "to the indoctrination of the more inarticulate sections of the community." In his equally concise and cryptic reply, Miles remarked that "it is astonishingly naive for anyone to suppose the existence of such a thing as theory-free observation," and that it "is unreasonable to expect all visitors to a public museum to provide their own conceptual structures." One would have to read between these lines to discern what was really meant, and in fact the significance of the exchange between Halstead and Miles was lost to all but a few enlightened individuals. As we shall see, two years were to pass before the true issues in this controversy would be brought out into the open.

Cladistics

Shortly following this brief exchange, Halstead attacked in another direction. The subject was a special session of the 26th Symposium of Vertebrate Palaeontology and Comparative Anatomy at the University of Reading. The session was devoted to *cladistics*—a school of evolutionary reconstruction and taxonomy that departs methodologically from traditional evolutionary systematics. As we will see later, the new exhibits would use cladistics to teach hypothesis formulation in evolutionary reconstruction. In a review paper, Halstead (1978b) expressed severe doubts about the appropriateness of cladistics for determining taxonomic relationships and understanding evolutionary history. In particular, he objected to cladism's rejection of certain taxonomic practices traditionally used in working out phylogenetic relationships: grade classification, ancestor recognition, and adaptive explanation. Unfortunately, Halstead's adverse criticism revealed some basic confusion about cladistic goals, methods, and assumptions. Rather than present cogent reasons to demonstrate why cladistic theory and practice are poorly conceived, Halstead merely asserted his own dogmatic and largely traditional taxonomic beliefs (Halstead 1978b, p. 760):

> *Major evolutionary events can best be understood in terms of major structural grades. . . . If it were possible to trace the ancestry of man back in time to a rhipidistian fish then the entire sequence of stages would be by definition a single monophyletic species [and] most zoologists and palaeontologists would surely accept the reasonableness of dividing such a lineage into a number of arbitrary divisions. . . . Evolution is a gradual process that takes place through time and man simply imposes on it his own arbitrary system of classification.*

All of these statements are highly debatable; many taxonomists (and all cladists) would agree that they are false. Halstead presented these statements as conclusions backed by scientific consensus, when in fact they are assumptions that are being increasingly rejected by modern systematists. Halstead concluded his review by remarking that cladists adhere to their theory and methodology with "religious fervour and are already entrenched in some of the major museums in the world." He thought that it would be a "severe error of judgement" if the new evolution exhibits in the Natural History Museum were organized to show relationships solely by means of cladograms, omitting traditional charts showing stratigraphic distribution and ancestral-descendant relationships (see Figure 1 in the Appendix to this reading). In this manner Halstead's critique began to center on specific theoretical issues, and the disagreements sparking his initial antagonism began to merge.

Why would a modern biosystematist such as L. B. Halstead attack cladistics in such strong terms? To answer this question we must first review the theoretical bases of opposing schools of evolutionary reconstruction. Cladistics is a relatively new taxonomic theory and method of classification that attempts to construct hierarchies of "sister groups" that reveal the relative order of branching in evolutionary history. Sister groups are two taxa hypothesized to share an ancestral species not shared by any other taxon; that is, a sister group is a species or higher monophyletic taxon hypothesized to be the closest genealogical relative of another species or higher taxon. Cladistics is often called a method of searching for sister groups rather than for ancestors. The phenomenon of branching or splitting in evolutionary history is formally termed *cladogenesis*; thus, a speciation event is a cladogenetic event. Both the terms cladistics and cladogenesis are derived from the term *clade*, which is a synonym for monophyletic taxon. A monophyletic taxon is a group of organisms (a species or group of species) that exists in nature as a result of a unique history of evolution (shared common ancestry). *All* organisms sharing this history are members of the taxon. It is also possible to recognize paraphyletic taxa (those omitting some members that share the unique evolutionary history) and polyphyletic taxa (those combining members of two or more unique evolutionary histories). These latter taxa are not clades, but are often grades characterized by adaptive similarities (see Figure 2 in the Appendix). Cladistics attempts to avoid them in classifications.

It is common knowledge that all organisms in nature exist as groups within groups. This empirical hierarchical arrangement of nested groups is one of the fundamental expressions of the evolutionary process and is one of the best pieces of evidence for the occurrence of evolution. The purpose of cladistics is to analyze these groups, correctly recognize them as clades, and thereby infer the genealogical evolutionary history that produced the groups. From this history, expressed most simply as a cladogram showing the sequence of branching among sister groups, a classification is directly and unambiguously derived. Most of the theory and methodology of cladistics are directed toward constructing hypothetical but rigorous cladograms capable of being falsified or corroborated. To do this, one analyzes the presence or absence of shared derived characters among the taxa of interest, and this results in a cladogram susceptible to testing. The utilization of shared derived characters alone among all the characters available for any taxon is a distinguishing characteristic of cladistics, because all other taxonomic methods also utilize ancestral characters and uniquely derived characters. In taxonomy, there are two concepts of similarity or relationship: (1) genealogical or genetic relationship, and (2) resemblance or phenetic relationship. Phenetic relationship, based on overall appearance or similarity, is not a rigorous criterion on which to build an evolutionary classification, because convergence can increase phenetic similarity sufficiently to confound its reflection of genetic relationship. Cladistics makes use of the fact that speciation, the branching mode of evolution, creates new taxonomic characters; the degree to which these newly derived characters are shared among the taxa determines their sequence on a cladogram and position in a classification. Thus, although explicit ancestors and descendants never enter the picture, a cladistic classification is a purely genealogical classification based solely on the relative recency of common ancestry. Noncladistic taxonomic methods utilize phenetic relationship as the sole or additional criterion in the construction of classifications. The theory and methodology of cladistics is logically simple and straightforward, but as with all things involving living organisms, complications quickly enter and both theory and practice can become complex. Today a large literature exists explaining cladistic methodology (Cracraft and Eldredge 1979; Eldredge and Cracraft 1980; Nelson and Platnick 1981; Wiley 1981; Duncan and Stuessy 1984).

Cladistic taxonomy is opposed by *evolutionary taxonomy*, although the name of the latter is misleading, since both taxonomies can be explicitly based on evolution. The widespread acceptance of evolutionary taxonomy is a consequence of the success of the synthetic theory of evolution. The two primary exponents of evolutionary taxonomy are George Gaylord Simpson (1961) and Ernst Mayr (1969), two of the foremost architects of the synthetic theory. Mayr (1981) has recently reviewed the modern evolutionary taxonomist position. Evolutionary taxonomy has been immensely influential and was for many years practiced and endorsed by the leading taxonomists, although this status is changing.

To explain why evolutionary taxonomy differs from cladistic taxonomy, I must first explain that there are three modes of evolutionary change, and that cladogenesis is only one of them. The other two are stasigenesis (stasis, equilibrium, or no change) and anagenesis (more or less gradual, progressive, or continuous change without splitting or branching). It is currently a matter of debate among cladists whether or not anagenesis can result in the creation of derived characters. Apparently some cladists do not believe anagenesis occurs in higher taxa at all, claiming that the observed progressive change visible in either the fossil record or among hierarchical groups of living organisms is the result of accumulated cladogenetic change, that is, the selection of species through time (see Eldredge, this volume).

The occurrence and relative importance of anagenesis is irrelevant to cladistic taxonomy; but evolutionary taxonomy considers anagenesis to be as important as cladogenesis, and its method of phylogenetic inference and classification allows taxonomic units to be constructed based on either. For example, evolutionary taxonomy allows gradually evolving single lineages to be subdivided arbitrarily into different species that are phenetically different. Evolutionary taxonomy considers grades to be as important as clades, and major taxonomic divisions are often made using grade criteria. The degree or amount of evolutionary divergence (anagenesis) of the branches (clades) following a speciation event is considered to be as important for taxonomic purposes as the speciation event is itself. Evolutionary taxonomy recognizes incompletely monophyletic taxa (that is, paraphyletic taxa) as valid. It permits explicit identification of ancestral taxa, especially paraphyletic supraspecific ancestral taxa, in genealogy construction, and allows adaptive explanations and evolutionary rates to be inferred for phylogenetic reconstruction. Finally, evolutionary taxonomy uses *both* genealogical and phenetic similarity to determine taxonomic relationships. Overall similarity of the taxa of interest is considered important because evolutionary taxonomy wishes to analyze and classify organisms on the basis of all genetic relationships, and evolutionary taxonomists believe that a taxon's phenotype is a suitable reflection of its genotype for taxonomic purposes. To the cladist, all this flexibility introduces an undesirable ambiguity into the process of generating hypotheses about evolutionary relationships.

The evolutionary taxonomist allows grades to assume the same taxonomic status as clades and phenetic similarities to assume the same importance as genealogical similarities because evolutionary taxonomy is implicitly derived from the synthetic theory of evolution. In effect, the synthetic theory of evolution must be assumed valid for evolutionary taxonomy to work. Only if the mechanism or process of evolution is known is it possible to assume that phenotype adequately reflects genotype, that evolutionary divergence along branches is taxonomically significant, and that it is possible to recognize supraspecific ancestors and grades. In contrast, cladistic taxonomy is based solely on the *fact* of evolution, not on any specific *theory* of evolution. If evolution occurs, then taxa split from evolving lineages (just as offspring split from parents), and new taxa are recognized and classified by derived characters. Cladistics assumes or requires nothing about mechanisms of speciation, evolutionary progression along grades, adaptive value of phenetic features, relationship between genotype and phenotype, or the possibility of recognizing ancestors (Platnick 1977; Gaffney 1979). Cladistics does not claim that these issues are unimportant, only that cladistics will work whether or not they are addressed. The major cladist criticism of evolutionary taxonomy is that it requires a great deal of detailed knowledge about evolution in order to work, and, lacking that, it must assume the truth of much that it really does not know. Evolutionary taxonomy is more of an art than a science, something freely admitted by evolutionary taxonomists themselves. The original objective of the man who invented cladistics, Willi Hennig (1966), was to give taxonomy a scientific legitimacy it had always lacked. This goal continues to motivate cladistic taxonomists in their work.

Cladistics has undergone a considerable metamorphosis since 1966, when it was first introduced to taxonomists in the United States. Because of the advocacy and stimulating writings of a number of museum taxonomists in the United States, England, and the rest of Europe, many of its original tenets have been examined, changed, and improved (Platnick 1980; Patterson 1980a). The theoretical basis of cladistics is noticeably stronger than a decade ago, and its adoption by increasing numbers of taxonomists reveals that a major revolution is occurring within biosystematics. In fact, cladistic taxonomy is only one facet of a new research program, *phylogenetic systematics*, which is competing against the traditional and still strong research program of evolutionary systematics. *Phylogenetic systematics* includes the new "phylogenetic" and "vicariance historical biogeographies" (Nelson and Rosen 1981; Wiley 1981) and, naturally enough, is critical of the synthetic theory of evolution. Evolutionary systematics has wholeheartedly adopted the synthetic theory and embraces the classic "dispersalist historical biogeography" (Darlington 1957) as well as evolutionary taxonomy.

These two opposing research programs are distinguished by two major factors. First, phylogenetic systematics is not wedded to any particular evolutionary theory, whereas evolutionary systematics is tied to the synthetic theory. For example, vicariance biogeography is founded on the analysis of geographic patterns in the form of area cladograms and the degree of congruence with taxon cladograms. Dispersalist biogeography, on the other hand, requires the same assumptions about the evolutionary process as does evolutionary taxonomy to explain dispersal from centers of origin and resulting cosmopolitan or disjunct distributions. For example, Briggs (1981), an evolutionary systematist, states that, "If species do not become regularly dispersed from centers of origin, then our general concept of how evolution works at the organismal level will have to be changed" (p. 307).

I am not suggesting that the synthetic theory is wrong, only that it is untenable for a system of biosystematics to be so closely identified and constrained by a particular evolutionary theory. Taxonomy and biogeography utilize methods that work with empirical data to analyze evolutionary patterns and relationships, and an underlying evolutionary theory, being subject to change, will only generate taxonomic and biogeographic confusion as it does in fact change. For example, the adaptationist program of the synthetic theory is being called into question (Lewontin 1978; Gould and Lewontin 1979; Gould 1980b); what will ultimately happen to all the taxa created and dispersal patterns explained by adaptation to one niche or another? Or, if macroevolution is successfully decoupled from microevolution (Stanley 1979, 1981; Eldredge, this volume; Gould and Eldredge 1977; Gould 1980a), and the origin of the higher taxa is no longer thought of as a simple extrapolation from population genetics, how will paraphyletic ancestral taxa based on grades and higher taxa dispersed from centers of origin be newly interpreted? These possibilities make it imperative that biosystematic theory should be as independent as possible from evolutionary theory. Phylogenetic systematics is clearly preferable to evolutionary systematics in this regard.

The second major distinguishing feature of the two research programs concerns their analytical rigor. Evolutionary systematics utilizes eclectic or intuitive methods in the practice of taxonomy and biogeographical analysis. Narrative explanations involving adaptation, amount of phenetic resemblance, and even subjective degree of evolution are frequently used to explain distribution patterns or taxon differentiation. Since eclectic criteria inherent in narrative explanations are usually arbitrary as well as intuitive, different hypotheses are immune to decisive criticism and thus may be accepted or rejected on the basis of authority. Phylogenetic systematics, on the other hand, makes use of simple analytical methods, hypothetical results of which are accessible to criticism by explicit testing and are judged solely by how parsimonious they are. Arbitrary criteria and authoritarian acceptance simply do not enter in. Thus again phylogenetic systematics is preferable to evolutionary systematics. Some authors have claimed that cladistics is only a formalization of methods that good evolutionary taxonomists have followed intuitively but have not properly acknowledged. There is some validity to this statement, since a few evolutionary taxonomists have occasionally used cladistic methods in an intuitive and nonrigorous manner. But to the cladists this sort of performance hardly constitutes the ideal research program taxonomists should emulate.

Halstead is an evolutionary taxonomist, and it is therefore not surprising that he should criticize cladistic taxonomy (Halstead 1978b); many other evolutionary taxonomists have done so (for example, see Mayr 1976, p. 433). Halstead's critical review was answered by Gardiner et al. (1979), a group of scientists including several taxonomists at the British Museum. They cogently remarked that "Halstead's report reveals several assertions and misunderstandings about aims and methods that were common in the early days of the controversy [between cladists and evolutionary taxonomists]" (p. 175). The arguments between evolutionary and cladistic taxonomists about grades, ancestors, and relationship are pointless because they are generated by fundamentally different assumptions that each group of taxonomists makes about scientific method. From these assumptions, largely philosophical in nature, each taxonomy derives its respective theory, goals, and methods, and since the assumptions each group makes are, in many respects, antithetical, it is no wonder that the resulting taxonomies are radically different. To object to specific aims and methods of cladistic taxonomy because they do not agree with those of evolutionary taxonomy, as Halstead did, is simply to miss the point of the cladists' arguments altogether.

Cladistic taxonomy was initially developed as an attempt to free taxonomy from the subjective, authoritarian, narrative explanations and paraphyletic taxa common in evolutionary taxonomy. It uses shared, derived characters to identify nested groups, and it relies on parsimony (the only nonauthoritarian criterion available) to justify preferred cladograms. It is perhaps understandable that some specialists trained in evolutionary taxonomy would censure such a simple strategy. Nevertheless, the rationale for cladistic taxonomy that Halstead reproves is a scientific imperative with an underlying philosophical derivation: the desire among taxonomists to bring scientific rigor into taxonomy by making taxonomic hypotheses objective and testable by application of logic and empirical evidence. Cladistics undeniably ignores such interesting evolutionary phenomena as anagenesis, stasis, rates of phyletic change, modes of speciation, shifts of adaptive zones, grades, degree of evolutionary divergence, and ancestral-descendant relationships during the procedure of classification construction. But these phenomena are themselves subjects of scientific investigation; and to intermingle inferences from these with a hypothetical classification will only lead to confusion and lack of scientific rigor, and not, as evolutionary taxonomists would claim, to classifications with greater theoretical content.

Furthermore, as phylogenetic systematics matures, evolutionary tempos, modes, and processes will increasingly fall under its purview. But this will happen only to the extent that systematic hypotheses (hypotheses about patterns of evolutionary and biogeographical relationship) can be tested independently of a specific theory of evolution. Of course the resulting corroborated biosystematic hypotheses may then be incorporated into a new or existing evolutionary theory. It is as if, in the words of Gareth Nelson (Patterson 1980a, p. 239), we are "rediscovering preevolutionary systematics." Eldredge and Cracraft (1980) explicitly investigate the relationship between biosystematic pattern and evolutionary process.

L. B. Halstead's antipathy to cladistics is the central motif in his controversy with the British Museum (Natural History); we may term this theme the *taxonomic argument*. But it is only one of three themes in the dispute, and, since it has been and is being debated by numerous other scientists, it is not unique to the present situation. Despite Halstead's objections, the British Museum (Natural History) went ahead and constructed pervasively cladistic exhibits. Knowing this is both relevant and indispensable to understanding the succeeding controversy. But the other two themes in the controversy attracted all the publicity, polemics, and philosophical commentary, and they best serve to reveal the human face behind the scientific mask.

Popper and Evolution

The second theme in the Halstead–British Museum controversy can be called the *philosophy of science argument*. This problem involves Sir Karl Popper, probably the foremost philosopher of science in the world (Magee 1973, 1974). Although Popper has many achievements, his greatest is that he developed a criterion to separate scientific statements from metaphysical and pseudoscientific statements. The basis of his criterion was that scientific statements cannot be proved or verified because proof or verification requires complete knowledge of all possible conditions, causes, and relationships of the subject—knowledge that science just does not possess. Only within disciplines, such as mathematics and logic, possessing defined axioms and constrained possibilities, is it possible to verify or prove something. Science is a method that must utilize empirical evidence, natural materials, and processes manifested in sense data to construct statements about nature; we impose these statements on the world and assume them to be true until they are shown to be otherwise. This fallibilist or tentative scientific truth, always subject to change and improvement, is the reason for science's great success and serves to distinguish science from other knowledge systems claiming absolute truth, such as those based on definition and logic (metaphysics) or intuition, revelation, and authority (theology). Therefore, Popper stated that a scientific statement is recognized by its ability to be empirically tested and falsified, whereas a metaphysical statement, by definition, will not be falsifiable by empirical evidence. Scientific statements, such as theories and hypotheses, that escape falsification despite repeated testing are said to be corroborated, but are never proved or verified. Thus, the best and most rigorous scientific hypotheses are those that are most susceptible to testing and falsification. In Popper's view, science gains knowledge by *falsifying* hypotheses, not by *verifying* hypotheses. Since what are actually tested and falsified are deductions from the hypotheses, this procedure is known as the hypothetico-deductive method. Popper's view of scientific method has become very influential among scientists and philosophers, and some scientists have guided their research programs and their practices of hypothesis formulation by it. The cladists are one such group of scientists.

As discussed earlier, cladistics was explicitly developed by Hennig (1966) to increase the objectivity, testability, and scientific rigor of taxonomy. Therefore, when the cladists discovered that Karl Popper's criterion of scientific demarcation demanded precisely the same qualities for scientific hypotheses that the cladists had already adopted (qualities such as simplicity, testability, direct correspondence between cladogram and classification, and nonarbitrariness), they used Popper's philosophy as additional justification for their new taxonomic theory (Wiley 1975; Platnick and Gaffney 1977, 1978a, 1978b; Gaffney 1979).

At this point, three questions immediately arise: First, does cladistics or any other new scientific method or theory require explicit philosophical justification over and above the scientific explanatory or methodological value it may possess? Second, is it legitimate for scientists to invoke philosophical justification in support of a new theory or method; rather, isn't empirical evidence alone called for? Third, why do the cladists insist on adopting Popper's philosophical views when these views have been severely criticized by other philosophers of science and are in no respect overwhelmingly preferred by the majority of philosophers and scientists? Indeed, it is probable that many scientists have never heard of Popper. Walter Bock (1974) even believes that evolutionary taxonomy better follows Popper's hypothetico-deductive method.

I will answer these questions here, but I cannot adequately justify my answers in the space available. [David Hull, one of the foremost philosophers of biological science, is preparing a book on the cladistic revolution in taxonomy and the cladists' employment of Popper's philosophy (Hull, personal communication, 1981; but see Hull 1980a); undoubtedly he will thoroughly investigate these questions.] First, I fail to see why cladistics needs any philosophical support, for its scientific success will be judged by its ability to provide useful, natural, and predictive classifications of organisms. Any favorable scientific attributes cladistics has over evolutionary taxonomy, whether logical or methodological, will contribute to its increased adoption by taxonomists. Most cladists apparently want the battle judged by philosophy and logic alone (see, for example, Gaffney 1979, p. 79); but it is premature to eliminate external or subjective (sociological, economic, cultural, psychological) factors from our explanations of how science works. Philosophers and historians of science are only now beginning to grapple with such questions, and it is by no means the consensus that scientific knowledge issues forth solely from objective perusal of empirical evidence and straightforward application of logical reasoning and scientific method. Science is a human enterprise, and somewhere in that process our human intellects are involved.

To answer the second question, of course it is legitimate for scientists to invoke philosophical justification for their theories; many scientists, including Darwin, do precisely this. But this does not mean that such justification is wholly logical or epistemological in its support. The philosophy's psychological or sociological impact may be just as important. In fact, we will soon examine an example of just such an effect.

As for the third question, Popper's description of scientific method does indeed support cladistic taxonomy better than evolutionary taxonomy. The cladists have examined Popper's critics to some extent (Platnick and Gaffney 1978b), but they tend to dismiss the criticisms too easily. Popper's critics (Lakatos and Musgrave 1970; Schilpp 1974; Ackermann 1976; Suppe 1977; Mackie 1978; Ziman 1978; Beveridge 1980; Caplan 1981; and, for that matter, all the works of Carnap, Reichenbach, Nagel, Hempel, and a host of other logical empiricists) have much of interest to say, but I will not attempt to deal with the philosophical complexities here. Popper's effort was limited to distinguishing scientific from nonscientific statements. He deliberately avoided such topics as the process of scientific discovery, aspects of creativity, history, intuition, or subjectivism in scientific method, and any attempt to define or understand absolute knowledge ("truth") as distinguished from strictly scientific knowledge. My own view is that Popper's criterion for the demarcation of science is necessary but not sufficient, that falsifiability is as slippery as verifiability, and that there is more to scientific method and reliable knowledge than distinguishing science from metaphysics, as vital as this distinction is.

The discussion of Popper's influence among cladists is a necessary prelude to an examination of the second theme in the controversy of Halstead versus the British Museum. The volumes edited by Schilpp (1974) contained an intellectual autobiography by Popper, later published separately (Popper 1976). In this work, Popper (Schilpp 1974, pp. 134, 137) made the following statements:

> *I have come to the conclusion that Darwinism [in Popper's usage, the synthetic theory of evolution] is not a testable scientific theory, but a* metaphysical *research programme—a possible framework for testable scientific theories.*
>
> *Now to the degree that Darwinism creates the same impression [that an incontrovertible explanation of adaptation has been reached], it is not so much better than the theistic view of adaptation; it is therefore important to show that Darwinism is not a scientific theory, but metaphysical.*

These remarkable statements were met with incredulity by evolutionary scientists. Had they been engaged in *metaphysics* all their working lives? Popper (1963, p. 108) believed that "The evolution of life on earth, or of human society, is a unique historical process," and was thus not repeatable, thus not subject to law, thus not predictable, thus not testable, and thus not scientific. He also believed that natural selection was a tautology. Popper's errors in not perceiving that processes involving unique events can be universal, and thus lawlike and testable, and that natural selection, correctly understood, is not tautologous, were discussed by Michael Ruse (1977) (see also Caplan, this volume). Ruse claimed that "Popper can draw his conclusions only because he is abysmally ignorant of the current status of biological thought." Gerhard Wasserman (1978) also explicitly criticized Popper's assertion that modern evolutionary theory was nontestable and therefore metaphysical. These two papers, at least, quickly led Popper to reconsider his previous statements (Popper 1978, pp. 344–345):

> *The fact that the theory of natural selection is difficult to test has led some people . . . to claim that it is a tautology. . . . I mention this problem*

*because I too belong among the culprits. . . . I have in the past described
the theory as "almost tautological," and I have tried to explain how the
theory of natural selection could be untestable (as is a tautology) and yet
of great scientific interest. My solution was that the doctrine of natural
selection is a most successful metaphysical research programme. . . . I still
believe that natural selection works in this way as a research programme.
Nevertheless, I have changed my mind about the testability and the logical
status of the theory of natural selection; and I am glad to have an opportunity to make a recantation.*

Popper's perspicacious and salutary admission of error should
have ended the matter at once, but it did not. Popper's original views
had already gained a widespread notoriety, and because of his distinguished stature among philosophers of science, many scientists
and nonscientists had already come to believe that evolutionary
theory was untestable and therefore unscientific. The creationists
were especially pleased: They frequently invoked Popper's authority
in their books and magazines by the usual quotations, only this time
not out of context! Popper's 1978 retraction, published in an obscure
philosophical journal, was missed by most scientists, and confusion
persisted for years.

The American cladists Platnick and Gaffney (1978a) evaluated
Popper's views on the untestability of evolutionary theory. They
concluded (p. 140) that Popper was "wrong about the absolute untestability of evolutionary theory itself, [but] right about the untestability of much conventional (narrative) evolutionary biology."
Wassermann (1978) had independently reached the same conclusion.
It should be mentioned that the problem of the theory of evolution's
testability is one that long antedates Popper's 1974 written critique.
Williams (1970, 1973a, 1973b), Ruse (1973), and Hull (1974) had
examined this problem in depth; all concluded that the theory is
testable, and Popper (1978) now agrees.

Some of the English cladists of the British Museum (Natural
History) did not see Popper's retraction and were apparently unaware
of the extensive literature opposing Popper's claim of nontestability.
These cladists therefore took the extraordinary opportunity of constructing the new exhibits in the British Museum (Natural History) to
reflect what they believed to be the new scientific status of evolutionary theory. For example, the British *Creation News Sheet* (cited
in Halstead 1980, p. 215) reported that:

*R. S. Miles, the Head of the Department of Public Services at the British
Museum (Natural History) states that the Museum is preparing a new exhibition on evolution for 1981 and that in this exhibition it will be stated
that evolution is not a scientific theory in the sense that it cannot be tested
and refuted by experiment. Mr. Miles says in his letter that evolution is a*

metaphysical theory but concludes that 'it [nevertheless] has proved to be
of enormous value over the last 100 years in stimulating Man's inquiry into
his origins and those of his fellow creatures.'

Similarly, in his book *Evolution*, published by the British Museum
(Natural History), Colin Patterson wrote (1978, pp. 145-151):

> *If we accept Popper's distinctions between science and nonscience, we*
> *must ask first whether the theory of evolution by natural selection is sci-*
> *entific or pseudo-scientific (metaphysical). . . . Taking the first part of the*
> *theory, that evolution has occurred, it says that the history of life is a single*
> *process of species-splitting and progression . . . like the history of England.*
> *This part of the theory is therefore a historical theory, about unique events,*
> *and unique events are, by definition, not part of science, for they are un-*
> *repeatable and so not subject to test. . . . Turning now to the second aspect*
> *of the theory, that natural selection is the cause of evolution, many critics*
> *have held that this is not scientific because the expression 'survival of the*
> *fittest' makes no predictions except 'what survives is fit,' and so is tautolo-*
> *gous. . . . In this sense, natural selection is not a scientific theory. . . . Using*
> *Popper's criterion, we must conclude that evolutionary theory is not test-*
> *able . . . and not scientific by Popper's standards. . . . Yet today's neo-*
> *Darwinian theory, with all its faults, is still the best we have. It is a fruitful*
> *theory, a stimulus to thought and research, and we should accept it until*
> *someone thinks of a better one.*

In a fascinating essay in *New Scientist*, Halstead (1980a) brought
this unfortunate situation to the attention of the public. After quot-
ing Miles and Patterson, Halstead expressed the following (p. 215):

> *It is evident that Popper's position in all this is central and his influence is*
> *due in no small measure to the extravagant and exaggerated claims made*
> *for his contributions to our understanding of the scientific method. . . .*
> *Popper's pre-eminent position among the philosophers of scientific method*
> *seems to have inhibited many scientists' critical faculties.*

Halstead perceptively and forthrightly recognized an irresponsible
distortion of evolutionary theory that would undoubtedly have a significant impact on innocent museum visitors. He also correctly identified the cause of the distortion: the uncritical acceptance of erroneous philosophical beliefs about evolution by a number of ranking
Museum scientists. The British Museum cladists were not using the
same objective methods to evaluate evolutionary theory as they insisted on using to evaluate taxa. Instead, they apparently based their
conclusions on the authority of a distinguished philosopher.

Unfortunately, Halstead was as unaware as the British Museum
cladists that Popper had corrected his early misunderstanding two
years prior to Halstead's (1980a) article. If he had known of Popper's

1978 paper in *Dialectica*, Halstead could easily have refuted Miles
and Patterson outright. Instead, Halstead went through the motions
of refuting Popper himself, by declaring that Popper's antipathy to
historical sciences such as evolution was due to Popper's intense dis-
like of Marxism and other disciplines claiming laws of historical development. This part of Halstead's article was ludicrous, and Popper
(1980) correctly identified it as a personal attack on himself, refusing
to answer "what are in my opinion hardly excusable misunderstandings, and wild speculations about my motives and their alleged history."
However, since his current views on the testability of evolutionary
theory were still not widely recognized, Popper (p. 611) did have this
to say:

> *[I fully support] the scientific character of the theory of evolution, and of
> palaeontology. . . . Some people think that I have denied scientific char-
> acter to the historical sciences, such as palaeontology, or the history of the
> evolution of life on Earth. . . . This is a mistake, and I here wish to affirm
> that these and other historical sciences have in my opinion scientific char-
> acter: their hypotheses can in many cases be tested. It appears as if some
> people would think that the historical sciences are untestable because they
> describe unique events. However, the description of unique events can very
> often be tested by deriving from them testable predictions or retrodictions.*

The exchange between Halstead and Popper brought forth a number
of excellent papers on scientific method (Little 1980; Sparkes 1981;
Ruse 1981; Ridley 1981). These papers, all published in *New Scientist*, performed the admirable service of amplifying the discussion
of both the philosophical and scientific issues initiated by the debate.

The same debate about the scientific status of the theory of
evolution was simultaneously taking place in the pages of *Nature*.
The editorial staff (1981a, p. 735) of this illustrious journal objected
to a phrase used in one of the Museum's exhibit brochures: "If the
theory of evolution is true. . ." To this the editorial staff commented:

> *If the words are to be taken seriously, the rot at the museum has gone
> further than Halstead ever thought. . . . This passage nicely illustrates what
> has gone wrong at the museum. The new exhibition policy, the museum's
> chief interaction with the outside world, is being developed in some degree
> of isolation from the museum's staff of distinguished biologists, most of
> whom would rather lose their right hands than begin a sentence with the
> phrase, 'If the theory of evolution is true. . . .' Nobody disputes that, in the
> public presentation of science, it is proper whenever appropriate to say
> that disputed matters are in doubt. But is the theory of evolution still an
> open question among serious biologists?*

Thus the debate now became *Nature* versus British Museum
(Natural History), but *Nature's* editor was participating under a

severe handicap: He was, apparently, totally unaware of the dissatisfaction many evolutionary scientists today hold for the synthetic theory of evolution. This ignorance was extremely curious, since an editor of one of the foremost scientific journals in the world should be aware of the remarkable new ideas and challenges to evolutionary theory. (Refer to Gould 1980a, for a summary of challenges, and Stebbins and Ayala 1981, for a defense of the synthetic theory.) Although scientists consider the occurrence of evolution to be a fact, the theory of evolution is subject to modification just like any other scientific theory, and today it is being modified. Contrary to *Nature's* opinion, most scientists would prefer to keep their right hands rather than dogmatically hold fast to any specific theory; evolutionary *theory* is still an open question.

The response by the British Museum's biologists was immediate. Patterson (1981) defended writing the phrase, and twenty-two of his colleagues (Ball and others 1981) asked "How is it that a journal such as yours that is devoted to science and its practice can advocate that theory be presented as fact?" But the twenty-two biologists also stated that "we have no absolute proof of the theory of evolution." Of course we don't, and we never will. In their reply, Ball and others were writing under the influence of a mistaken notion: that it is possible to prove something in science. They ask, "Are we to take it that evolution is a fact, proven to the limits of scientific rigor? If that is the inference then we must disagree most strongly." As discussed earlier in this chapter, proof is found only in disciplines such as mathematics and logic, and is alien to science. Science deals with empirical evidence and theoretical constructs, and thus absence of proof in no way disqualifies something from being called scientifically true or factual. As far as I know, no one has yet proved the existence of a material universe, although scientists and almost everyone else believe it to exist in fact. Ball and others (1981), in the quote above, object even to the fact of evolution. Here I must disagree with them most strongly. That evolution has occurred *is* known to the limits of scientific rigor; evolution is a fact of science because there is no legitimate scientific alternative. Species of organisms either emerge from other species, the phenomenon of evolution, or all were created by some other process, usually described as supernatural, vitalistic, or finalistic. These latter explanations do not have a material basis that can be tested.

An exact analogy can be made with the fact of gravity. Scientists believe that gravity exists, but they do not postulate that invisible, immaterial, and ineffable supernatural entities miraculously pull objects toward bodies of greater mass. Both the *theories* of evolution and gravity are subject to change, so neither is termed factual; but the *existence* of evolution and gravity *is* scientifically factual. At higher levels of philosophical skepticism, of course, we can doubt the factual existence of everything. But we are dealing here at the level of science, not arch-skeptical epistemology, and I have invoked the standard scientific working hypotheses of materialism, actualism, and causality. Thus the statement by Ball and others about the non-factuality of evolution is flawed, and they may quickly find themselves quoted by the creationists as the biologists at the British Museum who do not believe that evolution is a fact. A fact such as evolution is not an absolute fact, but it is nevertheless a scientific fact and can be fairly presented as such.

Nature responded to Patterson (1981) and Ball and others (1981) in the same issue (1981b). In its desire to uphold the factuality of the theory of evolution, the Editor made the following remarkable statements:

> *[Theories that cannot be falsified, Popper] called metaphysical. One obvious example of such a theory is that the world was made by God. Another is Darwinism.*

> *Darwinism is not the only theory afflicted by [lack of falsifiability]. Cosmological theories are similarly incapable of falsification and are thus, in Popper's language, metaphysical. But metaphysical theories are not necessarily bad theories. Plainly it would be absurd if Popper's work were to be held to invalidate theories of evolution in general.*

Thus the Editor of *Nature*, unaware of Popper's new view to the contrary, took the unusual position that although evolutionary theory (Darwinism) was not falsifiable and was therefore metaphysical, this did not constitute an impediment to its status as a valid scientific theory. This astonishing position was strongly criticized by Caplan (1981), who observed that "Popper's views [on the untestability of evolutionary theory] have been roundly and soundly criticized by numerous philosophers interested in the scientific status of evolutionary theory." Furthermore, it was difficult to comprehend how *Nature* could explicitly accept the notion that Darwinism is metaphysical, yet be ready to accept it as scientific—and factual to boot!

The British Museum cladists had not changed their philosophical views since 1978 about the untestability of evolution theory. Consider Barry Cox's (1981) review of the new Origin of Species exhibit, the latest of the Museum's permanent exhibitions. He quotes some of the film-loops that explain different aspects of evolutionary theory to a public eager for enlightenment from scientists (p. 373):

> *Many critics feel that not only is the idea of evolution unscientific, but the idea of natural selection also. There's no point in asking whether or not we should believe in the idea of natural selection, because it is the inevitable logical consequence of a set of premises. The idea of evolution by natural*

> *selection is a matter of logic, not science, and it follows that the concept*
> *of evolution by natural selection is not, strictly speaking, scientific. If we*
> *accept that evolution has taken place, though obviously we must keep an*
> *open mind on it . . . [and so on].*

Needless to say, Cox was quite unfavorably impressed by the message
these film-loops communicated to a public trying to understand the
scientific explanation of evolution. But the denouement, when it
came, was more spectacular than anyone could have hoped for. In a
brief letter to *Nature*, R. S. Miles (1981, p. 530) wrote:

> *In providing this audio-visual we were trying to avoid dogmatism in our*
> *presentation of the theory of evolution by natural selection. The inten-*
> *tion was to reproduce the arguments set out in Chapter 12 of Colin*
> *Patterson's book,* Evolution *(British Museum [Natural History], 1978).*
> *Before the opening of the exhibition the Museum was aware that as a*
> *consequence of compression of the subject matter and transference to a*
> *new medium the audio-visual might give an impression other than that*
> *intended. Subsequent experience of the audio-visual as part of the exhibi-*
> *tion has shown this misgiving to have been justified. A new version is being*
> *prepared.*

Let us hope that this is the final word. Clearly, no more need be said.

Cladism and Marxism

The third and final episode in the "great museum debate" will undoubtedly enter future history of science books as one of the most
fascinating displays of scientific contrariety in the twentieth century.
The theme of this episode is the *ideological argument*. Four months
after indicting the museum biologists for slavishly following Karl
Popper's mistaken notions about evolutionary theory, Halstead
(1980b) returned to the topic that had earlier piqued his interest and
drawn his disapproval: the cladistic exhibits in the British Museum.
In the two years since his 1978a critique, the Museum scientists had
constructed two new exhibits with accompanying booklets: *Dinosaurs
and Their Living Relatives* (1979) and *Man's Place in Evolution*
(1980). Halstead (1980b) complained that these "new exhibits are
simply vehicles for the promotion of a system of working out relationships known as cladistics [and the] accompanying booklets . . .
explain with startling clarity the essence of cladistics." He was especially derisive of the reluctance of the human evolution exhibit and
booklet to state that *Homo erectus* was directly ancestral to *Homo
sapiens*; Halstead believed there to be no "serious doubt" about this.
He claimed that "what the creationists have insisted on for years is

now being openly advertised by the Natural History Museum": that "there are no actual fossils directly antecedent to man." Halstead's antipathy to cladistics has been discussed in detail, along with the assumptions and procedures of the cladistic method, including the reasons why cladists avoid specifying direct ancestors. As an evolutionary taxonomist, Halstead has his own valid complaints against cladistic taxonomy. But the fact is that cladistic taxonomy is equally as scientific as evolutionary taxonomy, and the British Museum scientific staff had legitimately decided to construct cladistic exhibits instead of evolutionary taxonomic ones. It is hardly fair to object to exhibits by claiming they give solace to creationists, when in fact there is no reason why they should. Cladistics is based on the fact of evolution, as the exhibits and guidebooks state, and Halstead was throwing red herrings because he could not produce a logical objection to cladistics.

But Halstead (1980b, p. 208) was not finished; he felt compelled to explain *why* the Natural History Museum scientists were forcing cladistic exhibitions on an innocent public.

> *If a national museum is concerned with aspects of social engineering, by promoting concepts that happen to be current in the present climate of opinion, are there not sinister implications? . . . What exactly is the cladistic framework to which the Public Services Department is so fervently dedicated? Why is there such a fanatical insistence that data should be presented within such a framework?*

By posing such provocative questions, Halstead was clearly implying that a conspiracy was afoot. He wanted to know "what actually is going on and what is behind it all?" He was also quite ready to provide the answers:

> *The answers can be found by reading the literature of cladistics. The tenor of [cladism is firmly opposed] to the concept of gradualism and to the idea that the processes that can be observed at the present day, when extrapolated into the past, are sufficient to explain changes observed in the fossil record. The [synthetic theory of evolution] is anathema to cladists.*

Here Halstead was simply mistaken. As previously discussed in great detail, the synthetic theory is not anathema to cladists, but merely irrelevant. To evolutionary taxonomists, however, the synthetic theory is essential, and Halstead was illogically attempting to defend evolutionary taxonomy by making it appear that cladism is necessarily opposed to gradualism and the synthetic theory, which it is not. But Halstead (1980b, p. 208) saved his master argument for last:

> *Why should the notion of gradualism arouse passions of such intensity. The answer is to be found in the political arena. There are basically two*

contrasting views with regard to human society and the process of change through time: One is the gradualist, reformist and the other is the revolutionary approach. The key tenet of dialectical-materialism, the world outlook of [Marxism], is in the recognition of "a development in which the qualitative changes occur not gradually but rapidly and abruptly, taking the form of a leap from one state to another" (Engels). This is the recipe for revolution. If this is the observed rule in the history of life, when translated into human history and political action it would serve as the scientific justification for accentuating the inherent contradictions in society, so that the situation can be hurried towards its [inevitable conclusion] . . . . If it could be established that the pattern of evolution was a [punctuated] one after all, then at long last the Marxists would indeed be able to claim that the theoretical basis of their approach was supported by scientific evidence. . . . If the cladistic approach becomes established as the received wisdom, then a fundamentally Marxist view of the history of life will have been incorporated into a key element of the educational system of the country. Marxism will be able to call upon the scientific laws of history in its support. . . .

This remarkable critique of cladistics at the British Museum began a lengthy controversy in the correspondence section of *Nature* and attracted international attention (Wade 1981). Many individuals felt compelled to enter the fray at this point, to express disagreement or incredulity over different aspects of Halstead's ideological argument.

First, Halstead misunderstood the theory and practice of cladistic taxonomy. Rather than making the authoritative pronouncements on human evolution that Halstead (1980b) advocated, Patterson (1980b) thought the British Museum should use methods encouraging the visitor "to understand, and to take part in, the reasoning that underpins the story of human evolution." Patterson emphasized that cladistics "is not about evolution, but about the pattern of character distribution in organisms, or the recognition and characterization of groups." Patterson was supported by Janvier (1981) and McKenna (1981), who reiterated the nature of Halstead's fundamental misunderstanding. Indeed, as McKenna stated, the "British Museum (Natural History) is to be congratulated for bringing epistemology into its exhibits and teaching visitors that science is a method, not a body of revealed knowledge." This is the most important message conveyed by the format of the new exhibits; the opposite opinion—that science is a mass of authoritative knowledge—is sadly all too common among students and laypeople. It is this unfortunately common opinion that Halstead perpetuates by dogmatically asserting that the experts know exact evolutionary pathways and ancestors, and need only inform the public.

Halstead's second error was his equation of cladism with Marxism. This mistake drew the most withering criticism from the correspondents, for it was clearly illogical as well as untrue. To explain why this is so, I will divide Halstead's argument into its two component parts. First, Halstead linked cladism with punctuationalism, the anti-gradualistic model of fossil evolution. In response, Patterson (1980b) pointed out that there is no "necessary connection between cladistics and one view of the evolutionary process." Marks (1980) emphasized that "at least one articulate spokesman for punctuated equilibrium is not a cladist, and therefore it is incorrect to lump the two schools together." However much Halstead may disagree with cladism, the method does not make any claims about evolutionary tempos and modes; indeed, one of cladism's most salutary features is its independence from such evolutionary hypotheses. Halstead (1981a) replied that the museum exhibits were based on "the classic version of cladistics as set out originally by Hennig in *Phylogenetic Systematics* (1966)," and that Patterson was defending a special "transformed cladistics" advocated by Patterson (1980a) and Platnick (1977, 1980). Halstead (1981a) insisted that there is a "long recognized connection between cladistics and punctuated equilibria [as] has recently been emphasized by Cracraft (1979) and Hull (1980a, 1980b)." But the museum exhibits do not embrace an evolutionary theory-based classic version of cladistics; the exhibits and guidebooks were too elementary to discuss epistemology and evolutionary mechanisms in detail. As for "transformed cladistics," cladistics is still undergoing transformation, and in its exhibits the Natural History Museum presented only the essentials. The "long recognized connection between cladistics and punctuated equilibria" is a Halsteadian chimera; it simply does not exist in the Cracraft and Hull references Halstead cites. Although Cracraft and Hull do discuss both cladistics and punctuational evolution, they do not dogmatically link them. Compatible ideas do not necessarily possess a common origin or mutual dependency; to imply, as Halstead did, that they have such an origin or dependency, because they are compatible, is illogical.

Halstead's second linking, of punctuationalism to Marxism, is slightly more accurate, but nevertheless irrelevant. It is true that the punctuational model of evolution is consistent with the tenet of dialectical materialism stating that evolution takes place in leaps, not gradually, such that evolution or development passes suddenly from a succession of slow quantitative changes to a radical qualitative change. Gould himself said as much in Gould and Eldredge (1977, p. 145). (I must emphasize here that the leaps are visible as such only in geological time; the punctuational model is not advocating saltations —genetic leaps in ecologic time. Genetic transitions are gradual, although the rate of change is variable, and may be quite rapid.) Nevertheless, Halstead's link of punctuationalism to Marxism is still tenuous at best, for at least four reasons.

First, Eldredge (1971) initially elucidated the basic tenets of the modern punctuated evolution model, although Gould had independently reached the same conclusion. This is why they coauthored their seminal 1972 paper (Eldredge and Gould 1972). Since Eldredge is not a Marxist, and since most of the model's tenets came from earlier non-Marxist sources, Halstead's explicit connection vanishes. Second, Gould (1981) referred to the controversy as "Halstead's glorious uproarious misunderstanding," and repeated what he had clarified earlier, that the main reason for his developing a punctuated model was "not conscious Marxism" (Gould 1979, p. 11), "but rather as an attempt to resolve the oldest empirical dilemma impeding an integration of palaeontology into modern evolutionary thought: the phenomena of stasis within successful fossil species, and abrupt replacement by descendants" (1981). Gould (1981) also emphasized what others had noted, that "Under cladism, branching events may proceed as slowly as the imperceptible phyletic transitions advocated by the old school, [and the punctuated model is] a theory about the characteristic rate of . . . branching—an issue which cladism does not address." Halstead (1981b) replied by simply reasserting his earlier claims.

The third reason Halstead's linking of Marxism and punctuation is misguided is because whatever link there might be is irrelevant to the scientific validity of the punctuated model (Patterson 1980b; McKenna 1981). The inspiration or source of a scientific hypothesis is unrelated to its scientific veracity. The punctuational model of evolution will be corroborated or refuted by empirical evidence and scientific analysis, not by how well it conforms to the tenets of Marxist doctrine. Even Gould (1980b), an outspoken advocate of the subjectivist or externalist school of philosophy of science, stated that "The pervasive influence of culture upon science is depressing only to those who still advance the discredited myth that knowledge so constrained is tainted and impure." Whatever the cultural context of the punctuated model, its scientific legitimacy is unsullied. Would Halstead condemn Darwinism because it is Smithian, Malthusian, or even Marxist? In fact, this leads to the fourth objection to Halstead's argument—that Halstead's understanding of both the history and content of Darwinism and Marxism is simplistic (Hughes-Games 1980; Rothman 1980; Howgate 1981). Historically, Marxism has given as much support to gradual change as to punctuated change, and Darwinism has been invoked to support right-wing as much as left-wing ideologies (Hofstadter 1955, Stanley 1981). Rothman (1980) made the telling observation that Halstead's actions match those of Stalin by "encouraging the application of political criteria, rather than scientific ones, to assess scientific theories." Indeed, the only conclusion that one can reach from this debate is that Halstead, wishing to support evolutionary taxonomy and gradualism, used illogical, irrelevant, and irresponsible arguments to associate cladistics and punctuationalism with Marxism, in his view a disreputable doctrine. By failing to criticize cladistics and the punctuational model with legitimate scientific arguments and evidence Halstead earned the contempt of many scientists. Finally, in his response to their protestations—his "defence against irrelevancy" (1981c)— Halstead did not adequately answer his critics, but only reviewed and reasserted his charges.

Despite the public clamor that erupted over the issue of Marxism in the British Museum exhibits, only a few of Halstead's scientific peers took Halstead's arguments in this regard seriously. After a few months even *Nature's* editorial staff, whose lack of perspicacity throughout the controversy was noted by a number of commentators, managed to conclude that Halstead's "claim that cladism is a cloak for Marxism because Marxist-evolutionists tend to be cladists is illogical (and has been disowned)" (1981c). This being the case, I want to turn to what I believe to be the most serious issue in the entire controversy, that of Halstead's implicit belief that scientific support of Marxism would lead to Marxism's greater success in society. Halstead's earlier (1978a) veiled reference to this in his exchange with R. S. Miles (1978b) on the public responsibility of a national museum finally became clear: By 1980 the essence of Halstead's indictment of "cladism as Marxism" was explicit. Halstead (1980b) claimed that if the "cladistic approach becomes established as the received wisdom, then a fundamentally Marxist view of history of life will have been incorporated into a key element of the educational system of this country, [and] Marxism will be able to call upon the scientific laws of history in its support. . . ."

Even if we ignore the McCarthyistic tone of this claim, we cannot ignore Halstead's appeal to the existence of scientific laws of history. Hughes-Games (1980) claimed that the emptiness of such laws "has been elegantly demonstrated by Sir Karl Popper" in his books. Whether this is true or not, Halstead (1980b) believes that this Marxist "recipe for revolution," if found to be the "observed rule in the history of life," will serve as the scientific justification for imposing Marxist imperatives on society. Halstead, however, is unaware that even if scientific evidence and theory support Marxism at every turn, and even if scientific laws of history really exist, we still would not inevitably have to adopt Marxist tenets in our social, political, and economic life. Halstead implicitly believes in the dominion and supremacy of the "is/ought" principle, that what *is* true, *ought* to be. This principle usually takes the form that what is true in nature ought to be adopted or continued by humanity in its social, political, and ethical affairs; that is, it is a form of biological determinism. Unfortunately, the is/ought principle is a fallacy. Philosophers call this the *naturalistic fallacy*.

Halstead is not alone in his espousal of the naturalistic fallacy. Some sociobiologists have suggested that our modern understanding of evolutionary theory allows us to describe ethical human behavior in strictly scientific terms. For example, consider this quotation from E. O. Wilson's book *Sociobiology* (1975a, p. 562):

> *Scientists and humanists should consider together the possibility that the time has come for ethics to be removed temporarily from the hands of philosophers and biologicized.*

Although this suggests that Wilson accepts the is/ought principle as valid, he is actually only saying that science can now rigorously investigate and understand human ethics, not that we must begin to obey the biological imperatives we might discover. In fact, Wilson (1975b, p. 50) explicitly recognizes that the is/ought principle is a naturalistic fallacy, and that this is a "dangerous trap in sociobiology" that many can and have fallen into. This trap is not new. Julian Huxley (1947) believed that evolution provided an objective and reliable code of ethics that humans could and should adopt. Although Huxley was one of this century's greatest humanists, I, also both a humanist and evolutionary scientist, believe that evolutionary ethics in whatever guise, humanist or sociobiological, are a great and tragic mistake. The is/ought principle was found to be fallacious by David Hume and George Moore in decades past, but like any philosophical topic with social implications favorable to special interest groups it reappears in its law-like guise with dismaying regularity. Today the is/ought principle is supported by a small number of philosophers and scientists, the latter group including Halstead and a number of extreme sociobiologists. The best introduction to the topic is the book *Evolutionary Ethics* by Antony Flew (1967); he shows quite clearly that the naturalistic fallacy is precisely that—a fallacy, and not a law.

Contrary to Halstead's fears, there is no reason to conclude that humans are bound by biological necessity to follow a certain predetermined path or to choose a world view consistent with known scientific truth (when, of course, we determine what that truth is). Nondeterministic processes and stochastic elements in evolution and the rest of nature may in fact provide grounds for believing in free will. This then allows human judgment, in the realm of individual or societal choice, to ignore natural imperatives regardless of their scientific justification. Since Halstead has stated many times that he relies on the authority of George Gaylord Simpson in matters scientific, perhaps he will follow Simpson (1966, 1967, pp. 309, 311-312) in matters philosophic:

> *The point is that an evolutionary ethic* for man . . . *should be based on man's own nature, on his evolutionary position and significance. It cannot be expected to arise* automatically *from the principles of evolution in general, nor yet, indeed, from those of human evolution in particular. It cannot be expected to be absolute, but . . . must be the result of responsible and rational choice in the full light of such knowledge of man and of life as we have.*

> *Man . . . can choose to develop his capacities as the highest animal and to try to rise farther, or he can choose otherwise. The choice is his responsibility, and his alone. There is no automatism that will carry him upward without choice or effort and there is no trend solely in the right direction. Evolution has no purpose; man must supply this for himself. . . . It is futile to search for an absolute ethical criterion retroactively in what occurred before ethics themselves evolved. The best human ethical standard must be relative and particular to man and is to be sought rather in the new [cultural] evolution, peculiar to man, than in the old [biological evolution], universal to all organisms. The old evolution was and is essentially amoral.*

I fully support these views of Simpson and recommend that arch-selectionists, arch-reductionists, and biological determinists take them to heart. No scientific humanist, such as Simpson, Flew, Wilson, Gould, or myself, would endorse a claim that an ideology or doctrine supported by massive scientific evidence *must* be adopted or allowed to continue in humans' ethical or socioeconomic affairs. To think otherwise is to deny our own humanity. To think otherwise is to deny that "science is a human enterprise."

APPENDIX

FIGURE 1. This figure illustrates six types of evolutionary diagrams frequently used in systematic biology and paleontology. Each diagram depicts taxonomic or evolutionary relationships among five species (labeled A through E).

CLADOGENY. A *cladogeny* is the pattern created by the distribution of derived (apomorphic) characters among the recognized taxa. A *cladogram* depicts a cladogeny, which hypothesizes the distribution of shared derived (synapomorphic) characters among the taxa. There are two slightly different types of cladograms, both illustrated here. The more common form (the larger cladogram) does not indicate hypothetical ancestors at the nodes of the branching network. Such hypothetical ancestors are unnecessary in practice and often do not exist in fact, since a terminal species could be the ancestor of its sister species. Hypothetical

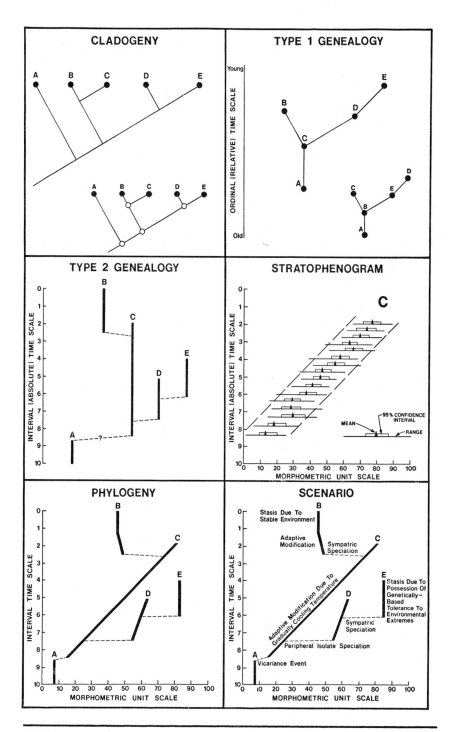

FIGURE 1. (see opposite)

ancestors represented by open circles at nodes (the smaller cladogram) can be either of the two terminal (sister) species or a third unknown species. In fact, a long-ranging terminal species could exist from node to node far down into the cladogram, although if a taxonomist inferred that this is indeed the case and plotted the species at these nodes, the diagram would no longer be a cladogram, but would become a genealogical tree. Therefore, any terminal species can be the ancestor of any or all of the other terminal species, but the extreme difficulty of inferring the ancestral-descendant relationships of the species, and the constant problem of undiscovered ancestral species, has led cladists to perform taxonomic classifications at the level of the cladogeny and to ignore the other types of evolutionary diagrams shown here except for special purposes. Note that cladograms are not plotted within time or morphology axes; the lengths and angles of the cladogram's branches are meaningless, and no specific pattern of ancestry and descent or branching sequence is indicated.

TYPE 1 GENEALOGY. If, by inference from some set of data, one decides which of the species is ancestral to others and brings certain terminal species down to nodes formerly occupied by open circles, one has constructed a *genealogy* of the simplest (first) type. The problem here is that a large number of type 1 genealogies can be derived from a single cladogram, and only one can be correct. For example, both genealogies shown here are consistent with the original cladogeny, and many other examples are possible, especially if unknown ancestors are invented and stationed at the various nodes. A genealogy is the pattern of ancestry and descent among the recognized taxa. A *genealogical* or *family tree* depicts a genealogy, so the two diagrams depicted are two different trees. (We will assume the larger is correct.) Such trees have a *polarity* from old to young; that is, they lie on an *ordinal* (relative) time scale, as shown in the figure. The branch nodes indicate the pattern of ancestry and descent, but the length and angle of the branches are meaningless. Since numerous assumptions, not discussed here, are needed to proceed from a cladogram to a family tree, type 1 genealogies are often speculative and highly subject to modification, and thus are not a reliable basis by which to classify organisms.

TYPE 2 GENEALOGY. A more specialized type of genealogy utilizes stratigraphic data derived from the fossil record. Type 2 genealogies are commonly found in paleontological publications and are often constructed solely from fossil phenetic and stratigraphic data without the necessary preliminary steps of a cladistic analysis and a type 1 genealogical inference. Type 2 genealogies require additional assumptions over those of type 1 genealogies (for example, that the stratigraphic and fossil records are relatively complete). A type 2 genealogy may be plotted against an *interval* (absolute) time scale, as in this figure, or against an ordinal time scale with units such as biozones or chronostratigraphic stages. By this point in a biosystematic analysis (which proceeds from cladogram to type 1 tree to type 2 tree to phylogram to scenario), we are searching for patterns to examine the tempo and mode of evolution that can only be recognized by constructing nonrigorous diagrams higher than cladograms. Also note that type 2 genealogies are frequently plotted against rock thickness or against lithostratigraphic units, although these trees are practically useless for comparative purposes. Furthermore, the horizontal axis for both types of genealogies is dimensionless and does not indicate degree or type of morphologic change.

STRATEOPHENOGRAM. A *stratophenogram* is a plot of a morphometric datum (measurement of a univariate character, bivariate ratio, or multivariate factor) of one species (single lineage) or higher monophyletic taxon (clade) against an interval time scale. In other words, a stratophenogram shows phenetic data plotted against stratigraphy. Stratophenograms plotted against rock thickness (core or measured section length) or against an ordinal time scale are essentially useless for comparative work and are useful for recognizing only the most generalized phyletic patterns. To be valuable in the investigation of evolutionary tempo and mode, a rigorous stratophenogram must be plotted against an interval time scale. In some cases it is necessary to construct stratophenograms before performing cladistic analysis, so that both static and gradually changing characters may be recognized and avoided in the subsequent cladistic analysis. Such characters are ancestral (plesiomorphic), and might appear to the investigator to be derived if an evolving lineage is not completely sampled and plotted by stratophenograms. Some paleontologists derive classifications directly from stratophenograms without performing a cladistic analysis; this practice is not theoretically valid and should be discouraged.

PHYLOGENY. A *phylogeny* is probably the most controversial of all evolutionary patterns, since it seeks to represent the pattern of branching, ancestry, descent, and divergence (progression along a branch) of the recognized taxa. It seeks to illustrate the entire evolutionary history of the taxa: all cladogenetic, anagenetic, and ancestral-descendant relationships. A phylogeny is depicted by a phylogenetic tree, or *phylogram*, a diagram by which the lengths and angles of branches (single lineages) convey anagenetic information in addition to the cladogenetic and genealogic information conveyed by the splitting branches and the location and sequence of the branch nodes. Anagenesis, also called phyletic evolution, is progressive evolution within a single branch (lineage). This component of evolutionary change is distinguished from cladogenesis, the splitting of lineages that yields the other component of evolutionary change. The appearance of a phylogram depends heavily on the author's preferred models of evolution and speciation. For example, the quite atypical example illustrated here assumes a punctuated model of evolution: that speciation occurs at a tempo that would appear instantaneous on a geologic time scale. The assumption of a gradualistic model, on the other hand, would result in a phylogram showing species gradually splitting and diverging from one another, with no dashed lines between species to indicate a speciation event. Such phylograms have appeared in the paleontological literature for decades, because the gradualistic model of evolution was universally held. A second assumption about evolution implicit in the figured phylogram is that a single lineage (ancestral-descendant sequence of populations) remains a single species, no matter what amount of gradual divergent evolution (anagenesis) occurs. Thus, species C remains one species for 6.5 units of time, whereas its great degree of progressive change (in a character, ratio, or factor) during this time would lead most paleontologists to divide it into two or more paleospecies or chronospecies (that is, arbitrarily subdivided parts of a gradually changing lineage), so that the phylogram would show ancestral species gradually transforming into new descendant species.

A rigorous phylogeny utilizing fossil data is simply a combination of a type 2 genealogy and stratophenograms of each species (taxon) in the genealogy. It should be obvious that a phylogeny, which purports to express the type and amount of evolutionary divergence (anagenesis) by the lengths and angles of the branches, is essentially useless for such a purpose unless it is constructed within an interval or ratio time scale and morphometric unit scale that accurately presents such anagenetic data. The phylogeny illustrated here is therefore an ideal that has yet to be reached in the systematic paleontologic literature. All published phylograms are really quasi-phylograms that are nonrigorous, speculative diagrams that omit the interval scale axis, the morphometric scale axis, or both. They reflect their authors' particular beliefs about a fossil group's evolutionary history. The difficulty of two people reaching the same phylogeny by examining the same data makes the construction of phylograms an exercise in authoritarianism. (The reader should be aware that the cladist literature frequently confounds genealogies and phylogenies by calling both family trees and phylogenetic trees simply "trees." For some reason, modern cladistic taxonomists tend to discount the occurrence of anagenetic evolution, so the possibility of constructing phylogenies is ignored, and the term is frequently used interchangably with genealogy. Obviously, if anagenesis does not occur, genealogies *would* be phylogenies.)

SCENARIO. A *scenario* is simply an annotated phylogram that strives to present an environmental or adaptive explanation for every cladogenetic event (speciation, in the strict sense used here) and anagenetic change or stasis. A scenario depicts a *narrative explanation*, a history of evolution of the recognized taxa with an adaptational and environmental narrative explanation for every gradual change, episode of speciation, or extinction event. Now that stasis is recognized to be an important attribute of a lineage, this also must be explained. It is not unusual for different paleontologists to propose the same environmental explanation for both speciations and extinctions; different adaptive explanations for evolution of the same species or the different evolutionary histories of two sympatric species; and different modes of speciation for similar species—all depending on which circumstances the paleontologist wishes to consider. The problem with all these explanations is that they are paleontological overgeneralizations requiring extrapolation of neontological microevolutionary processes, themselves often poorly understood and controversial. Thus scenarios have justifiably been described as "fairy tales."

FIGURE 2. These two diagrams will help illustrate the concepts of monophyly, paraphyly, and polyphyly. The upper diagram is a cladogram depicting cladistic relationships among the eight recognized taxa portrayed in the example. The lower diagram is a specialized type of phylogram portraying a number of additional items: a single genealogy (one of many that could be extracted from the cladogram), hypothetical ancestors, and the amount of morphological divergence that has occurred through time. A *monophyletic* taxon is a group that includes a common ancestor and all of its descendants. The cladogram (upper diagram) tells us that CD, EF, GH, BCD, A-D, E-H, and A-H are monophyletic taxa. For each of the monophyletic taxa we may assume either that one of the known species in the taxon is the common ancestor of all species in the taxon, or that the common ancestral species is unknown.

In the phylogram (lower diagram), seven hypothetical ancestral species are shown. Let us assume that this phylogram accurately depicts the actual phylogeny of the species and their extended lineages. Note that species B has diverged considerably from its sister taxon CD and converged toward species A, and that species F has diverged from its sister species E and converged on taxon GH. An evolutionary taxonomic analysis utilizing shared ancestral (symplesiomorphic) characters as well as uniquely derived (autapomorphic) characters could result in a classification containing the paraphyletic taxa, such as AB, ABC, and GFH, and polyphyletic taxa such as DE, A-E, and D-H. A *paraphyletic* taxon is a group that includes a common ancestor and some but not all of its descendants. For example, paraphyletic taxa AB and ABC include common ancestor 2, but

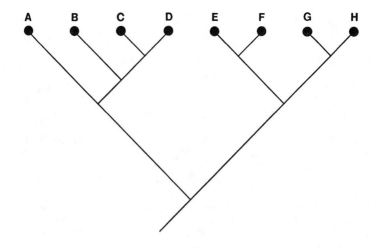

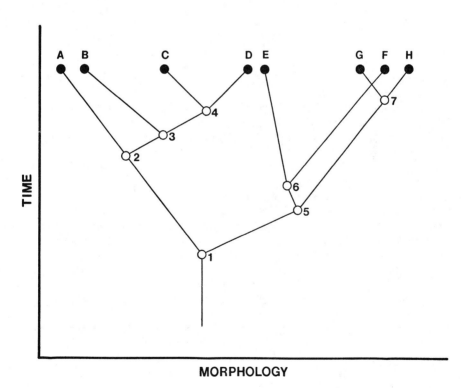

FIGURE 2. (see opposite)

ABC leaves out descendant D and AB leaves out both C and D; paraphyletic taxon GFH includes common ancestor 5, but omits descendant E. A *polyphyletic* taxon is a group that omits its most recent common ancestor (which is assigned to some other taxon). For example, 1 is the most recent common ancestor of polyphyletic taxa DE, A-E, and D-H, but this ancestor would be assigned to either paraphyletic taxon ABC or GFH if the polyphyletic taxa were accepted.

Both evolutionary and cladistic taxonomists agree that polyphyletic taxa are unnatural, but unlike cladists, evolutionary taxonomists accept paraphyletic taxa as natural. The class Reptilia is an excellent example of such a paraphyletic taxon. The reptiles are a grade characterized by many shared ancestral characters. In the diagram, paraphyletic taxon GFH could represent reptiles, with F representing dinosaurs, E representing birds, and G and H representing some other reptiles. Monophyletic taxon EF would group the dinosaurs and birds together, since they share a common ancestor that other reptiles do not share. Although the amount of morphological divergence between E and F is immense, a cladistic classification that logically emerges solely from recency of common ancestry is better in many ways than one that separates related groups subjectively by degree of morphologic change.

NOTE

The editor wishes to thank L. B. Halstead for granting permission to quote extensively from his work.

REFERENCES

Ackermann, R. J. *The Philosophy of Karl Popper.* Amherst: University of Massachusetts Press, 1976.

Ball, H. W., and others. "Darwin's Survival." *Nature* 290 (1981):82.

Beveridge, W. I. B. *Seeds of Discovery.* New York: W. W. Norton, 1980.

Bock, Walter. "Philosophical Foundations of Classical Evolutionary Taxonomy." *Systematic Zoology* 22 (1974):375-392.

Briggs, J. C. "Do Centers of Origin Have a Center?" *Paleobiology* 7, no. 3 (1981):305-307.

Caplan, Arthur L. "Popper's Philosophy." *Nature* 290 (1981):623-624.

Cox, B. "Premises, Premises." *Nature* 291 (1981):373.

Cracraft, Joel. "Phylogenetic Analysis, Evolutionary Models and Paleontology." In *Phylogenetic Analysis and Paleontology*, edited by Joel Cracraft and Niles Eldredge, pp. 7-39. New York: Columbia University Press, 1979.

Cracraft, Joel, and Eldredge, Niles, eds. *Phylogenetic Analysis and Paleontology.* New York: Columbia University Press, 1979.

Darlington, P. J. *Zoogeography: The Geographical Distribution of Animals.* New York: Wiley, 1957.

Duncan, Thomas, and Stuessy, Todd, eds. *Cladistics: Perspectives on the Reconstruction of Evolutionary History.* New York: Columbia University Press, 1984.

Eldredge, Niles. "The Allopatric Model and Phylogeny in Palezoic Invertebrates." *Evolution* 25 (1971):156-167.

Eldredge, Niles, and Cracraft, Joel. *Phylogenetic Patterns and the Evolutionary Process.* New York: Columbia University Press, 1980.

Eldredge, Niles, and Gould, Stephen J. "Punctuated Equilibria: An Alternative to Phyletic Gradualism." In *Models in Paleobiology*, edited by T. J. M. Schopf, pp. 85-115. San Francisco: Freeman, Cooper, 1972.

Flew, Antony G. N. *Evolutionary Ethics*. London: Macmillan, St. Martin's Press, 1967.

Gaffney, E. S. "An Introduction to the Logic of Phylogeny Construction." In *Phylogenetic Analysis and Paleontology*, edited by Joel Cracraft and Niles Eldredge, pp. 79-111. New York: Columbia University Press, 1979.

Gardiner, B. G.; Janvier, P.; Patterson, C.; Forey, P. L.; Greenwood, P. H.; Miles, R. S.; and Jefferies, R. P. S. "The Salmon, the Lungfish, and the Cow: A Reply." *Nature* 277 (1979):175-176.

Gould, Stephen Jay. "The Episodic Nature of Change Versus the Dogma of Gradualism." *Science and Nature* 3, no. 2 (1979):5-12.

——. "Is a New and General Theory of Evolution Emerging?" *Paleobiology* 6, no. 1 (1980a):119-130.

——. "The Evolutionary Biology of Constraint." In Intellect and Imagination, *Daedalus* 109, no. 2 (1980b):39-52.

——. "Museum Debate." *Nature* 289 (1981):742.

Gould, Stephen Jay, and Eldredge, Niles. "Punctuated Equilibria: The Tempo and Mode of Evolution Reconsidered." *Paleobiology* 3, no. 2 (1977): 115-151.

Gould, Stephen Jay, and Lewontin, Richard C. "The Spandrels of San Marco and the Panglossian Paradigm: A Critique of the Adaptationist Programme." *Proceedings of the Royal Society of London* B 205 (1979):581-598.

Halstead, L. B. "Whither the Natural History Museum?" *Nature* 275 (1978a):683.

——. "The Cladistic Revolution—Can It Make the Grade?" *Nature* (1978b): 759-760.

——. "Popper: Good Philosophy, Bad Science?" *New Scientist* 87 (1980a): 215-217.

——. "Museum of Errors." *Nature* 288 (1980b):208.

——. "Halstead Replies." *Nature* 289 (1981a):106-107.

——. "Last Word?" *Nature* 289 (1981b):742.

——. "Halstead's Defence Against Irrelevancy." *Nature* 292 (1981c):403-404.

Hennig, Willi. *Phylogenetic Systematics*. Urbana: University of Illinois Press, 1966.

Hofstadter, Richard. *Social Darwinism in American Thought*. Philadelphia, University of Pennsylvania Press, 1955.

Howgate, M. "Evolutionary Thought." *Nature* 289 (1981):344.

Hughes-Games, M. J. "Museum Pieces." *Nature* 288 (1980):430.

Hull, David. *Philosophy of Biological Science*. Englewood Cliffs, N.J.: Prentice-Hall, 1974.

——. "The Limits of Cladism." *Systematic Zoology* 28 (1980a):416-440.

——. "Cladism Gets Sorted Out." *Paleobiology* 6, no. 1 (1980b):131-136.

Huxley, Julian. "Evolutionary Ethics." In *Evolution and Ethics 1893-1943*, edited by T. H. Huxley and J. Huxley, pp. 103-152. London: The Pilot Press Ltd., 1947.

Janvier, P. "French Museums." *Nature* 289 (1981):626.

Lakatos, I., and Musgrave, A., eds. *Criticism and the Growth of Knowledge*. Cambridge: Cambridge University Press, 1970.

Lewontin, Richard C. "Adaptation." *Scientific American* 239, no. 3 (1978): 212-230.

Little, J. "Evolution: Myth, Metaphysics, or Science?" *New Scientist* 87 (1980): 708-709.

Mackie, J. L. "Failures in Criticism: Popper and His Commentators." *British Journal of the Philosophy of Science* 29 (1978):363-387.

Magee, B. *Karl Popper*. New York: Viking Press, 1973.

———. "Karl Popper: The Useful Philosopher." *Horizon* 16, no. 5 (1974):52-57.

Marks, Jon. "More on Museums." *Nature* 288 (1980):638.

Mayr, Ernst. *Principles of Systematic Zoology*. New York: McGraw-Hill, 1969.

———. *Evolution and the Diversity of Life*. Cambridge: Harvard University Press, Belknap Press, 1976.

———. "Biological Classification: Toward a Synthesis of Opposing Methodologies." *Science* 214 (1981):510-516.

McKenna, Malcolm. "More Museums." *Nature* 289 (1981):626-627.

Miles, R. S. "The Public's Right to Know." *Nature* 275 (1978a):682.

———. "Whither the Natural History Museum?" *Nature* 276 (1978b):10.

———. "Film Loop Evolves." *Nature* 291 (1981):530.

Nature. "Darwin's Death in South Kensington." Volume 289 (1981a):735.

———. "How True is the Theory of Evolution?" Volume 290 (1981b):75-76.

———. "Loose Ends on Evolution." Volume 292 (1981c):1.

Nelson, G., and Platnick, N. *Systematics and Biogeography*. New York: Columbia University Press, 1981.

Nelson, G., and Rosen, D. E., eds. *Vicariance Biogeography: A Critique*. New York: Columbia University Press, 1981.

Patterson, Colin. *Evolution*. London: British Museum (Natural History), 1978.

———. "Cladistics." *Biologist* 27, no. 5 (1980a):234-240.

———. "Museum Pieces." *Nature* 288 (1980b):430.

———. "Darwin's Survival." *Nature* 290 (1981):82.

Platnick, N. "Cladograms, Phylogenetic Trees, and Hypothesis Testing." *Systematic Zoology* 26 (1977):438-442.

———. "Philosophy and the Transformation of Cladistics." *Systematic Zoology* 28 (1980):537-546.

Platnick, N. I., and Gaffney, E. S. "Systematics: A Popperian Perspective." *Systematic Zoology* 26, no. 3 (1977):360-365.

———. "Evolutionary Biology: A Popperian Perspective." *Systematic Zoology*, 27, no. 1 (1978a):137-141.

———. "Systematics and the Popperian Paradigm." *Systematic Zoology* 27, no. 3 (1978b):381-388.

Popper, Karl R. *The Poverty of Historicism*. London: Routledge and Kegan Paul, 1963.

———. "Darwinism as a Metaphysical Research Program." In *The Philosophy of Karl Popper*, vol. 1, edited by P. Schilpp, pp. 133-143. LaSalle, Ill.: Open Court, 1974.

———. *Unended Quest: An Intellectual Autobiography*. LaSalle, Ill.: Open Court, 1976.

———. "Natural Selection and the Emergence of Mind." *Dialectica* 32, nos. 3-4 (1978):339-355.

———. "Evolution." *New Scientist* 87 (1980):611.

Ridley, M. "Who Doubts Evolution?" *New Scientist* 89 (1981):830-832.

Rothman, H. "Museum Pieces." *Nature* 288 (1980):430.

Ruse, Michael. *The Philosophy of Biology*. London: Hutchinson University Library, 1973.

——. "Karl Popper's Philosophy of Biology." *Philosophy of Science* 44 (1977): 638-661.

——. "Darwin's Theory: An Exercise in Science." *New Scientist* 89 (1981): 828-830.

Schilpp, P. A., ed. *The Philosophy of Karl Popper*. 2 vols. LaSalle, Ill.: Open Court, 1974.

Simpson, George Gaylord. *Principles of Animal Taxonomy*. New York: Columbia University Press, 1961.

——. "Naturalistic Ethics and the Social Sciences." *American Psychologist* 21 (1966):27-36.

——. *The Meaning of Evolution*. Revised Edition. New Haven: Yale University Press, 1967.

Sparkes, J. "What is This Thing Called Science?" *New Scientist* 89 (1981): 156-158.

Stanley, Steven M. *Macroevolution: Pattern and Process*. San Francisco: W. H. Freeman, 1979.

——. *The New Evolutionary Timetable*. New York: Basic Books, 1981.

Stebbins, G. L., and Ayala, F. J. "Is a New Evolutionary Synthesis Necessary?" *Science* 213 (1981):967-971.

Suppe, F., ed. *The Structure of Scientific Theories*. 2d ed. Urbana: University of Illinois Press, 1977.

Wade, N. "Dinosaur Battle Erupts in British Museum." *Science* 211 (1981): 35-36.

Wassermann, G. "Testability of the Role of Natural Selection within Theories of Population Genetics and Evolution." *British Journal of the Philosophy of Science* 29 (1978):223-242.

Wiley, E. O. "Karl R. Popper, Systematics, and Classification—A Reply to Walter Bock and Other Evolutionary Taxonomists." *Systematic Zoology* 24 (1975):233-243.

——. *Phylogenetics: The Theory and Practice of Phylogenetic Systematics*. New York: John Wiley and Sons, 1981.

Williams, M. B. "Deducing the Consequences of Evolution: A Mathematical Model." *Journal of Theoretical Biology* 29 (1970):343-385.

——. "The Logical Status of the Theory of Natural Selection and Other Evolutionary Controversies: Resolution by Axiomatization." In *The Methodological Unity of Science*, edited by M. Bunge, pp. 84-102. Dordrecht: D. Reidel, 1973a.

——. "Falsifiable Predictions of Evolutionary Theory." *Philosophy of Science* 40, no. 4 (1973b):518-537.

Wilson, E. O. *Sociobiology, The New Synthesis*. Cambridge: Harvard University Press, 1975a.

——. "Human Decency is Animal." *The New York Times Magazine*, October 12 (1975b):38-50.

Ziman, J. *Reliable Knowledge*. Cambridge: Cambridge University Press, 1978.

SECTION FOUR

The Edge of
Discovery

The Origin of
the Cosmos and the Earth

GEORGE O. ABELL

Introduction

A learned professor of astronomy had just delivered an inspiring popular lecture on cosmology, in which he described the expanding universe, the big bang, and the like. During the question period an elderly lady raised her hand, was recognized, and said, "You're all wrong, Mister—that's not the way it is!"

"Oh," he said politely, "how is it?"

"The earth," she said, "is supported on the backs of four elephants standing on a turtle."

"Why, that's interesting," he replied. "Tell me, what is the turtle standing on?"

" 'Nother turtle," she snapped promptly.

"I see; and what," the astronomer responded, "is the second turtle standing on?"

"It won't work, Mister! It's *turtles*, all the way down!"

From the earliest times we have wondered about the origins of the earth and the universe. For reasons that I do not fully understand, most people seem to *need* to have answers to these grand questions. The more creative individuals simply invented those answers, and the rest of us most often have accepted those inventions, which are generally expressed with more conviction than we could have mustered. Thus all cultures have their myths of the creation. But like the turtles, these speculations lead nowhere because they cannot be tested or built upon, save by more story telling. They are not, of course, within the realm of science.

Science, a method of inquiry rather than a body of knowledge, operates by simple rules: Information is gathered by experiment or observation; hypotheses are generated to synthesize or organize that information; and the hypotheses are tested by using them to predict new observations or the results of new experiments. Without testing, or even the possibility of testing, hypotheses are not part of science. As knowledge accumulates, more and more sophisticated hypotheses —eventually theories—are needed to complete the synthesis. But *truth* is never involved—only models describing the way nature behaves.

I think, though, that science does give a rational person some basis for judgment. Whereas we can never prove the absolute correctness of something (after all, we may all be dreaming, the rest of you may not even exist, or God may have perpetrated an elaborate hoax on us all), reasonable assumptions about the reality of our senses and of the concrete and repeatable results of our research do, after all, lead to some informed conclusions based on mature experience.

Most things seem to have an origin and a finite age. The earth does, and the sun, and the stars. Thus things age and, in general, evolve with time—not just life on earth, but the earth itself and presumably the universe as well. So do our ideas about nature. As our knowledge evolves, there forms a foreground that is pretty well—even very well—understood. Beyond lies the scientific frontier, where all things are *not* yet clear, and where debate goes on about the proper interpretation of available data. Gradually, as investigation (science) progresses, more and more of that frontier joins the well-trodden foreground, and the true frontier retreats; but a frontier is always there. In the following brief sketch of the origin and evolution of the universe, I shall try to distinguish between what is in the well-understood foreground (what informed, reasonable people are likely to accept, at least provisionally), and what is truly at the scientific frontier and ought not to be taken as well-established at present.

Evolution of Our Ideas about the Universe

The ancient Greeks believed there were four elements—earth, water, air, and fire—and the heavens above. The heavens were of different substance, and not subject to terrestrial laws. Yet it was in the heavens that science had its beginnings, for a regularity was discovered in the seemingly eternal motions of the celestial sphere and planets. The interpretation of the rules of planetary motion, and the motivation for their investigation, may have been far removed from our modern ideas, but that infant science and its continual refinement eventually led, in the seventeenth century, to Kepler's precise laws of planetary motion. Meanwhile terrestrial physics developed, as exemplified by Galileo's investigations of falling and moving bodies.

Newton had the genius to realize that Kepler's laws describing the falling of the planets around the sun and Galileo's laws of falling bodies on earth are different manifestations of the same thing—universal gravitation. From this realization he formulated mathematically the precise behavior of gravitation. The heavens and earth were seen to be united by the same and far more basic rules of nature. Modern science was born; and astrology, based on the planet-gods of antiquity, no longer played a credible role to those knowledgeable of the new natural philosophy.

Moreover, it was eventually shown that the same naturally occurring chemical elements (nearly one hundred, not the ancient four!)
comprise not only the earth but all objects in the universe; analysis
of moon rocks and meteorites show this, as does spectroscopic analysis
of light from the most remote galaxies. We are all of the same stuff
and subject to the same universal laws, the understanding of which
has enabled us to thread Voyager 2 through the rings of Saturn and
about its moons, and on its way to future encounters with Uranus
and Neptune.

By the eighteenth century it was known that the sun is just a
star among countless others, most of which are too faint to see without a telescope. Thomas Wright (1750) speculated that the sun and
the other stars about us make up a vast system or *galaxy*. By the end
of the century, William Herschel (1785) demonstrated that to be the
case, although it was Harlow Shapley (1918) who showed that the
sun is thousands of light years from the center of the galaxy. Today
we know that just as the earth revolves about the sun each year, the
sun revolves about the center of the galaxy with a period of some
200 million years.

The sun's eccentric (but typical) location in the galaxy was not
discovered earlier because interstellar space is not quite empty and
transparent—even though it is a far purer vacuum than any that can
be realized on earth. There are widely scattered atoms of gas, mostly
hydrogen and helium, and an even sparser distribution of microscopic
grains we call cosmic dust. The dust, thin though it is, extends through
thousands of light years of space and absorbs the light from remote
stars in the direction of the flat plane of our wheel-shaped galaxy,
dimming those stars in the distance as would a fog. This produces the
impression that we are in the center. This interstellar matter plays a
vital role in the evolution of stars.

Writing in 1755, Immanuel Kant speculated that there are other
galaxies, like our own but far removed from it and extending through
the depths of space (Kant 1969). Faint patches of light discovered in
telescopic surveys were prime candidates for these "island universes,"
as Kant called them; but it was Edwin Hubble (1925), at the Mount
Wilson Observatory in Southern California, who identified certain
stars in the nearest of those nebulous patches, and showed from the
faintnesses of those stars that Kant's idea is essentially correct. Our
own galaxy of at least several hundred billion* stars is of such great
size that light requires at least a hundred thousand years to cross it.
The distance to nearest external galaxies is several times the size of
our own system. Galaxies tend to clump into groups and clusters, but

---

*Following American practice, by one billion I mean one thousand million, not
a million million, as in Great Britain.

otherwise extend in all directions as far as we can observe—certainly for billions of light years.

Some of these ideas about the universe at large were guessed at in the nineteenth century, or even earlier. But no one had the faintest idea how old the galaxies were, or even how old the earth was, let alone how it formed. Yet respect for the success of science led serious investigators to hypothesize models of genesis that were consistent with what had been learned about physical law. Matter cannot be created from nothing, for example, and angular momentum must be conserved. One early idea for the origin of the planets was that they were drawn from the sun by the tidal action of a passing star. But the dynamics were wrong: Such pulled-out material, in addition to having the wrong chemical composition, would also have dispersed to interstellar space, and would not have ended up in nearly circular orbits about the sun. The basically correct idea, which dates at least to Laplace in 1796, is that the planets and sun condensed together from the same cloud of gas—a cloud now called the *solar nebula*.

But the solar system and its origin are inextricably tied up with the evolution of the sun and stars, so we must digress a moment to review what we have learned of stellar formation and evolution.

Stellar Evolution

Spectroscopic analysis shows that the sun and stars are mostly made up of the two lightest elements: hydrogen and helium. All of the heavier elements familiar on earth (oxygen, silicon, carbon, nitrogen, and iron, for example) are also present in the sun and in most other stars, and in roughly the same relative abundances in which they are found on earth; but they make up only about 2 percent of the total mass of the sun. Of the remaining 98 percent, the ratio (by mass) of hydrogen to helium is about 3 to 1. (Note this hydrogen-to-helium ratio, for we shall return to it later.)

Since the 1930s it has been recognized that the sun and stars derive the energy by which they shine from the thermonuclear conversion of hydrogen to helium. In the sun, every second about 600 million tons of hydrogen undergo fusion to helium, and about 4 million tons of matter are lost in the transaction—converted to energy according to Einstein's famous formula of special relativity, $E = mc^2$. Yet, compared to the total amount of hydrogen in the sun, this is an extremely gradual conversion.

On the other hand, it cannot go on forever. There is a finite store of potential nuclear energy, even in the stars. Some stars, in fact, pour energy into space a million times faster than the sun does, and so must be fusing hydrogen into helium a million times faster than does the sun. Such stars can shine at that rate for no more than about a million years—a short period of time for stars. The fact that we observe them at all is evidence that these stars must be young. We have realized since the 1940s that stars are forming even today. Since then, we have discovered ample evidence for that star formation from the clouds of gas and dust in space between the stars.

Astronomers commonly follow the evolution of a star by plotting a point representing it on a diagram that displays stellar luminosities (energy output) and surface temperatures. The points representing the overwhelming majority of stars fall into a fairly narrow band across such a diagram. That band is called the *main sequence*; it represents stars of different total mass but whose chemical elements are roughly uniformly mixed and which derive their energy from conversion of hydrogen to helium in their deep interiors, where temperatures range up to tens of millions of degrees. The sun is such a main sequence star.

Stars are so hot that all of their matter must be in the gaseous phase. Thus they are relatively simple, in that we pretty well understand the physical laws dictating their structure. We can also calculate with pretty fair confidence how stars must change their overall structure, including their luminosities and surface temperatures, as they alter their chemical compositions with nuclear reactions. We now understand quite well, we believe, how stars slowly evolve while they are on the main sequence, and how long they can stay there before so much hydrogen is converted to helium at their centers that they undergo far more drastic evolution.

When about 10 percent of its central hydrogen is exhausted, a star leaves the main sequence, expands, and cools to a greatly distended *red giant*. How long this takes depends on its total mass. A star like the sun will remain on the main sequence for a total time of about 10 billion years, but will slowly change a little during that time. From the state of the sun's present evolution, we calculate its age to be roughly five billion years.

A star of high luminosity exhausts 10 percent of its hydrogen and becomes a red giant much faster than the sun; one of lower luminosity takes longer than the sun will. There are many star clusters in the galaxy, and presumably stars in the same cluster have a common origin and age. Thus comparison of the luminosities and temperatures of the stars in a cluster indicates which stars have left the main sequence, and hence indicates the age of the cluster. Some clusters have ages of only a few million years; others are estimated at from 11 to 16 billion years. The sun (and the solar system) is thus considerably younger than the oldest systems of stars found in the galaxy, and so of course much younger than the galaxy itself.

Significantly, the oldest systems of stars have a far lower proportion of heavier elements (that is, elements heavier than hydrogen and helium) than does the sun—down to only 1 percent or less of the solar ratio—while younger stars have a greater abundance of the heavy elements. We now understand how this can be in terms of the more advanced stages of stellar evolution. The central cores of red giants become extremely hot, reaching hundreds of millions of degrees—hot enough for helium to fuse into carbon, and subsequently into still heavier elements. Moreover, late in their lives some stars explode in violent *supernova* eruptions, during which nuclear reactions can "cook up" all chemical elements.

In any case, eventually a star must exhaust its store of nuclear fuel and die. The final stages of stellar evolution are now believed to be white dwarfs for most stars (compact objects with a mass similar to the sun's but a size similar to the earth's); neutron stars for some (highly compressed bodies only a few miles across and consisting entirely of neutrons); and possibly, for certain stars, black holes (bodies of such high surface gravity that even light cannot escape). We cannot go into detail here, but in many cases, before reaching those final states, stars must eject some of their matter into space, either in an orderly ejection of a shell of gas known as a *planetary nebula*, or in a more violent outburst such as a supernova. In either event, that matter, enriched in heavy elements by nuclear reactions in the star during its late evolutionary stages, is returned to the interstellar medium, so that future generation stars that form from that material will have a greater abundance of those heavier atoms than did the original stars. Thus heavy elements comprise 2 percent of the mass of the sun, a later generation star, while the oldest stars are more nearly pure hydrogen and helium. This nucleosynthesis of matter in the galaxy is, of course, very slow. Throughout the galaxy's history, the ratio of hydrogen to helium would not be expected to vary much from 3:1, despite the gradual conversion of hyrodgen to helium in stellar interiors.

Stellar evolution theory dates from 1920, but it has developed rapidly since 1950. The theory is far from complete, and there are many unanswered questions. For example, the ages of the oldest star clusters are still uncertain; there are still unresolved problems concerning the low emission of neutrinos by the sun; the many late stages of evolution, including stages of variability, are only partly understood; and many other problems remain. Nevertheless, we have made enormous progress, and we believe we know the general picture, despite the many loose threads. Our lack of complete knowledge does not imply complete ignorance.

For example, suppose your neighbor buys a new car but jealously hides it from your view. Finally, one day you catch a glimpse of it as the neighbor leaves for work. It is, you note, a four-door sedan, not a coupe. It is a large car, not a compact. It is blue, certainly not white, red, or black. You think, but are not sure, that you noticed a radio antenna. Probably, but not certainly, the car has a radio. You have no idea, though, what color the upholstery is, whether it has a real spare tire or one of those little "space savers," how many cylinders it has, or whether it has a regular carburator or fuel injection. At least, though, you can say it is *not* a two-door white Fiat!

Origin of the Solar System

We have seen that the sun formed relatively recently in the history of the galaxy. Moreover, there is convincing evidence that the solar system and the sun formed at the same time. Analysis of the relative abundances of radioactive elements and their decay products in moon rocks, meteorites, and the earth all lead to total ages for the parent bodies of 4.5 billion years, in excellent agreement with the age of the sun as deduced from stellar evolution theory.

Today there is pretty general agreement on the broad outline of the formation of the solar system. The details are uncertain and parts of the picture are still somewhat speculative, not because the subject is particularly mysterious but because we simply do not yet have enough information to choose among the possibilities. Thanks to the great successes of our recent space probes, however, there are far fewer uncertainties now than there were a decade ago.

Now to return to the solar nebula, that cloud of interstellar gas that eventually became the sun and planets a little under 5 billion years ago. Originally it had to have a diameter thousands of times that of the orbit of the most distant present planet—perhaps as much as a light year or so. It also had to have some original net rotation, probably due to the rotation of the galaxy itself. The original cloud rotation could have been exceedingly slight, merely a tiny net imbalance of the many random motions of the gases within it.

Perhaps the solar nebula represented a fluctuation of density, so that it was very slightly more dense than the gas in the interstellar medium surrounding it. In any case, it must have been gravitationally unstable, in that its own gravitation was enough to pull its parts together. So it began to contract under its own gravity, and to conserve its angular momentum as it contracted it rotated faster and faster, as an ice skater spinning on the toe of a skate pulls her arms to her body. After a time the rotation began to produce an orderly structure.

Eventually matter in the outer equatorial region of the rotating cloud, moving ever faster as it contracted, attained a high enough speed to stay in a circular orbit about the center of mass of the cloud. Subsequently, material in that part of the cloud could not come closer to the center—just as an artificial satellite well outside the earth's atmosphere remains in perpetual orbit, never falling to the ground. Thus material in the equatorial region of the nebula was simply left behind in a roughly circular orbit as the rest of the cloud continued to fall inward. As time went on, more and more material was left behind the shrinking cloud, moving in circular orbits and forming a roughly disk-like accretion of material. Matter in this region could no longer contract toward its center, but matter on either side could fall toward it (falling toward the disk in a direction parallel to the axis of rotation). In this way the rotating solar nebula flattened itself into a disk.

The infalling atoms picked up speed as they fell, and when the gas density became high enough for them to collide with each other, the kinetic energy was distributed among the atoms, becoming heat. Most of this heat was radiated away from the disk, but in the central condensation—which would become the sun—the density grew until the gases of the protosun became opaque. The opacity trapped the heat inside, and the pressure produced by the heat slowed the contraction. The shrinking nebula had become a great globe of hot gas that could contract only very gradually as it slowly radiated away the heat trapped in its interior. Thus a star (the sun) was born at the center, containing perhaps half or more of the material of the original cloud. The rest of the nebula was in the form of a relatively cold rotating disk, from which the planets and their satellites formed. Much later, the gas of the nebula that did *not* find its way into the sun or the small solid bodies was blown away by solar radiation.

In the cooler disk many of the atoms combined to form molecules (although most of the matter was still hydrogen and helium), and some of the molecules condensed to form solid grains of such materials as ice, frozen carbon dioxide, silicates, and metallic substances. It was cold enough to allow retention of all these volatile substances, and water ice was probably the dominant solid material. But in the inner part of the solar nebula the high luminosity of the new sun would have evaporated those grains composed of volatile substances, leaving only rocky and metallic particles.

In all parts of the rotating disk the orbiting particles were constantly colliding and often sticking together, and many began to grow by this accretion. A few became large enough to produce a gravitation effect on those that came near. Sometimes smaller particles would pass close enough to bump into them and stick. But if they did not pass close enough to hit, they could be gravitationally deflected to another part of the disk, or even out of the solar system altogether. In this way a few large chunks gradually won out over their neighbors, either capturing them or getting rid of them, and thereby sweeping out ring-shaped swaths in the solar nebula, all centered on the sun. These large chunks became the planets. In the final stages of this accretion the young planets swept up the last of the solid particles remaining in the disk, some of which had accreted to fair size. There had to have been many crater-producing explosions as these chunks smashed into the planets. On all planets without dense atmospheres to erode away these scars, we observe the heavy cratering produced during this final accretion process between 4 and 4.5 billion years ago.

Those planets in the inner part of the solar system—Mercury, Venus, Earth, and Mars—were built up of rocky and metallic particles. They have a lot in common and are called *terrestrial* (earthlike) planets. Indeed, Mercury, nearest the sun where the solar nebula would have been the warmest, has a high mean density indicating that it has a large proportion of iron and other metals, as expected for the particles that could survive in that part of the nebula. Far out, on the other hand, it was cool enough for icy grains to exist in addition to rocky and metallic ones. The planets that accreted out there—Jupiter, Saturn, Uranus, and Neptune—thus formed out of lots of ices as well as of rocks and metals, and became much more massive. With their greater masses and gravitation, they could grab and hold a great deal of the gas in the solar nebula as well. Thus they now contain large abundances of hydrogen and helium; Jupiter, in fact, has a present chemical composition similar to that of the sun, and very likely reflects, as the sun does, the original composition of the solar nebula. These giant planets also have a lot in common with one another, and are called *Jovian* (Jupiter-like) planets. Because they are largely composed of hydrogen and helium the Jovian planets are often called *gas planets*, although throughout most of their interiors the hydrogen and helium must be compressed to at least a liquid (if not solid) state.

The favored theory of the moon's origin is that it and the earth formed together, the moon accreting from material in orbit about the primordial earth. Some theorists, however, suggest that the moon and earth could have formed independently in different parts of the solar nebula, but at about the same distance from the sun. In this case the earth and moon would have been trapped in each other's mutual gravitational fields at a later time, a scenario a little difficult (but not impossible) to reconcile with the moon's present near-circular orbit. Most other planets have satellites, and it is believed that most of them formed by accretion from material in orbit about their parent planets. In particular, the inner satellite systems of Jupiter and Saturn strongly resemble miniature solar systems, suggesting that they formed about their planets as the planets did about the sun. Most of those satellites display heavy cratering, evidently scars from their final accretion processes. As would be expected, Voyager measurements show that the satellites of Jupiter and Saturn contain a great deal of water ice. Some of Saturn's satellites appear to be nearly entirely ice, as are the particles of Saturn's rings. Some of the satellites, however, such as Jupiter's outer ones, have eccentric orbits and even revolve from east to west (opposite to the revolution of the planets and most satellites); these were probably captured subsequently to their formation.

The terrestrial planets could not have gravitationally captured or held onto the gases present about them in the solar nebula. The present atmospheres of these planets are presumed to have come from *outgassing* of their crustal layers. Some of the solids that accreted to these worlds contained volatiles in chemical combination with other substances, such as hydrates and carbonates. Natural radioactivity in the outer layers of the young planets heated these solids and released such gases as water, carbon dioxide, and nitrogen, and these substances outgassed to the surface, especially through volcanism (which continues today). On the earth the water reached the cooler exterior and recondensed to form the oceans; most of the carbon dioxide that did not dissolve in the oceans recombined with surface rocks, leaving nitrogen as the principal constituent of the present atmosphere. (Oxygen, now about 21 percent of our atmosphere, arose from photosynthesis by green plants during the past billion years.) Argon, making up about 1 percent of the earth's atmosphere, also outgassed, produced by the radioactive decay of potassium-40 in the crust. Outgassing must have been similar on the other terrestrial planets, but the subsequent evolutions of their atmospheres have differed from planet to planet; in particular, Mercury is too small to hold an atmosphere at the temperatures prevalent there, and so has lost its outgassed materials to space.

That is not the entire story. Most (but not all) geophysicists and biologists believe that the primordial earth had a reducing atmosphere, containing ammonia, methane, and perhaps hydrogen, in addition to water, carbon dioxide, and nitrogen. These latter gases may have been formed by chemical activity at the surface of the young planet. In any event, when a mixture of such gases (called a *soup* by biologists) is irradiated with ultraviolet radiation or subjected to electrical discharges such as lightning, sugars and amino acids form in large quantities—some of the basic building blocks of living organisms (see, for example, Ponnamperuma 1972). But theories of the origin of life are addressed in the following reading.

The above scenario is taken seriously in its broad outline. There are, needless to say, many as yet unanswered questions, some of which have possible answers but lack means of verification. For others, we can only speculate. Among these questions are those of the origin of the outer satellites of the Jovian planets, and of the asteroids and comets. Other subjects for speculation include: What happened to the water that must have outgassed from the surface of Venus? What is the internal heat source of Jupiter and Saturn? Why is there an excess of Argon-36 (compared to Argon-40) in the atmosphere of Venus? What is the origin of the rings of Jupiter? What maintains the tens of thousands of discrete ringlets of Saturn revealed by the Voyager spacecraft? Is there another planet beyond Pluto that may account for small discrepancies in the motions of the Jovian planets? There are many other problems, and of course always will be, but at least we have a model that can account for most of the general characteristics of the solar system and give us a means for approaching the problem of the origin and evolution of life.

We turn now to the grandest and most difficult subject of all—the origin and evolution of the universe itself.

Cosmology

Let us review for a moment the structure of the universe. The planets of the solar system revolve about a typical star, the sun. Light requires minutes or hours to travel the distances from the planets to the sun, or from one planet to another. In contrast, light takes years to traverse the separations between the sun and other stars, and between the stars. Stars are *light years* apart. One light year is slightly less than six million million miles, not a distance that conveys much feeling to the average person. Probably a good fraction, perhaps as many as half, of those other stars may have planetary systems, but they are too remote for us to know about, given existing techniques for investigation. Some hundreds of billions of these stars, or suns, make up our galaxy, a gigantic wheel of stars, gas, and dust extending at least a hundred thousand light years across. Our galaxy is one member of a small cluster of about two dozen galaxies, most smaller than ours; that cluster extends across some three million light years, and we rather affectionately call it our Local Group. Far beyond the boundaries of the Local Group there are other, similar small clusters, and, farther still, some great clusters. Even clusters of galaxies are parts of larger units, *superclusters*, consisting of perhaps hundreds of groups and clusters of galaxies—some tens of thousands of galaxies in all—and having overall sizes that are guessed to be one to three hundred million light years. The superclusters themselves occupy perhaps 5 or 10 percent of the space of the universe but, so far as we can tell now, are themselves more or less randomly scattered through space for as far as we can see. On the largest scale, over an expanse of space that must encompass at least thousands of superclusters, space appears to be homogeneous—the same everywhere.

We know the distances to the planets in the solar system with extraordinary precision—far better than one part in a million. But our ability to survey distances accurately fades with distance. So we know the distances to the neighboring stars to within only a few percent, and to most stars in our galaxy to perhaps 10 or 20 percent; we are fairly confident of the distances to the nearest galaxies, also to about 20 percent; but to the most remote galaxies and clusters in the universe our estimates of distance are uncertain by about a factor of two. Perhaps that seems sloppy science, but remember that before 1925 most astronomers thought that our own galaxy was the entire universe. There are always uncertainties of measurement, but we are also constantly refining the techniques and improving our estimates. At least we cannot be off by a factor of hundreds or thousands, as was the case three-quarters of a century ago.

So we are situated in what, so far as we can tell, is an unbounded universe of large-scale uniformity—sameness everywhere. What does our best knowledge of physics say it should be doing? That best knowledge is provided by Einstein's general relativity theory, which agrees very well with Newton's theory, except where gravity is extraordinarily strong. However, relativity, at least in its simplest form, does *not* permit an infinite (or finite) homogeneous universe to remain static. It should collapse of its own gravitation. But why *should* the universe be static? In the 1920s several physicists and mathematicians looked carefully at relativity theory, and predicted that the universe should be expanding (Friedmann 1922; Lemaître 1927). Then, even though gravitation tries to pull everything together, if the universe is expanding fast enough we can understand why it has not already collapsed.

Let us consider what we would expect to observe if the universe were expanding uniformly. Imagine an infinite universe of balls, all spaced at random. We are sitting on one ball (the earth, perhaps); the balls do not expand, because they are held together by their own gravity, but they are separating from one another as the whole system expands. Since the universe is unbounded, we cannot be at any center; the concept has no meaning. Let the whole universe double in size, expanding to a greater infinity (you need not worry about visualizing that, because nobody can—nor the alternative, for that matter!) in a given interval of time. The balls close to us must double their distance, but do not have to move too far to do so. Those farther away, however, must move farther in that same time—that is, must go away from us at a faster rate—to double their distance. The farther away something is, the faster away from us it must move to double its distance in the same time, which is what uniform expansion means. It does not matter where we are, for there is no middle. All other observers, everywhere, would see the same thing. So it was realized in

the mid-1920s that if the real universe is uniformly expanding all remote galaxies should be moving away from each other and from us,
with speeds that are greater in proportion to their distances.

After 1925 Hubble had found ways to estimate the distances to
galaxies. There is also a simple way to measure their motions in the
line of sight. We spread out the light of a galaxy (or star, or planet)
and photograph it with a spectrograph. We find its light to be made
up of a continuous rainbow of colors, or wavelengths of light; but
the atoms of the outer layers of the stars contributing to the galaxy's
light absorb certain wavelengths, leaving dark lines at certain places
in the spectrum—darkness at those wavelengths where discrete colors
of light are absorbed. Now if the source is moving away from us the
waves of light from it are spread out (the Doppler effect), like the
sound waves from the horn of an automobile moving away; and the
light from the galaxy is observed at lower frequencies (or longer
wavelengths), just as the sound from the automobile horn is heard at
lower than normal pitch. (The reverse is noted, of course, if the source
approaches us.) If the universe is expanding, the light from remote
galaxies should show this characteristic Doppler shift to longer
wavelengths (lower frequencies), and this shift should be in proportion to the distances of the galaxies observed.

It happens that the spectra of galaxies had been under observation in a painstaking program carried out since 1912 by V. M. Slipher
(1917) at the Lowell Observatory in Arizona, long before the galaxies
were even known to be galaxies. Slipher was puzzled that most of the
faint "nebulae" (as he then regarded them) seemed to be moving
away from us at extremely high speeds—up to nearly 2000 km/s.
Hubble (1929) estimated distances to more than forty "nebulae"
whose velocities had been observed by Slipher, and found that indeed the more remote were moving away systematically faster. The
case was not convincing in 1929, but by 1931, aided with additional
observations by Milton Humason at Mount Wilson's 100-inch telescope, the velocity-distance relation (now known as the *Hubble law*)
had been extended to objects moving away at speeds of up to 30,000
km/s (Hubble and Humason 1931). It had, by then, been observa-
tionally verified that the universe is expanding. An important theoretical prediction had been realized! Victory Number 1 for twentieth
century cosmology. The Hubble law has now been extended to objects moving away at speeds of up to half that of light, and is thoroughly established.

But what about the future? If there is gravitation in the universe,
the pull of gravity between the various galaxies and other matter (if
any) should tug at the expansion and slow it down. I can throw a
baseball into the air, but gravity always wins out, and the ball soon returns to earth. On the other hand, NASA can put that ball in a rocket

and give it such speed that gravity does not win, and the ball can keep going out forever. Similarly, the universe can either stop expanding some day and give way to contraction, or it can expand forever. It depends on whether the present rate of expansion is great enough to win out over the combined gravitation of the universe.

In principle, there are ways we can tell from observations what the future of the real universe should be. One way is to look back in time, to see whether the expansion in the past was faster than it is now, and how much faster. We look back into time very simply—by looking off into the distance, for we see distant objects as they were long in the past when light left them to start its long journey across space to reach our telescopes. Unfortunately, the crucial measurements are very difficult to make, and the results are highly uncertain.

One kind of observation that is more definitive is that of the mean density of matter in the universe. We can measure the masses of galaxies by how fast their stars are moving within them, and of clusters of galaxies by how fast the member galaxies of a cluster are moving, for those speeds are dictated by the gravitational forces that accelerate those stars and galaxies, and those gravitational forces in turn depend on the total masses of the systems. This enables us to make a fairly confident estimate of the mean density of matter in the universe. That estimate, in turn, tells us how important gravitation can be, and whether it is great enough ever to stop the universal expansion. When we carry out this exercise, we find that there is far too little matter in the universe to have enough gravity to ever stop the expansion, and it thus appears that the expansion must go on forever.

If correct, this would rule out the alternative, that someday the expansion will give way to contraction, and that the universe will eventually collapse to enormous density again. Many people like the apparently ruled-out alternative, because if we can get the matter together again, we can imagine that a new cosmic explosion might start things over again, perhaps leading to a pulsating universe with many billions of years separating alternate expansions and contractions. The trouble is that even if there were enough matter to stop the expansion, there is no known physical theory that could lead to a new expansion. All that we know would lead us to expect the universe to collapse into a cosmic black hole from which it could never escape. The oscillating universe theory is thus not really a theory at all but a speculation based on wishful thinking. On the other hand, we do not have any idea how the original expansion got started either, so perhaps we should not be too smug.

But, the available evidence does suggest that the universe will go on expanding forever, into an ultimate darkness and emptiness—a sort of thermodynamic Götterdämmerung. But here we are truly at the frontier, so we should not take this result too seriously. Perhaps, for example, there is dark matter in the universe of which we have no knowledge that may add gravitation but not reveal its presence otherwise. One remote possibility is neutrinos, subatomic particles emitted in certain nuclear reactions. Theory predicts that there should today be several hundred neutrinos per cubic centimeter everywhere in space. Neutrinos are generally thought to be massless, and they are very hard to detect (although they have been detected in the laboratory), but a few recent experiments suggest that they may have a tiny bit of mass. If so, it is possible that they might add enough mass to the universe to stop the expansion. This is doubtful, however, because, first, the experiments suggesting that they have mass are highly uncertain; and second, even if they do have mass, they probably would clump up in clusters or superclusters of galaxies, in which case their contribution has already been measured. But such doubts remain, and any month new results might drastically alter our conclusions about the future of the universe. But, then, what about its past?

About the past we can say more. If the universe is expanding, we need only extrapolate backward to find that it was denser in the past. At some point all of the matter was packed together in a superdense state, and that had to have occurred at a finite time in the past; how long ago can easily be calculated from the present rate of expansion. Unfortunately, the expansion rate itself is uncertain, because of the uncertainty of distances of remote galaxies; we know how fast they are moving, but until we know accurate distances, we cannot say how long it took them, at their present speeds, to reach those distances. We can, though, make a rough estimate, and that estimate places the time of the dense universe at between 8 and 20 billion years ago.

One of the first people to consider the physics of that early universe was the Belgian priest Abbé Georges Lemaître, who was also highly trained in physics and mathematics, and who had made a special study of relativity theory. Lemaître (1945) postulated that the universe began in a hyperdense state that he called the *primeval atom.* His idea was that the primeval atom fissioned into many smaller parts, and each of them into still smaller ones, and so on, until eventually the present distribution of various atoms observed about us resulted. It was probably the first quantitative postulate of a universe that evolved from an explosive and finite beginning.

As knowledge of nuclear physics progressed, it was clear that Lemaître's idea of a universe starting with nuclear fission was not possible. In the late 1940s George Gamow and his associates (Alpher, Bethe, and Gamow 1948), put forth a new model assuming that the universe started in a hot dense state and consisted only of fundamental subatomic particles. In Gamow's model, nuclear fusion built up the various atoms we find today. Note that Gamow still postulated an explosive beginning, which he dubbed the "big bang."

There are also problems with Gamow's model, however. More detailed calculations show that at the densities that would have had to exist in the early universe no atoms heavier than those of helium can be formed. But then where did the heavy elements of which *we* are composed come from? This problem concerned Fred Hoyle, British astrophysicist, and led him to investigate the possible properties of the carbon-12 nucleus that would allow its fusion from helium at temperatures of a few hundred million degrees in the centers of red giant stars. Hoyle (1954) predicted that carbon-12 must have a nuclear resonance at 7.7 million electron volts, a prediction that proved to be correct, and that led to the realization that nucleosynthesis can occur in stars late in their evolution (as described earlier). Hoyle's brilliant deduction, by the way, gave us the insight that the atoms of our own bodies were originally synthesized in the centers of earlier-generation stars; we are quite literally made of stardust.

At this writing the most generally accepted calculation of conditions for the early universe is that by Wagoner, Fowler, and Hoyle (1967) at Caltech. This *standard model* for the big bang starts off much like Gamow's. It shows, however, that only hydrogen, helium, and a trace of deuterium (heavy hydrogen) survived the primeval fireball. The heavier elements, in this theory, must have formed later in stars. All of this may seem terribly academic and far removed from reality, but there is one highly significant point: The theory predicts that the ratio of hydrogen to helium, by mass, should be 3:1. Chalk up another victory for cosmology!

But there are problems, nevertheless. For one thing, an upper limit to the time since the big bang is given by the present rate of the expansion of the universe—uncertain, as we have said. However, the most recent, and seemingly promising, calibrations of the extragalactic distance scale suggest that the universe is less than 10 billion years old. This turns out to be less than the age estimated for the oldest star clusters in our own galaxy, and to allow time for galaxy formation, to say nothing of the slowing of the expansion since the big bang, we should have another few billion years cushion, anyway. So there may be a problem with the age of the universe; perhaps the recent distance scale determinations are wrong, or perhaps stellar evolution theory leading to the ages of the oldest clusters is offbase. Or perhaps the whole theoretical structure is more complex than we have so far considered.

There are also problems of understanding how the entire universe managed to go off together in the big bang. Light travels at a finite speed, and it would seem that different parts of a virtually (if not actually) infinite universe would have no way of communicating with themselves, in order to set the clock to go off in unison everywhere; or, perhaps they didn't. Moreover, we have no idea how the universe could have gotten into the state it had to be in to make the big bang. Science, in other words, has by no means all of the answers, nor does it pretend to.

So the whole idea, you may be thinking, is no better than that of the turtles. But I think it is. It may be no nearer the truth, whatever that means. But our current ideas are closer to producing a self-consistent model that is testable, and the testability is what makes it science. Note that two tests of the most seriously considered idea of the origin of the universe have been realized: its expansion, and the hydrogen-helium ratio resulting from the big bang. But there is yet one more!

Alpher and Herman (1948) pointed out that the hot universe Gamow envisioned (and that we envision) would be an opaque gas. Matter and radiation would be interacting in equilibrium with each other. The hot gas would also be ionized, with nuclei of hydrogen (protons) and electrons moving about separately, as they do in the interiors of stars. However, as the hot universe expanded, it would have to cool, and eventually the gas would reach a temperature at which the protons and electrons could recombine and form neutral hydrogen. From then on, the matter would no longer interact much with radiation, and each would go its own way. The matter would cool, and eventually condense into galaxies or stars, whichever came first.

But what about the radiation? It should still be around! When last emitted by hot matter it was in the form of visible light, like that from a star. But the radiation released from our part of the universe has long since flowed away at the speed of light to remote regions. If we want to see any of the remaining glow of the big bang, we must look at least 8 billion, perhaps 20 billion, years into the past.

But we can and *do* look into the past by looking off into space, to see those parts of the universe as they were when light left them far in the past. Thus there is a shell surrounding us, at a distance of 8 or possibly 20 billion light years, which we are seeing as it was 8 or 20 billion years in the past.

But, as Alpher and Herman realized, those remote parts of the universe are receding from us at great speed because of the expansion of the universe—at nearly the speed of light. At such a speed for the source, its radiation would be Doppler shifted from visible light to radio waves. It would, however, have a very characteristic spectrum—that is, a well-defined intensity at various wavelengths.

The Alpher-Herman prediction did not attract much attention in the late 1940s because there was then no way to observe such radiation; by the 1960s, when there was a way, the work had been overlooked. But Princeton physicist Robert Dicke and his associates (Dicke et al. 1965) looked at the matter independently of Alpher and Herman and arrived at essentially the same conclusion. The Princeton team even built a special radio antenna to detect the signals from the "creation" that they expected to be present.

But before they had their antenna fully operative they were scooped, by accident, by Arno Penzias and Robert Wilson (1965) at the Bell Laboratories at Holmdel, New Jersey, only a few miles away. Penzias and Wilson had been attempting to use a delicate horn antenna for absolute calibration of galactic radio sources and had run into problems with unexpected interference. After much effort and ingenious analysis, they had concluded that the signal they were observing was of cosmic origin. It was, of course, the radiation from that dying glow of the explosion that began the expansion of the universe. Since then the radiation has been measured at many different wavelengths with ever greater accuracy, and in many different directions in the sky. New subtleties have been discovered, but the basic interpretation of the observation is not generally disputed: Evidence of a hot primordial universe has been detected. A third point for cosmological theory!

Of course, there is a host of uncertainties, problems, and unanswered questions: The hydrogen-helium ratio and microwave background radiation can be interpreted, albeit with some difficulty, by alternate explanations, and there could be something far more subtle at work that has not yet been considered. We are especially cautious about concluding whether or not the universe is open (will expand forever) or closed (will contract again someday). There is concern about the problem of the ages of the oldest star clusters and the best evidence (at this writing) on the age of the universe itself. Our general conclusions rest on certain simplifying assumptions about the homogeneity of the entire universe (whatever that means). There are some questions about whether or not the galaxy began its existence with pure hydrogen and helium. We may be unjustifiably extending laws of science learned in local environments to the universe as a whole, where they may be entirely inapplicable. We are playing games—cosmology is the best sport of all, because it is the ultimate game. We are at the frontier, and we make no claims of omniscience. But we do insist that all who play the game, and expect to be taken seriously, obey the rules, and stick to hypotheses that can be tested by rigorous, objective criteria.

And for all of the uncertainty (which I regard as enjoyable, for it is the food of science), we have learned something:

1. Almost certainly the universe is expanding.
2. There is now strong evidence that it had a hot beginning, or at least a hot earlier era.

3. There is very strong evidence for the evolution of the chemical composition of the galaxy (and presumably of the universe as well); in particular, the original ratio of hydrogen to helium is very close to the predictions of cosmological theory.

4. Certainly the universe is very old, as is the younger earth (unless we are prepared to accept that we are dreaming, or that God has created a gigantic hoax).

It seems to me that a rational, properly informed person, given the evidence, will seriously consider (with proper skepticism for details) the general picture of an old, expanding universe, and of a more recently formed, but still old, earth, formed by accretion, along with the other planets, in a solar system more than 4 billion years old; and that he will certainly recognize the overwhelming evidence for the evolution of the universe, the stars, the solar system, and the earth itself.

Obviously we do not know all yet, not even very much; we are scratching the surface. But surely we have come a long way, and can rule out a world that is six thousand years old, a small static universe centered on the earth, only four elements, separate laws for the heavens and earth, and turtles all the way down.

REFERENCES

Alpher, Ralph A.; Bethe, Hans; and Gamow, George. "The Origin of Chemical Elements." *Physical Review* 73, no. 4 (1948):803-804.

Alpher, Ralph A., and Herman, Robert C. "Evolution of the Universe." *Nature* 162, no. 4124 (1948):774-775.

Dicke, Robert H.; Peebles, Peter J. E.; Roll, Peter G.; and Wilkinson, David T. "Cosmic Black-Body Radiation." *Astrophysical Journal* 142, no. 1 (1965): 414-418.

Friedman, Aleksandr. "Über die Krümmung des Raumes." *Zeitschrift für Physik* 10 (1922):377-386.

Herschel, William. "On the Construction of the Heavens." *Philosophical Transactions of the Royal Society of London* 75, no. 1 (1785):213-266.

Hoyle, Fred. "On Nuclear Reactions Occurring in Very Hot Stars. I. The Synthesis of Elements from Carbon to Nickel." *The Astrophysical Journal Supplement Series* 1, no. 1 (1954):121-146.

Hubble, Edwin P. "Cepheids in Spiral Nebulae." *Publications of the American Astronomical Society* 5 (1925):261-264.

———. "A Relation between Distance and Radial Velocity among Extra-galactic Nebulae." *Proceedings of the National Academy of Sciences USA* 15 (1929):168-173.

Hubble, Edwin P., and Humason, Milton L. "The Velocity-Distance Relation among Extra-galactic Nebulae." *Astrophysical Journal* 74 (1931):43-80.

Kant, Immanuel. *Universal Natural History and Theory of the Heavens.* 1755. Ann Arbor: University of Michigan Press, 1969.

Laplace, Pierre Simon (Marquis de). *Exposition du Système du Monde*. 1796. Oeuvres Complètes de Laplace, Publiées sous les auspices de L'Academie des Sciences, par Mm. les Secrétaires Perpetuels, tome sixième. Paris: Gautier-Villars, 1884.

Lemaître, Georges (M. L'Abbé). "Un Univers Homogène de Masse Constante et de Rayon Croissant, Rendant Compte de la Vitesse Radiale des Nébuleures Extra-galactiques." *Annales de la Société Scientifique de Bruxelles (Série A)* 47 (1927):49-60.

——. *The Primeval Atom, an Essay on Cosmogony*. New York: Van Nostrand, 1950 edition. (Based on an address delivered to the Société Helvétique des Sciènces Naturelles, 1945.)

Penzias, Arno A., and Wilson, Robert W. "A Measurement of Excess Antenna Temperature at 4080 Mc/s." (Letter to the Editor) *The Astrophysical Journal* 142, no. 1 (1965):419-421.

Ponnamperuma, Cyril. *The Origins of Life*. New York: Cutton, 1972.

Shapley, Harlow. "Studies Based on the Colors and Magnitudes in Stellar Clusters. VII. The Distances, Distributions in Space, and Dimensions of 69 Globular Clusters." *The Astrophysical Journal* 148, no. 3 (1918):154-181.

Slipher, Vesto M. "Nebulae." *Proceedings of the American Philosophical Society* 56 (1917):403-409.

Wagoner, Robert V.; Fowler, William A.; and Hoyle, Fred. "On the Synthesis of Elements at Very High Temperatures." *The Astrophysical Journal* 148, no. 1, 1 (1967):3-49.

Wright, Thomas. *An Original Theory or New Hypothesis of the Universe*. 1750. Facsimile reprint with *A Theory of the Universe*. London: MacDonald; New York: American Elsevier, 1971.

The Origin of Life

HAROLD J. MOROWITZ
Department of Molecular Biophysics and Biochemistry
Yale University

Introduction

In seeking life's origin, there are two directions of inquiry that seem most plausible in view of the hierarchy of biological organization. We may start with the properties of contemporary organisms and fossils and work back, or we may start with the nature of atoms and molecules and work forward. The first approach begins with paleontological evidence, phylogenetic data, and biochemical generalizations, and moves toward recovering the nature of the earliest forms. Alternatively, physics, chemistry, and planetology can be taken as starting points and an attempt made to formulate a probable sequence of processes leading to biogenesis. In a completely successful formulation these two approaches will converge.

There are several tacit assumptions underlying efforts to investigate biogenesis in this way, and it is best to try to make them explicit at an early stage. First, by *origin of life* we mean the formation of bounded self-replicating entities, or *cells*. The prior chemistry of the earth may have involved related processes, and other life forms are conceptually possible, but the only life known with certainty is cellular in nature. A second assumption is that life did, in fact, originate on earth from inorganic materials. The one other possibility is that living forms migrated here from elsewhere in the universe. In the absence of evidence of space travel by such panspermia, it seems best to exhaust the possibility of earthly origin before looking for more distant explanations. In any case immigration does not solve the basic problem but only changes the question to how life originated on Krypton or in spiral galaxy M81 or wherever the panspermia came from.

A third assumption is that the origin of life is a scientific problem. This does not mean that it is solved but that it is solvable using methods that characterize the scientific endeavor. New principles may be sought, but these are postulated to be of the same philosophical (epistemological) character as the existing laws of science. A

The writing of this manuscript was supported by a fellowship from the Guggenheim Foundation.

243

fourth assumption is that the origin of cellular life is an accessible scientific problem. A number of investigators have believed that the origin required so many chance events of such low probability that we have no way of studying it within the framework of science, even though it involved perfectly normal laws of nature. According to this view the origin can only be studied as a problem in history, an unfolding in time whose traces have been all but obliterated by subsequent events. The chance postulate precludes the possibility of investigating the subject experimentally. The assumption of accessibility, on the other hand, provides the best intellectual climate for exploring the problem to its limits. It is our point of departure.

The view that life's origin cannot be predicted from physics because of the dominance of chance factors was elaborated by Jacques Monod in his book *Chance and Necessity*. The chance he discussed was largely genetic, but he also extrapolated back to the prebiotic chemical epoch—the period before life began on earth. A later section of this reading develops the counterargument that many of the features leading up to life can be predicted from physics. It is premature to rule out life as a deterministic rather than chance phenomenon, particularly since we are only beginning to develop those branches of physical sciences (nonequilibrium thermal physics, theoretical organic chemistry, and network theory) necessary to study the problem. To assert that biogenesis cannot be predicted from physics is a self-fulfilling prophecy because it discourages us from the very hard work necessary to pursue the problem to its limit.

Working Down

Starting from the top, the examination of present-day biota presents us with two great classes of organisms, the prokaryotes and the eukaryotes. The prokaryotes are unicellular and lack membrane-bounded organelles such as nuclei. They include bacteria, blue-green algae, methanogens, and mycoplasma. The taxonomic relationships of these organisms to one another are unclear, but there is no doubt that prokaryotes form a cohesive group distinct from all other organisms in their mode of cellular organization. The eukaryotes are characterized by internal cellular organelles such as mitochondria, chloroplasts, and nuclear membranes. They also have chromosomes and undergo the elaborate processes of cell division characteristic of those structures. The eukaryotes include plants, animals, algae, fungi, and protozoa.

Because of their greater simplicity it is widely assumed that the prokaryotes preceded the eukaryotes, and the next step back in time would be the ancestors of these unicellular forms. But we cannot rule out the possibility that eukaryotes came first, or that both forms had a common ancestor that was neither prokaryote nor eukaryote. At this point we move from cytological to biochemical considerations.

Regardless of their specific structural form, all cells have certain features in common that characterize life as we now know it. These features thus constitute the irreducible minimum specification of all known life. The boundary that separates each cell from its surroundings is the plasma membrane, a closed shell about one ten-millionth of an inch in thickness. The membrane is largely made up of special part-lipid (oily), part-polar (water-loving, or *hydrophilic*) molecules that fit together in a regular way. The membrane forms a very thin, oily layer made of the lipid portions of the molecules, and this barrier separates the watery interior of the cell from the watery exterior. On the average the membrane is the thickness of two polar lipid molecules and is thus called a *bimolecular leaflet* structure. Such molecular aggregates require components with long, thin, oily (lipid) parts attached to a hydrophilic (polar) group. The condensation of these molecules into a sheetlike structure is the universal physical process used in constructing biological membranes.

The essential function of a membrane is to separate a cell from its surroundings. The membrane defines a living entity by providing a geometric and chemical boundary—chemical in the sense that it forms a barrier to the free flow of molecules. Present-day membranes have numerous proteins associated with the structural polar lipids. These proteins carry out a variety of functions, including catalysis (speeding up of chemical reactions), transport, and energy transformation. Primordial membranes may have been constructed almost entirely of polar lipid molecules, and thus may have lacked many of the diverse associated proteins.

On the surface and within the membrane, chemical events take place that are responsible for the functions of transport, energy transformation, molecular rearrangement, macromolecule synthesis, and organelle formation. Among the macromolecules synthesized is DNA, which forms the structures within the cell that carry hereditary information. Each molecule of DNA consists of two linear polymers of nucleotides of the bases adenine, thymine, guanine, and cytosine. The nucleotide bases are paired between the polymers so that the two polymers complement each other; adenine is always paired with thymine and guanine is always paired with cytosine. Thus the DNAs exist as double helical structures made of linear sequences of paired nucleotides. The molecules can be synthesized outside of the cell using primer DNA, nucleotides, enzymes, and energy-providing molecules.

Many investigators of the origin of life have assumed that self-replicating nucleic acids occurred in the primordial soup before the formation of primitive cells—and it is true, as noted above, that such replication can occur outside cells. Others (including myself) postulate that the formation of membrane vesicles was the primary event in biogenesis. There is a sharp dichotomy of views on this issue: Bioenergeticists favor the sequence of membrane → metabolism → macromolecule synthesis, and geneticists favor the order of metabolism → macromolecule synthesis → membrane. This issue will eventually have to be resolved both experimentally and theoretically. For now, one should be aware of the divergence of opinions, although the rest of this reading follows the membrane hypothesis.

Returning to ubiquitous cellular functions, we next examine the process by which nutrient molecules are transported into the cells and waste materials are transported out. This process is usually carried out by protein molecules associated with the membrane. Carrying materials across the membrane often requires energy expenditure, so these two functions may be closely coupled.

Energy within cells is usually liberated by oxidation-reduction reactions (electron transfers from a reduced to an oxidized molecule), and transformed into a small number of storage forms. Most molecular reactions requiring energy are linked to the breakdown (or hydrolysis) of adenosine triphosphate (ATP) into adenosine diphosphate (ADP) and phosphate (P). ATP molecules serve as universal energy exchange elements in cellular systems and must therefore be generated constantly by cellular metabolism. This is the primary mechanism by which cells store energy. A second method of energy storage is in the separation of electrical charge and pH gradients across the membrane. The two methods of storage are connected by enzyme systems associated with membranes. Highly reduced compounds, such as reduced nicotinamide adenine dinucleotide ($NADH_2$) and reduced flavin adenine dinucleotide ($FADH_2$), also store energy. Oxidation of these compounds occurs at membranes and is associated with energy being changed to other forms. While the processes listed above are common to all cellular systems, in prokaryotes they take place at the plasma membrane while in eukaryotes they tend to be associated with the inner mitochondrial membrane.

The molecular rearrangements of intermediary metabolism perform two basic functions. First they carry nutrient molecules through a number of transformations leading to those substances necessary for the synthesis of cellular materials. Amino acids and nucleotides are among the kinds of molecules that must be produced. Second, some of the chemical reactions of metabolism must lead to the making of ATP, $NADH_2$, and $FADH_2$ to provide the energy that all subsequent living processes require. The reaction networks for these two functions are exquisitely interrelated, so as to optimize the value of ingested molecules in the cellular economy.

The syntheses of macromolecules of DNA, RNA, and protein from their metabolic precursors are highly interrelated. Starting from double stranded DNA with its pair of complementary chains, two possible processes occur. The strands may unwind, each acting as a template for the formation of a new complementary strand. This leads to two identical double stranded DNA molecules, each containing the complete hereditary information, and constitutes the process of replication of the genetic material.

Alternatively, one strand of the DNA may act as a template for the synthesis of its complementary RNA. This RNA is released and acts as a messenger specifying the sequence of amino acids in proteins. Protein synthesis occurs at ribosomes (large structures made of proteins and RNAs). It is an elaborate process involving ATP, amino acids, and activating enzymes in solution, as well as other enzymes that act at the ribosomal surface. The synthesized proteins include both cellular enzymes and structural proteins.

The biochemical steps just briefly listed appear to be an irreducible minimum set of operations for modern organisms. All present-day living forms grow and replicate using the same molecular mechanisms and the same basic pathways. The unity-within-diversity characteristic of modern biology has its basis in this ubiquitousness of molecular hardware and chemical reactions in all living things.

The Minimum Free-Living Organism

In examining present-day biota, biogenesis may be approached by seeking the simplest known free-living organism consistent with all the generalizations of biochemistry and molecular biology. Such an organism can be more complex than the first cells, but it establishes an upper limit of sophistication for primordial systems. Since all hereditary information in prokaryotes is linearly encoded in DNA genomes, the modern free-living organism with the smallest genome may be presumed to be the simplest one. Obligate intracellular parasites are excluded because they may use part of the host cell's genetic information. Rickettsiae, for example, have very small genomes. Mitochondria and chloroplasts, which some biologists believe to be derived from endosymbionts (organisms that entered host cells from outside and then adapted to life within), now contain very minimal amounts of DNA.

The search for genetic simplicity is presently focused on the mycoplasma, a group of prokaryotes lacking a cell wall and of extremely small cell size. Some species of mycoplasma have genome sizes in the neighborhood of 440–600×10^6 daltons (molecular weight units). Since on average it requires about 800,000 daltons of

DNA to encode a single functional protein, the smallest known mycoplasmas specify about 550 biochemical processes. The organism's complexity is limited by the amount of genetic information.

A mycoplasma cell, which may be as small as one-half of a micron in diameter, consists of:

1. A lipid bilayer plasma membrane with attached proteins and carbohydrates;
2. A single closed loop of double stranded DNA containing the entire genetic information;
3. A small number of ribosomes;
4. A few thousand protein molecules, messenger RNAs, and a larger number of ATPs and assorted small molecules.

Calculating theoretically from the known generalizations of molecular biology to the smallest, simplest organism that could carry out absolutely necessary functions, such an organism would require a genome size at least half that of mycoplasma. In other words, *the simplest free-living organisms discovered to date are close to the theoretical limit of simplicity based on generalizations derived from starting at the top and working down.* This is not to suggest that mycoplasma are necessarily primitive; they may be degenerate forms of bacteria. They have, however, achieved great simplicity while retaining the ability to exist as free-living forms.

The search for the simplest living cell is always open-ended. Current cell culture techniques may not be adequate, or the search may not have been exhaustive. However, the closeness between the theoretical and experimental sizes suggests that such a search would be a matter of refinement unless organisms were found using presently unknown methods of carrying out known functions.

It is possible to extrapolate from the present structure of molecular biology and move back one step toward earlier systems. Since there are viruses that encode their genetic information in double stranded RNA, and since in principle all known hereditary processes could be carried out using RNA in place of DNA, we can envision an even simpler cell than the existing ones: a cell that uses no steps involving DNA. The apparent limit of simplicity, working backward from the top, is a simplified mycoplasma-like cell containing double stranded RNA as the coding material. We can, however, note the ubiquity of certain functions such as specific catalysis, transmembrane charge separation, and template complementarity.

The next step is to work up from the bottom from first principles of the physical sciences and then focus on the gulf between the two views.

Working Up

In introducing the physical-chemical approach to the origin of life, we trace out certain aspects of the subject going back to the elegant experiments of Louis Pasteur, who showed that previous claims for the spontaneous origin of bacteria were false and represented microbial contamination of the growth medium. These experiments were so convincing that they tended to table the question of the origin of life for a substantial number of years.

In the 1920s A. I. Oparin and J. B. S. Haldane reopened the issue of biogenesis by noting the possibility of the spontaneous synthesis of biochemically interesting compounds in a reducing environment (one dominated by an excess of hydrogen, in contrast to our present oxygen-rich atmosphere). Their ideas were finally subjected to experimental test by Stanley Miller and Harold Urey in 1951. The long delay between the proposal and the experiments is of interest from the point of view of the history of science. I would like to suggest two reasons for the thirty-year interval, one conceptual and one technological. The conceptual difficulty stemmed from the paradigm of organic chemistry, which was the synthesis of pure crystalline compounds. The idea of a mixed synthesis with a variety of product compounds in varying concentrations was contrary to the method of approach. The technological problem stemmed from the difficulty of analyzing such a rich mixture of products. By the 1950s paper chromatography had gone a long way toward solving the analytical problem, and a new approach was undertaken.

The Urey-Miller synthesis was carried out by a gas phase spark discharge in an atmosphere of hydrogen, methane, ammonia, and water. It produced a surprising array of amino acids and various possible metabolic intermediates. Their approach has initiated an extensive investigation of mixed syntheses starting with a wide variety of compounds of carbon, hydrogen, nitrogen, and oxygen. These experiments are usually run under relatively reducing conditions with external energy inputs. In addition to spark discharge the energy sources have included ultraviolet light, ionizing radiation, heat, shock waves, and chemical potential. Some experiments have added compounds of phosphorus and sulfur. The variety of investigations have been almost uniformly successful in producing a rich mixture of product molecules that were possible participants in the origin of life. Indeed the very success of so many of these experiments in generating potential biochemicals makes it difficult to choose among them as models of the actual precursors, energy sources, or boundary conditions of the primitive planet. At first this inability to use mixed synthesis experiments to identify the actual chemistry of the primordial earth was a disappointment. Their universal success may, however, yield another, unexpected, type of information. If the reaction products are generated over such a wide range of conditions and starting materials, then there are *system features* governing the process. This leads to an even more deterministic view of the origin of life. The current understanding is that this family of gas phase syntheses is dominated by free radical reactions and hydrogen abstractions leading to the synthesis of molecules of hydrogen cyanide, formaldehyde, and ethane. These molecules then strongly influence the synthesis of subsequent products.

A second series of experiments, initiated by Sidney Fox and his coworkers, has demonstrated, in the absence of water, the synthesis of polymers possessing many of the properties of proteins. These polypeptides are nonrandom in composition and sequence, and under favorable circumstances demonstrate catalytic function. Again certain system properties appear to be operative.

These series of investigations have led to a proposed scheme of the following sort:

precursors ⟶ small molecules ⟶ polymers ⟶ functional macromolecules ⟶ organelles ⟶ cells.

At this point a note on the logical status of theories of the origin of life is in order. In the absence of laboratory biogenesis or overwhelming theoretical arguments, all theories of the origin of life have a scenario aspect. They do not have that kind of certainty that some people like to associate with science. Nevertheless the favored scenario should be the most probable one, given the known laws of science and the known astrophysical and geophysical constraints. If life is a general phenomenon, as distinguished from a chance event, then our procedures should be able to narrow in on understanding its origin. The answers should be somewhat independent of the details. On the other hand, if life is unique, we can only do our best to reconstruct a history that had no witnesses and left few remains of its earliest days.

It is my contention that the conventional path from reducing molecules to cells pays insufficient attention to the origin and character of bioenergetics; it focuses on chemistry, with inadequate consideration of the idea that chemical structures are intimately associated with energy processing, and their character must reflect that association. In modern organisms this is best seen in intermediary metabolism, which is the core of biological unity. I shall proceed to reformulate a view of life's origin and incorporate the highly significant results of the last twenty years of research in bioenergetics.

First, the modern biosphere is almost entirely powered by radiation from the sun. The global ecosystem is run by absorbing solar photons, capturing the energy in chemical form, using that energy to drive all processes, and eventually releasing the energy as heat. This energy-flow point of view provides the framework within which all large-scale biological phenomena must be understood. We have the choice of assuming either that the solar energy flow process has been continuous since the origin of life, or that there was a primordial energy source that has since been replaced by solar radiation. Using the principle of continuity in the absence of any contradictory evidence leads to postulating that the earliest ecosystem was photosynthetically driven. This does not deny the possibility that a Urey-Miller type of synthesis of precursors used other power sources, such as lightning or volcanoes; it asserts that by the time a cellular biosphere existed, the energy to drive it came from sunlight.

The existence of a chemical system with an input of solar electromagnetic energy and an output of thermal energy allows us to apply some results from statistical mechanics and network theory. The theorems state that when such chemical systems approach steady states they will have material cycles in which the lowest-energy small molecules are converted to larger, higher-energy intermediates. The intermediates are then degraded back to the original precursors. This is a description of the carbon or nitrogen cycle in ecology. Cycles do not necessarily require living organisms and will occur on any planet with the appropriate input spectrum and availability to reactants. The existence of the great global chemical-ecological cycles could thus have predated the origin of life and indeed have provided a favorable milieu for biogenesis.

The cycling theorems on which these ideas are based are rather straightforward results of physics. They indicate one of the ways in which a planet can be prepared for life in a precellular epoch. Investigators in this field have not given a great deal of consideration to this prebiotic nature of chemical-ecological cycles, but I believe it to be a point of greatest importance in developing a systematic view of biogenesis. This preparation of the planet for life stresses the sense in which the property of being alive is a reciprocal relation between organisms and environment. Although this reading focuses on the properties of the organism, we must remain cognizant of the meteorological, hydrological, and geological features that are part of the origin and perpetuation of life.

Returning to planetary energy sources, there appear to be two ways in which photochemical reactions store energy. In ordinary photochemistry a molecule absorbs a photon and is elevated to an upper electronic energy level. This excited state structure then reacts, leading to products of higher available energy than the initial reactants. The energy of the photon has been converted to the chemical potential of the products. In biological systems the absorbed photon energy causes electrical charge separation. The resulting difference of electrochemical energy drives chemical reactions leading to high-energy chemical intermediates.

A recently investigated example of biological photoconversion is provided by the salt bacterium, *Halobacter halobium*. This organism lives in brine ponds and normally gets its energy from respiration using carbohydrates in the aqueous (watery) surroundings. In the absence of free oxygen, under conditions of heavy growth, the cells produce patches of purple membrane whose principal component is the protein bacterial rhodopsin. When photons are absorbed in these purple patches, energy is stored by pumping hydrogen ions across the membrane from the cell interior to the exterior. This generates a difference of electrochemical potential across the membrane, such that the exterior is positively charged and at a lower pH than the interior. The backflow of protons down the difference of potential is linked to the production of ATP in a process similar to that taking place in mitochondria. (In the mitochondrial case the electrochemical potential difference is produced by a linked series of oxidation-reduction reactions.)

The synthesis of ATP in mitochondria and chloroplasts is called oxidative phosphorylation or photophosphorylation. The mechanism of phosphorylation that appears to be operative in all cases is the backflow of energetic protons coupled to the synthesis of high-energy ATP. This conversion mechanism, first postulated by Peter Mitchell, is one of the modern developments in bioenergetics that suggests a reexamination of the problem of biogenesis. Such a mechanism requires a nonaqueous transmembrane proton semiconductor coupled to a catalytic site for the condensation of phosphate esters. The process appears to be sufficiently general so that in primitive systems inorganic polyphosphates, rather than specific nucleotides such as ATP, could have been synthesized.

All biological photosynthesis is associated with the movement of protons across membranes. The ubiquity of this phenomenon, as well as its overwhelming importance in powering the present-day biosphere, suggests the probability of its primitive nature. We will next focus on the simplest molecular hardware capable of carrying out the anaerobic photophosphorylation we have been discussing. (The process is anaerobic because oxygen is neither required nor synthesized in the energy fixation.) At the same time we will consider the likelihood of finding such components on an early planet.

The essential structure for a two-phase separation of hydrogen ions is a closed membranous vesicle separating the aqueous interior and exterior. To be a barrier to the flow of ions in general and protons in particular, the vesicle needs to be made of material with low dielectric constant and low electrical conductivity. The dielectric constant reflects the charge asymmetry and charge mobility within the molecules. All compounds are characterized by a dielectric constant ranging from two to three for pure hydrocarbons to about eighty for water. Miscibility and solubility depend on molecules having similar dielectric properties. Thus the familiar adage, "oil and water don't mix," reflects the large difference in the dielectric properties of these materials. Nonpolar substances with low dielectric constant are called lipophilic (oil-loving), whereas substances with asymmetric charge and high dielectric constant are hydrophilic (water-loving).

If the early seas had sufficient lipophilic molecules, such as hydrocarbons or other material of very low dielectric constant, they would have condensed into droplets and surface oil slicks. There have been numerous suggestions that the early earth had such oily substances, including long-chain hydrocarbons, on its surface.

In addition to the hydrophilic and lipophilic molecules there is a third class called *amphiphilic* molecules. Structures of this type have two connected portions, one hydrophilic and one lipophilic. One end of the molecule is normally stabilized by association with aqueous environments while the other end is usually stabilized by association with oily environments. In water these molecules may form a wide variety of aggregates because of their ability to interact with both of the other major classes of molecules as well as with each other. Amphiphilic molecules can form substances known as colloids and coacervates. All of these unusual structures are predictable from physics, in that they represent free-energy minima for the systems under study. Examples of the versatility of such molecules are seen in the cleaning power of soaps, the stabilizing of mayonnaise, and the structural basis of biological membranes.

If long hydrocarbon chains of the oily material of the primitive earth combined chemically with hydrophilic groups dissolved in the aqueous solution, they would have given rise to amphiphilic molecules capable of forming bilayer membrane structures. Such membranes would seal at the free ends and spontaneously form vesicles. Such protocells allow the distinction between interior and exterior aqueous phases, and can accumulate interior reaction products because the membrane presents a barrier to diffusion. This is extremely important because diffusion constantly dilutes reaction products, thus interferring with the orderly development of continuous reaction sequences.

Among the reaction products formed in a mixed synthesis in a reducing atmosphere will be a number of light-absorbing molecules. Experimentally this is shown by the build-up of dark color in the Urey-Miller type of experiment. The existence of such molecules can be argued theoretically from the expected appearance of pi bonds in carbon chains and the high probability of generating conjugated and aromatic hydrocarbons. The light-absorbing groups of atoms, or *chromophores* formed in these systems tend to be of reasonably low dielectric constant. One would therefore expect that they would be soluble in the lipid portions of the vesicles. Thus the protocells would be capable of absorbing visible light in the membranes.

In order to form a closed vesicle a membrane must be concave on the inner surface and convex on the outer. This necessary asymmetry will lead to a statistical imbalance in the orientation of light-absorbing molecules in the membrane. The axes of the molecules will tend to be parallel to the radii of the protocells, and there will be a nonrandomness in the direction in which the molecular dipoles are pointing. When a chromosphore absorbs light the electrical charge of the molecule becomes redistributed. This leads to the generation of an electrical dipole moment in the excited electronic state. (The dipole moment is due to the separation of positive and negative charges within the molecule.) A group of such excited molecules, embedded in the membrane with a preferred orientation, will cause an electrical field to form across the membrane. If appropriate ion semiconductors are coupled to the dipoles, protons can be transported across the membrane. This in turn leads to an electrochemical potential difference of hydrogen, of the type we have previously seen in chloroplasts, *Halobacter*, and mitochondria. Recent studies have demonstrated the possibility that such ion semiconductors have played such a role in protocells.

Given a photochemically generated transmembrane potential, an apparatus such as that invoked in the Mitchell hypothesis is needed to convert that potential into high-energy phosphate bonds. As noted, the requirements are for a proton-conducting channel coupled to a catalytic site. Research on proton conductors indicates that any contiguous chain of hydrogen bonds of the form

is capable of transporting protons by a mechanism first elucidated by Lars Onsager. Such chains occur in ice and in many inorganic and organic crystals. They all occur in certain polypeptides and other possible transmembrane molecules.

What is being envisioned is the spontaneous, even the likely, formation of closed vesicles capable of forming high-energy phosphate bonds in the interior of the protocell. Such a device could carry out anaerobic photophosphorylation in much the same manner as *Halobacter halobium*. It represents the bioenergetic precursor of a living cell, but lacks any of the genetic and macromolecular apparatus of extant minimal organisms such as mycoplasma.

From Protocells to Cells

There is a high probability of successfully synthesizing the type of energy-converting vesicles we have been describing. They involve known thermodynamic and chemical principles; it is a matter of putting the system together in the right way. Even if such probable structures can be made in the laboratory there is a large gulf between their limited activities and the much greater complexity of the simplest living cells.

One feature that characterizes contemporary biochemistry is that, from the vast potential of possible compounds, a very limited subset of small molecules and reaction pathways dominates the whole system. The model suggests some reasons for this limitation in terms of chemical selection. This feature might set the stage for the next step in biogenesis.

First, as discussed earlier, the Urey-Miller type of synthesis is not random, but tends under a wide variety of conditions to favor the production of certain molecules such as hydrogen cyanide, formaldehyde, and ethane. This considerably narrows the possibilities of the starting materials. Once vesicles form and anaerobic photophosphorylation takes over, the primary energy flows, according to the model being proposed, will be through the input of high-energy phosphate bonds. Among the vast array of possible organic reactions there will be an immediate and highly directed selection for that subset that occurs through phosphate transfer reactions. The interior of the protocells will have a chemical character determined by the chemical specificity of the energy inputs.

Modern-day biochemistry tends to be a network of organic reaction sequences dominated by phosphorylations and dephosphorylations. My suggestion is that this dependence on phosphorylation reactions is not accidental—that high-energy bonds from pyrophosphates and higher polymers have been the source of cellular energy since prebiotic times. The sequence of events is from primordial chemicals, to an energy processing system, to a chemical selection and specification based on the compounds involved in energy input. The validity of this conjecture can be explored both experimentally and theoretically. In the meantime it is interesting to realize that, in principle at least, the character of the biochemical network could have been strongly influenced by the energy source.

Even granting the possibility of a rather defined metabolic network, our thermodynamically likely protocells do not yet possess a combined genetic and macromolecular synthesizing apparatus. In thinking about the *de novo* formation of such a system two logical difficulties are encountered. First, present-day cells require an entire related series of cycles of DNA, RNA, and protein sequences, so that no isolated step in a cycle appears to be of use to a cell lacking the entire machinery. Second, the present components are mostly large, complex macromolecules; this poses the question of whether smaller units could have been of functional value. The initial need for very large, highly specific molecules poses formidable problems.

The reasons for the large size of enzymes, ribosomes, and similar hardware are incompletely understood. It is known that large structures provide rigid, defined, catalytic surfaces for orienting substrates with the appropriate degree of precision. In addition, low-frequency vibrations require a substantial number of coupled oscillators. If such soft modes of oscillation are needed for polymer formation, then a second reason for large structures exists.

Contemporary biological systems use two types of large-sized structures: (1) macromolecules that are precise and sufficiently specified to allow crystallographic location of atoms; and (2) membranes that are a thermodynamics phase of a much lower degree of atomic order. Primitive cells might have achieved sufficient functional regularity by adsorbing short-chain polymers onto bilayer membranes. Such small adsorbed polymers might possess sufficient catalytic and template function to maintain the synthesis of other small polymers. This would remove the necessity for macromolecules at the very beginning, and allow the functional molecules to grow evolutionarily in size to the point where they no longer require membrane stabilization. The suggestion is that a small molecule adsorbed on a surface may be the functional analogue of a large molecule.

Thus, if catalytic function is available with an adsorbed tripeptide, then tripeptides and nonanucleotides would have been a sufficiently complex genetic system to start a protocell on the way to developing toward a full genetic system. The postulate that the membrane came first obviates the need for having large molecules before there was a method for synthesizing them. The physical aspects of this proposal will have to be studied in detail, but for the moment it does overcome a logical difficulty in theories requiring a macromolecular replicating system prior to a membrane-bounded vesicle.

The scenario starts with a moderately reducing atmosphere and an ocean of dissolved organic molecules produced by an energy-driven synthesis. This synthesis uses the sun's ultraviolet energy, together with terrestrial energy sources capable of causing electronic transitions in substrate molecules. Some of the primordial carbon and hydrogen is in oil droplets and surface oil slicks associated with the ocean. Under these conditions amphiphilic molecules and chromophores are produced and condensed into vesicles with polar-lipid bilayer membranes. Under the influence of sunlight, these membranes pump protons from the interior to the exterior of the protocells. This energy is used in the backflow of protons to synthesize high-energy phosphate bonds. The pyrophosphate and polyphosphates formed drive the chemical network toward a specific set of chemical intermediates. Among the products are short chains of amino acids and nucleotides. These adsorb on the vesicle surface, and in the process some of them acquire catalytic and template functions.

The postulated primitive cell has, in some degree, most of the important functional properties of the simplest contemporary cells. In principle we can envision a series of evolutionary changes linking the protocells to their modern descendants.

While this scenario fails to provide a large number of details and only vaguely suggests how the genetic code could have originated, it is consistent with the biology and biochemistry from above and the physics and chemistry from below. By the successive detailing and sharpening of both of the approaches we can hope to develop an ever more realistic picture of life's origin.

The Evolution
of Complex Animals

JAMES W. VALENTINE
Department of Geological Sciences
University of California, Santa Barbara

> *Where are the remains of those infinitely numer-*
> *ous organisms which must have existed long be-*
> *fore the Cambrian system was deposited?*
> —Charles Darwin, *On the Origin of Species*

Introduction

Charles Darwin was convinced that evolution is a slow and gradual process. He therefore inferred that the earliest fossil record of which he knew, from the early Cambrian period, must be of great antiquity. Whenever events in life history appeared to occur abruptly, Darwin was inclined to argue that such appearances were deceiving, due to a telescoping of events caused by the incompleteness of the geological record. These views clearly influenced Darwin's interpretation of what is now termed the Precambrian-Cambrian boundary, which is approximately the horizon where skeletons of animals belonging to living phyla begin to make their appearance, nearly 570 million years ago. Darwin expected those animals to have had a long Precambrian history. Going backward in time, ancestors of the Cambrian animal groups should at first be similar to the Cambrian forms and then be increasingly more primitive in progressively earlier times, eventually converging on some ancestral stock at some very remote period. No such ancestral history could be found, so Darwin suggested that the geological record of the appropriate Precambrian time period was missing.

Today we have identified an abundant geological record of those times, and we have recovered enough fossils to be able to form scenarios of the early evolution of major animal groups. It now seems that complex organisms did appear and diversify relatively abruptly,

The research from which many of these ideas have come was supported by NASA grant NAG 2-73.

without the long prehistory Darwin imagined. The rates of evolution that can be inferred from the fossil record of this period are so high that they are difficult to account for even today, and they call for a careful evaluation of evolutionary mechanisms. This reading reviews the fossil evidence of the rise of complex animals and discusses the mechanisms proposed in explanation.

The Rise of Multicellularity

Organisms are usually divided into five kingdoms (modified from Whittaker 1969). The simplest organisms (Kingdom Monera) include bacteria and blue-green algae among living groups. The oldest known fossils are representatives of this kingdom; several Precambrian associations are known, and the earliest has been discovered by Stanley Awramik in rocks about 3.5 billion years old. The cells of Monera are of the relatively simple sort called *prokaryotic*, lacking nuclei, chromosomes, large organelles, and other attributes of the more complex *eukaryotic* cell types. It is now believed that the simplest eukaryotic kingdom, the Protoctista, arose from the Monera about 1.5 to 1.4 billion years ago (for a review, see Awramik 1981). Protoctists include protozoans, unicellular algae, and multicellular algae that are not organized at the tissue grade of construction. All three advanced multicellular kingdoms (animals, plants, and fungi), the members of which are all or nearly all constructed at the tissue grade, have eukaryotic cells and evidently evolved from Protoctistan ancestors (Figure 1).

The multicellular level of organization was reached independently many times. G. L. Stebbins has conservatively estimated that there are at least seventeen independent inventions of multicellular groups, and the actual figure may be higher. This raises the question of why no complex organisms evolved from prokaryotes. Eukaryotes seem to achieve a multicellular grade easily enough, and the prokaryotes were present over 2 billion years before eukaryotes appeared. During some of that time the earth's environment may have been unsuitable for multicellular forms, but it is reasonable to suspect that the differences between prokaryotic and eukaryotic cell organization are also critical for the origin of complex organisms.

It is difficult to trace the origin of eukaryotic organization from the prokaryotic condition. Margulis (1975) and others have worked out a model that seems successful in accounting for the origin of some eukaryotic organelles (mitochondria and plastids). She suggests that these organelles were originally independent, free-living prokaryotes that came into symbiotic association with a host cell that was normally an ingestor; these symbionts were eventually amalgamated

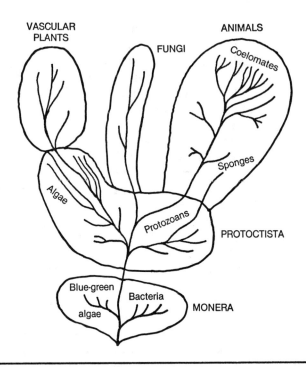

FIGURE 1. Kingdoms of organisms. It is believed that the prokaryotic Monera gave rise to eukaryotic unicellular Protoctistans, from which numerous multicellular lineages developed. Most of these were algal forms (the lineages are depicted very diagrammatically), but two or more lineages gave rise to animals, and one or more other lineages gave rise to vascular plants. (Modified after Robert H. Whittaker, "New Concepts of Kingdoms of Organisms," *Science* 163, © 1969 by American Association for the Advancement of Science.)

to form a more complex unicell. However, the evolution of some eukaryotic features, such as the nucleus with characteristic eukaryotic chromosomes, has never been satisfactorily explained. Indeed, whether or not the host cell was closely allied to living prokaryotes is open to question.

Even though these problems are unresolved, it is possible to advance a hypothesis to explain in a general way why eukaryotes rather than prokaryotes have been able to give rise to complex organisms (Awramik and Valentine, in press). In amalgamating symbiotic prokaryotic cells (or in otherwise evolving organelles that are as complicated as many entire prokaryotic organisms), eukaryotic cells have developed the ability to integrate and regulate the operations of these organelles to form harmoniously functioning whole organisms. The regulatory apparatus that achieves this harmony should be much more sophisticated in eukaryotes than are regulatory systems in relatively simple prokaryotes. It is known that eukaryotes do in fact have elaborate systems of gene regulation when compared with prokaryotes, although their workings have not yet been elucidated on the molecular level. To be complex in the sense that animals are, an organism must at least differentiate cells into a number of types, control cell divisions and associations to form tissues, and control the topology of tissues so as to produce harmoniously functioning organs within a fully integrated organism. In going from a unicellular eukaryote to an animal, the organization rises from the phenotype of a single cell to the phenotype of a complex organism that subsumes many different cell structures and functions. This clearly requires a great regulatory advance. In the broadest sense, all the Protoctista differ from the Monera in being multicellular—that is, they include cell-derived organelles. Therefore it is proposed that the eukaryotic regulator abilities evidenced, and perhaps enhanced, by the evolutionary changes to promote the acquisition of organelles through cell amalgamations proved pre-adaptive to the evolution of complex multicellular organisms. Indeed it is possible that a predisposition to heightened regulatory abilities grew in turn from the animal-like ingesting functions proposed for the host cells, which had to cope with the ingestion and assimilation of particulate materials. This proposed sequence of events is illustrated in Figure 2.

Since unicells have given rise so many times to multicellular organisms, it is reasonable to infer that conditions in which multicellularity confers an adaptive advantage are not uncommon. Complex multicellular organisms generally differ from unicellular ones in having increased body size, increased longevity, and increased homeostasis—features that would take the early multicellular animals, at least, into a distinctive adaptive zone. Additionally, cellular differentiation and the development of tissue-like cell associations are found in the simplest living animals. Differentiation may have begun at a stage preceding the rise of integrated multicellular body plans, perhaps in arrays of cell phenotypes within protoctistan colonies. Cell differentiation is certainly another advantage of multicellularity, permitting specializations of cell function that may enhance metabolic efficiency and lead to geometrically advantageous arrangements of the specialized cell types.

It is likely that a shift in reproductive strategy accompanied the rise of multicellular animals from protoctistan ancestors. Generally, unicellular organisms have relatively short time spans between reproductive events. The number of new individuals produced by any parent during a given reproductive event is, however, relatively small. In multicellular animals, by contrast, there is usually a significantly longer span between the generations, although an individual may produce many more reproductive products per reproductive event. However, the reproductive potential of unicellular populations is generally

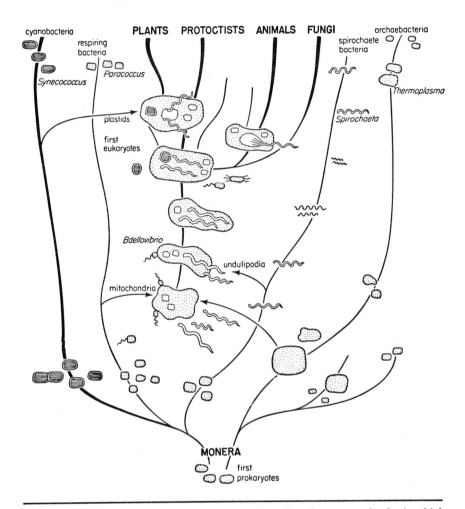

FIGURE 2. The origin of eukaryotic (or nucleated) cells as co-evolved microbial communities. (© 1981, Lynn Margulis.)

higher than for multicellular populations, by virtue of their much shorter generation lengths.

It is unclear which of these several differences between unicellular and multicellular forms were more important in determining the selective pressures that gave rise to obligatory multicellularity. Probably different properties were important to the rise of different multicellular lineages, and more than one property may have commonly been selected. Indeed, most of these properties seem coadaptive and together they create a characteristic form/function complex adapted to modes of life unavailable to unicellular forms. When they arose in motile multicellular ingestors, they led to animals.

The Rise of Animal Body Plans

It is not certain how many times multicellularity was achieved independently by animals. Most workers today suggest that living animals have had at least two or three independent origins; a few workers have called on many more. Nearly all authorities now agree that Porifera—sponges—arose from different Protoctistan ancestors than did other living animal phyla. The sponge ancestor was probably a colonial protozoan of the suborder Choanoflagellata; choanoflagellates closely resemble certain sponge cells (see Hanson 1977 for a good discussion). Within the kingdom Animalia, then, the sponges are usually separated as the subkingdom Parazoa, while the remaining animals are placed in the subkingdom Metazoa (or Eumetazoa). The origin of the Metazoa is subject to much dispute. The Cnidaria (jellyfish, corals, and so on) and Platyhelminthes (flatworms) are certainly among the simplest of living Metazoan phyla. Some workers believe these two phyla arose independently from different Protozoan ancestors. If so, zooflagellates are likely cnidarian ancestors, while ciliates are claimed as likely ancestors for flatworms (Hanson 1977). Other scenarios include the Cnidarians as primitive metazoans, with flatworms eventually evolving from their descendants (Marcus 1958), a primitive flatworm stock with cnidarians evolving from them (Hadzi 1963), or a primitive metazoan stock preceding each and giving rise to them both (Barnes 1980). Clearly, the nature of the earliest Metazoan forms will depend on whether they evolved along a pathway from ciliates to flatworms or from zooflagellates to cnidarians, or along some other route altogether.

Most authorities do agree that metazoan phyla more complex than flatworms have all (or perhaps nearly all) descended at least indirectly from flatworm-like stocks, since they all share many features. However, there is no agreement on the actual pathways of descent; nearly every remotely possible ancestral-descendant combination has been suggested by one or another worker. Again, the nature of forms intermediate between known groups will obviously have been different for one ancestor-descendant pair than for another.

The fossil record is of little use in providing direct evidence of the pathways of descent of the phyla or of invertebrate classes. Each phylum with a fossil record had already evolved its characteristic body plan when it first appeared, so far as we can tell from the fossil remains, and no phylum is connected to any other via intermediate fossil types. Indeed, none of the invertebrate classes can be connected with another class by series of intermediates. The relationships among phyla and classes must be inferred on the basis of their resemblance. However, even the most sophisticated techniques of phylogeny analysis have thus far failed to resolve the great differences of opinion concerning the relationships among phyla (or among many classes as well).

There is one approach that avoids some of the problems of phylogeny reconstruction. This method concentrates on the evolution of the functions implied by the morphological features characterizing living phyla or classes, and attempts to trace evolution along functional pathways. Although this is just the opposite of the usual methods of phylogeny analysis, it has in fact improved our understanding of the course of the early diversification of animals. Clark (1964, 1979) has made particularly important contributions to this field. If the results of such studies are applied to interpreting the early fossil record of animals, a scenario of metazoan diversification can be postulated that brings some order to the data and that explains some otherwise enigmatic facts (Valentine 1973, 1977).

Burrows are among the earliest traces of Precambrian animals, dating from about 680 million years ago (Figure 3). Early burrow types include long horizontal ones and relatively short vertical ones. These tell us quite a bit about the state of metazoan evolution at that time, because the more primitive metazoans do not make burrows of this sort. In order to burrow strongly in the sea floor, an organism must be able to thrust sedimentary particles aside and enlarge a space to accommodate its body while moving through the sediment. Clark (1964) has argued that a hollow-bodied worm is an ideal solution to the burrowing problem. The hollow, a coelom, is filled with fluid to form a hydrostatic skeleton, antagonizing the muscles in the body wall. By squeezing down on one portion of the body, another portion is caused to bulge out, much as constricting a long balloon to form a local neck will cause bulging elsewhere. Coordination of constrictions and relaxations can produce waves of alternate necks and bulges and permit burrowing via peristalsis—the worm flows within the sediment as waves of bulges move along the body. Clark has made the point that most coelomic cavities were invented and first elaborated in order to promote burrowing. Most primitive members of coelomic worm groups are adapted to burrowing modes. Segmented worms such as annelids employ the coelom for prolonged burrowing, as required of most deposit feeders and predators. Unsegmented but regionated worms such as phoronids use a trunk coelom to create a burrow in which to live, commonly a vertical burrow as a home for suspension feeding. Flatworms cannot make such burrows, and other noncoelomates burrow only weakly (some cnidarians and nemerteans), or are minute (nematodes) and would not leave the sorts of burrows that appear in the early animal record.

When the late Precambrian burrows appear, then, they probably indicate that coelomic animals had evolved. This implies that flatworm-like animals had preceded them; possibly cnidarians and other non-

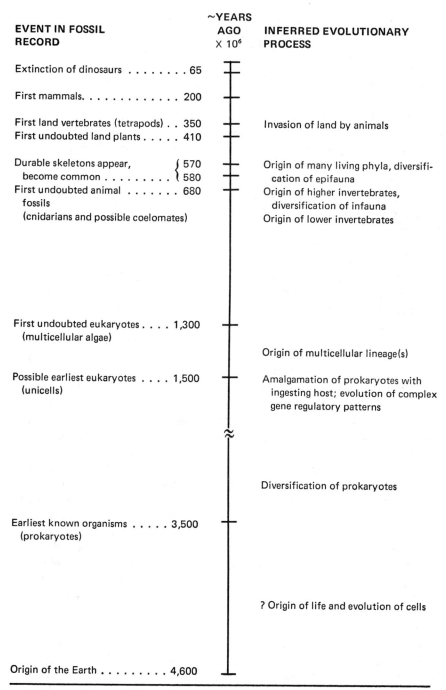

FIGURE 3. Benchmark events in the fossil record (left column) with interpretations of the important evolutionary processes underway (right column) during geological time.

coelomate phyla including pseudocoelomates had evolved earlier also, but on these points the fossil record has been silent. It is not surprising that the small to minute soft-bodied flatworms or the living pseudocoelomate groups have not fossilized (we have no certain indications of their existence until the Cenozoic); we are indeed fortunate to have a few fossils of soft-bodied metazoans from the late Precambrian. These are mostly jellyfish and other cnidarians, but they include a few worms that are almost certainly coelomates along with a number of enigmatic animals that cannot be placed with confidence in any living phylum.

Skeletons composed of durable material, such as chitin, calcium phosphate, or calcium carbonate, do not appear until just before the beginning of the Cambrian (Figure 3). It is certainly true that the explosive appearance of fossils in the Cambrian is due to the appearance of durable skeletons far more easily preserved than ordinary, soft animal tissues. The important questions are, Why were skeletons developed and why just then? There have been literally scores of suggestions, but most can now be ruled out. It is now quite certain that a major diversification of life forms accompanied the Cambrian appearance of numerous skeletonized fossils. The kinds and extent of burrowing activities increased greatly at that time, suggesting that soft-bodied animals, as well as those with hard parts, were diversifying. Furthermore, we have some marvelously preserved fossils of soft-bodied animals from the middle Cambrian—the famous Burgess shale fauna (for a fine popular account see Conway Morris and Whittington 1979). These mid-Cambrian remains include many normal sorts of fossils with durable skeletons (trilobites, for example), together with early records of some soft-bodied groups that are rarely fossilized (such as priapulids and annelids). Of even greater interest, there are a large number of animal types, perhaps a dozen, that probably represent wholly extinct phyla. Most of these new forms appear to be coelomates, and many are swimming or floating types. The contrast between this rich and diverse soft-bodied fauna of metazoans with the relatively depauperate late Precambrian fauna is striking. It certainly appears that the early Cambrian witnessed a great expansion in both types and numbers of complex animals at the highest levels of organization, levels we recognize as phyla and classes.

Part of the explanation seems to be that the coelomates invaded new adaptive zones at that time. Just as the coelomates seem to have evolved to exploit burrowing modes of life beginning 680 million years or so ago, the skeletonized forms that emerged near 570 million years ago seem to have evolved to exploit life *upon* (epifaunally) rather than *within* (infaunally) the sea floor (Valentine 1973). So far as we can tell, these durable skeletons were nearly or quite all coadaptive with body plans permitting locomotion (arthropods, for example), or provided a mode of sessile life (suspension-feeding brachiopods, for example) in epifaunal habitats. The appearance and elaboration of the durable skeleton signals the diversification of coelomates within epifaunal communities. Each of the phyla that developed durably skeletonized lineages during this period did so independently, suggesting that the opportunities for epifaunal life were open to a wide array of adaptive types. Furthermore, many of the durably skeletonized phyla appearing in Cambrian rocks are represented by a number of distinctive subgroups, classes, or orders, that appear suddenly without known intermediates.

When we take into account that many new soft-bodied forms as well as the better-known forms with hard parts all originated at some time in the late Precambrian or early Cambrian, we can get some estimate of just how extensive this episode of evolutionary invention was. There are about thirty living phyla; there are a few durably skeletonized extinct forms appearing in the Cambrian that may represent phyla; there are the dozen or so soft-bodied forms from the Burgess shale; and finally there are a few more soft-bodied fossil forms discovered in younger rocks that may represent distinctive phyla. We know of about fifty phyla all told, and it is highly unlikely that we have as yet found representatives of all the distinctive body plans ever evolved. It is doubtful that there were hundreds more phyla than have been discovered, but there may have been dozens. The number of distinctive Cambrian classes with novel subbody plans reaches over a dozen in some phyla (Echinodermata, Arthropoda), and even for a small phylum like the Brachiopoda there are at least seven orders (see papers in House 1980). Presumably the soft-bodied phyla, which are so spottily known, had similar numbers of classes or other major subtaxa. We do not know for certain that all coelomate phyla originated in late Precambrian–early Cambrian times (probably they did not), and we are certain that not all early classes began then. Nevertheless, if we guess that about fifty phyla did originate then, and that those phyla average six classlike subdivisions each, then about 300 new major body plans and subplans developed within that remote time interval. Clearly, those radiations were extensive.

Several lines of evidence indicate that the radiations may have been rapid as well. I trace one such line here as an example. The phylum Brachiopoda are small- to moderate-sized solitary organisms largely or entirely enclosed within two mineralized shells that are sometimes hinged at the rear (Figure 4; see Rudwick 1970 for a good account of this group). Inside the valves the viscera lie near the posterior, while the anterior is enclosed within an extension of the body wall termed the mantle, which lines (and secretes) the shell internally. The anterior space, the mantle cavity, contains the lophophore, a folded or coiled, tentacle-like apparatus used for feeding. Cilia-driven

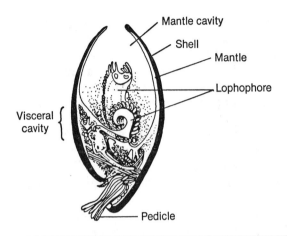

FIGURE 4. Longitudinal section of an articulate brachiopod. The lophophore may be coiled or folded into waves or loops; it creates currents that follow distinctive pathways within the mantle cavity. Pedicle is for attachment. (Modified after Alwyn Williams, "The Calcareous Shell of the Brachiopoda and its Importance to their Classification," *Biological Reviews of the Cambridge Philosophical Society* 31, no. 3, 1956, Cambridge University Press.)

currents circulate through the mantle cavity in well-defined paths, and the lophophore traps food items suspended in the currents. The special circulation of the mantle currents would not be possible without a rigid skeleton; indeed, without a rigid skeleton and the organs and muscles associated with it, the brachiopod ground plan could hardly be realized (Cloud 1949). Stripped of the mineralized skeleton and associated features, brachiopods become phoronid-like polypides; to function they would require differently shaped lophophores (perhaps circular or U-shaped) and would lose nearly all the distinguishing features that characterize them as the phylum Brachiopoda (Valentine 1973). Thus we cannot imagine a long period of existence of brachiopods lacking mineralized skeletons; when the first brachiopod skeletons appear in the fossil record we are witnessing the origination of the brachiopod ground plan, or as near to it as the spotty fossil record permits us to approach.

The earliest brachiopods are found near or at some localities at the base of rocks of the Tommotian stage, now usually regarded as earliest Cambrian age. Rocks of the preceding stage, the Vendian, contain rare indications of mineralized skeletal elements but have yielded no brachiopods. We cannot be sure whether there is always an unrepresented interval of time between the fossiliferous latest Vendian and earliest Tommotian rocks, but if so it is not likely to be more than a few million years, judging from the durations, completeness, and ages known or inferred for units near this boundary. The most likely estimate of the time available for the development of the brachiopod ground plan is a few million years at most. The brachiopods typify the phyla appearing in Cambrian rocks with durable skeletons in that they are adapted to epifaunal life and have developed, most likely, from burrowing worms (probably phoronid-like forms) of the late Precambrian.

One can conclude from such examples that evolution is capable of developing phylum-level ground plans within a few million years—less than the average duration of fossil invertebrate species! In the brachiopod example the ancestral and descendant ground plans are presumably at nearly the same grade of organization—both groups are presumably regionated (oligomerous) coelomates—and thus a major increase in complexity was not involved. This is true of many of the living phyla, probably including all those with durable skeletons: When they first appeared they had novel body plans but at about the same grade as their ancestral stocks. It is not certain that all such ground plans actually involved only a few million years for their evolution; but the fact that they seem to be capable of such rapid development helps to explain the sudden appearances of animals near 680 million years ago and of epifaunal phyla with hard parts near the beginning of Cambrian time.

To summarize and interpret the fossil evidence bearing on the origin of complex animals, then: The eukaryotic cell was probably developed sometime after 1500 million years ago and owed many of its advanced features to being an amalgamation of individuals into a "supercell," involving particularly the development of advanced gene regulatory mechanisms to cope with this level of organization. Subsequently, multicellular organisms developed many times. The organization of multicellularity was probably possible because of the regulatory capacity of the eukaryotes. Early animal lineages included bilateral flatworm-like organisms that gave rise to a number of coelomate metazoan lineages, beginning near 680 million years ago. There are thus 800 million years or more between the appearance of prokaryotes and the appearance of the earliest known animals. During this interval animals were invented and developed complex forms, but we do not know whether they developed gradually throughout that interval or rapidly during part of it. The early coelomates were chiefly burrowers and had diversified, perhaps from several non-coelomate ancestors, into a variety of wormlike ground plans by the close of Precambrian time, near 570 million years ago. Again, we do not know whether the diverse worm architectures arose gradually or rapidly and episodically. During or just before the early Cambrian the major phyla with durable skeletons appear, some already differentiated into many major classes, and it can be argued that this event marks a truly extensive diversification of body plans within a relatively short time. Not all of the phyla, nor all primitive classes, evolved during this interval, but a great many did—hundreds of body plans and subplans may have arisen within a few to several million years. When we examine the later fossil records for rapid bursts of evolutionary invention we find similar patterns, though not at quite so high a taxonomic level (the mammals, for example; see Gingerich 1977). Thus, reasoning by analogy, we may propose that it is likely that the first animals and the early coelomates arose in relatively sudden evolutionary bursts rather than over long intervals of slow change. There is still hope that evidence can be obtained, partly from the fossil record, partly from molecular "clocks," to decide what those patterns were really like.

Possible Mechanisms Underlying
Large Rapid Morphological Changes

The rapidity with which changes in complex organisms appear in the fossil record leads to the question, Can such change be accounted for by known evolutionary processes? Some workers have argued that when the processes we currently postulate to be involved in species formation are extrapolated to a longer time scale, they are quite sufficient to account for higher taxa such as phyla. This is a complicated proposition and we cannot do it full justice here, but it is probably true to say that even at the most rapid rates of morphological change usually considered likely between species, new phylum-level body plans cannot be evolved in the times available. The uncertainty here stems partly from the great difficulty in quantifying morphological change; how does one add up species-level changes to achieve a new phylum? In many ways, the changes between species and those between phyla are qualitatively different.

Since phyla differ from each other in their basic body plans, major differences occur in the numbers and/or kinds of cells that are differentiated during development, in the timing of their appearance, in the geometry of their elaboration. Phyla that are distantly related may differ in developmental plan from the earliest cleavages of the zygote. Even closely allied phyla that are similar in earliest development may differ considerably in their embryonic or larval stages, when it is common for the larval form to include structures that anticipate distinctive adult requirements. The phyla are constructed according to distinctive anatomical plans, or blueprints. The blueprints are encoded as genetic regulatory systems and make use of many self-organizing properties of developmental systems. According to Britten and Davidson (1971), who have done pioneering work on gene regulation in eukaryotes, over 90 percent of the gene functions in mammals are present in prokaryotes. Thus these very different kingdoms of organisms contain similar materials and even somewhat similar genes; it is the way the materials are organized and the genes expressed during development that creates the basic differences between them and between other major groups and organisms. Once again the explanation of major evolutionary developments—this time, the creation of diverse and complex metazoan body plans—is associated with the evolution of gene regulation.

If new body plans are based on new gene regulatory patterns, then we are much closer to accounting for their rapid appearance. A single regulatory change may involve change in the expression of large numbers of structural genes (those that code for polypeptides) associated in a gene battery (Britten and Davidson 1971). Morphological change may be brought about rapidly by reorganization of the regulatory pattern, using the gene products within batteries as building blocks, but placing them in novel arrangements to form a new body plan. Many such changes in expression could be effected by changes in the timing of appearance of gene functions in development—heterochrony—which includes neoteny and similar phenomena (Valentine and Campbell 1975). The ancestral gene batteries function harmoniously in the ancestral genome, so genetic modification might not need to be extensive to produce harmonious functioning at a new developmental stage within the same genome. Fitness between parental and descendant forms might remain sufficiently high to establish a novel organism during a rapid sequence of changes. Changes in patterns of expression could be extended backwards into the earliest developmental stages, by subsequent regulatory changes, if they improved the life cycle as a whole; prepared the way for the adult, ecologically or structurally; or simply improved the adaptation of the developing stages. Thus the divergences that we now see in early life stages of phyla can be accounted for in a general way. Of course this quasi-philosophical account is merely a generalized scenario of a possible explanation of mechanisms of the origin of phyla and classes. The regulatory systems of eukaryotes are not yet understood on a molecular level, and until the principles of the systems are discovered we cannot form more detailed hypotheses.

Despite this qualification, the evolution of complex organisms does appear to be a sequence of largely regulatory changes within genomes. The changes probably arose as solutions to immediate problems—how to cope with a number of symbiotic cells, how to coordinate and differentiate numbers of eukaryotic cells, how to exploit infaunal habitats and energy sources, and so on; and the solutions happened to create novel abilities and to be preadaptive to the exploration of myriad and diverse life modes. As for the reasons for the timing of the various steps in complexity, although there are many suggestions we do not have any convincing evidence. What is more certain is that once a new step had been accomplished, diversification could be exceedingly rapid, evidently because a vast range of opportunities were suddenly available. As these opportunities were exploited and the world filled up with the new types of organism, the rate of production of novelties slowed and stopped, and evolution continued only at lower levels, usually in response to environmental changes, until another opportunity happened to occur, usually involving a new step. This sort of explanation has long been made for adaptive radiations at intermediate taxonomic levels— mammals, for example, radiating into environments vacated by dinosaurs. Today the world is rather well-stocked with complex forms, and novel evolutionary inventions are only at low levels in most cases. So far as we can tell, the opportunity for the evolution of truly new body plans has passed, barring catastrophe.

Without much doubt, evolution of gene regulatory systems continues today. However, without broad opportunities for novel life modes, it is likely that most regulatory changes that do prove adaptive have relatively small morphological effects, on the same order as the effects of structural gene changes. Not that regulatory changes are necessarily unimportant today. King and Wilson (1975) have developed evidence suggesting that humans differ from chimpanzees chiefly in pattern of gene regulation, which fits nicely with the hypothesis that humans are neotenic (for a review, see Gould 1977). Thus, perhaps the origin of phyla is not much different from the origin of species after all, scale aside. Perhaps, indeed, there are lessons in speciation to be drawn from the evolution of major steps in the rise of complex animals.

REFERENCES

Awramik, Stanley M. "The Pre-Phanerozoic Biosphere—Three Billion Years of Crises and Opportunities." In *Biotic Crises in Ecological and Evolutionary Time*, Matthew H. Nitecki, ed., pp. 83-102. New York: Academic Press, 1981.

Awramik, S. M., and Valentine, J. W. (in press) "Adaptive Aspects of the Origin of Autotrophic Eukaryotes." In *Geological Factors and the Evolution of Plants*, edited by B. H. Tiffney. New Haven, Conn.: Yale University Press.

Barnes, R. D. "Invertebrate Beginnings." *Paleobiology* 6 (1980):365-370.

Britten, R. J., and Davidson, E. H. "Repetitive and Non-repetitive DNA Sequences and a Speculation on the Origins of Evolutionary Novelty." *Quarterly Review of Biology* 46 (1971):111-138.

Clark, Robert B. *Dynamics in Metazoan Evolution.* Oxford: Clarendon Press, 1964.

——. "Radiation of the Metazoa." In *The Origin of Major Invertebrate Groups*, edited by M. R. House, pp. 55-101. London: Academic Press, 1979.

Cloud, Preston E. "Some Problems and Patterns of Evolution Exemplified by Fossil Invertebrates." *Evolution* 2 (1949):322-350.

Conway Morris, S., and Whittington, H. B. "The Animals of the Burgess Shale." *Scientific American* 241, no. 1 (1979):122-133.

Gingerich, Philip D. "Patterns of Evolution in the Mammalian Fossil Record." In *Patterns of Evolution as Illustrated by the Fossil Record*, edited by A. Hallam, pp. 469-500. Amsterdam: Elsevier, 1977.

Gould, Stephen Jay. *Ontogeny and Phylogeny*. Cambridge, Mass.: Harvard University Press, 1977.

Hadzi, Jovan. *The Evolution of the Metazoa*. New York: Pergamon Press, 1963.

Hanson, Earl D. *The Origin and Early Evolution of Animals*. Middletown, Conn.: Wesleyan University Press, 1977.

House, M. R., ed. *The Origin of Major Invertebrate Groups*. London: Academic Press, 1980.

King, Marie-Claire, and Wilson, Allan C. "Evolution at Two Levels: Molecular Similarities and Biological Differences Between Humans and Chimpanzees." *Science* 188 (1975):107-116.

Marcus, E. "On The Evolution of the Animal Phyla." *Quarterly Review of Biology* 33 (1958):24-58.

Margulis, Lynn. *Origin of Eukaryotic Cells*. New Haven, Conn.: Yale University Press, 1970.

——. "Symbiotic Theory of the Origin of Eukaryotic Organelles: Criteria for Proof." In *Symposia of the Society for Experimental Biology Number XXIX: Symbiosis*, pp. 21-38. Cambridge: Cambridge University Press, 1975.

——. *Symbiosis in Cell Evolution*. San Francisco: W. H. Freeman, 1981.

Rudwick, M. J. *Living and Fossil Brachiopods*. London: Hutchinson, 1970.

Valentine, James W. *Evolutionary Paleoecology of the Marine Biosphere*. Englewood Cliffs, N.J.: Prentice-Hall, 1973.

——. "General Patterns of Metazoan Evolution." In *Patterns of Evolution as Illustrated by the Fossil Record*, edited by A. Hallam, pp. 27-57. Amsterdam: Elsevier, 1977.

Valentine, James W., and Campbell, Cathryn A. "Genetic Regulation and the Fossil Record." *American Scientist* 63 (1975):673-680.

Whittaker, Robert H. "New Concepts of Kingdoms of Organisms." *Science* 163 (1969):150-160.

Williams, Alwyn. "The Calcareous Shell of the Brachiopoda and its Importance to their Classification." *Biological Reviews of the Cambridge Philosophical Society* 31, no. 3 (1956):243-287.

Human Origins

KENNETH H. JACOBS
Department of Anthropology
University of Texas, Austin

The Human Fossil Record

Less than a century and a half ago, the idea of human evolution belonged more to the realm of fantasy or philosophy than to the realm of science. While creative souls such as Lamarck or Erasmus Darwin might conclude from their philosophical meanderings that *Homo sapiens* simply had to be the product of some sort of evolutionary process, no hard evidence supported their assertions. The Baron Georges Cuvier, founder and still patron saint of French paleontology, could survey the known paleontological record and confidently opine that "fossil man does not exist." Today, however, fossil human remains are known in abundance from sites spanning four million years and three Old World continents. These remains have permitted the construction of a broad outline of the course of human evolution that is worth considering briefly.

The earliest unambiguous fossil hominid (from *Hominidae*, the taxonomic family that includes *Homo sapiens* and all directly ancestral and collaterally related species) is a form called *Australopithecus afarensis* (Johanson and White 1979). It is known from two sites in East Africa that are dated between 3 and 4 million years ago and includes many well-known specimens, among them Lucy and the so-called First Family. As might be expected from its relatively early date, *A. afarensis* is the most primitive hominid yet known—that is, it is the least changed from the form of the common ancestor of hominids and pongids (the great apes).

Its brain size was small, averaging little more than 400 cubic centimeters (cc). This is little different from the value for modern chimpanzees, slightly less than that for modern gorillas (ca. 500 cc), and considerably less than the modern human average of about 1400 cc. The form of its jaws and teeth was also primitive, being much like that of the sivapithecines, a diverse group of generalized apes that roamed Eurasia and Africa between 14 and 8 million years ago and from one of which *A. afarensis* most likely descended. The least primitive feature of *A. afarensis*, and the one that clearly marked it as a hominid, was its mode of locomotion. This has been deduced from the bony remains of its pelvis and lower limb, as well as from a set of remarkably well-preserved fossil footprints (Leakey and Hay 1979). These traces leave no doubt that *A. afarensis* was a fully accomplished biped, standing, walking, and running on two feet in a manner virtually indistinguishable from that of modern *Homo sapiens.*

Fossil material after *A. afarensis* is best viewed as falling within two distinct phyletic lines (Figure 1). One line consists of three further species of the genus *Australopithecus: A. africanus, A. robustus,* and *A. boisei.* Known from nearly a dozen sites in both East and South Africa, these species adapted to an increasingly arid and treeless habitat by emphasizing diets of tough, hard-to-chew terrestrial vegetation. Their cranial and dentognathic (tooth and jaw) morphologies reflect this dietary specialization. Cranial architecture was often dominated by bony structures accommodating large chewing muscles. Mandibles were massive and well-buttressed in order to withstand prodigious chewing forces. The anterior teeth (incisors and canines) were greatly reduced and nearly afunctional, while the posterior dentition (premolars and molars) was a monstrous grinding surface. These hominid herbivores arose about three million years ago, and became extinct for unknown reasons by one million years ago (Wolpoff 1980).

The second phyletic line is that of the genus *Homo.* In its several-million-year existence, this lineage evolved culturally at least as impressively as it evolved biologically. Beginning with *Homo habilis* approximately two million years ago, *Homo* has increasingly relied on cultural solutions to adaptive problems. There have certainly been some morphological changes within the genus, but these typically involved features most likely correlated with some precedent cultural change: an increase in brain size, for example, or a change in tooth size and cranial shape resulting from an increased efficiency of stone tools and decreased use of the mouth as a third hand.

In any event, the association of stone tools and remains of butchered animals between 2 and 1.5 million years ago in East Africa suggests that *Homo habilis* had already acquired some of the habits of later hominid hunter-gatherers (Isaac 1980). Gathering and hunting led *Homo erectus,* the next step in this lineage, to colonize much of the Old World. *Homo erectus* remains found in East and South Africa and in Indonesia date from 1.5 million years ago. Although no early *Homo erectus* fossils have yet been found in Europe, early European archaeological remains indicate that *Homo erectus* was there as well by this time. In all of these geographic regions, *Homo erectus* continued little altered until around 200,000 years ago. At that point, an increase in brain size and other correlated cranial shape changes combined to produce a form that can be classified as *Homo sapiens.*

That all hominid fossils since 200,000 years ago can be called *Homo sapiens* does not mean that they were all thoroughly indistin-

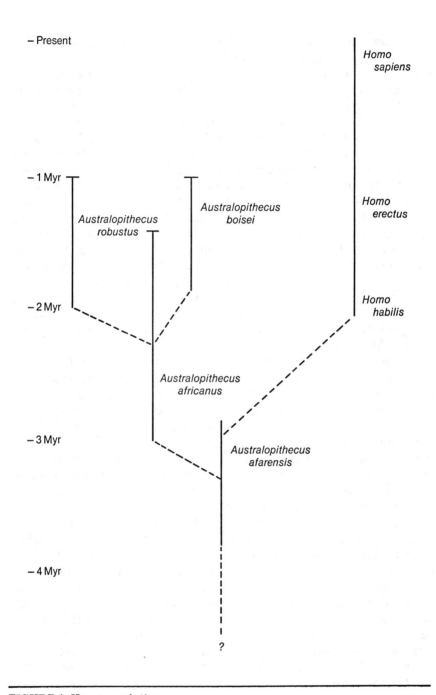

FIGURE 1. Human evolution.

guishable each from the other. On the contrary, regional variants of fossil *Homo sapiens* are readily recognizable. The best-known of these is the much-maligned Neandertal. That prototypical caveman was nothing more than the European variant of archaic, or early, *Homo sapiens* (Wolpoff 1980). Nor does the *Homo sapiens* designation imply that these forms were indistinguishable from ourselves. It means simply that our phyletic roots can be traced back to them with only the sort of minor morphological transformations that normally occur within the limits of a single species.

Most paleoanthropologists would agree, at least in principle, on such a broad outline. But this does not mean that every aspect of human evolution is either known or interpreted uniformly. There are indeed persisting gaps in the fossil record. And there are certainly interpretive disputes, some of which are sufficient to generate impressive displays of agonistic behavior whenever two or more paleoanthropologists gather. Is *Australopithecus afarensis* the basal hominid? Or is *A. africanus* still sufficiently generalized to be considered ancestral to both the later australopithecines and the *Homo* lineage? Does *Homo erectus* really persist for over a million years with little or no evolutionary change? Or is there a discernible but gradual trend toward *Homo sapiens*? Is Neandertal just a regional variant of archaic *Homo sapiens* and ancestral to later European fossil hominids? Or is it an overly specialized dead-end, with more recent European hominids having moved in from elsewhere?

Each of these is a significant dilemma confronting students of human evolution. As such, the attempt to deal with each of them would be a useful object lesson in paleoanthropological problem solving: the application of the evolutionary paradigm at the level of the explanation of a specific evolutionary event. Nevertheless, there is an even more fundamental question vexing paleoanthropologists, and the ways in which it has been temporarily answered during recent decades might prove to be even more illustrative. This question is, in a nutshell: Why are there hominids? What evolutionary pressures caused a group of early apes to diverge from the adaptive patterns characterizing other such apes and to elaborate that suite of features that are recognized today as hominid? The changing answers to this question are the focus of this reading, and the desire to define *hominid* is the starting point.

Linnaeus's Dilemma

By the early 1700s, two centuries' accumulation of traveler's tales of human-like creatures in the wilds of Africa and Asia had led to the scientific recognition of a striking biological similarity between humans and the great apes. So great was this similarity generally considered that Carolus Linnaeus, the founder of scientific taxonomy and no stranger to the art of identifying morphological minutiae, could complain to a friend: "What is the difference between man and ape, based on natural history? Most definitely I see no difference. I wish someone could show me even one distinction."

Subsequent natural historians leapt to the challenge and, by the dawn of the Darwinian era, had generated a list of features thought to be uniquely human. Among the more significant were: our habitual use of and reliance on tools; our erect posture and two-footed mode of locomotion; our lack of natural biological weapons, such as large protruding canines; our large brains and intellectual powers; and our complex social behavior, learned during a long infancy and childhood.

With the advent of Darwinian evolutionary thought came the logically necessary realization that the differences and similarities characterizing apes and humans were not merely fortuitous. Quite the contrary, they were the inevitable and predictable consequence of both groups having diverged from a shared common ancestor. At some point in the remote past, portions of an ancestral group must have become isolated from one another and begun to adapt in differing fashions to different environments. During the subsequent evolution of these newly distinct lineages humans must have developed their unique features, all the while retaining the common ancestral features that make them so clearly similar to living apes.

Within this context, the list of uniquely human features took on a new and ambiguous significance. If humans indeed possessed a phylogenetic history linking them with the apes, then there ought to be a fossil record documenting that history. As the fossil record was uncovered, it would demonstrate whether all of our distinctive features were in place from the beginning or, if not, which of them came first, thereby earning recognition as the keystone of hominid uniqueness. At the same time, however, this list of features constituted a sort of litmus test, determining whether or not a new fossil might even be accepted as a hominid. Deeply held prejudices about which feature was indispensable to humanness have been as significant in the search for hominid origins as the well-intentioned desire to let the fossil record reveal what it might about the emergence of humankind.

In this sense, changing perceptions of the origin of the Hominidae have been at least partially the result of attempts to reconcile the increasing completeness of the fossil record with a checklist of criteria for humanness that predates the discovery of any significant hominid fossils. Numerous fossils *were* found during the last half of the nineteenth century and the first decades of the twentieth century, but these were all sufficiently similar to *Homo sapiens* to be fairly easily dismissed, either as pathological specimens or as representatives of a previously unknown and primitive race of modern humans. The first hominid form to have a serious impact on notions of hominid origins remained undiscovered until the 1920s.

Raymond Dart's Hominid

In 1925 Raymond Dart described a new species of hominid, *Australopithecus africanus*, and proposed that it was the long-sought missing link, documenting the phylogenetic unity of apes and humans. Although Dart (1925) had only one specimen on which to base his conclusions, the subsequent discovery of dozens more in the next twenty-five years lent weight to his arguments. The unexpected blend of ape and human features in *A. africanus* was indeed tantalizing; so much so, in fact, that many could not accept it as a hominid.

The most disturbing feature was its small brain size, averaging around 450 cc. To a species such as *Homo sapiens*, much impressed with its own intellectual prowess, accepting a small-brained primate as ancestral was initially very difficult. This was especially true for a scientific community that, until 1953, was still largely taken in by the Piltdown fraud. Piltdown's coupling of a modern human braincase with the lower jaw and upper canine of an ape suitably appealed to rampant cerebrocentric vanities—the idea that of all human traits, large brain size simply had to be of prime importance.

Admittedly certain other features of *A. africanus* were also pongid-like. The lower part of the face jutted out moderately from the rest of the skull. This prognathism was more ape- than humanlike; in modern humans the face is tucked away neatly under the braincase. The browridges of *A. africanus* were also well-pronounced, another typically pongid feature. Furthermore, bony crests or ridges at the back of the skull implied the presence of very powerful, very nonhumanlike neck muscles.

Still, the vast majority of the remaining *A. africanus* features were distinctly humanlike (Le Gros Clark 1967). The posterior teeth, for example, while very large by modern human standards, were hominid in shape, proportions, and detailed form. The all-important canine was a short tooth and nearly spatulate in shape, mimicking the incisors in form and function. This contrasted starkly with both monkeys and apes, in whom the canine is subconical and, in males especially, almost fanglike. The lower first premolar, an elongated, high-cusped tooth that shears scissors-like on the upper canine in pongids, was low-cusped and squarish in *A. africanus*—another hominid feature.

Aside from the teeth, the most compelling evidence for the hominid status of *A. africanus* concerned its mode of locomotion, which was clearly bipedal (Lovejoy 1974). The foramen magnum (where the spinal cord enters the brain) was more or less centered in the base of the skull, indicating an habitual posture in which the head sits perched on top of a spine held perpendicular to the ground. In nonbipeds, by contrast, the foramen magnum is situated further back on the skull, reflecting the normally angled or horizontal orientation of the spine.

Other parts of the skeleton also showed the sorts of architectural adjustments that one would expect in a primate that had to support itself on only two feet. The spine had the characteristic human double curve (concave in the small of the back and convex in the shoulder region) that helps support the weight of the arms and trunk. The pelvic blades were short, broad, and facing sidewards. The muscles that attach here and then connect to the femur were thus in a position to stabilize the body when it was being supported on only one foot. This potentially precarious position is the one in which we find ourselves during most of the time spent bipedally walking. Chimps, for example, do not possess this stabilizing structural adjustment; this is the reason for the characteristic side-to-side wobble of their torso during bouts of bipedality. Finally, both the knee and foot of *A. africanus* exhibited features stressing stability and weight-bearing strength over the flexibility emphasized in most pongids.

Even the brain, on closer analysis, was thought to be not so depressingly ape-like (Holloway 1974). While it certainly was small, some scholars felt that the convolutions of the surface of the brain, as well as the relative proportions of the brain's various lobes, were more similar to the human than to the ape condition. In other words, it was argued that despite its small size the brain of *A. africanus* had undergone a structural reorganization along hominid lines. This in turn suggested that *A. africanus* might have been capable of behaviors considered specifically human.

What these behaviors might have been was surmised from associated materials discovered in many of the the same deposits that contained the hominid fossils themselves. Raymond Dart (1957), for example, argued that many of the broken animal bones, teeth, and horns found in the South African sites were actually deliberately manufactured tools—remnants of a tool culture he termed *osteodontokeratic*. He further argued that many of these pieces belonged to animals that had been killed directly by hunting activities of *A. africanus*. Many anthropologists disagreed; they argued that other predators or even scavenging species might have been responsible for the accumulation and modification of animal remains in the South African cave sites. But no one doubted the evidence of early human cultural activities emerging from East African Olduvai Gorge.

Here the Leakeys had documented a very early *stone* (rather than bone or horn) tool industry, long before their first discovery of a fossil hominid there (Leakey 1971). Most of the tools were little more than a fist-sized pebble with a few flakes knocked off—simple choppers or cleavers. Often the resulting flakes seemed to have been used as well, perhaps as knives or scrapers. More important than the form of the tools, however, was the fact that they were not found scattered randomly across the landscape. Instead, they were found together in high-density clusters. These clusters were usually located near water sources, sometimes in association with the partial skeleton of a relatively large animal, and, in one case, in association with a rough circle of large stones that may have functioned as a windbreak.

This patterning seemed to suggest three things. First, as noted by Glynn Isaac (1978), most primate species eat, drink, sleep, and socialize in different places. Only in humans do these activities customarily take place at the same location: the home base or camp. The spatial distribution of A. africanus cultural debris would make sense only if it resulted from such an integrated set of behaviors. Second, if culture was an important part of A. africanus's adaptation, the potential importance of learning, and therefore of a long preadult learning period, was obvious. Following this lead, Alan Mann (1975) discovered that the apparent timing of tooth eruption (which is linked to the general "clock" guiding growth and development) is much delayed in A. africanus relative to modern pongids, and closely resembles that of modern humans. Finally, the association of stone tools with large animal remains suggested to some, notably Sherwood Washburn, that A. africanus had engaged in systematic hunting or, at the very least, scavenging (Washburn and Lancaster 1968). Neither of these activities was thought to be within the behavioral repertoire of the extant apes.

By the early 1960s, then, Australopithecus africanus was portrayed as satisfying, at least marginally, nearly all the classic criteria of hominidhood. It was clearly bipedal; it possessed a dentition that was perhaps large in some respects, but that was human in its shape and lack of protruding canines; its brain was small, but organized in a human fashion; and its social life seemed to be a significant part of its overall adaptive strategy. The only remaining puzzle of human origins appeared to be why this virtually complete hominid pattern had so suddenly arisen.

The Tool Use Hypothesis

The most widely accepted solution to this puzzle focused, as had Darwin nearly a century before, on the importance of tools (Washburn 1960). It was argued that the climate had been changing rapidly prior to the reign of *A. africanus* and that the forests in which the prehominid apes had thrived dwindled with the advance of vast grass-lands or savannas. In such a situation, tools might have been the key to survival for a newly and begrudgingly terrestrial ape. They would have been an effective defense against roaming predators, assuming the function that the large canines of nonhuman primates were pre-sumed to serve. Thus, reduction of the canine in *A. africanus* was thought to have accompanied the cultural acquisition of superior and flexible tools and weapons. In turn, bipedalism was seen as a neces-sary biological adjustment to this change in cultural behavior. Bi-pedalism would free the hands for making, carrying, and using these implements.

Tools would also have been effective as *offensive* weapons for hunting large animals, especially if employed by several cooperating individuals. A highly integrated social organization, and perhaps even linguistic communication, would have been strongly selected in order to facilitate the necessary cooperation. Increasing social and techno-logical complexity would have placed a premium on learning and intelligence. This would lead to selection for, on the one hand, larger, more effective brains and, on the other, an even more cohesive social unit. The latter would provide for the education of socialization of the young, who now had so much more to learn than the average chimpanzee.

This tool use hypothesis was a tightly woven, highly satisfying scenario, seeming to account well for all the known data and leading one observer to remark: "Give me a stone tool and two million years, and I'll give you the atom bomb." It could only be refuted by the discovery of nonhominid tool users, or of hominids that did not use tools. This is, of course, precisely what happened.

First the sanctity of tool use as an exclusively human domain was violated. Jane Goodall's (1965) observations showed that the use of a variety of simple tools, from leaf sponges to termiting sticks, is a relatively common event among the Gombe Stream chimpanzees. Other field studies demonstrated occasional tool use in different chimp populations, including the use of a large tree branch to threaten a potential predator. Later laboratory studies showed that chimpan-zees, gorillas, and orangutans all have the ability to fashion and use simple tools. Their lack of tool use in the wild thus seems to stem more from a lack of a *need* to use them than from an inability to do so (Beck 1975). How could tools be the key factor in the origin of the hominids, if pongids seemed to be able to use them or not, as the situation warranted?

In addition, it became widely suggested that an apparently non-tool-using hominid was present more than ten million years before *A. africanus*. This form, called *Ramapithecus*, was known only from jaws and teeth, so nothing could be said about its brain size or mode of locomotion. But its principal advocate, Elwyn Simons (1977), asserted that these jaws and teeth matched in nearly every feature the pattern present in *A. africanus*. The canine appeared to be small in both males and females, barely extending above the level of the other teeth. The first lower premolar was claimed to be at least incipiently squarish and molar-like. The outline of the dental arcade was said to define a parabola, as in all known hominids, rather than a 'V' as in contemporaneous apes, or a 'U' as in modern pongids.

If *Ramapithecus* was indeed a hominid (and the consensus view, with some vociferous exceptions, said that it *was*), the cluster of typical hominid dental features was in no way related to tool use. Reduced canines and molarized premolars could no longer be attributed to the replacement by material culture of the typical pongid large canine and canine/premolar shearing complex. But if tool use was not the definitive human feature, then what was?

The Seed Eater Hypothesis

Clifford Jolly (1970) proposed a possible answer, the seed eater hypothesis. Jolly had studied the behavior and morphology of various baboon species in East Africa and had noted some interesting differences between two of them: the hamadryas baboon, living on the flat savanna of Tanzania and Kenya, and the gelada, occupying much drier and more mountainous terrain in Ethiopia.

Compared to the hamadryas, the gelada possesses a much shorter snout and a deeper, more robust jaw. The posterior teeth are much larger in the gelada and tend to be wider than they are long, thereby increasing tooth surface area without lengthening the jaw (which would reduce the mechanical efficiency of the chewing muscles). Jolly attributed these differences to the fact that geladas subsist on a diet of small, gritty, and extremely hard items (mostly grass seeds) that require far more chewing and are far more abrasive than the leaves, grass blades, and shoots that comprise the hamadryas diet.

It was suggested that the distinctiveness of the *Ramapithecus/ Australopithecus* dentition relative to modern or fossil apes might be due to a similar dietary differentiation. Large molars and molarized premolars would grind more effectively and wear out less rapidly if the diet consisted of small, tough-to-chew items. Short canines, Jolly argued, might be selectively advantageous, since longer teeth might tend to lock the jaws and prevent the side-to-side or rotatory motions necessary for effective grinding. Noting further that geladas feed in a squatting position, shuffling along on their buttocks with their torso held vertically, Jolly suggested that such an incipiently erect posture might preadapt an early hominid to completely erect, bipedal locomotion. Finally, the increased hand-eye coordination and manual dexterity required for small-object feeding could presage the neuromuscular reorganization on which later tool manufacture and use might depend.

While many argued that the emphasis on seed eating was overly restrictive, the dentognathic morphology of *Ramapithecus* was widely accepted as the result of what came to be called a terrestrial dental shift. A previously forest-dwelling and arboreal form, probably one of the earlier, putatively very pongid-like dryopithecines, had been forced to adapt to a diet of small, abrasive, terrestrial food items and ultimately developed a hominidlike chewing complex. With the defensive canine reduced, tools might have been an appropriate response to the increased predator pressure of savanna life. In turn, bipedality would have evolved to facilitate constant tool use, and *Ramapithecus* would have become a creature very much like *A. africanus* in all respects. This, then, was the consensus scenario of the early to mid-1970s.

As with the tool use hypothesis, the seed eater model could not withstand the assault of an expanding database. *Ramapithecus* had originally been defined on the basis of a relatively scanty sample of fragmentary jaws from the Indian subcontinent. Subsequent excavations produced a much expanded sample of more complete, clearly similar specimens from several other locations in Europe and Asia. These stimulated a few authors, notably Leonard Greenfield, to undertake a systematic reevaluation of *Ramapithecus* and its contemporaries in the 14–8 million-year-ago time range. As a result, it soon became clear that *Ramapithecus* was neither so distinctively hominidlike nor so different from other contemporaneous apes as had been previously asserted (Greenfield 1979). It did indeed possess relatively large molars and robust jaws, but the canine was often large and projecting, and the first lower premolar could be considered "incipiently molar-like" only to the extent that a molehill is incipiently mountainlike. Furthermore, many other species in this time range, placed in the genus *Sivapithecus*, exhibited the same or a very similar cluster of features. The terrestrial dental shift seemed to have been a more widespread and less dramatic phenomenon than once assumed. Designating one of these sivapithecines as the earliest hominid seemed arbitrary at best, and, at worst, wishful thinking.

Other inconsistencies within the consensus model soon arose. Preliminary paleoecological information had indeed suggested that *Ramapithecus* inhabited savanna or grassland zones. But later, more complete analyses of a variety of sites demonstrated a range of habitats, from woodland/grassland mosaic to canopy forest zones (Kennedy 1978). The forced terrestrialization of a prehominid ape seemed increasingly unlikely. The form of *Ramapithecus* limb skeleton remains, discovered in Pakistan and Hungary, supported this newer view. Rather than suggesting any sort of terrestrial locomotory mode, these remains are indicative of a generalized arboreal quadrupedality, with some features perhaps suggesting even limited brachiation or arm-swinging (Morbeck 1979). Finally, a recent study by Richard Kay demonstrates that the dental and jaw features of the sivapithecines (including *Ramapithecus*) are highly suggestive of a diet consisting of hard nuts and fruits (Kay 1981). The evidence thus mounts that the terrestrial dental shift may actually have transpired in the trees and that, in any event, it had nothing to do with the advent of the Hominidae.

Not that the seed eater hypothesis turned out to be totally without relevance, however. On the contrary, it seemed to explain well the evidence for two hominid lineages beginning about 2.5 to 2 million years ago. "Hyper-robust" types of australopithecines (*A. robustus* and *A. boisei*) were well known from somewhat later deposits and showed an almost exaggerated adaptation to dental crushing and grinding: massive molars and premolars; bony crests running down the center of the skull, anchoring what must have been impressive chewing muscles; huge and exceedingly well-buttressed mandibles. Some analyses suggested, however, that the earlier species, *A. africanus*, had already diverged in this quasi-herbivorous direction and that it too was well-adapted to very heavy grinding and crushing of food items (Wolpoff 1973). Its lack of bony crests and the like was simply a function of its smaller overall body size, much as the smaller female gorilla lacks the various crests of the much more massive male, despite consuming the same diet.

Paralleling the known representatives of the australopithecine lineage was thought to be the lineage representing the genus *Homo*. The earliest member of this lineage, *Homo habilis*, lacked the dental specializations characterizing *A. robustus*, *A. boisei*, and, some argued, *A. africanus*. It was said to be the maker of the stone tools appearing in 2-million-year-old deposits at Omo, East Turkana, and Sterkfontein, as well as responsible for the occasional finds of butchered animals. The *Homo* lineage was thus asserted to be culture-bearing and omnivorous, in stark contrast, at least metaphorically speaking, to the seed-eating australopithecines (Walker and Leakey 1978).

Lucy

The *Hominidae* was thus back in the position of being a family without a known progenitor. *Ramapithecus* was nothing more than one of a broad group of Old World-wide, nut-crunching, probably arboreal apes. *Australopithecus africanus* was already on a phyletic line emphasizing herbivory and heading for a mid-Pleistocene extinction. If the basal hominid were to be found, it would have to be in deposits between 8 and 2.5 million years old. Ironically, biochemists had long argued that the hominid/pongid split was within this time range (Sarich and Wilson 1967). Measuring the molecular differences between extant apes and humans, and then assuming a set rate for the accumulation of those differences, they suggested that the split might be as recent as 5 million years ago. As long as *Ramapithecus* reigned as the earliest fossil hominid, paleoanthropologists could (and did) smugly ignore the molecular evidence and choose to let the "fossils do the talking." The fossils had indeed spoken, if only to throw open once again the debate on hominid origins.

From this perspective, the discovery of *Australopithecus afarensis* can only be seen as an example of greatly needed serendipity. Since its deposits at Laetoli, Tanzania are between 3.6 and 3.8 million years old, and those at Hadar, Ethiopia between 2.8 and 3.2 million years, *A. afarensis* is clearly the oldest hominid yet known. Its significance derives less from this, however, than from its totally unexpected blend of specifically hominid and more generally pongid features (Johanson and White 1979).

Like all later hominids, *A. afarensis* was a biped. Although small (Lucy—the best-known and remarkably complete specimen from Hadar—was perhaps $3\frac{1}{2}$ feet tall), the various limb and pelvic remains are all functionally indistinguishable from those of modern humans. Footprints preserved in hardened volcanic ash at Laetoli are also small, but are again indicative of a thoroughly efficient bipedality. At least one of the classic criteria of hominidhood thus seems to have evolved by 4 million years ago.

In all other aspects, however, *A. afarensis* is manifestly more primitive than even *A. africanus*. The teeth and jaws differ only slightly from those of the much earlier sivapithecines. The canine is large and commonly extends, often appreciably, above the level of the other teeth. The first lower premolar retains a single high cusp that exhibits wear from shearing in a pongidlike fashion on the upper canine. The outline of the tooth row is not parabolic, as in all later hominids, but often V-shaped as in many of the earlier pongids. The two reconstructable crania give an average brain size of 417 cc, somewhat less than the *A. africanus* average of 457 cc. Skull form is also primitive, with considerable prognathism and, in at least one known specimen, a complex pongid-like nuchal crest. Finally, there is no evidence of stone tools in deposits associated with *A. afarensis*.

Aside from bipedality, *A. afarensis* lacks all the features long thought to distinguish the *Hominidae* from other primates, thus forcing us to recognize that these are relatively late innovations in our evolution. Our large and complex brains are not even foreshadowed until the appearance of *Homo habilis* by 2 million years ago. The oft-cited reorganization of the australopithecine brain is not evident in *A. afarensis*, nor, according to more recent studies by Dean Falk (1980), even in *A. africanus*. The use and manufacture of stone tools seems to be of similarly recent origin. Aside from scatters of stone tools at 2.8 million years ago in strata at Hadar (far above those containing *A. afarensis*), the densest evidence for early stone tool use clusters at about 2 million years ago (Isaac 1980). Stone tool use may thus explain the origin of *Homo*, but it was apparently an irrelevant factor in the origin of the hominids.

Nor are the traditional dental trademarks of small canines and molarlike premolars actually features of all hominids. As noted above, *A. afarensis* differs little in its jaws and teeth from the clearly pongid sivapithecines. Reliance on some sort of dietary shift as the key to hominisation is also thereby ruled out. Thus, bipedalism exists in relative isolation. Rather than the consequence of the development of some other hominid trait, as prior models suggested, it must be seen as underlying all other traits and its origin must be explained accordingly.

Lovejoy's Reproductive Hypothesis

An attempt to do just this has recently been made by Owen Lovejoy (1981), who sees the origin of bipedality as part of a broader shift in early hominid reproductive behavior. His model is based in part on the assumption that prehominid pongids (such as the sivapithecines) were demographically similar to the modern apes, specifically the chimpanzees. The latter are in an extremely precarious position, measured in terms of the ability of a given population to replenish itself reproductively from generation to generation.

As in any sexually reproducing population, each female chimp must, on average, produce two offspring that survive to reproductive age if the breeding population is to remain stable. A female chimpanzee, with an age of 10 years at sexual maturity and a spacing of 5.5 years between successive births, must survive to the age of 21 in order to accomplish this reproductive task. Yet the limited demographic data now available on wild chimpanzees (from the Gombe preserve) suggest that very few females actually survive to or beyond that age. Chimpanzee populations thus possess very little reproductive reserve with which to compensate for any increase in mortality due to, for example, environmental deterioration.

But environmental deterioration, of a sort, is precisely what was going on during the crucial period between 8 and 4 million years ago.

The widespread forests of earlier periods were breaking up, creating tropical islands of still-stable rain forest surrounded by more temperate forest/woodland/grassland mosaics. Some of the affected pongids, Lovejoy argues, retreated to the stable sanctuaries, avoiding what he calls the "demographic dilemma" and ultimately giving rise to the modern apes. However, according to this new model, at least one group—the future hominid—reacted in a more dynamic fashion to the potential reproductive crisis.

The key to this adaptive reaction was a reduction in the birth spacing interval, the amount of time between successive births. Since potential lifespan and the length of the period to sexual maturity are physiological/genetic factors not easily altered by the individual, a change in birth spacing is the only relatively easy behavioral adjustment of reproductive strategies. By producing more offspring within a given period of time, a group's and (in a highly social group such as pongids) an individual's vulnerability to increased mortality risks would be lessened.

Such a response would in turn have other consequences. Lovejoy argues that, given the exceedingly immature state in which pongids (and hominids) are born, the length of the birth spacing interval is largely a function of the amount of time it takes a female's previous offspring to reach a state of relative independence and self-sufficiency. Shortening the former interval without shortening the latter (which is generally not possible) would mean that a female would be encumbered with two or perhaps more highly dependent offspring. This might be expected to reduce her mobility somewhat, an especially crucial consideration for a species whose dietary resources are becoming more and more scattered in an increasingly mosaic habitat.

Analogizing from the strategies adopted by other vertebrate species with similar reproductive schedules, Lovejoy suggests that these incipient hominids would most likely have evolved a response consisting of home base and provisioning behaviors. Provisioning of less mobile females with dependent offspring by more mobile group members (perhaps mostly, but not exclusively, males) would have entailed a minor change from behavior evinced by modern male chimpanzees. The latter routinely roam far and wide, scouting for clusters of food sources, and summoning the rest of the group with a food call when they have found something. Were they to simply gather the food items and return with them to a central location, the net effect would be provisioning.

This central location would be the equivalent of a home base, a place from which females might range limited distances, gathering food items in their own right. It would also be the locus of the distribution and consumption of group-gathered foods, sleeping, and, as always occurs whenever primates congregate, socializing. As noted above, the spatial concentration of these activities seems to be a distinctive hominid behavior.

According to this model, bipedalism might arise to facilitate the carrying of infants and/or gathered food items. In the latter case, bark trays or scavenged animal skins might ultimately have proven to be useful carrying devices, laying the foundation for further elementary tool use but not leaving a discernible archaeological record. No significant dental or gnathic changes would be expected, since the nature of the dietary items being consumed was not changing. Only their spatial distributions, and thus the appropriate means of obtaining them, were seriously altered.

This reproductive hypothesis effectively interrelates and reasonably explains the unique and previously unexpected suite of features characterizing *A. afarensis*. One should recall, however, that previous models were no less aesthetically pleasing, yet both quickly succumbed to falsification based on new fossils and/or living primate data. It might be profitable, therefore, to anticipate a similar fate for Lovejoy's model by attempting to consider the possible conditions of its falsification.

Given the model's emphasis on behavioral factors having no morphological or archaeological manifestations, this is no easy task. Without a cultural tradition employing lithic, nonperishable materials, home bases could not reasonably be expected to be archaeologically preserved. Bipedalism may indeed have arisen to facilitate provisioning of a home base, or it may be related to some entirely different behavior. The proposition can be neither verified or falsified; it is plausible, but not logically compelling.

The thorough downgrading of the importance of tool use in hominid origins is similarly contingent on negative evidence. It is true that *stone* tools are a relatively late innovation in hominid evolution. Still, the widespread tool-using ability of pongids (and, obviously, of hominids) make it extremely likely that the common ancestor of pongids and hominids also possessed such an ability and perhaps even occasionally exercised it. The potential significance of a prelithic technology in the divergence and early evolution of the hominids, despite its wholly expected lack of archaeological manifestation, cannot be dismissed *a priori*.

A less problematical area, in which the model might be tested in the future, may be its demographic assumptions. The quantitative discussion of pongid reproductive scheduling relies solely on the Gombe chimpanzees, yet theirs is a highly unique and hardly pristine pongid group. During the past decades nearly as many primatologists have visited their territory as there have been new chimps born. There is little assurance that the demographics of such a disturbed group accurately reflect those of other apes. Indeed, in contrast to the Gombe chimps' 5.5 years, gibbons seem to exhibit a birth spacing interval of only two years (Schultz 1969), while orangs may vary from 3 to 8 years (MacKinnon 1974). Pygmy chimps (a different species than the Gombe chimps) seem to have a shorter birth interval as well, approximating that of many human groups (Kano 1980). It is also equally plausible to argue that the long birth spacing of chimps may have evolved after the pongid-hominid split in response to the high stability of chimp habitats. As the demography of extant pongids becomes better known, it is entirely possible that the demographic dilemma may turn out to be an alluring mirage.

Similarly, some of the causality in the model's tracing of the consequences of reduced birth spacing may prove to be amenable to testing. Is female mobility and effective range size seriously reduced as a result of more frequent births, thereby compelling the development of provisioning? The ethnographic literature on modern human hunter-gatherers uniformly paints a picture in which females give birth every two to three years, yet bear the brunt of the food quest, bringing in up to 80 percent of the calories and travelling far greater average distances than the males (Lee 1979). A comparison of average subsistence-round length in human hunter-gatherer females with those of supposedly less child-laden, more mobile female chimps, for example, should prove to be a significant test of the model's assumptions.

Getting Closer

In concluding this brief overview of hominid origins models, it is important to recognize that all such models operate under the same constraint: Armed with a scientific paradigm based on dynamism and change, we must interpret the static data of the fossil record in order to answer an essentially historical question. The fossil record is not conducive to experimentation, and the discovery of a fossil form that falsifies prevailing hypotheses is less a matter of sound science than it is of pure, dumb luck. In dealing with hominid origins, perhaps the best one can hope for is an internally consistent argument, tying up the known loose ends: What some would call a "just-so story."

Still, there is increasingly less concern with the classic checklist of hominid criteria that has far too long dominated consideration of hominid origins. As epitomized by Lovejoy's scenario, newer models will focus on subtle shifts in a set of behavioral characteristics, emphasizing less the qualitative, essentially typological, distinctions between hominids and pongids, and more the continuously variable adaptive responses potentially available to both. Evolution does not respect typological boundaries, so while we may never know the precise causes of the origin of the hominids (any more than those of the Industrial Revolution), it is perhaps reasonable to believe that we're getting closer all the time.

REFERENCES

Beck, Benjamin B. "Primate Tool Behavior." In *Socioecology and Psychology of Primates*, edited by Russell H. Tuttle, pp. 413–447. The Hague: Mouton, 1975.

Dart, Raymond A. "*Australopithecus africanus:* The Man-Ape of South Africa." *Nature* 115 (1925):195–199.

——. "The Osteodontokeratic Culture of *Australopithecus prometheus*." *Transvaal Museum Memoirs* 10 (1957):1–105.

Falk, Dean. "Hominid Brain Evolution: The Approach from Paleoneurology." *Yearbook of Physical Anthropology* 23 (1980):93–107.

Goodall, Jane. "Chimpanzees of the Gombe Stream Reserve." In *Primate Behavior*, edited by Irven DeVore, pp. 425–473. New York: Holt, Rinehart & Winston, 1965.

Greenfield, Leonard O. "On the Adaptive Pattern of *Ramapithecus*." *American Journal of Physical Anthropology* 50 (1979):527–548.

Holloway, Ralph L. "The Casts of Fossil Hominid Brains." *Scientific American* 231, no. 1 (1974):106–116.

Isaac, Glynn Ll. "The Foodsharing Behavior of Protohuman Hominids." *Scientific American* 238, no. 4 (1978):90–108.

——. "Casting the Net Wide: A Review of Archaeological Evidence for Early Hominid Land-Use and Ecological Relations." In *Current Argument on Early Man*, edited by Lars Konig Konigsson, pp. 226–251. Oxford: Pergammon Press, 1980.

Johanson, Donald C., and White, Tim D. "A Systematic Assessment of Early African Hominids." *Science* 203 (1979):321–330.

Jolly, Clifford J. "The Seedeaters: A New Model of Hominid Differentiation Based on Baboon Analogy." *Man* 5 (1970):5–26.

Kano, T. "Social Behavior of Wild Pygmy Chimpanzees (*Pan paniscus*) of Wamba: A Preliminary Report." *Journal of Human Evolution* 9, no. 4 (1980): 243–260.

Kay, Richard F. "The Nut-crackers—a New Theory of the Adaptations of the Ramapithecinae." *American Journal of Physical Anthropology* 55 (1981): 141–151.

Kennedy, G. E. "Hominoid Habitat Shifts in the Miocene." *Nature* 271 (1978): 11–12.

Leakey, Mary D. *Olduvai Gorge*, Vol. 3. Cambridge: Cambridge University Press, 1971.

Leakey, Mary D., and Hay, Richard L. "Pliocene Footprints in the Laetoli Beds at Laetoli, Northern Tanzania." *Nature* 278 (1979):317–323.

Lee, Richard B. *The Kung San: Men, Women and Work in a Foraging Society*. Cambridge: Cambridge University Press, 1979.

Le Gros Clark, W. E. *Man-Apes or Ape-Men? The Story of Discoveries in Africa*. New York: Holt, Rinehart and Winston, 1967.

Lovejoy, C. Owen. "The Gait of *Australopithecus*." *Yearbook of Physical Anthropology* 17 (1974):147–161.

——. "The Origin of Man." *Science* 211 (1981):341–351.

MacKinnon, J. R. "The Behavior and Ecology of Wild Orangutans (*Pongo pygmaeus*)." *Animal Behavior* 22 (1974):3–74.

Mann, Alan E. *Paleodemographic Aspects of the South African Australopithecines.* Philadelphia: University of Pennsylvania Publications in Anthropology, 1975.

Morbeck, Mary Ellen. "Hominoid Postcranial Remains from Rudabanya, Hungary." (Abstract) *American Journal of Physical Anthropology* 50 (1979): 465–466.

Sarich, Vincent M., and Wilson, Allan C. "Immunological Time Scale for Hominid Evolution." *Science* 158 (1967):1200–1203.

Schultz, Adolph H. *The Life of Primates.* New York: Universe, 1969.

Simons, Elwyn L. "*Ramapithecus*." *Scientific American* 236, no. 5 (1977): 28–35.

Walker, Alan, and Leakey, Richard E. F. "The Hominids of East Turkana." *Scientific American* 239, no. 2 (1978):54–66.

Washburn, Sherwood L. "Tools and Human Evolution." *Scientific American* 203, no. 3 (1960):62–75.

Washburn, Sherwood L., and Lancaster, C. S. "The Evolution of Hunting." In *Man the Hunter*, edited by Richard B. Lee and Irven DeVore, pp. 293–303. Chicago: Aldine, 1968.

Wolpoff, Milford H. "Posterior Tooth Size, Body Size, and Diet in South African Gracile Australopithecines." *American Journal of Physical Anthropology* 39 (1973):375–394.

——. *Paleoanthropology.* New York: Knopf, 1980.

Glossary

adaptive landscape A surface plotted on a three-dimensional graph, with all possible combinations of frequencies of different alleles plotted in the plane, and fitnesses for each combination plotted on the third dimension. Adaptive peaks are the high points on an adaptive landscape.

adenine A purine base that occurs in nucleosides, nucleotides, and nucleic acid (DNA and RNA). Adenine pairs with thymine in the DNA double helix.

ADH Alcohol dehydrogenase; an enzyme that catalyzes the oxidation of ethanol to acetaldehyde.

ADP Adenosine diphosphate; a compound that serves as a coenzyme, or coupling agent, between different enzymatic reactions in cellular metabolism. ADP is composed of the nucleoside adenosine and two molecules of phosphoric acid.

aerobic metabolism The common form of cellular respiration. In contrast to *anaerobic* metabolism, which occurs in the absence of oxygen, aerobic metabolism requires oxygen. It results in the biochemical transformation of much more energy from food than does anaerobic metabolism.

Agnatha Jawless fishes, including hagfishes and lampreys.

allele One of two or more forms of a gene that occupy a particular locus on a chromosome.

allopatric Living in different areas.

alpha chain (α chain) See *hemoglobin.*

amino acid An organic acid that contains one or more amino groups and one or more carboxyl groups. Amino acids have diverse and essential biological functions; of prime importance is their role as building blocks for protein molecules.

amphiphilic Pertaining to molecules with hydrophilic (water-loving) and lipophilic (oil-loving) ends.

anaerobic metabolism See *aerobic metabolism.*

anagenesis Gradual cumulative evolutionary change within a lineage that is not undergoing speciation.

Animalia The animal kingdom; one of three advanced kingdoms of multicellular organisms.

Annelida The segmented worms, including marine bristle worms, leeches, and earthworms. A phylum of the subkingdom Metazoa.

Anthropoidea A suborder of the Order Primates. Anthropoidea includes Old World monkeys, New World monkeys, apes, and humans.

293

Arthropoda The largest phylum in the subkingdom Metazoa, including insects, crustaceans, horseshoe crabs, spiders, trilobites, and other groups.

ATP Adenosine triphosphate; adenosine diphosphate with an additional phosphate group. Like ADP, ATP is a coenzyme of prime importance in cellular metabolism. Most molecular reactions requiring energy are linked to the breakdown of ATP to ADP and phosphate (P).

australopithecines The extinct hominid species belonging to the genus *Australopithecus.*

autapomorphic character A derived character that is unique to the taxon being described. Because it is not shared by others, it cannot be used to construct hypotheses concerning genetic relationship. See also *synapomorphic characters.*

balanced polymorphism At a genetic locus, the maintenance of a stable genetic polymorphism by natural selection for a species, the maintenance of morphologically discrete, nonintergrading segments (intraspecific polymorphism).

balancing selection Selection in favor of heterozygotes. Balancing selection occurs when both homozygotes are at a selective disadvantage.

belemnites Belemnoidea; an order of extinct mollusks.

Beta chain (β chain) See *hemoglobin.*

bioenergetics The study of energy transformations in organisms.

biogenesis The origin or generation of life.

biogeography The science concerned with the geographical distribution of life on earth.

biome A geographic region featuring a distinct and relatively stable combination of life forms, as well as distinct and relatively stable climatic, geological, and hydrological conditions; ecological zone.

biostratigraphy Separation and differentiation of rock units based on the stratigraphic sequence of their contained fossils. The study of paleontological aspects of stratigraphy.

biosystematics The study of organic diversity through space and time, especially the study of the relationships among species and historical aspects of their distribution.

biota Life forms; all unicellular and multicellular organisms (Monera, Protoctista, animals, plants, and fungi).

biozone The range of a single taxonomic group in geologic time as reflected by its occurrence in fossiliferous rocks.

Brachiopoda A phylum of marine metazoans that superficially resembles bivalve mollusks. Also called lamp shells.

Cambrian Earliest subdivision of the Paleozoic era.

carbohydrates The group of organic compounds composed of carbon, hydrogen, and oxygen; including sugars, starches, and celluloses.

carbon 14 See *radiometric dating.*

catalysis The process whereby the velocity of a chemical reaction is increased in the presence of a substance that remains apparently chemically unaffected throughout the reaction.

Cenozoic A geologic era comprising the Tertiary and Quaternary Periods (about 65 million years ago to the present).

central dogma The hypothesis that genetic information flows in one direction only, via *transcription* from DNA to RNA and via *translation* from RNA to protein. Reverse transcription (RNA to DNA) is now known to occur.

Some researchers believe that reverse translation (protein to RNA) may also occur, but this has not been confirmed.

chimera An individual composed of tissues containing a mosaic of two or more genetically distinct cell types.

chloroplast A chlorophyll-containing plastid found in the cells of most green plants. The site of photosynthesis.

Choanoflagellata A suborder of the Protozoa; the group of colonial protozoans that probably gave rise to the sponges.

chromophore   An arrangement of atoms that results in the appearance of color in organic compounds.

chromosome A rod-shaped body that carries the genes conveying hereditary information.

chronostratigraphy   The study of geologic *time* units. The construction of a geologic time scale based on the study of the stratigraphic succession of rocks.

cilia   Microscopic hairlike structures that project from the surfaces of certain cells and are capable of moving rhythmically. Cilia function in the locomotion and feeding of some organisms.

cistron   The ultimate unit of genetic *action*—as opposed to the ultimate units of *recombination* (recons), or of *mutation* (mutons). Generally, the equivalent of the gene.

clade A monophyletic taxon; a taxon whose members include *all* of the descendants of a single common ancestor.

cladistics   A school of evolutionary reconstruction and taxonomy. Cladists construct taxonomies that attempt to reflect the hierarchical pattern of descent of monophyletic groups of organisms. They do so by searching for sister groups based on the distribution

pattern of presumed shared derived characters (synapomorphies). See *sister groups; synapomorphic characters; monophyletic taxon.* See also *evolutionary taxonomy.*

cladogenesis   The multiplication of species via speciation (the branching or splitting of lineages).

cladogram A hypothesis concerning the structure of nature's hierarchy for a group of organisms; a hierarchical branching diagram that indicates the hypothesized pattern of shared derived similarities for the taxa included.

clone A group of genetically identical cells asexually derived from a single ancestral cell.

Cnidaria The coelenterates (hydroids, jelly fishes, sea anemones, and corals) excluding the sponges. A phylum of the animal subkingdom Metazoa.

coacervate A coagulation of colloidal droplets bound together by electrostatic attraction.

codon A sequence of three adjacent nucleotides (a triplet) in DNA or RNA that designates a specific amino acid or indicates that translation is to be terminated.

coelom The hollow body cavity of advanced metazoans; the "true" (mesodermally lined) body cavity of animals higher on the evolutionary scale than flatworms and nonsegmented roundworms. Coeloms are present in many phyla, including Bryozoa, Brachiopoda, Phoronida, Chaetognatha, Echinodermata, Mollusca, Annelida, Priapulida, Arthropoda, and Chordata.

coelomate An animal possessing a coelom.

coenzyme A nonprotein substance that is closely associated with or bound to the protein component of an enzyme. Coenzymes are necessary for enzyme activity.

colloid A suspension of finely divided particles in a continuous medium.

cytochrome c One of a group of complex respiratory pigments, called cytochromes, that generally occur in the mitochondria of aerobic organisms. Cytochrome c functions as an electron carrier in biological oxidation, and therefore plays an important role in the production of the high-energy coenzyme ATP.

cytosine A pyrimidine base that occurs in nucleosides, nucleotides, and nucleic acids (DNA and RNA). Cytosine pairs with guanine in the DNA double helix.

dalton An arbitrarily defined atomic mass unit (equal to 1/12th of the mass of the carbon-12 atom).

dentognathic Pertaining to teeth and jaws.

dephosphorylation The breakdown of high-energy phosphate bonds.

deuterium An isotope of the element hydrogen.

dielectric Pertaining to material in which an electric field can be sustained with minimal dissipation of power—a nonconductor of electricity.

dielectric constant A property of compounds that reflects the electrical charge assymetry and charge mobility within their molecules. The lower the dielectric constant, the greater the insulating properties of the material.

dimorphism A polymorphism involving only two forms.

diploid A cell or individual having two chromosome sets (that is, having *pairs* of homologous chromosomes).

dipole An electric dipole is formed by two equal electric charges of opposite sign ($+q$ and $-q$), separated by a small distance (d). The *dipole moment* is the vector qd. It is thus generated by the separation of positive and negative charges within a molecule.

directional selection Selection that changes the frequency of an allele in a constant direction, toward either fixation or elimination of that allele.

dispersalist historical biogeography The school of biogeography that developed before plate tectonics were known, and that therefore assumed that dispersal across preexisting relatively stable barriers must explain the distribution of organisms on the earth today. While modern dispersalists accept plate tectonics (and continental drift), they nevertheless ascribe a primary role to *dispersal* from point of origin rather than earth history (rifting, drifting, and so on) in explaining modern disjunctions of organisms. See also *vicariance historical biogeography*; *phylogenetic historical biogeography*.

DNA Deoxyribonucleic acid; the main carrier of genetic information in living organisms (except in viruses, which contain RNA).

Doppler effect The change in the observed frequency of a wave due to the relative motions of the source and the observer.

drift See *random drift*.

Echinodermata A taxon of marine invertebrates that includes starfishes, sea cucumbers, brittle stars, sea urchins, and other related forms. A phylum of the animal subkingdom Metazoa.

ecosystem A natural biotic community (assemblage of organisms living in a given area) and its environment, treated together as a system of complementary functional relationships and of transfer and circulation of matter and energy.

electromagnetism The branch of science dealing with the relationship between electricity and magnetism, based on the fundamental observation that a moving electric charge produces a magnetic field.

electrophoresis A technique for separating the charged components of a mixture of macromolecules under the influence of an electric field.

endemic Native to a particular geographic region.

endosymbionts Symbionts that live *within* their hosts. Some biologists believe that some modern cellular organelles (such as mitochondria and chloroplasts) were originally independent prokaryotic organisms that entered a host cell and then adapted to live within it. If so, these cellular organelles would have evolved from endosymbionts.

enzyme Any of a group of catalytic proteins that drive chemical reactions without themselves being altered.

epifauna The fauna that lives *on* (as opposed to *within*) the sea floor.

epigenesis The process by which characteristics of the adult arise anew during the ontogeny of the individual and are not, therefore, preformed in the egg (as pre-early-nineteenth century preformationism held). Today, developmental epigenesis refers to the interactions between the developmental environment and developmental processes, and their influence on morphology and the expression of genes. Epigenetic events are everything that happens to the embryo after fertilization. The embryogenetic process is known to be influenced by the embryogenetic substrate, and may be influenced by external factors as well.

evolutionary systematics A research program in systematics that includes evolutionary taxonomy and dispersalist historical biogeography.

evolutionary taxonomy A school of evolutionary reconstruction and taxonomy that seeks to produce classifications that reflect hypotheses concerning grades, ancestors, and adaptations as well as the pattern of shared derived traits among the taxa included. See also *cladistics*.

FADH$_2$ Reduced flavin adenine dinucleotide; a compound that stores energy and can be changed into other forms when oxidation occurs.

fibrinopeptides A group of proteins that aid in the blood clotting process.

fitness, Darwinian The relative probability of survival and reproduction of a genotype, based on the interaction between its phenotypic expression and the environment.

fixation An allele is said to be fixed in a population when all other alleles for its locus have been eliminated and all members of the population are homozygous for that given allele.

foramen magnum The opening at the base of the skull for the passage of the spinal chord into the vertebral column.

gamete A sexual reproductive cell, or germ cell, that normally unites with another to produce a new individual.

gelada baboon *Theropithecus gelada*; a particular, relatively short-muzzled, species of baboon that lives today in the arid Ethiopian highlands.

gene A segment of a chromosome providing information for carrying out a particular task, such as dictating the amino acid sequence of a protein.

genetic drift Fluctuations in allele frequencies resulting from chance factors and independent of natural selection and mutation.

genetic relationship Nearness of common ancestry.

genome The genetic material in a cell.

genotype The genetic constitution of an individual organism at one or more loci; the specific allelic composition of a gene, set of genes, or the entire genome.

geomorphology The branch of geology dealing with the characteristics, origin, and development of topographic features.

globin A soluble histone protein obtained from animal hemoglobin.

grade A taxon or group of organisms defined by a set of adaptive characteristics without regard to whether those characteristics represent shared derived traits. Because monophyly is not a criterion for the definition of a grade, grades are usually polyphyletic or paraphyletic.

gradualism See *phyletic gradualism*.

guanine A purine base that occurs in nucleosides, nucleotides, and nucleic acids (DNA and RNA). Guanine pairs with adenine in the DNA double helix.

hamadryas baboon *Papio hamadryas*; a particular species of baboon that lives in arid environments in Ethiopia today.

haploid A cell or individual having a chromosome complement consisting of only *one* copy of each chromosome instead of the normal two.

hemoglobin A blood protein that transports oxygen; generally, a tetrameric protein—that is, one that contains four polypeptide chains. The major hemoglobin molecules in adult vertebrates consist of two different types of polypeptide chains called α and β chains, associated with an iron porphyrin moiety, or *heme*. Because there are two of each type of polypeptide chain, these molecules are described as $\alpha_2\beta_2$ hemoglobins.

heterochrony An evolutionary shift in the time of onset or rate of development of one feature relative to another in an organism's ontogeny.

heterozygote A cell or individual that has *different* alleles at a given locus on homologous chromosomes.

histones Basic proteins occurring in the nuclei of both plant and animal cells, in close association with DNA.

homeostasis The maintenance of a rather constant internal environment in an organism throughout its encounters with varied external conditions, or the process whereby such stable conditions can be maintained.

Hominidae The family of primates that includes modern humans and our closest extinct relatives.

homologous chromosomes In diploid cells or individuals, pairs of chromosomes that are identical in shape, size, and function.

homologous traits Structural similarities inherited from a common ancestor. Homologous similarities are usually constrasted with convergent similarities, which are repeatedly derived. Homologous similarities may be plesiomorphic or synapomorphic—that is, primitive or derived.

homozygote A cell or individual that has the *same* allele at a given locus on homologous chromosomes.

hydrocarbon A polymer unit consisting of carbon and hydrogen.

hydrophilic Water-loving (attracting, adsorbing, or absorbing water).

hydrostatic Pertaining to a liquid in a state of equilibrium.

infauna The fauna that burrows into and thus lives *within* the sea floor.

inorganic Nonorganic chemical compounds. Inorganic compounds generally do not contain carbon and are derived from mineral sources.

intron Intervening sequence; a segment of unknown function within a gene. The segment may be initially transcribed, but it is not found in the functional mRNA.

isotope One of several forms of a chemical element, differing from the others in the number of neutrons in the atomic nucleus but not in its chemical properties.

Jurassic The middle of the three periods comprising the Mesozoic era.

light year The distance light travels in a year (9.454×10^{12} kilometers).

lipid One of a class of organic compounds that includes waxes, fats, and derived compounds.

lipophilic Pertaining to molecules with an affinity for lipids.

lophophore The crown of tentacles surrounding the mouth in the Bryozoa, Phoronida, and Brachiopoda; a coiled or folded, tentacle-like apparatus used for feeding.

mRNA Messenger RNA; a molecule of RNA transcribed from the DNA of a gene, which functions in protein synthesis on the site of ribosomes.

macroevolution Large-scale, long-term evolutionary change; evolution in a geological framework.

mantle In biology, the flap or extension of the body wall of organisms such as mollusks and brachiopods that contains glands that secrete a shell-forming fluid.

Markov chain A sequence that fluctuates stochastically. The accumulation of small random fluctuations results in a system whose future states are greatly influenced by the preceding states.

metabolism The physical and chemical processes by which food energy is made available for use by an organism.

Metazoa All of the multicellular animals except the sponges (Parazoa). A subkingdom of the kingdom Animalia.

methanogens Simple organisms thought to be among the oldest extant organisms on the earth. Found in ocean trenches, mud, and sewage, these organisms require no oxygen; they produce methane from carbon dioxide and hydrogen.

microevolution The short-term evolution of populations that can be studied by population geneticists working under the constraints of ecological, rather than geological, time.

Miocene The fourth epoch of the Cenozoic era. The Miocene precedes the Pliocene, Pleistocene, and Recent epochs.

miscible Pertaining to liquids that are mutually soluble or capable of being uniformly blended.

mitochondria Eukaryotic cellular organelles. Energy-liberating processes are generated in mitochondria, generally in association with their membranes.

molecular clock A means of measuring the time involved in molecular evolution. Calibration of the clock is based on the empirical observation that point mutations are fixed in the genome at reasonably regular rates.

Monera The kingdom that includes the bacteria and blue-green algae; the simplest prokaryotic organisms.

monophyletic taxon A clade. A group of organisms that share a unique evolutionary history (common ancestry).

Monte Carlo (game theory) A method for resolving mathematical or statistical problems using random numbers or samples.

morphology The form of an organism or part of that organism at any stage of its life history.

mRNA Messenger RNA; a ribonucleic acid molecule that transfers genetic information transcribed from nuclear DNA to the ribosomes, where it functions (with tRNA) in the production of proteins.

mycoplasma Simple, poorly known, prokaryotic organisms that lack cell walls, are very small, and contain tiny genomes.

myoglobin An oxygen-carrying protein found in muscle tissue. A special type of hemoglobin.

$NADH_2$ Reduced nicotinamide adenine dinucleotide; a compound that stores energy and that can be changed into other forms when oxidation occurs. A coenzyme.

N_e Effective population size, that is, the portion of the total population that is reproducing. In human populations, this is roughly one-third the census size of the population.

nebula Interstellar clouds of gas or small particles. The term *nebula* is used to describe any luminous spot that remains fixed relative to the stars.

nematodes A group of unsegmented worms; the roundworms or threadworms.

nemerteans Unsegmented marine worms with long, ribbonlike bodies.

neoteny The retention of what were *juvenile* characteristics in ancestors as *adult* characteristics in descendants; produced by a relative retardation of somatic development.

neutrinos A hypothetical elementary particle with an extremely small mass and carrying no electric charge.

neutron An elementary particle with approximately the same mass as the proton but without electric charge.

nonequilibrium thermophysics The study of irreversible thermophysical processes and the rates at which they occur.

nucleoside See *nucleotide*.

nucleotide A compound composed of a base, sugar, and phosphate group. The basic chemical unit in nucleic acids (DNA and RNA). A nucleotide consists of a nucleoside (purine or pyrimidine base attached to deoxyribose or ribose sugar) plus a phosphate group.

organelle A subcellular structure with a specialized function, such as ribosomes, nuclei, mitochondria, and chloroplasts.

organic Pertaining to any aspect of living matter. The term is also applied to any chemical compound that contains carbon.

overdominance Overdominance is said to occur when the phenotypic expression of the heterozygote is greater than that of either homozygote, or when the heterozygote is superior in fitness to both homozygotes.

oxidation A chemical reaction that increases the oxygen content of a compound; technically, one involving relative loss of electrons.

oxidative phosphorylation The synthesis of the high-energy compound ATP through a series of chemical reactions involving oxidation. Oxidative phosphorylation occurs in subcellular organelles known as mitochondria.

Paleozoic The era of ancient life, or the age of invertebrates. The Cambrian period is the first subdivision of the Paleozoic era. The Paleozoic era preceded the Mesozoic and Cenozoic eras.

pangenesis Darwin's theory of Lamarckian inheritance. Darwin proposed that an organ altered by use or disuse will release minute altered particles (or *gemmules*) that circulate in the blood and then collect in the germ cells to contribute to the form of the offspring.

paper chromatography A method used to separate mixtures into their constituents by preferential adsorption on a strip of filter paper.

paraphyletic taxon A taxon that represents only part of a clade; generally, a taxon that excludes some members of a clade because of their adaptive dissimilarities to others in that clade. See also *monophyletic taxon*.

Parazoa The sponges (Porifera); a subkingdom of the kingdom Animalia. While sponges are multicellular animals, they are so different in structure from the other multicellular animals (Metazoa) that they are often distinguished by this special name. Some researchers believe that the Parazoa and Metazoa had separate protoctistan ancestries; if so, the kingdom Animalia is a polyphyletic taxon.

peptide The chemical bond that links amino acids in proteins. Molecules composed of many sequential peptide bonds are called *polypeptide chains*; those composed of two, three, or four peptide bonds are called di-, tri-, and tetrapeptides.

peristalsis A rhythmic, progressive wave of muscular contraction, as in the intestines.

*p*H The chemists' system for expressing the acidity of water solutions in terms of the concentration of hydrogen ions. It ranges on a 14-point scale from extremely acidic (pH=0) to extremely basic (pH=14). All values above 7 are alkaline; all values below 7 are acidic; 7.0 is the neutral point.

phenetic relationship The overall similarity of one organism to another, based on physiological or morphological appearance. Such overall similarity may be based on any combination of convergent (nonhomologous), symplesiomorphic, and synapomorphic characteristics, and therefore need not closely reflect genetic relationship.

phenotype   The observable characteristics of an individual organism.

phenotypic (somatic) flexibility   The broad range of physiological and morphological responses of organisms to environmental stresses or to changes in environmental conditions.

Phonorida   A phylum of metazoans with elongate bodies and a crown of tentacles surrounding the mouth.

phosphorylation The formation of high-energy phosphate bonds.

photon Light quantum, or unit of radiant energy.

photophosphorylation The synthesis of high-energy ATP via light-energy-induced phosphorylation; occurs in chloroplasts.

photosynthesis   Metabolic processes by which light is trapped and its energy used to synthesize energy-rich compounds such as glucose or ATP.

phyletic gradualism A school of macroevolutionary theory, based on the notion that macroevolutionary change is gradual, constant, and constrained primarily by natural selection operating on variations among individuals *within* populations.

phylogenetic historical biogeography Also called cladistic biogeography. A school of biogeography that seeks to reconstruct the location of the ancestral group and pathways of dispersal from prior phylogenetic analysis rather than from present-day diversity and distribution gradients. Thus, *historical* biogeography depends on a reconstruction of the group's phylogenetic history.

phylogenetic systematics A research program in systematics that includes cladistic taxonomy, phylogenetic historical biogeography, and vicariance historical biogeography.

phylogeny The evolutionary history of a lineage or series of related lineages.

phylum A taxon that is a subdivision of a kingdom and that is in turn subdivided into classes.

plastid A plant organelle that functions in food storage and food manufacture.

Platyhelminthes A phylum of nonsegmented worms; the flatworms. A phylum of the animal subkingdom Metazoa.

Pleistocene The Ice Age, or the first epoch of the Quaternary period, following the Tertiary period and preceding the Holocene or Recent epoch.

plesiomorphic characters   Primitive characters (inherited from the common ancestor of a broad taxon).

polymer A macromolecule; a chemical of high molecular weight.

polymorphism The existence of several discrete forms in a population. In genetics, the occurrence of two or more alleles at a given locus, where at least two of these alleles appear with frequencies of more than 1 percent.

polypeptide chain A chain of amino acids linked together by peptide bonds. See *peptide*.

polyphyletic taxon A group whose members do not share a unique evolutionary history. Rather than comprising all of the descendants of a single common ancestry, polyphyletic taxa combine members of two or more evolutionary histories, generally when they share some important though repeatedly derived adaptive similarities.

polyploidy The existence of three or more sets of chromosomes in a cell or in all cells of an organism.

Pongidae The family of Primates that includes the great apes (gorilla, chimpanzee, and orangutan) and their extinct relatives.

Porifera The sponges (see *Parazoa*).

Precambrian   The geologic era predating the Paleozoic.

Priapulida A phylum of wormlike marine invertebrates.

prognathic An anatomical term referring to forward protrusion of the jaws.

prokaryote A unicellular organism whose genetic material is distributed throughout the cell rather than confined within a membrane-bound nucleus. Includes bacteria and blue-green algae (the Monera).

protocells Hypothetical predecessors of cells; the earliest cells.

Protoctista The simplest eukaryotic kingdom, including eukaryotic organisms that lack differentiated tissues, such as protozoans, unicellular algae, and multicellular algae that are not organized at the tissue grade of construction.

proton A positively charged elementary particle.

protovirus Hypothetical normal cellular genetic elements that can escape the nucleus and transfer genetic information from one somatic cell to another.

provirus A portion of chromosomal DNA that has been integrated into the nuclear genome via the reverse transcriptase activity of a retrovirus.

punctuated equilibria The theory of punctuated equilibria was proposed in 1972 by Eldredge and Gould as an alternative to phyletic gradualism. It argues that organisms evolve in fits and starts punctuating periods of relative stasis (that is, in punctuated equilibria), and that cladogenesis, far more than anagenesis, is responsible for the more dramatic shifts in form. See also *phyletic gradualism*.

punctuationalism A school of macroevolutionary theory. Proponents of the theory of punctuated equilibria are called punctuationalists (also, punctuationists).

pyrophosphate Inorganic phosphate; a salt of pyrophosphoric acid.

quantum evolution Rapid macroevolutionary change, possibly but not necessarily associated with rapid rates of speciation. Simpson defined quantum evolution as a special form of phyletic evolution that occurs when a population shifts from one adaptive peak to another new or previously unoccupied adaptive peak, across an adaptive valley.

quantum speciation A very rapid speciation event.

radiometric dating Methods of measuring the age of rocks or remains of living organisms using the decay properties of radioactive substances contained within them. Radiocarbon dating, for example, reflects the relative proportion of the isotope carbon 14 ($_{14}C$) to the total carbon contained in the substance to be dated.

random drift Changes in allele frequency in a population due to sampling error.

random walk (game theory) A succession of movements along line segments where the direction and length of each move is randomly determined.

recombination The formation of new combinations of genes on a chromosome or in individuals. A variety of processes, including independent segregation and crossing over, lead to this genetic reshuffling.

reduction Chemical reaction in which an element gains an electron.

regulatory gene A gene that controls development by turning protein-manufacturing genes (structural genes) on and off.

retroviruses RNA tumor viruses—a group of viruses sharing similarities in structure and mode of replication. Some retroviruses can induce tumors (for example, mammary cancer and leukemia). DNA copies of these RNA-containing viruses are synthesized in infected cells, and these copies are able to integrate into the cellular DNA, becoming part of the genetic complement of the cell.

reverse transcriptase An enzyme that can catalyze the synthesis of a DNA copy from an RNA template.

ribosomes Cellular organelles that are the sites of protein synthesis.

Rickettsiae A group of small and simple intracellular parasites.

RNA Ribonucleic acid; the main carrier of genetic material in some viruses. In other organisms RNA is first transcribed from a DNA template and then used in translating genetic information into protein structure. Reverse transcription of DNA from an RNA template is known to occur in the life cycles of some organisms, and this process has become a key element of modern Lamarckian theories of inheritance.

saltationism Literally, evolution by jumping; Goldschmidt's proposed mechanism for macroevolutionary change, involving genetic macromutations that simultaneously initiate reproductive isolation and result in the appearance of morphological discontinuities in short intervals of time.

selection Darwin's proposed mechanism for evolutionary change by the differential reproduction of naturally occurring variations in specific environmental contexts. Today, selection is described in terms of *values* or *coefficients* for individual genotypes—that is, the proportional excess or deficiency of one genotype relative to another. Different forms of selection are recognized, including frequency-dependent selection, where the value of the selection coefficient depends on the frequency of the genotype in the population; density-dependent selection, where the value of the selection coefficient depends on population density; truncation selection, where individuals above or below a certain phenotypic value are selected; and so on.

sivapithecines A group of extinct Miocene apes that share certain anatomical features with modern orangutans.

somatic Pertaining to the body; for example, somatic (body) cells are contrasted with germ (reproductive) cells.

somatic recombination A rearrangement of the chromosomal DNA (to reassemble genes or parts of genes) during the course of differentiation and development of somatic or body cells.

somatic selection hypothesis The hypothesis that DNA mutations occurring in somatic cells of organisms can be picked up by endogenous retroviruses and incorporated into the chromosomal DNA of that organism's germ cells.

stasigenesis The generation of evolutionary stability or stasis in a lineage over long periods of time.

stratigraphy The branch of geology concerned with the description, organization, classification, and temporal sequence of stratified rocks.

supernovae A stupendous explosion of a star that increases its brightness hundreds of millions of times in a few days. Some supernovae become as bright as the whole galaxy in which they are observed.

symbiosis Symbiosis occurs when two or more species live together in a prolonged intimate ecological relationship.

sympatric Living in the same area.

symplesiomorphic characters Shared primitive traits. Homologous similarities that do not distinguish members of one subgroup of a particular taxon from members of another, because they were present in the common ancestor of both subgroups.

synapomorphic characters Shared derived traits; homologous similarities that do distinguish members of one subgroup of a particular taxon from members of another subgroup, because they uniquely appeared in the common ancestor of only that one subgroup.

synthetic theory The great synthesis of the work of the Mendelian population geneticists and Darwinian naturalists that formed the basis of neo-Darwinism. The synthetic theory (or modern synthesis, as it is called) developed in the period 1930–1950. It rejects use inheritance and is nonvitalistic. According to the synthetic theory, evolution is the gradual accumulation of small genetic changes, largely point mutations. These mutations are themselves randomly produced. Natural selection is the primary mechanism of evolution, and is the source of its directionality. The synthetic theory is largely Darwinian, incorporating Darwin's emphasis on competition, fitness, and adaptation.

systematics See *biosystematics*.

taxon   A group of organisms of specific rank within a hierarchical classificatory scheme. Kingdoms, phyla, classes, orders, families, genera, species, and so on represent different taxonomic ranks; the phylum Chordata and family Hominidae are examples of specific taxa of different rank.

teleost A member of a group that includes all bony fishes except the sturgeons, lobe-fin fishes, alligator gars, bowfins, coelacanths, and lungfishes.

tetramer   A protein containing four polypeptide chains; a polymer that results from the union of four monomers.

thermodynamics   The branch of physics that seeks to describe the conversion of energy from one form to another and to derive relationships between properties of matter (especially those affected by temperature changes).

thymine   A pyrimidine base occurring in nucleosides, nucleotides, and the nucleic acid DNA.

Tommotian A geologic stage, usually regarded as earliest Cambrian.

translation In genetics, the ribosome-mediated process by which a polypeptide is produced following the codon sequence of an mRNA molecule.

transposable elements In eukaryotic organisms, DNA sequences that are able to move around *inside* the cell genome and that may catalyze chromosomal deletions and rearrangements.

Trilobita An extinct group of arthropods.

tripeptide See *peptide*.

tRNA Transfer RNA; small ribonucleic acid molecules that function in transferring free amino acids to the ribosomes, where they can be inserted into growing polypeptide chains. The structure of tRNA is complementary to the ribosomal mRNA, whose codon sequences control the sequences of amino acids in the polypeptide chains.

uracil A pyrimidine base that occurs in nucleosides and nucleotides, and substitutes for thymine in the nucleic acid RNA.

Vendian A geological stage, immediately preceding the Tommotian stage.

vertical congenital infection The infection of an offspring with tumor viruses derived from the mother via the placenta or milk.

vertical genetic transmission The infection of an offspring via the direct passage of a viral genome from parent to offspring. The virus is inherited as a cellular genetic element in DNA form.

vicariance historical biogeography The school of biogeography that developed from the writings of Leon Croizat. Croizat maintained that dispersal events from numerous centers of origins do not best account for the present-day distribution of organisms on earth. Vicariance biogeographers ascribe a primary role to vicariant events—that is, to geologic and geographic changes in the environment, such as continental movement, tectonic events, transgressions and regressions of the sea, changes in climate. Vicariance historical biogeography offers an alternative to traditional dispersalist biogeography (which developed before plate tectonics were known) and to cladistic or phylogenetic biogeography. See also *dispersalist historical biogeography; phylogenetic historical biogeography*.

Weismann's germ theory August Weismann's theory of the independence of the *germ line* from the soma. The germ line is the lineage of cells from the fertilized egg to the germ cells of succeeding generations. The soma is the cell lineage from the fertilized egg to the body or somatic cells of the adult organism. Weismann's evidence for independence of the germ line from the soma argued strongly against the notion of the inheritance of acquired characteristics.

zoophyte One of a group of invertebrate animals (including corals, sea anemones, bryozoans, hydroids) that resemble plants in appearance, especially by growing as a branching colony attached to a substrate.

Index